D1553676

HANDBOOK OF FIXTURE DESIGN

McGRAW-HILL HANDBOOKS

ABBOTT AND STETKA · National Electrical Code Handbook, 10th ed.

ALJIAN · Purchasing Handbook

AMERICAN INSTITUTE OF PHYSICS · American Institute of Physics Handbook

AMERICAN SOCIETY OF MECHANICAL ENGINEERS · ASME Handbooks:

    Engineering Tables   Metals Engineering—Processes

    Metals Engineering—Design   Metals Properties

AMERICAN SOCIETY OF TOOL AND MANUFACTURING ENGINEERS:

    Die Design Handbook   Tool Engineers Handbook, 2d ed.

    Handbook of Fixture Design

BEEMAN · Industrial Power Systems Handbook

BERRY, BOLLAY, AND BEERS · Handbook of Meteorology

BLATZ · Radiation Hygiene Handbook

BRADY · Materials Handbook, 8th ed.

BURINGTON · Handbook of Mathematical Tables and Formulas, 3d ed.

BURINGTON AND MAY · Handbook of Probability and Statistics with Tables

CARROLL · Industrial Instrument Servicing Handbook

COCKRELL · Industrial Electronics Handbook

CONDON AND ODISHAW · Handbook of Physics

CONSIDINE · Process Instruments and Controls Handbook

CROCKER · Piping Handbook, 4th ed.

CROFT AND CARR · American Electricians' Handbook, 8th ed.

DAVIS · Handbook of Applied Hydraulics, 2d ed.

DUDLEY · Gear Handbook

ETHERINGTON · Nuclear Engineering Handbook·

FACTORY MUTUAL ENGINEERING DIVISION · Handbook of Industrial Loss
    Prevention

FINK · Television Engineering Handbook

FRICK · Petroleum Production Handbook

GUTHRIE · Petroleum Products Handbook

HARRIS · Handbook of Noise Control

HARRIS AND CREDE · Shock and Vibration Handbook

HENNEY · Radio Engineering Handbook, 5th ed.

HUNTER · Handbook of Semiconductor Electronics, 2d ed.

HUSKEY AND KORN · Computer Handbook

JASIK · Antenna Engineering Handbook

JOHNSON AND AUTH · Fuels and Combustion Handbook

JURAN · Quality-control Handbook

KALLEN · Handbook of Instrumentation and Controls

HANDBOOK OF FIXTURE DESIGN

A Practical Reference Book of Workholding
Principles and Designs for All Classes of
Machining, Assembly, and Inspection

Prepared under Supervision of

NATIONAL TECHNICAL PUBLICATIONS COMMITTEE
AMERICAN SOCIETY OF TOOL AND MANUFACTURING ENGINEERS

FRANK W. WILSON, *Editor-in-Chief*
JOHN M. HOLT, JR., *Associate Editor*

First Edition

McGRAW-HILL BOOK COMPANY, INC.
New York   Toronto   London
1962

HANDBOOK OF FIXTURE DESIGN

Copyright © 1962 by American Society of Tool and Manufacturing Engineers. Printed in the United States of America. Published by the McGraw-Hill Book Company, Inc. All rights reserved, including those of translation. This book, or parts thereof, may not be reproduced in any form without permission of the copyright owners. The Society does not, by publication of data in this handbook, ensure to anyone the use of such data against liability of any kind, including infringement of any patent. Publication of any data in this handbook does not constitute a recommendation of any patent or proprietary rights that may be involved. *Library of Congress Catalog Card Number:* 61–14046

INDUSTRIAL SCREENING AND REVIEW COMMITTEE

RAYMOND H. MECKLEY, CHAIRMAN
  Vice President, Flinchbaugh Products, Inc., York, Pa.

FRANCIS L. EDMONDSON, *Assistant Supervisor, Tool and Operations Planning, General Dynamics Corp., Fort Worth, Texas*

SAMUEL E. GEISELMAN, *Supervisor of Tool Design and Control, Bearings Company of America, Inc., Div. of Federal-Mogul-Bower Bearings, Inc., Lancaster, Pa.*

H. J. GERBER, *Head, Machine Shop Department, College of Engineering, Oklahoma State University, Stillwater, Okla.*

CURTIS E. GROVE, *Shop Superintendent, Davey Products Company, Inc., Red Lion, Pa.*

HAROLD J. HARTLIEB, *Sales Engineer, Precision Metals Division, Hamilton Watch Company, Lancaster, Pa.*

J. V. JUCKER, *Superintendent of Manufacturing, Caterpillar Tractor Company, York, Pa.*

ROBERT E. NAUTH, *President, Detroit Engineering Institute, Detroit, Mich.*

SYDNEY H. PARSONS, JR., *Senior Engineer, Tool and Equipment Sec., Wasatch Div., Thiokol Chemical Corporation, Tremonton, Utah*

WILLIS J. POTTHOFF, *Tooling Supervisor, Emerson Electric Company, St. Louis, Mo.*

LEON K. YEISER, *Project Engineer, Connector Devices, General Products Div., AMP, Inc., Harrisburg, Pa.*

LIST OF CONTRIBUTORS

*Sectional
Author Group*

PREFACE

In all fabricated manufacturing, there is no single problem so universally encountered as that of holding the workpiece for machining, forming, assembly, and inspection operations.

Nor is there any other problem that demands more ingenuity of the tool and manufacturing engineers for its solution. Characteristically they are suddenly confronted with a largely unalterable product design, a preselected class of machine tool for which the fixtures must be designed, and a preestablished production rate and total volume. Finally, while planning within such restrictive parameters, they must work within sharp budgets and short lead times.

To meet a specific fixture requirement, engineers will necessarily fall back upon accumulated personal experience, designs of earlier fixtures for similar duty, their little black books, company standards, and the like.

From this, it is a giant step forward to utilize the proved, compressed experience of hundreds of other fixture designers. That is what this book is all about.

Except for certain simple and fundamental types of fixtures described, it will seldom happen that a complete given design can be lifted out and used unaltered in a given application. More commonly—and this is a prime purpose of the book —the designer will find some one or few design *details* which, used as-is or adapted, will significantly reduce his fixture design problems and time.

As with other ASTME books, this book has been built on the basis of all-member and all-industry cooperation. Individual contributions are sometimes therefore lost sight of in the massed effort but are nonetheless valued and appreciated. Specific acknowledgments are gratefully made

To the many dedicated members who helped us define the scope of the book and supplied the raw data.

To the many authors and coauthors previously listed.

To the staff editors who fulfilled their lengthy and heavy responsibilities with high credit.

To the National Technical Publications Committee for planning and policy that established the book.

Frank W. Wilson

xi

CONTENTS

Section 1

PREDESIGN ANALYSIS AND FIXTURE-DESIGN PROCEDURE

By COMMITTEE FOR FIXTURE PLANNING*

Jigs and fixtures are not mainly designed on the drawing board. While the details of a design are developed as drafting proceeds, its main features will have been conceived in the designer's mind before he started sketches and working drawings.

A successful fixture design is the result of the designer's ability to analyze all information and conditions which are in any way pertinent to a given manufacturing operation and to incorporate design features that offset or eliminate all difficulties or problems associated with the operation.

If a fixture fails, it is either because of a faulty analysis or because an analysis, substantially correct throughout, was followed by a fixture design that did not overcome the problems and difficulties clearly shown by the analysis.

Irregular workpieces, such as castings or forgings, nonhomogeneous strip or sheet stock, or workpieces having variations in size, properties, etc., can be a main cause of improper functioning of a fixture. The characteristics and properties of the workpiece are known at the outset of fixture planning; therefore all possible nonuniformities and variations in a work material will have to be considered in its analysis as a basis for subsequent decisions in planning the fixture as a whole, as well as its details.

The main concern of this section is with procedures for tool designers to follow in analyzing and assessing all conditions which can influence, to any degree, the design of a fixture.

Of necessity, all tool designers conduct some form of analysis when confronted with a tool-design problem. A systematic analytical approach, consisting of a procedure in a certain chronological order presented in written form, may help the beginner or improve the experienced designer's method.

It is found desirable in design practice to consistently follow a chronological analytical pattern, because each phase of the analysis is dependent upon or influenced by preceding phases, as are design decisions made during each phase.

There is no infallible procedure that can be applied to any design problem and

---

* The members of the committee are: Edward Aldous, Sales Engineer, Charles Churchill Co.; Thomas Atkins, Safety Engineer, Ford Motor Co. of Canada; James Barlow, Tool Engineer, Kelsey Wheel Co.; Isaac Barsky, Methods Engineer, Ford Motor Co. of Canada; Graham Jones, Tool Engineer, Ford Motor Co. of Canada; Paul Orr, Tool Engineer, Electroline Mfg. Co.; Stanley Rice, Tool Engineer, Chrysler Corp.; Louis Schlappner, Tool Engineer, Ford Motor Co. of Canada; Gordon Way, Tool Engineer, Chrysler Corp.; Richard Poultney, Process Supervisor, Ford Motor Co. of Canada, Chairman.

that, on being compared to all the variables found in check lists and questions, will automatically ensure the conception of a perfect or nearly perfect design of a tool. There is no formula in which the fixture designer can insert values and variables associated with the five major phases of design (Fig. 1-1) and similarly evolve perfection in the design of a fixture.

It is not to be inferred that the outlined approach to and suggested procedure for designing are unique or error-proof. There are many capable and experienced designers who may desire to start planning by first considering machine and equipment characteristics (Phase III, Fig. 1-1). We have no quarrel with this attitude and action, since all the many variables relating to the five phases are not entirely independent. Major decisions are not always final; and since later considerations may affect earlier decisions, some steps in the procedure may have to be retraced and previous decisions reevaluated. It does not seem illogical to start design planning with Phase I, because the quality of the product, as specified by the product designer, is considered during this phase. Few tool designers can change the specifications of a product (or workpiece), and since the fixture must ensure that the specifications are met, an examination of the product can be the first order of business for the designer. An examination of the product, Phase I, is an analysis, based upon certain criteria (product variables listed in Table 1-1), which suggests fixture-design ideas. Some of these ideas and concepts are immediately rejected; others will be rejected during the four phases shown in the chart of Fig. 1-1; while the other remaining fixture ideas and designs will survive the analyses and tests by the designer as one or more of the finalized and justified designs.

DESIGN PROCEDURE

A systematic and orderly procedure for jig and fixture design consists of five major phases or steps (Fig. 1-1):

First Phase. The examination of all information pertinent to the product (workpiece) as given by engineering and/or manufacturing drawings and operation or process sheets (see Tables 1-1 and 1-2).

Second Phase. From the analysis of all information obtained in Phase I, some general design concepts are arrived at, as related to design considerations listed in Table 1-4.

Third Phase. The examination and evaluation of criteria associated with the operation (process) (see Table 1-2) further determines or modifies some design concepts which were previously reached in Phase II, which considered only workpiece characteristics. During this third phase, some design concepts, tentatively proposed and based exclusively on product analysis, are retained and others eliminated. Those which are retained are subject to decisions that are wholly dependent upon operation criteria (as they affect fixture design) unique to (1) the type of operation, (2) the sequence of operations, and (3) specific machine characteristics (bed size, tooling areas, etc.), as listed in Table 1-3.

Generally, decisions to design either a single fixture or a number of fixtures, based upon operation and machine considerations and characteristics, result in tentative alternate fixture-design concepts which may appear in preliminary rough sketches.

The proposed alternate designs are further modified according to the assigned production quantity and rate.

Product quality for required production has now been established by these tentative design concepts that have been retained in the designer's mind and perhaps illustrated by rough sketches.

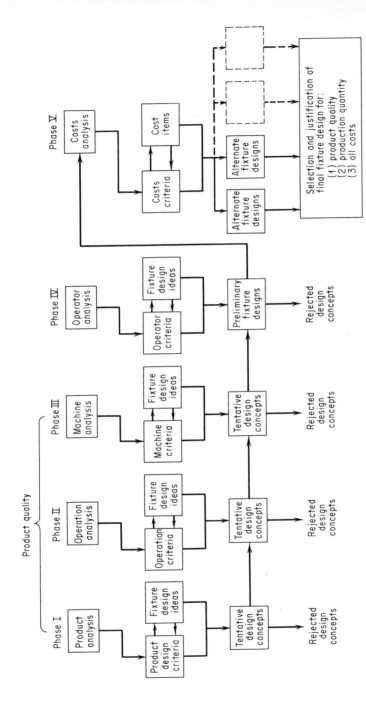

FIG. 1-1. Dependent flow of analytic design criteria, idea and concept variables.

Fourth Phase. This phase consists of the examination of all accumulated design concepts and their possible change because of operator considerations, which consist of the elements of time, fatigue, and safety.

These elements, as fixture-design criteria, are directly related to the loading, clamping, and unloading of the workpiece, as well as to the cleaning of the proposed fixture(s), and form the basis of design decisions made during this phase to synthesize one or more preliminary fixture designs.

Fifth Phase. This final phase is the evaluation of the tentative design(s) for lowest fixturing cost per part, which includes fixture design and fabrication costs, costs of fixture operation, amortization, and all other costs that are applicable wholly or in part to the design(s).

It is certainly true that the fixture design must provide the necessary quality, safety, production per hour, etc., so that up to this point in the design, the economic factors are not considered. It is therefore recommended that the design be begun by fulfilling these necessary requirements and then its estimated cost be compared with that allowed. Should the minimum design for required workpiece quality be under the allowable expense, it is suggested that further design improvement be justified on the basis of additional savings.

Though there are many methods of determining whether or not the expenditure is justifiable, the following method is recommended because of its relative simplicity.

The formula is

$$S_G \geqq \text{(equals or is greater than) } KT + \frac{T}{N}$$

where S_G = gross annual saving to be realized by the improvement. By gross we mean the savings before any deduction for expense in order to realize the savings

K = return expected on the investment after tax

T = estimated tool building expense

N = estimated life of the product or tool

Should the above be fulfilled, then the expenditure would provide at least the specified return on the investment *after tax*. Note that N varies with company policy but is usually a constant once established. The formula then becomes (if 15 per cent is used)

$$S_G \geqq .15T + \frac{T}{N}$$

Example:

S_G = $75.00 per year savings in direct labor

K = 15 per cent

T = $120.00 (additional tool building cost to allow machining of two pieces instead of one)

N = 2 years (the part will be obsolete in this time)

$$75.00 \geqq .15 \times 120.00 + \frac{120.00}{2}$$

$$75.00 \geqq 18.00 + 60.00$$

$$75.00 \geqq 78.00$$

Since $75.00 is not equal to nor is it greater than $78.00, the expenditure would not provide 15 per cent return on the investment and therefore should not be undertaken.

FIXTURE-DESIGN CHECK LISTS

In the foregoing discussion of a suggested procedure for fixture design, it is entirely impractical to treat thoroughly all design variables and their combinations. The variables listed in Tables 1-1 to 1-3 inclusive are given as items for the designer to consider in the combinations recognized during his procedural analysis; he must also estimate their effect on fixture-design considerations as listed in Table 1-4.

Table 1-5 lists the main function of the jig or fixture and related design factors, and it keys the group and section number to the list of check questions. These questions can be asked as a final review of the design before it is fabricated, or they can be introduced during a phase of the procedure as they apply to that particular phase.

FIXTURE-DESIGN QUESTIONS[1]

0.   Setting Up the Jig or Fixture

0.1. *Shop Layout*

Is there any obstruction in the shop layout which will affect setting up the fixture, *e.g.,* columns in the way?

Are the necessary services, such as air lines, available?

If a hoist is required, is it available; and can it be maneuvered into place?

0.2. *Machine*

Are the correct speeds and feeds available on the machine?

Is the machine accurate enough for the operation?

Is the machine sturdy enough for the operation?

Will the fixture fit into the machine for which it is intended?

Has the machine sufficient room and stroke length of the slide to perform the operation when the jig and cutting tools are in place?

Is there sufficient throat depth between spindle and column of the machine to accommodate the jig?

Is the weight of the fixture too great for the machine?

Do the T slots in the table line up with the clamping holes or slots in the fixture?

TABLE 1-1. Product Analysis Criteria for Fixture Predesign (Phase I)

1. Type
    a. Casting
    b. Stamping
    c. Mill shape
    d. Other
 	
2. Kind
    a. Ferrous
    b. Nonferrous
    c. Nonmetallic
 	
3. Properties
    a. Strength
    b. Hardness
    c. Ductility
    d. Machinability
    e. Weight
        (1) Amount
        (2) Distribution (center of gravity)
    f. Rigidity
    g. Resistance (electrical)
    h. Conductivity (thermal)
	4. Geometry (general shape and size)
	    a. Cylindrical
	    b. Flat
	        (1) Circular
	        (2) Rectangular
	    c. Spherical
	    d. Trapezoidal
	    e. Pyramidal
	    f. Conical
	    g. Combined shapes
	
	5. Specifications (holes, bosses, slots, other surfaces or points)
	    a. Numbers
	    b. Sizes
	    c. Location
	    d. Linear relations (tolerances)
	    e. Angular relations (tolerances)
	    f. Finish
	    g. Other

Is there enough clearance in these holes or slots to permit adjustment of the jig under the machine spindle?

Will the fixture overhang the end of the table when in place?

Are the register blocks in the fixture base the correct size for the machine, and are they correctly located?

Is there any projection, boss, bolthead, or other machine part which will foul the jig or fixture?

Will any operating handle of the machine strike on the fixture or be prevented from moving by the fixture?

Will the jig interfere with any other jig or fixture next to it on a multispindle machine?

Are jig-hole spacings within the range of adjustment of the spindles when a multispindle head is used?

0.3. *Cutters*

Can the setup man see whether the cutter or drill is correctly set?

Can cutting tools be adjusted when the fixture is in place?

Can cutters be readily removed for sharpening without disturbing the fixture?

TABLE 1-2. Operation Classification and Criteria for Fixture-predesign Analysis (Phase II)

Analysis of specified operations for criteria such as distribution, direction, and amount of machining or other forces, including considerations of vibration and chatter. For some assembly operations, such as welding, the analysis includes considerations of heat and electricity.

I. Type

    A. Machining
       1. Drill
       2. Ream
       3. Bore
       4. Grind
       5. Mill
       6. Hone
       7. Broach
       8. Brush
       9. Polish
      10. Tap
      11. Thread
      12. Plane
      13. Shape
      14. Slot
      15. Electromachine
      16. Manual
      17. Other

    B. Assembling
       1. Rivet
       2. Stitch
       3. Staple
       4. Braze
       5. Weld
       6. Solder
       7. Bond
       8. Fasten
         a. Bolt
         b. Screw
         c. Special types

       9. Press-fit
      10. Stake
      11. Tab-bend
      12. O ring, seal, and gasket-material insertion
      13. Other

    C. Inspection (qualification, gaging)
       1. Angular relations
       2. Linear relations
       3. Concentricity
       4. Surface conditions
       5. Others, such as leakage testing

    D. Miscellaneous fixtures for
       1. Heat-treating
       2. Plating
       3. Painting (masks)
       4. Foundries
       5. Cooling of plastic parts

II. Number and order

    A. Single
    B. Multiple
       1. Sequential
       2. Simultaneous

TABLE 1-3. Machine and Equipment Classification and Criteria Characteristics for Fixture-predesign Analysis (Phase III)

Class I. Material removal	Class II. Nonmachining
1. Milling type (vertical, etc.)	*A.* Assembling
2. Drilling type (sensitive, etc.)	1. Welding type (resistance, etc.)
3. Broaching type (pull-down, etc.)	2. Riveting type (pedestal, etc.)
4. Boring type (horizontal, etc.)	3. Stapling, stitching
5. Grinding type (surface, etc.)	4. Soldering, brazing
6. Turning type (automatic lathe, etc.)	*a.* Electrical induction
7. Reciprocating type (planer, etc.)	*b.* Furnace
8. Honing	5. Other
9. Electrical metal-removal type	*B.* Inspection
10. Polish	1. Optical (comparator, etc.)
	a. Stage area
	2. Fixture indicating elements
	a. Mechanical (geared indicator, etc.)
	b. Air, hydraulic (indicators, gages)
	c. Electric, electronic (pick-ups, meters)
	C. Miscellaneous equipment
	1. Painting
	2. Heat-treating
	3. Plating
	4. Foundry operations
	5. Peening
	6. Other

Criteria as applicable to machine and/or accessories: size, capacity, speed, feed, tooling area, coolant facilities, stroke, shuttle travel, other.

0.4. *Setting Aids*

Can setting blocks, bushings, stops, or collars be used in setting up the cutting tools?

If dial indicators are required for the setup, are there suitable places for mounting them on the cutters or fixture?

Have suitable locating plugs been provided for setting up?

TABLE 1-4. Fixture-design Considerations (as Determined or Affected by Product, Process, and Machine Analyses)

1. Locating considerations	4. Supporting considerations
a. Radial	*a.* Relation to tool forces
b. Concentric	*b.* Relation to clamping pressure
c. From surfaces	*c.* Relation to thin walls, sections of workpiece
d. From points	5. Loading considerations (including manual lifting and sliding; hoisting, unloading chutes, magazines)
e. Other	*a.* Rapidity
2. Positioning considerations (relation to tool and orientation in the fixture)	*b.* Ease
a. Indexing (linear and circular)	*c.* Safety
b. Rotating	6. Coolant considerations
c. Sliding	*a.* Direction
d. Tilting	7. Chip considerations
3. Clamping considerations	*a.* Accumulation
a. Rapidity	*b.* Disposal
b. Amount of clamping forces	
c. Direction of clamping forces	
d. Actuation (manual, power)	

TABLE 1-5. Checking Factors for Fixture Design[1]*

Group number	Function of jig or fixture	Related factors and section numbers				
0	Setting up	0.1 Shop layout	0.2 Machine	0.3 Cutters	0.4 Setting aids	0.5 Operator
1	Loading and location of part	1.1 Shop layout	1.2 Nature of part	1.3 Previous operations	1.4 Cutters	1.5 Operator
2	Clamping and support of part	2.1 Kind of operation	2.2 Nature of part	2.3 Machine	2.4 Cutters	2.5 Operator
3	Positioning tool to cutters	3.1 Tool features	3.2 Special equipment	3.3 Machine	3.4 Cutters	3.5 Operator
4	Cutter guiding	4.1 Nature of operation	4.2 Second operation	4.3 Coolant	4.4 Cutters	4.5 Operator
5	Chip control	5.1 Nature of part	5.2 Tool features	5.3 Machine	5.4 Cutters	5.5 Operator
6	Measurement of part	6.1 Cleaning	6.2 Clearance	6.3 Nature of measurements	6.4 Datum faces	6.5 Operator
7	Safe working	7.1 Part	7.2 Tool	7.3 Machine	7.4 Cutters	7.5 Operator
8	Handling and storage	8.1 Lifting aids	8.2 Loose parts	8.3 Fragile parts	8.4 Identification	8.5 Storage aids
9	Manufacture and maintenance	9.1 Cost	9.2 Standards	9.3 Manufacturing facilities	9.4 Design features	9.5 Provision for maintenance

* Superior numbers indicate specific references listed at the end of this section.

Is the accuracy of the part such that built-in adjustments are required in the fixture to compensate for machine misalignment?

Will an accurate sample part be useful as a setting master?

0.5. *Operator*

Does the setup man need more than one size of wrench? If so, can the number of sizes be reduced?

Are the hold-down bolts awkwardly placed, making their insertion or tightening difficult?

Is the setup man required to handle excessively heavy or awkward equipment?

1.   Loading and Location of Part

1.1. *Shop Layout*

Is there any obstruction in the shop layout which will hinder the loading of the part into the fixture?

Is the jig design correctly related to the flow line of the process?

Is the fixture to be used in conjunction with material-handling aids, such as hoists, hoppers, or conveyors?

If so, is the design correctly related to such equipment?

1.2. *Nature of the Part*

How will allowable variations in the shape of the part affect its location in the jig or fixture?

Is there enough clearance in the jig to allow for all lumps, fins, lugs, burrs, or protrusions on the part and for all normal variations in size and shape? (Castings and forgings often vary from the drawings.)

Will a profile plate on the jig base or sighting holes in the jig plate be useful in locating parts which are not consistent in shape or size?

If no previous operations have been done on the part, are there suitable datum faces or points from which to locate?

Can such points be properly related to the results required from this operation?

If the shape of the part makes location difficult, is it possible to have it modified to assist in locating it?

If the completed shape cannot be changed, can some temporary lug or other helpful feature be provided which can be machined off when its purpose has been fulfilled?

If the component is heavy, can arrangements be made to slide rather than lift it into place?

Where only one end of a long component has to be loaded into a fixture, has a suitable support or outrigger been provided to carry the free end?

Have V locators been placed in the correct plane so that variations in the locating diameters will not affect the accuracy of this operation?

Are the locating points as widely spaced as possible?

Are the locators affected by the material from which the part is made?

Is the component material so abrasive as to warrant the use of carbide locators?

Are the locating points those from which the result of this operation is dimensioned on the part drawing?

If the part is a rough casting, can a three-point location scheme be used?

If not, can a suitable jack pin or adjustable locator be used to provide the fourth point?

Should any other locators be adjustable to allow for casting variations?

Are centralizing devices required to compensate for part variations?

Are all locators on the same side of the parting line of a casting or of the flash of a forging?

If not, what effect on the location will mismatching have?

Is it possible to have all the locators on the bush plate of a drill jig, thus ensuring correct relationship between locators and holes?

Where several parts are located in the tool, should each one have its own locators, or will the accumulation of errors caused by parts resting on one another be acceptable?

1.3. Previous Operations

Do previous operations provide suitable datum and location points?

Is the tolerance on the locating points sufficiently close to obtain the accuracy required from this operation?

Can all subsequent operations be located from the same points?

If so, can the locators in all these fixtures be made identical in size and shape?

Have locators been relieved to accommodate burr thrown up by previous operations?

Have locating surfaces on the jig been kept as small in area as practicable?

Where they locate on a machine surface, do the rest pads come well within the boundaries of the machined area?

Are they well above chip-collecting surfaces?

Are they easy to keep clean?

Does the required accuracy demand expanding pins when locating from previously machined holes?

In boring fixtures where more than one hole is to be finish-bored after rough or intermediate boring, has the part been located from the smallest bore in order to minimize deflection of the slender boring bar with an eccentric cut?

Where location is from accurately machined or fine-finished surfaces, have steps been taken to avoid scratching or distortion of the part by locators?

1.4. *Cutters*

Are locators safe from damage by cutters overrunning or being set too deep?

Do any cutters, such as long drills, interfere with loading or location of the part? This sometimes happens when drilling on different levels with a multispindle head.

1.5. *Operator*

Can the jig be made easier to load and unload?

Is there plenty of room for the operator's hands when loading and locating the part?

Are the clamps well out of the way when loading and unloading?

Are the locating points easily visible to the operator?

Have locating pins been reduced to their shortest practicable length and smallest permissible diameter?

Have they been provided with effective bullet noses?

Where two locating pins are used, has one been relieved to a diamond shape and is one shorter than the other to make loading easier?

Is there enough clearance for the part to be easily lifted over or into locating and centering devices?

If the part is heavy and is to be located from previously drilled holes, is it possible to provide disappearing location pins which can be raised when the part has been slid into its approximate located position?

Can one end of a heavy part be rested in its approximate position while the operator loads and locates the opposite end?

Have sliding pins and other hand-operated locators been provided with comfortable handles, allowing a good grip?

Has it been considered that knurled knobs or screws, used continuously, will make the operator's fingers very sore?

Can all movable locators or jack pins be operated with one handle or one movement by the operator?

Can locators or jack pins be locked by the act of clamping the part in the jig?

Are all movable locators and adjustments on the side of the fixture nearest to the operator?

Should duplicate holding devices be provided so that one may be loaded during the machine cycle?

If the fixture is designed for several parts, can they be prepositioned during the machine cycle in some form of magazine or loading rack?

Is it possible to load the jig with one hand while the other hand is discarding the completed part?

Is there a fouling device to prevent the part from being loaded incorrectly?

Do the burrs thrown up by this operation interefere with unloading?

Is it desirable to provide an ejector?

If so, can it be operated automatically when the work is unclamped?

Can the finished part be ejected by loading the new part?

2.   Clamping and Supporting the Part

2.1. *Kind of Operation*

Is the cutting force heavy or light in this operation?

If it is light, is it possible to avoid clamping the part in the fixture?

If heavy, is the part rigidly supported and clamped in a manner best suited to resist the cutting forces?

Is the part supported as close as possible to the point where the load is applied?

Is the cutting force resisted by a solid support rather than by the clamp?

Will the cutting load distort or bend the part or the jig because of inadequate support?

Will the operation tend to tip or tilt the part in the jig?

Will it upset or twist the jig on the machine table?

Can the cutting force be used to help locate and secure the part in the jig?

Is the clamp strong enough to provide the necessary holding force?

If the fixture rotates, will centrifugal force tend to loosen the clamp?

2.2. *Nature of the Part*

Will the clamping force bend, crush, or mar the work?

Should a torque-limiting screw, or similar safety device, be built into the clamp in order to prevent overstraining of the frail parts?

Should brass, leather, or fiber faces be used on the clamps to avoid spoiling the surface finish of the work?

Has the clamp enough range to take care of allowable variations in the workpiece?

When more than one part is to be clamped, have suitable equalizing devices been included in the clamp to cover their variations in size?

If there is more than one clamping point on the part, are the points as widely spaced as practicable?

Is the work supported directly under the clamping points?

Will the clamping force distort the part enough to allow the surface machined in this operation to spring out of true when the clamp is released?

Will the clamping force bend the jig plate or other part of the tool and cause inaccurate work?

2.3. *Machine*

Can the movement of the machine table or quill be used to operate the clamp?

If an air-operated clamp is used, can the control valve be worked by the engagement of the machine feed lever?

Can a hydraulic clamping device be built into the circuit of the machine?

Does the clamping mechanism place any undue strain on the machine?

Will the clamp, whether open or closed, foul on any part of the machine?

When the clamp is thrown or dropped open, can it do any damage to the machine?

2.4. *Cutters*

Will the cutter be struck by the clamp when it is being opened or closed?

Will the cutter strike the supporting surfaces when it passes through the work?

Will cutter vibration or chatter tend to loosen the clamp?

2.5. *Operator*

Can the clamping be done easily and quickly?

Can all clamping devices be operated from the side of the fixture nearest to the operator?

Does the operator need a special wrench to clamp the work, or does he need more than one?

If so, is it possible to arrange for one standard wrench to tighten all the clamps?

Better still, can all clamps be self-contained, thus avoiding loose wrenches?

Can C washers or clamp plates be made captive by hinges or pins in order to do away with loose parts?

Can all clamping arrangements be combined so as to operate with the movement of one handle?

Would the clamp be easier to lift or move if a handle is attached?

Does the operator need a fixed handle, or similar grip, in order to hold the jig firmly while operating the clamp with his other hand?

Does clamping require much exertion by the operator?

Does the size of the work or the required clamping force warrant the use of compressed air or hydraulically operated clamps?

Can the clamping be speeded up by means of compressed-air, cam-operated, or quick-action toggle clamps?

Is it possible to clamp the jig with one hand, while the other is engaging the feed lever?

Has provision been made to prevent clamps from twisting or turning when tightened?

Have clamps been provided with springs or other means of lifting them clear of the part when loosened?

3.   Positioning Tool to Cutter

3.1. *Tool Features*

Have headed bushings been provided so that they project above the chips and coolant lying on the jig plate?

Are the jig feet large enough to span the T slots in the table?

Are the feet high enough to allow the drill to pass through the component without striking or injuring the machine table?

Have roll-over curves been provided to assist in turning the jig over?

Can the jig be clamped directly under the machine spindle?

If not, is it light enough to position easily under the spindle?

3.2. *Special Equipment*

Could the jig be more effectively presented to the cutters by mounting it on a rotary or indexing table or on trunnion mountings?

Would it be advantageous to rest the jig in an angle block clamped under the machine spindle when drilling holes on an angle?

3.3. *Machine*

When used on a multispindle machine, can the jig be nested into suitable table stops under each spindle as it is moved from one position to another?

Can suitable fences, or table stops, be used to prevent the jig from rotating with the cutter?

3.4. *Cutters*

Has the fixture been designed to keep the amount of cutter travel to a minimum?

Is it possible to design the jig so that all holes of the same size can be drilled to their correct depths with one setting of the cutter spindle?

Is the jig light enough to enable it to be pulled into place by a slender drill if it is not quite correctly positioned?

3.5. *Operator*

Can the operator see clearly all the bushings or cutter guides when positioning the jig?

Does the jig need a handle to allow the operator to control it easily and to resist its tendency to twist?

If the fixture is to index, can the index pin be withdrawn easily?

Can the index pin be unlocked and withdrawn by the one movement?

Will the index pin locate quickly and accurately when engaged?

Will a handle or handwheel assist the operator to index the fixture?

4.   Cutter Guiding

4.1. *Nature of Operation*

Do the cutters need guiding for this operation?

If so, are the guide bushings long enough to give adequate support to the cutting tool?

Are the bushings too long, thus giving excessive rubbing surface and restricting the escape of chips?

Is the required accuracy such that the bushings need to touch, or almost touch, the surface of the work?

Is the surface of the work contoured or on an angle so that the drill cannot enter squarely?

If so, does the end of the bushing need to follow the contour of the part in order to guide the drill effectively?

Would a bushing supported on ball bearings be an advantage for piloting a slender boring bar?

4.2. *Second Operations*

Do the tools need guiding for a second operation, such as countersinking or reaming?

If not, would a hinged or latch-type jig plate swinging out of the way after the first operation be better than removing slip bushings?

Is it possible to avoid slip bushings by using stepped drills for combining the drilling and counterboring operations?

If a stepped drill is used, has the largest diameter entered the bushing—and is it adequately guided—before the smaller leading end begins to cut?

If slip bushings are required, have hardened liner bushings been provided to locate them?

4.3. *Coolant*

Is the machine equipped with a coolant pump and tank?

Can the coolant reach the cutting edges of the tool?

Would suitable funnels or channels be an advantage to carry the coolant where it is required?

Are fences or guides necessary to prevent the used coolant from running to waste?

Is a guard required to protect the operator from coolant spray?

4.4. *Cutters*

Have chip flutes been provided in the pilots of counterbores, etc., to prevent them from binding in the guide holes?

When the cutters have been shortened by sharpening, will any part of the chuck, collet, or arbor foul on the jig or fixture body?

Can the heads of bushings be used as depth stops by allowing hardened collars on the cutter stems to contact them?

Have the bushings an adequate lead-in chamfer for the drills?

If a drill strikes a headless bushing hard and drives it a little way through the jig plate, will this affect the accuracy of the operation? Perhaps headed bushings would be better.

Long slender drills tend to whip when running at high speed. Is there any disadvantage to having them guided in the bushings all the time, even when the jig is being loaded and unloaded?

4.5. *Operator*

Has the bushing plate been correctly marked near the bushings with the drill sizes to be used in the respective holes?

Have slip bushings been marked "drill" or "ream" according to their function?

If slip bushings cannot be avoided, are the heads large enough and fluted (not knurled) to allow the operator to grip and turn them easily?

Is there room for his finger tips under the heads of the slip bushings?

Would it be an advantage to provide handles for extracting slip bushings?

Have the slip bushings been provided with an effective means of locking them in place?

When taking slip bushings out, can the operator turn them to a stop before lifting them, thus making it unnecessary to feel for the right place?

5.   Chip Control

5.1. *Nature of the Part*

Is the material of the part such that it will produce continuous chips (as in steel) or discontinuous powdery chips (as in cast iron)?

Will the accuracy of the part allow enough space between the drill bushing and the work to allow discontinuous chips to escape without having to pass through the bushing?

When drilling materials which produce stringy continuous chips, has the clearance between the bushing and the work been reduced to zero to enable chips to pass up through the bushing, thus avoiding chip tangles within the jig?

5.2. *Tool Features*

Do all supporting pads and pins stand well clear of chip-collecting surfaces?

Have all locating pins with rest shoulders been relieved in the corners to provide chip and burr clearances?

Have locating and supporting surfaces been kept as small in area as practicable?

Has chip and burr clearance been provided in V locators?

Have chip-collecting pockets and corners been eliminated as far as possible?

Have openings and ramps been provided to allow chips to escape from the jig?

Can channels or races be provided to allow the coolant to wash the chips away in a desirable direction?

Have suitable guards or shields been provided to prevent chips from fouling and wearing jack pins, index plates, and plungers?

Will chips foul the clamp lifting springs?

Have the jig feet been kept in as small an area as possible, consistent with their ability to bridge the T slots of the machine table?

Can the jig feet be secured to the jig from their top surfaces, thus avoiding holes in the bearing faces where chips may collect?

5.3. *Machine*

Is it desirable to fit chip-removal equipment to the machine?

Are chip tangles likely to interfere with operation of the machine?

Is an air blast desirable for cleaning out the fixture before reloading it?

5.4. *Cutters*

Has ample chip clearance been provided in flutes of the cutters?

Has the fixture been designed so that the cutter flutes are not prevented from discharging chips when covered up?

5.5. *Operator*

Are all locators and supports easy for the operator to see and keep clean?

If the operator cleans the chips out by knocking the jig on a bench or on the edge of the machine table, can suitable bumpers of fiber, hardwood, or Neoprene be provided to minimize damage to both jig and machine?

Should the operator be provided with a chip rake or cleaning probe?

6. Measurement of Part

6.1. *Cleaning*

Is it necessary to measure the part while it is still in the fixture?

If so, is it possible to clean it sufficiently for this to be done?

Will burrs prevent the accurate measurement of the part?

6.2. *Clearance*

Is there enough clearance between the tools and the part to admit the necessary scales, gages, or calipers?

Will the cutter be in the way?

6.3. *Nature of Measurement*

Is the nature of the measurement such that the whole jig, complete with part clamped in it, should be presented to the measuring device?

If so, has the tool been designed to suit the gaging device?

6.4. *Datum Face*

Is it desirable to provide measuring blocks, a datum surface, etc., from which to check?

6.5. *Operator*

Can the operator easily see the surface he is to measure?
Can he see the gage or scale in the measuring position?

7.   Safe Working

7.1. *Part*

Have all necessary steps been taken to prevent the parts from being damaged during the operation or in the handling to and from it?

7.2. *Tool*

Is the tool sturdy enough to prevent it from being damaged or broken during normal use and abuse?
Can it be damaged or rendered inaccurate through parts being inserted incorrectly?

7.3. *Machine*

Is the machine likely to be damaged by accidental breakage of part, tool, or cutter?
If the fixture rotates, has it been balanced to minimize machine vibration?

7.4. *Cutters*

Is it necessary for the operator to have his hands near the cutter while it is in motion?
If so, is the cutter properly guarded?
Could the cutter be damaged by striking the jig or fixture?

7.5. *Operator*

Can the operator see clearly what is going on at all times?
Have all unnecessary sharp edges and corners been removed from the fixture to avoid cutting or bruising the operator's hand?
Have screw heads been let into counterbores wherever possible?
Are there any sharp or awkwardly placed levers or handles to catch in clothing?
Is there ample clearance for fingers and knuckles around all handles, knobs, and slip bushings?
Is any leaf, cover, or clamp likely to fall on the operator's fingers?
Is the operator protected from flying chips or coolant spray?
If the clamp failed, could the part fly out of the jig and injure someone?
If the clamp is air-operated, should the mechanism contain a positive interlock so that if the air pressure failed, the clamp would not become loose?
Have suitable safety stops or guards been employed on air-operated clamps to avoid crushing the operator's fingers?
Should the tool be marked with a warning notice to caution the operator against improper or dangerous practice?

8.   Handling and Storage

8.1. *Lifting Aids*

Have lifting lugs, eyebolts, or chain slots been provided for slinging heavy tools?
Have lifting handles been attached to all awkward or heavy loose parts of the fixture?

8.2. *Loose Parts*

If loose parts such as spacing pieces, wrenches, or locating pins are unavoidable, can they be attached to the fixture with keeper screws or light chains to prevent loss in storage?

8.3. *Fragile Parts*

Is there any fragile part of the jig which needs a protective cover in storage?
Is the tool so delicate or highly finished as to require a special case, cover, or box to protect it in storage?

8.4. *Identification*

Has the tool, and all loose items belonging to it, been marked clearly with identification numbers or symbols?

8.5. *Storage Aids*

Can the tool be stowed safely without danger of tipping over?

Is a special storage stand or rack desirable for safe and convenient storage?

9.   Manufacture and Maintenance

9.1. *Cost*

Has the cost of the tool been properly related to the quantity and accuracy of the part to be produced?

Is it too expensive for low-volume production?

Are the production requirements high enough to warrant a better class of tool?

9.2. *Standards*

Have standard, or readily purchasable, parts been specified wherever practicable?

Have all parts been designed for manufacture from stock-size materials with a minimum amount of machining?

If the material is not carried in stock, is the right kind and size readily available?

9.3. *Manufacturing Facilities*

Can the tool be made with the available toolmaking labor and equipment?

Are the tool dimensional tolerances as wide as possible?

Has the design included suitable datum surfaces for toolmaking operations?

Is it easy to set up the fixture for grinding locators or supports which have to be sized in assembly?

If so, is there plenty of clearance for the grinding wheel and spindle?

Has provision been made for easy alignment and starting of pressed-in parts which need accurate location?

Have blind holes been avoided wherever possible?

Would it help the heat-treater to drill a small hole in each part, which normally has no holes in it, so that he may suspend it in a salt bath by a wire threaded through the hole?

9.4. *Design Points*

Are all parts well designed to take the loads imposed on them in service?

Is the tool sturdy enough to stand considerable abuse?

Is the fixture amply proportioned to damp out vibration and chatter? This applies especially to milling fixtures.

Is the design of all parts and mechanisms as simple as possible?

Have cylindrical plungers and holes been used in preference to square or polygonal ones?

Have holes for headed pressed-in parts (such as for accurate location of rest pins) been countersunk to allow any excess press lubricant to collect in the countersink (allowing the rest pin to vibrate slightly in service) instead of gradually squeezing out under the head?

Have spring pocket holes been countersunk on their open ends?

Are the dowel pins in each part as widely spaced as practicable?

Where detachable parts need very accurate location, have register keys or pins been used instead of dowels?

Is the accuracy of the operation such that the base of the fixture should be scraped to fit the machine table?

Have breather holes been drilled to allow air to escape from close-fitting plunger holes?

Is it possible to forecast any part design changes and to make allowance for them in the design of the fixture?

9.5. *Provision for Maintenance*

Has provision been made for lubricating the tool mechanisms?

Have all wearing parts been hardened?

Are these parts easily made and replaced?

Have correct materials and heat-treatment been specified?

Has provision been made for easy removal of pressed-in parts?

Can vulnerable parts be removed and replaced quickly without disturbing the setup of the fixture on the machine?

Throughout the examples of the application of predesign analysis and fixture-design procedure to specific operations, the criteria listed are only those which can in some way influence fixture-design concepts. While product data may include its electrical resistance, principally as a reference to its end use, this property can rarely be a criterion for designing a fixture for any purpose other than one directly using electrical energy, such as resistance welding or induction heating.

For the design of a fixture for any operation or process, it is the designer's function to decide whether any criterion associated with or intrinsic to the product, machine, operation, operator, or costs is a fixture-design consideration (Table 1-4) and to what degree.

APPLICATIONS OF PREDESIGN ANALYSIS AND PROCEDURE
Example 1. Press-fit Assembly Fixture Design

Product Data

Assembly components (Fig. 1-2, *A* and *B*) of SAE 32510 malleable iron casting
  Weight, approximately 2 lb each
Surface conditions (Fig. 1-6*b*)
  Surface *X* is flat and 90° to bore axis; chamfered mating diameters (Fig. 1-3)
Quality requirements
  Radial relation of the large holes to the small hole and mating diameters (press fit) as shown in Figs. 1-2 and 1-3
  Concentricity of ID (diameter *S*) of both parts to be held within 0.005 in. TIR to OD (diameter *T*) of both parts, after assembly (Fig. 1-4)

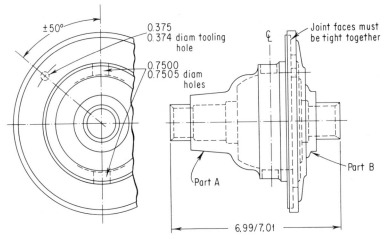

FIG. 1-2. Components to be assembled (press-fit) in the fixture of Fig. 1-8.

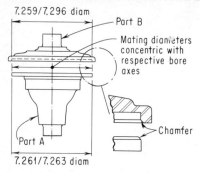

FIG. 1-3. Mating diameters, parts of Fig. 1-2.

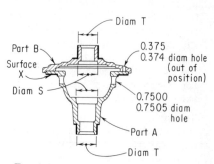

FIG. 1-4. After assembly, diameters T and S to be concentric within 0.005 in. TIR.

Joint faces to be tight after assembly (Fig. 1-2)
Quantity requirements
  50 assemblies per hr, net
  8,000 assemblies per year; 3-year period

Operation Data

Press-fit thrust of 500 lb is specified for interference fit

Machine Data

Arbor press, air-operated and of 1,000 lb capacity specified by process engineer, has T slots and a tapped hole in its arbor
Bed area; closed and open height are shown in Fig. 1-10

Operator Data

Manual loading and unloading of assembly fixture during operator's idle time allowed from another operation is required by work standards

I. PRODUCT ANALYSIS FOR FIXTURE DESIGN

Criteria		*Design Decision*
Size, fairly small		
Weight, light	5*	Manual handling
Distribution (c.g.)	1, 4	Part A to be supported for stability with small end down in fixture, part B with small end up (Figs. 1-5a and 1-6)
Surface X (part A)	1, 4	Placement of part A with small end down provides for its best support and ensures verticality (Fig. 1-6b)
Surface Y (part B)	3	Uneven, unmachined surface unsuitable for applying pressure (Fig. 1-7); therefore not used
Surface Z (part B)	3	Machined surface satisfactory for pressure to be applied by pressure ring (Fig. 1-7)
Surface of bore U (part B)	1	Incorporate locating plug held in pressure ring to engage bore U, locating part B vertically before pressure ring contacts part B (Fig. 1-7)
Outside surface of flange (part B)	1	This surface to be approximately located by a spring-loaded locating ring, which allows slight movement of part B to facilitate entry of locating plug into bore U (Fig. 1-7)
Chamfer on inside flange (part B)	2	Facilitates alignment and force fit of parts (Fig. 1-3)
Chamfer on OD (part A)	2	Facilitates alignment and force fit of parts (Fig. 1-3)
50° angle between axes of 0.375-in. hole in part B and the 0.750-in. hole in part A	1	Provides retractable spring-loaded swing locating pin (1) and removable locating pin (2) to establish required angle (Fig. 1-8)

* Numbers correspond to design considerations, Table 1-4.

II. OPERATION ANALYSIS FOR FIXTURE DESIGN

Criteria	Design Decision
Vertical press-fitting force directed downward with no torque or vibratory components	2 Fixture to be open at top for pressure ring's unobstructed contact with part *B* 4 Moderate unidirectional force requires fixture construction to withstand fairly low stresses

III. MACHINE ANALYSIS FOR FIXTURE DESIGN

Criteria	Design Decision
Tooling area	Does not affect fixture design; adequate for fixture accommodation (Fig. 1-9)
Open and closed height	
Capacity	Adequate per-process specification
Mounting	Fixture key to be included

IV. OPERATOR ANALYSIS FOR FIXTURE DESIGN

Criteria	Design Decision
Loading and unloading	5 Height of fixture allows space between pressure tool and top of fixture for parts insertion and removal
Ease of locator operation	5 Provided by swinging locator and removable locating pin, both having knurled handles; latter slides in slots rather than holes
Operator safety	No hazards to be reflected in fixture design

V. COSTS ANALYSIS FOR FIXTURE DESIGN

Criteria	Design Decision
Total costs per assembly with desired product quality	Fixture costs justified by amortization for production quantity

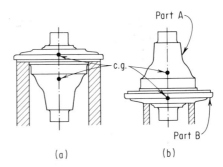

FIG. 1-5. Alternative positioning of assembly components in the assembly fixture; decision: as at *a* for best supporting and stability of both parts.

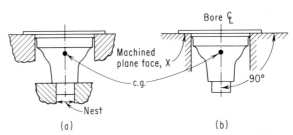

FIG. 1-6. Supporting decisions: at *a* a lower nest is not needed, since at *b* the part is adequately supported on its flat flanged surface *X*, which is also maintained at 90° to the bore axis.

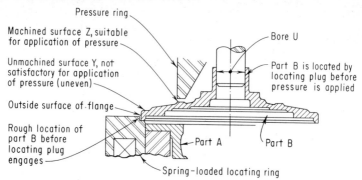

FIG. 1-7. Surface considerations for pressure application, part *B*.

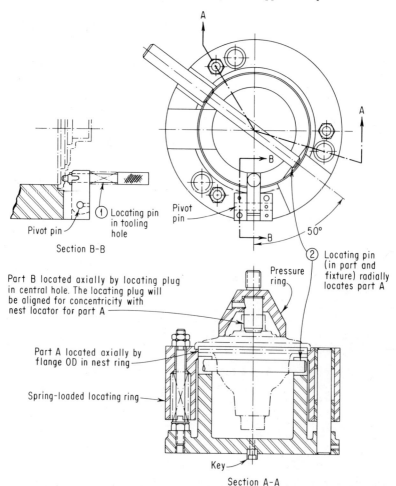

FIG. 1-8. A fixture for assembling parts *A* and *B*.

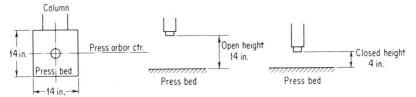

FIG. 1-9. Press data.

APPLICATIONS OF PREDESIGN ANALYSIS AND PROCEDURE
Example 2. Drill and Ream Fixture Design

Product Data

Connecting-rod cap (Fig. 1-10) SAE 1041 steel forging; surfaces *A, B, C,* and *D* are finish-machined

Weight, 4 oz

Quality requirements (Fig. 1-10)

Hole size, 0.3760 ± 0.0005 in.

Hole location, 0.510–0.514 in. from face *A*

Interhole distance, 3.265–3.270 in.; from center line, ±0.0025 in.

Quantity requirements

400 parts per hr, net

800,000 parts per year; 3-year period

Operation Data

Drill, ream, chamfer (2) holes, counterbore (1) hole, according to quality requirements (above)

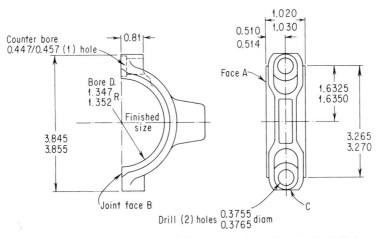

FIG. 1-10. Manufacturing drawing of a workpiece (connecting-rod cap) to be drilled, reamed, and counterbored.

Machine Data

Greenlee horizontal one-way-indexing drill machine time:

Index	3 sec
Rapid advance	2
Drill	34
Dwell	1
Rapid return	2
	42 sec

Index table to be drilled for bolting fixtures to it

I. PRODUCT ANALYSIS FOR FIXTURE DESIGN

Criteria		*Design Decision*
Weight	5	Manual handling
Hole location from face *A*	1	Locate against face *A* (1)
Interhole location (1.6325/1.6350 in.)	1	Locate from broached bore
Perpendicularity of holes with parting face	1	Locate on joint face *B* (2)
	1, 3	The tentative design decisions (1) and (2) necessitate a clamping force with consequent distortion (Fig. 1-11*a*). A preliminary locating design concept (Fig. 1-11*b*, *c*, and *d*) retains design decisions (1) and (2) and prevents distortion, without the need of clamping forces in more than one direction.
		Its depth will be nearly as thick as the edge of the part for maximum surface contact with it. Inside edges will be chamfered for ease of loading.
		It was concluded that the incorporation of a nest in the fixture would necessitate changes in product dimensions (length and width). The changes *A* and *B* listed below will not affect the function of the workpiece as discussed.

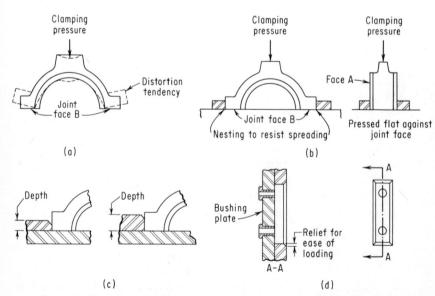

FIG. 1-11. Distortion considerations and their effect on tentative locating design.

Proposed Product Changes (Fig. 1-12)

A. Considerations for holding the 0.510/0.514 in. dimension and to arrive at a new part width, as well as nest dimensions, are:
   1. The mean part width is 1.024 in. (2 × 0.512 in.)
   2. Part-width tolerance, 0.002 in.
   3. Minimum clearance between part and nest to prevent difficult locating, 0.002 in.
   4. Part width, determined by (1) and (2), 1.023/1.025 in.
   5. Nest width, determined by (3) and (4), 1.027 in.

The establishment of a part width of 1.025 in. with drill bushings at 0.510 in. from the nest face will also establish a distance of 0.512/0.514 in. from hole centers to face A. A part width of 1.023 in. will permit a variation of 0.510 to 0.514 in. The 1.6325/1.6350 in. dimension will be maintained indirectly since the hole location will not be taken from the center of the bore radius.

B. Considerations for holding the part to a mean length of 3.8515 in.
   1. Part-length tolerance of 0.003 in. for machining.
   2. Minimum clearance between part and nest, 0.002 in.
   3. The part length, determined by mean length and tolerance (1), is 3.850/3.853 in. The distance from the center of the bearing radius to the end of the part is 1.9265/1.9250 in.
   4. The nest length, based on (2) and (3), is 3.855 in.
   5. The bushings are spaced 3.2670 in. center-to-center and 0.294 in. from the nest edges.
   6. The hole in the longer part (3.853 in.) will be from 1.631 to 1.633 in. from the center of the bore radius (Fig. 1-13a, b).
   7. The hole in the shorter part (3.850 in.) will be from 1.6325 to 1.6375 in. from the center of the bore radius (Fig. 1-13c, d).
   8. The nest location and dimensions (with the bushings spaced at 3.2670 in.) will consistently produce parts within tolerances if clamping forces do not distort it or disturb its location.

I. PRODUCT ANALYSIS FOR FIXTURE DESIGN

Criteria		Design Decision
Face A Face B	3	A single clamping force against these faces is not desirable and can cause tilting of the part (no particular squareness held in previous operation) and loss of accuracy in the 0.510–0.514 dimension and perpendicularity of the holes (Fig. 1-14a). Two clamping forces (Fig. 1-14b) are not desirable because perpendicularity of the holes will not be ensured.
Clamping points	3, 4	Boss faces were selected as clamping points (Fig. 1-15b) for more positive part support than a single force (Fig. 1-15a); there is less risk of part distortion.
Boss faces	3	Variations in boss thicknesses (not more than 0.005 in.) can result in nonuniform clamping with a nonequalizing clamp (Fig. 1-16a). A compensating-clamp design will be used (Fig. 1-16b). The type (Fig. 1-17a) is simpler than that of Fig. 1-17b, although it must withstand drilling pressure. Final design decisions: three clamps each to clamp two workpieces, each actuated by one toggle-clamp (for speed and locking action) and clamp yokes having a groove to restrict its swing (Figs. 1-18, 1-19).

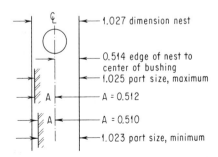

FIG. 1-12. Proposed dimensional part redesign for fixture planning.

Quantity
Cycle time

3, 5 Cycle time, including indexing time, confirms clamp design (above) for rapid clamping and suggests fixture mounting arrangements (Fig. 1-20) to drill 12 holes. Arrangement 3 (Figs. 1-20 and 1-21) will be used since it allows adequate room for each fixture and clamp, and for loading and unloading the workpieces.

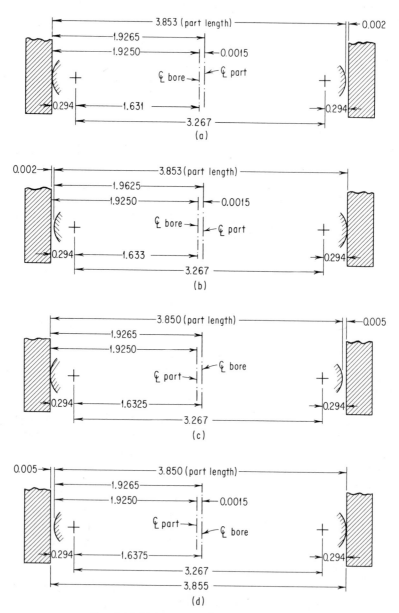

Fig. 1-13. Hole center to bore center variations.

II. OPERATION ANALYSIS FOR FIXTURE DESIGN

Criteria	Design Decision
Simultaneous drilling of 12 holes with a horizontal spindle and 12 drills	4 Fixture must withstand drilling pressure of 200 lb per drill
Coolant application	6 Coolant pipes on multiple-head side of index table direct coolant to bushings
Chip removal means	7 Not a part of fixture; air blast directed by operator into nests

III. MACHINE ANALYSIS FOR FIXTURE DESIGN

Criteria	Design Decision
Tooling area	2 Adequate for mounting fixtures on index plate, which is to be drilled for mounting holes
Clearance	2 Adequate between fixture and drill points

IV. OPERATOR ANALYSIS FOR FIXTURE DESIGN

Criteria	Design Decision
Ease and rapidity of loading, clamping, un-clamping, and unloading	5 Design decisions for locating nests and clamps permit easy fixture operation. An ejector, similar to that of Fig. 1-22, will be incorporated.
Safety	5 Fixture guards unnecessary since drills approach from side of index plate opposite to that of fixture. Spacing of clamps allows their manipulation without hazard to operator's hands.

V. COSTS ANALYSIS FOR FIXTURE DESIGN

Criteria	Design Decision
Total costs per workpiece with desired product quality	Fixture costs justified by amortization for production quantity

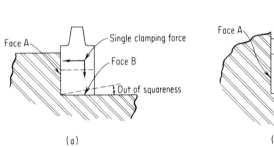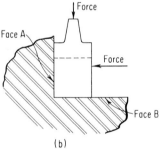

FIG. 1-14. Clamping-force considerations: (a) one force; (b) two independent forces.

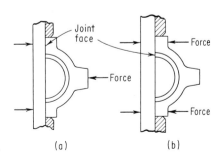

FIG. 1-15. Clamping-force selection.

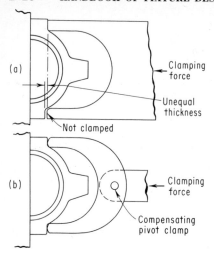

(a)

Clamping
force

Unequal
thickness

Not clamped

(b)

Clamping
force

Compensating
pivot clamp

FIG. 1-16. Boss-thickness considerations
for clamp design.

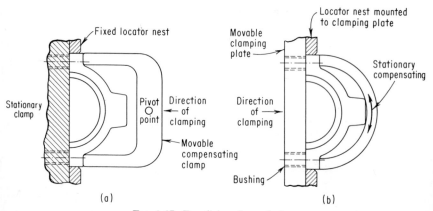

Fixed locator nest

Stationary
clamp

Pivot
point

Direction
of
clamping

Movable
compensating
clamp

(a)

Locator nest mounted
to clamping plate

Movable
clamping
plate

Stationary
compensating

Direction
of
clamping

Bushing

(b)

FIG. 1-17. Equalizing-clamp design.

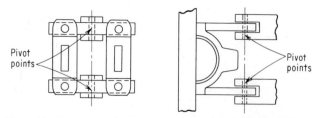

Pivot
points

Pivot
points

FIG. 1-18. Compensating (equalizing) clamp to hold two workpieces.

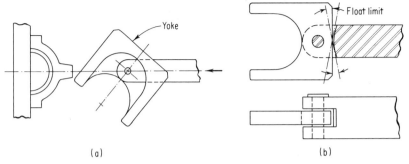

(a)   (b)

FIG. 1-19. Equalizing-clamp design details: (*a*) clamp can interfere with workpiece; (*b*) radial movement (float) is limited to ensure clamp engagement at boss faces.

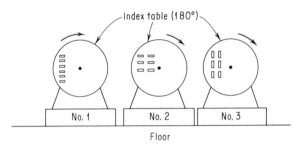

FIG. 1-20. Fixture arrangements on index plate at load-unload station for six workpieces (working stations are duplicates, oriented 180°).

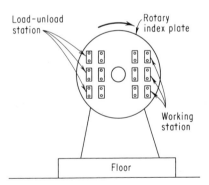

FIG. 1-21. Design decision for fixture placement on index plate (arrangement 3, Fig. 1-20).

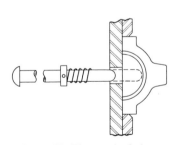

FIG. 1-22. Ejector-pin design.

Reference

1. Tindale, G. R.: Check List for Jig and Fixture Design, *Am. Machinist,* Sept. 12, 26, 1955.

Section 2

PRINCIPLES OF LOCATING AND POSITIONING

By J. I. KARASH

Manufacturing Engineer
Reliance Electric & Engineering Co.

A working knowledge of workpiece locating is not a mere refinement or a fine point in the art of manufacturing but is instead utterly basic to the practical solution of manufacturing problems.

Treatment of the subject will be limited to (1) the metal-cutting industry, (2) workpiece examples of basic geometric forms to minimize possible misunderstandings due to irrelevant complexities or size contrasts, and (3) illustrative examples of manufacturing facilities limited to ordinary machine shop equipment, such as conventional drill presses, lathes, milling machines, etc., and their related common auxiliary devices, such as vises, chucks, simple jigs and fixtures, etc.

The limitations described here are in reality very broad, for the fundamentals of workpiece locating are basic and universal and apply in some degree to all manufacturing operations, whether they are manual or machine, crude or precise, simple or highly automated complexities.

Our present-day technology produces astronomical quantities and myriad varieties of manufactured goods. At first impression this would seem to constitute overwhelming evidence that there must be in existence uniform and universally accepted principles of manufacturing. The principles of workpiece locating are not clearly defined and fully described even though the manufacturing industry is profuse in its verbal and written dissemination of its knowledge and experience.

In the field of manufacturing, because of the many different and contrasting meanings of the one word "locating," no universal and clear definition has been evolved. The word locating (and its many derivatives) does mean different things to different people, and it may mean different things to any one person under different circumstances. A few of the many shop-talk usages of the generic word locating are:

1. In the manual operation of layout (scale measure and scribe), it is commonly said that these lines are located.
2. In center punching the intersection of scribed lines (to create a drill start indentation), it is commonly said that the center punch mark has been located.
3. In positioning a workpiece to the drill spindle, or vice versa, it is ordinarily said that the hole is being located.
4. When manipulating cutting tools for a lathe, milling machine, planer, cylindrical grinder, etc., it is common shop talk to say that the operator is locating to diameter, to depth, to length, or to merely say "locating" without qualification.

5. When using a workpiece-manipulating device, such as the table of a jig-boring machine (positioning in the X-Y axis) or a precision-indexing device (a dividing head), shop talk commonly describes these positioning functions as locating.
6. When using precision indicators to check concentricity, squareness, parallelism, etc., common usage refers to these operations as locating.
7. When setting up a job (changing the auxiliary mechanical devices which supplement the basic machine tool) the adjustment or trueing up of the positional relationships may be called locating.
8. Placing of a workpiece into a workpiece-holding device (mating) is ordinarily referred to as locating.

Definition of Locating. Workpiece locating will relate to the considerations involved in achievement of a desired dimensional and positional relationship (mating) between the workpiece and the workpiece-holding device.

Relationship between Workpiece Locating and Clamping. The definition of workpiece locating may be further refined by clarifying what it is not. Locating and clamping are different though related subjects (problems). In the performance of a manufacturing operation, it is generally necessary to provide some kind of a clamping mechanism to maintain the workpiece in a desired position and to resist the effects of gravity and/or operational forces. Very often the workpiece locating and clamping may be simultaneously accomplished by the same mechanism.

The proper solution of the workpiece-locating problem requires certain points (or surfaces) of contact between the workpiece and the workpiece-holding device, and may also require a definition of direction and degree of holding force. In this sense, locating and clamping are related; but whether the clamp mechanism is actuated by a screw, wedge, cam, toggle, power cylinder, etc., selection of the proper actuation is a problem in itself and is a separate consideration from the fundamental problem of workpiece locating.

Failure to recognize or to properly apply the fact that locating and clamping are separate problems can cause considerable indecision and design rework. If the tool designer begins by first designing the clamp mechanism for a specific tool (jig, fixture, etc.), the later workpiece-locating considerations may then bring out the fact that the clamp already designed is not compatible with the logical method of workpiece locating. Such a clamp may be acting in the wrong direction or with improper force, or it may interfere with loading or unloading the workpiece.

The proper initial decision is to resolve the problems of workpiece locating; their solution will define a direction and degree of required clamping force. A suitable clamping mechanism can then be contrived, thus completing a compatible locating and clamping scheme.

Empirical Aspects of the Workpiece Locating Problem. Workpiece-locating procedures would be difficult to explain or to understand if there were no recognition of the difference and the essential relationships between an art and a science.

To illustrate the basic difference between the art of manufacturing and a pure science, if a purely mathematical problem of reasonable complexity is separately submitted in written form to different mathematicians, each will end up with the exact same numerical solution. In the event of a discrepancy, any one of the mathematicians will then be able (by universally standardized procedures) to recheck the figures and to irrefutably prove the accuracy or error of conflicting calculations. There is, in this instance, no leeway for bias or personal opinion, no basis for argument and emotions; none can have the slightest effect on problem solutions.

Contrasted to this convenient, orderly, and impersonal scientific procedure is a parallel experiment in the field of manufacturing. If a manufacturing problem of normal complexity is similarly submitted in recorded form, including drawings, to different manufacturing engineers for careful study of the problem, their individual recorded recommendations for the best method of manufacturing will differ. Although each engineer possesses the same data, it is highly probable that each method will differ from the other either entirely or in detail (the method of workpiece locating could be one critical difference of detail). None of the engineers could, by any universally accepted criteria, prove that he was right or that others are wrong. Invariably, there are seemingly logical grounds for inconclusive argument, and emotions can have profound effects on manufacturing-method decisions.

The implications of such an experiment (actual or imaginary) should not be construed as a reflection on the ability of manufacturing engineers, but should rather be regarded as an illustration of some of the inherent empirical aspects of manufacturing problems.

If experienced manufacturing engineers can have such basic differences of opinion (and they often do), the problems of the newcomer in highly competitive industrial areas are perplexing. Even though he be intelligent and well-educated (in a formal sense), when confronted with an on-the-job problem, such as a workpiece locating problem, he will have prolonged periods of uncertainty and indecision.

The fact is that manufacturing is now, and in the foreseeable future will continue to be, an evolutionary and dynamic mixture of science and judgment. The scientific and empirical considerations should not conflict but should complement each other, each in its proper function and each in its proper degree of influence to best solve the problem in hand.

Tangible and Intangible Factors of Workpiece Locating. The manufacturing engineer is constantly confronted with many conflicting objectives. Due to intermittent economic fluctuations and technological evolutions, these conflicting objectives have patterns that are each seemingly logical and orderly but are ever-changing, ever-different. Some of these conflicting objectives are as follows (not listed in any related sequence):

Capital equipment cost (minimum)
Tooling costs (minimum): tool-design time, toolmaking time
Tool material cost
Manufacturing cost (lowest): setup time, per-piece operation time
Required productive capacity
Required workpiece accuracy

All these objectives are related and interdependent. All can be affected directly or indirectly, favorably or adversely, by the selected method of workpiece locating.

To illustrate some of the tangible and intangible factors involved, required workpiece accuracy will be analyzed, as normally recorded on the product drawing, in terms of dimensions and tolerances. A tolerance is the permissible dimensional variance. Thus, dimensional tolerance is a goal, whereas actual dimensional variances are the results of operations. If a dimensional variance is not within the dimensional tolerance, then by that standard the product is not made according to the drawing (scrap).

Drawings sometimes do not, and for practical and economic reasons cannot, show all possible dimensional interrelationships. To illustrate this, an extremely simple geometric form, such as a Jo block or a paving brick (a parallelepiped), is considered. Actually, normal product configurations are far more complex than such a simple six-sided body, but it will serve for purposes of discussion.

Such an oblong body is made up of 6 faces, 24 angles, and 12 edges. A product drawing which actually recorded a dimension and a tolerance for every possible dimensional interrelationship, from any face to any face, any edge to any edge, any angle to any angle, and any face to any edge to any angle, would be fantastically complicated, expensive, and in a practical sense, incomprehensible in the shop.

Because of the astronomical number of possible dimensional interrelationships, product drawings tend to show only the essential information related to the problems of product design (those dimensions which control product appearance and its mating to other parts).

Typical product drawings carry a footnote such as "Unless otherwise stated all dimensions to be held to plus or minus 0.010 in." or some similar generalization. In actual practice, such footnotes enjoy or endure a considerable amount of interpretation and, like other generalizations, may sometimes result in some fantastic interpretations or misinterpretations.

It is evident that the manufacturing engineer must (in addition to that shown on the product drawing) have knowledge of certain, and sometimes considerable, supplementary data, such as an intimate knowledge of the end use of the product.

Some of the common causes of dimensional variance in the finished product are:

1. Raw material dimensional variances (for example, castings, forgings, weldments, bar stock, etc., will vary within drawing or mill specifications)
2. Workpiece-locating dimensional variance (chucking or fixturing positioning variance)
3. Workpiece-relocating dimensional variance (most products are not made in one operation but in a series of consecutive operations to most effectively utilize the skills of men or machines)
4. Workpiece-clamping distortion which may not be apparent until the machined workpiece is released. While clamped it may be of desired size and to shape but not when released
5. Workpiece warpage, due to release of internal strains by cutting away material
6. Basic-machine dimensional inaccuracy (machines have acceptable or inacceptable inherent dimensional error)

The manufacturing engineer has no standard reference tables to determine dimensional variances. If dimensional variances are known, there is the added problem that they act in cumulative (additive) and differential (subtractive) combinations.

The purpose of describing the general problems of dimensional tolerance and dimensional variance is not to criticize existing drawing conventions (for no better system is proposed) nor to overemphasize shop problems, but to discuss the causes and effects of dimensional tolerances and variances.

Problem-solving Procedure for Workpiece Locating. The procedure that the manufacturing engineer uses to resolve workpiece-locating problems can be compared to the technique used by the chemist.

The skilled chemist assumes that the test specimen is made up of some combination of known basic chemical elements. The chemist has systematic procedures for establishing the presence or absence of any of these basic chemical elements.

Similarly, the manufacturing engineer analyzes the workpiece to see whether or not it is made up of some combination of familiar elemental workpiece surfaces. Since he knows how to locate to these elemental workpiece surfaces, the manufacturing engineer extends and implements this know-how to solve workpiece-locating problems related to the particular combination of elemental workpiece surfaces.

Language of the Shop. Workpiece-locating problems (the mating of the workpiece and the workpiece-holding device) are solved by the practical application of the principles of conventional geometry. There can be considerable difficulty in reconciling the classical Euclidean theorems with the language of the trade as it is commonly used when discussing workpiece-locating problems.

Shop talk was coined and is commonly used for aptly stating certain specialized or certain combinations of geometric terms, which include words and phrases which may have no single direct counterpart in classical geometry.

Since it is impractical or impossible to convert the manufacturing industry to the use of pure Euclidean expressions, the prevailing idioms that are indigenous to the trade are explained.

Elemental Workpiece Surfaces. For the purpose of workpiece-locating analysis, the four basic kinds of workpiece surfaces (which in various combinations make up the total configuration of any workpiece) are as follows:

1. Flat surface
2. Inside diameter
3. Outside diameter
4. Irregular surface

The condition of each of these four elemental surfaces in regard to relative smoothness and/or dimensional variance will be later discussed.

The definition of a flat surface is considered to be self-evident. In the shop, flat surfaces are also referred to by a variety of different names all meaning some specialized variation of this elemental surface, for example, face, shoulder, flange, plane, wall, etc.; but they are all flat surfaces.

An example of an inside diameter (ID) is the inside (concave) face of a drilled or bored hole.

An example of an outside diameter (OD) is the outer (convex) face of a turned cylinder.

An irregular surface is any surface which is neither a flat, an inside diameter, nor an outside diameter. A simple example of an irregular surface is that of a vane of a ship propeller.

Inasmuch as the definition of an irregular surface is defined by exception (not a flat, an OD, or an ID) and is all-inclusive, any one individual workpiece surface can be classified as belonging to one, and only one, of the above four elemental workpiece surfaces.

Degree of Workpiece-surface Smoothness and/or Dimensional Variance. Any one of the previously described four elemental workpiece surfaces can individually have any conceivable degree of smoothness and/or dimensional variance.

Some problems can be most practically explained by using clear-cut, contrasting examples rather than by becoming involved in an explanation of all of the infinite degrees between these contrasts.

For that reason terms shall apply to only two contrasting workpiece surfaces: (1) rough or (2) finished.

Thus, a flat workpiece surface may be rough or finished. An ID surface may be rough or finished. An OD surface may be rough or finished. An irregular surface may be rough or finished.

The term "rough" is intended to designate a workpiece surface common to raw materials such as castings, weldments, forgings, hot-rolled bar stock, boiler plate, etc. A rough surface by definition has inherent dimensional variance to the degree that it cannot be ignored in considering workpiece locating.

The term "finished" is intended to mean a smooth machined surface (this section is limited to the metal-cutting industries). For the purpose of discussion, a finished surface has negligible dimensional variance unless otherwise specifically stated.

A typical shop part can be, for example, a casting which is made up of some combination of the four elemental surfaces (flat, ID, OD, and irregular surfaces), and each of these elemental workpiece surfaces may be either rough or finished.

The tooling most practical to locate to rough surfaces may have to be different from tooling to locate to finished surfaces. This difference in tooling may not be merely one of degree but rather one of more basic difference.

Locating Nomenclature. In locating to the four previously defined elemental workpiece surfaces (and their rough and finished surface variations), certain specialized descriptive words and phrases are commonly used by manufacturing personnel; for example:

Locating to a flat workpiece surface is usually referred to as plane locating.

Locating to an outside diameter or inside diameter is ordinarily referred to as concentric locating.

After a workpiece has been concentrically located, there may be a supplementary locating requirement which is called radial locating. There are only two locating considerations involved in placing an ordinary phonograph disk on a record-player turntable. The small center hole in the record is engaged downward over the mating pin in the center of the turntable. The record is now internally concentrically located. When the face of the record and the face of the turntable are in contact, the record is now properly concentrically and plane located. The direction of clamping force (gravity) is down. In this example, there is no requirement for radial locating.

When a wheel of chance has similarly been properly located, plane and concentrically (Fig. 2-1), and if it stops with the ratchet finger pointing to a desired number, the wheel can be said to be properly located radially. These three criteria for locating are independent, which the following various combinations of conditions of locating demonstrate.

1. The record could be true concentrically while simultaneously off-plane, since the plane of the record could wobble when rotating.
2. The record could be true with respect to plane locating (the plane does not wobble), but at the same time it could be off concentrically if the center pin of the turntable does not coincide with the center of rotation of the turntable; the record would then rotate eccentrically.
3. For the wheel of chance, the radial location either could be true (the one winning number) or it could be off (any losing number) regardless of whether (within reasonable limits) the plane of the wheel is wobbling or whether the wheel is rotating eccentrically.

The logical analysis of a workpiece-locating problem will be resolved into some combination or multiple of these three different locating requirements: (1) plane locating, (2) concentric locating, (3) radial locating.

There have been so far some combinations illustrated but not a multiple of locating axes. To illustrate multiple locating, a common paving brick, made up of six faces, would be located to one face and to two edges (lengthwise and crosswise), thus locating it in three plane axes. Since it does not have a diametrical surface, there can be no concentric locating. Since radial locating is a supplement to concentric locating, there can be no radial locating.

A cylindrical shaft that has been center-drilled in both ends and is located between the centers of a lathe is located internally concentrically on each end. The driving dog would normally not be considered a radial locator.

Analysis of Workpiece Surfaces. Before consideration of workpiece locating (and the subsequent problem of clamping), the workpiece must first be analyzed to very clearly identify the essential workpiece-locating surfaces.

A workpiece may be made up of any conceivable number or variety of elementary surfaces, but for any one locating problem, often only a very few such surfaces can be used.

To help identify these few key workpiece surfaces, a general pattern of questions follows:

1. What is the end use of the product?
2. What work is to be accomplished in the proposed operation?
3. What are the dimensional interrelationships between the surfaces to be machined and the other workpiece surfaces?

The answer to these and other necessary questions will usually lead to the identification of the workpiece-locating surfaces.

Workpiece-locating surfaces are those surfaces which are to be the basis of alignment for workpiece locating.

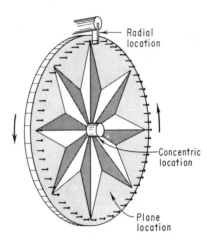

Radial location

Concentric location

Plane location

FIG. 2-1. Plane, concentric, and radial locating.

Pure (Individual) Locating Problems. The manufacturing engineer seldom, if ever, encounters a workpiece-locating problem that is of such simplicity that it can be solved by locating to only one single surface, point, or axis of the workpiece. Almost invariably there is present some combination of plane, concentric, and radial locating surfaces to be considered in the design of locators.

Each of these problems will be explained individually not in combination, but each as a pure problem. Illustrations of the specific problems will be schematic.

PLANE LOCATING

Plane locating is defined as the achievement of a predetermined positional and dimensional relationship between the cutting tool (limiting the scope of this discussion to metal cutting) and a specific flat surface of the workpiece.

Plane Locating to a Finished Workpiece Surface. Shown in Fig. 2-2 is a simple example of a workpiece which is finished all over and has no significant dimensional variations. A hole is to be drilled as shown. Inasmuch as the opposite faces of the workpiece are parallel, a hole drilled perpendicular to either work face will also be perpendicular to the other (parallel) work face. Either the top or bottom face of the workpiece can therefore be used as a basis of plane registration.

One of the problems of metal cutting is the inaccuracy which results from the presence of chips between the workpiece and the plane-locating face of the

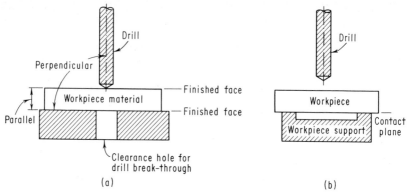

FIG. 2-2. Plane locating.

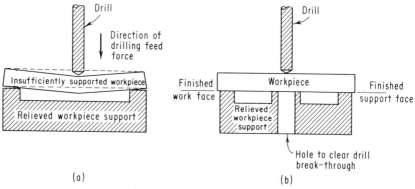

FIG. 2-3. Workpiece locating and supporting.

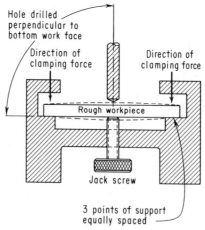

FIG. 2-4. Plane locating to the rough surface of a workpiece.

work support. The design of the work support (plane locator) cannot eliminate the problem of stray chips, but the design of the work support can help minimize this chip problem.

At *b* in Fig. 2-2 is pictured the same work support as that shown at *a* except that it is relieved, which reduces the potential area on which stray chips can accumulate and makes the locator easier to clean.

Relieving the face of a plane locator should not result in undue deflection or distortion of the workpiece due to insufficient support; that condition is illustrated in Fig. 2-3*a*.

A modification of the design is shown at *b*, with workpiece support closer to the pressure point and allowing clearance for drill break-through.

Plane Locating to a Rough Workpiece Surface. The rough faces of workpieces such as castings have appreciable dimensional variation which are not truly parallel and have minute casting inperfections. Under such a condition, the workpiece is unstable under drill pressure, and a hole cannot be drilled perpendicular to the bottom work face.

Shown in Fig. 2-4 is a type of adjustable support, a thumbscrew (jackscrew), that is suitable to rough-plane locating.

In operation, the proper sequence in loading and clamping the fixture must be followed or the jackscrew will not serve the purpose intended. The proper procedure follows: (1) the jackscrew is backed off to positively clear the workpiece for its loading into the fixture; (2) the clamps (represented by arrows) are secured; (3) the jackscrew is then adjusted upward to touch the workpiece; (4) the hole is then drilled which will be perpendicular to the bottom work face, because there is a specification for three equally spaced points of support around the periphery of the workpiece. The jackscrew is not a clamp but is instead an adjustable anvil.

As shown, the jackscrew would interfere with the drill bit if the hole is a through hole. In an actual application, the jackscrew would be located to clear the drill break-through area.

A plane-locating arrangement for drilling a hole perpendicular to the top work face is schematically illustrated in Fig. 2-5. It may need three point rough-plane contact and adjustable jackscrews below the workpiece to prevent workpiece distortion.

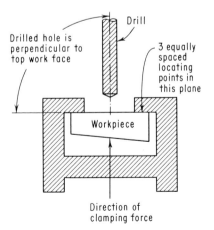

FIG. 2-5. Locating for drilling the top face of a workpiece.

While a drill is the cutting tool in the examples of locating discussed, the same general problems exist in almost any metal-cutting operation.

Variations in Plane Locating. The fundamentals of plane locating when applied to different operations may seem to be entirely different, but actually the basic principles involved are the same.

Finished work material is frequently clamped on two finished faces in an ordinary milling vise. Because the work material is flat, smooth, parallel, and to size (between parallel vise faces), workpieces of consistent quality are machined.

The faces of an ordinary casting are not straight, smooth, or parallel. Castings, as they are loaded, may fully locate (plane locate) against the stationary vise jaw, against the movable vise jaw, or not fully against either vise jaw, depending on workpiece-material variations.

It is not normal procedure to relieve the vertical faces of a milling vise, because workpiece deflection may result from cutter forces.

To control plane locating, some modification of the vise jaws can be made similar to that schematically shown in Fig. 2-6. The stationary vise jaw is relieved, and the movable vise jaw is crowned to direct the clamping force to hold the workpiece against (plane locate) the stationary vise jaw. It is not good practice to plane-locate against the movable vise jaw. It is good practice to plane-locate to the stationary milling vise jaw, thereby maintaining a constant relationship of the milling cutter to the identified rough work face.

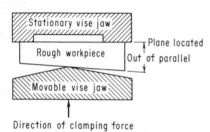

Fig. 2-6. Plane location of a rough workpiece in a vise.

Relieved vise jaws may need some form of an adjustable jack to prevent work distortion due to the clamping forces. Milling-machine operators frequently set the vise clamp screw with a lead hammer after tightening it. The impact of a hammer blow on the end of a vise crank lever creates a relatively high clamping force which can readily distort a seemingly rigid workpiece.

Shown in Fig. 2-7 at *a* is another variation in plane locating using an ordinary chuck, normally used with a vertical turret lathe or a vertical boring mill. The identified finished work face uniformly contacts the face of the chuck, which can be checked by a feeler gage. Such a locating procedure permits the workpiece to be face-cut parallel to the identified work face and is most suitable for locating to a finished work face. The identified workpiece face is located to but is not clamped by the chuck jaws and is not to be machined.

If the workpiece has a reasonably flat (though rough) identified plane, it may be practical to use the chucking procedure described. However, if the identified work face has a very rough surface, it may be desirable to support the workpiece on the step of each of the jaws of a three-jaw chuck (Fig. 2-7b). Since three points of support establish a plane, the workpiece will be equally supported.

With a four-jaw chuck, three equally spaced support blocks mounted to the face of the chuck but independently of the four chuck jaws will properly plane-locate the workpiece.

When a cut of uniform depth is to be made from the rough surface of a work-piece, it may be necessary to use a plane-locating method similar to that shown schematically in Fig. 2-8 in which three jackscrews operate in blocks secured in the T slots of the chuck. The process of securing correct plane locating is one of trial and adjustment. The operator spins the workpiece, and with chalk, he marks the high spots of the work face. Then he adjusts the jackscrews to position the top face of the workpiece in correct plane location. The identified work face is not contacted by the locating mechanism, the leveling jackscrews, but is indirectly positioned and located.

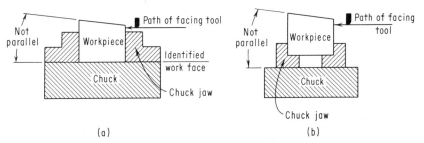

FIG. 2-7. Plane locating in chucks.

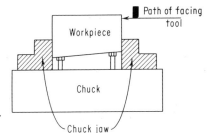

FIG. 2-8. Chuck leveling screws.

CONCENTRIC LOCATING

The condition of the workpiece surface, rough or finished, may in itself dictate design of the locating device, particularly for concentric locating.

For concentric locating there is an infinite variety of locating mechanisms, but for purposes of discussion, only two general types are included: (1) chucks and (2) fixtures.

Types of Chucks for Concentric Locating. While there are many different types of chucks, the discussion will include the four common types of wrench-operated chucks: (1) three-jaw scroll universal type with self-centering jaws (Fig. 2-9b); (2) four-jaw independent type with independent jaws (Fig. 2-9a); (3) three-jaw combination type with independent and self-centering jaws (Fig. 2-9c); and (4) four-jaw combination with independent and self-centering jaws (Fig. 2-9d).

For the purpose of this discussion, it is most practical to assume that each of the four basic chucks are equipped with master jaws and that the hardened reversible top jaws or reversible soft jaws can be interchanged as shown in Fig. 2-10.

There are inherent workpiece-locating advantages and limitations peculiar to each of these four basic chuck types.

Workpiece Examples for Discussing Chucks. The discussion of chucks is limited to workpiece examples which require external concentric locating, excluding

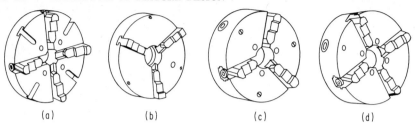

(a)   (b)   (c)   (d)

Fig. 2-9. Common types of wrench-operated chucks. (*Horton Chuck Co.*)

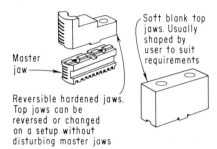

Master jaw ⟶

Soft blank top jaws. Usually shaped by user to suit requirements

Reversible hardened jaws. Top jaws can be reversed or changed on a setup without disturbing master jaws

Fig. 2-10. Types of chuck jaws. (*Horton Chuck Co.*)

chucks for internal concentric locating for these reasons: (1) the basic locating fundamentals are the same; (2) there should be no difficulty in visualizing internal concentric counterparts of the external type; and (3) chucks for external-concentric-locating applications far outnumber those for internal concentric locating.

Concentric Locating with Three-jaw Scroll Chuck (with Hard Jaws). A washer-shaped workpiece is concentrically located externally in a three-jaw scroll chuck with hard jaws, as shown in Fig. 2-11. The chuck has the following operating characteristics: (1) by its inherent geometry, it is best suited to circular, triangular, or related work shapes which will mate with its three jaws; it is awkward or imprac-

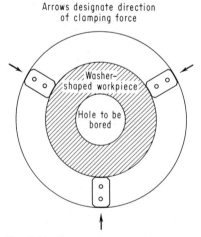

Arrows designate direction of clamping force

Washer-shaped workpiece

Hole to be bored

Fig. 2-11. Concentric external locating in a three-jaw scroll chuck.

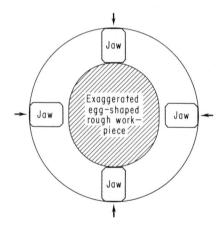

Jaw

Jaw

Exaggerated egg-shaped rough work-piece

Jaw

Jaw

Fig. 2-12. Nonuniform clamping in a four-jaw scroll chuck.

tical to chuck a square workpiece in a three-jaw scroll chuck; (2) the combination of a scroll and hard jaws is practical for jobs not requiring individual jaw correction as part of the concentric locating; (3) a scroll chuck having three hard jaws is suitable for rough concentric locating but not for finish concentric locating. The scroll, when new, does not move the three master jaws with precise uniformity and tends to wear unevenly after repetitive operations on one work-diameter setting. It also tends to develop irregularities from the impact of work cutting forces or from extreme clamping pressures. The hard jaws contribute to inaccurate settings, because they are designed for rough work and, for precise assembly to the master jaws, need not be accurately concentric to the center line of the rotating spindle; (4) the 120° spacing between jaws makes this chuck suitable for firmly holding circular, slightly egg-shaped or lobed workpieces. The clamping force of each jaw tends to push the workpiece between the other two jaws, with the result that the clamping forces are directed to the workpiece in diametric opposition (as compared to a self-centering four-jaw chuck); (5) since there is no provision for individual jaw correction, this concentric-locating device is only suitable for those operations in which the bored hole needs to be concentric with the average rough OD of the workpiece; and (6) the absence of means for individual jaw adjustment makes the three-jaw scroll chuck (with hard jaws) readily adaptable to power actuation for clamping. As a result, it is widely used for high-production applications.

Four-jaw Scroll Chucks. Figure 2-12 shows that a four-jaw chuck is impractical for chucking rough work. The simultaneous tightening of the four jaws does not result in their uniform clamping of the workpiece. The workpiece will tend to tear loose under cutting and centrifugal forces.

A four-jaw scroll chuck may be practical for second-operation work if the workpiece machined surface is accurate and if the soft jaws are accurately cut.

Concentric Locating with a Four-jaw Independent Chuck (with Hard Jaws). The four-jaw chuck, by its inherent geometry, is best suited for circular, square, or rectangular workpieces but not for triangular workpieces. It is best suited to those jobs requiring individual jaw adjustment and for locating to rough workpieces. Each workpiece (because of the four separate jaw adjustments) must generally be individually trued up by use of a dial indicator or by the chalk-marking method (Fig. 2-13).

The procedure for moving the workpiece toward true center in a four-jaw chuck

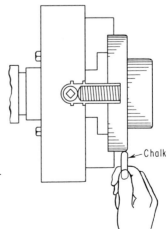

Fig. 2-13. Locating in a four-jaw independent chuck.

is that of holding it with two opposite jaws while adjusting the other two jaws. Thus, each pair of jaws alternately holds the work while the other pair makes a correction, a time-consuming operation. With a four-jaw independent chuck, either the external or the internal diameter of the workpiece (or some other identified surface) can be used as a locating surface. The individual adjustment of jaws for trueing up the workpiece is usually too sensitive for present power-chuck clamping devices and is not economically suited to high production.

Combination Chucks. A combination chuck is one in which the jaws can be operated in unison (self-centering action) by the operation of the scroll plate or in which the jaws may be moved independently; therefore, this chuck has the operating characteristics of either a scroll or an independent-jaw chuck.

Concentric Locating with Fixtures. The discussion of concentric locating related to chucks extends to simple drill jigs because chucks and fixtures for turning, boring, and drilling (including tapping, counterboring, spot facing, countersinking, etc.) operations present to the manufacturing engineer many actual problems of location.

Internal Concentric Locating of Finished Workpieces. The drill jig illustrated in Fig. 2-14a has an internal concentric locator which locates to the machined bore of the workpiece. A hole is to be drilled a specified distance from the center of the bored hole. It shows a basic design to accomplish this interhole relationship by establishing both plane and concentric location.

External Concentric Locating of Finished Workpieces. External concentric

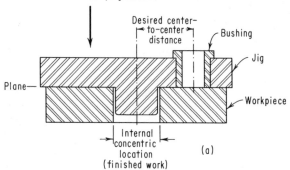

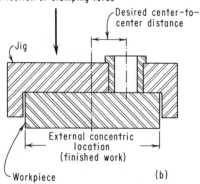

FIG. 2-14. Locating concentrically in fixtures.

locating of a workpiece which had been previously turned on its OD and faced is shown in Fig. 2-14*b*. A hole is to be drilled a specified distance from the center line of the workpiece. This arrangement will establish plane and concentric locating.

Jamming. Close-fitting concentric locators, whether internal or external, may have a tendency to jam or lock with the work. Jamming illustrated in Fig. 2-15 is exaggerated to show the basic condition of engaging two close-fitting concentric parts regardless of which is the locator and which is the work.

The diameter of the male part is smaller than any diagonal, such as that shown by the arrows. This diagonal is the hypotenuse of a right triangle. The two parts cannot engage in skewed position but will jam. The application of force may only cause the two to jam more tightly.

If an attempt is made to disengage the two after they have been hopelessly jammed, instead of straightening out and retracting, the parts may tilt past the perfect alignment point and jam in the opposite relation, as shown in Fig. 2-15.

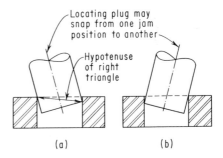

FIG. 2-15. Jamming or sticking of locators.

(a)   (b)

When the two parts are engaged beyond jamming depth side-wall contact will prevent tilting. Once this depth is reached, the two will slide together easily; but on disengaging, just before the parts come apart, the two may again start the jamming cycle.

Prevention of Jamming. There are several different methods of eliminating or minimizing jamming relating to clearance, length of fit, spherical internal locators, aligning shoulders, and cutting the side of the concentric plug.

Clearance Allowance. The closer the fit between the two concentric members, the greater the inclination to lock. The situation can sometimes be remedied by allowing ample clearance as dictated by work tolerance. This practice, however, should not be carried to excess; beyond a certain point, increased clearance will merely contribute to a poor fit.

The closeness of fit has a direct relation to the size of the parts being engaged. The entrance of a 0.246-in.-diam plug into a 0.250-in.-diam hole allows 0.004 diam clearance. The two parts should show almost no tendency to jam; in fact, they should enter so readily as to feel excessively loose. On the other hand, if a 15.996-in.-diam plug is entered into a 16.000-in.-diam hole, which also has 0.004 diam clearance, the parts will have a decided tendency to lock if slightly misaligned. Thus the amount of clearance in itself will not necessarily determine the ease of engaging, for this also depends on the diameter of the members. Small pieces require less clearance than large pieces.

Length of Fit. The relative length of fit of the engaging parts also has an important bearing on the ease with which the close-fitting concentric parts can be engaged. By length of fit is meant the distance the two overlap, as shown in Fig. 2-16*a*.

There are three fundamental conditions that occur as the length of fit is increased to the point where the parts are engaged deep enough to be unable to jam.

1. If the length of fit is short enough, the parts will be unable to jam.
2. There is a critical point at which maximum jamming action is reached.
3. Beyond this depth, the parts engage freely.

For a very short distance, the two parts can be engaged without any possibility of jamming; this is illustrated in Fig. 2-16b.

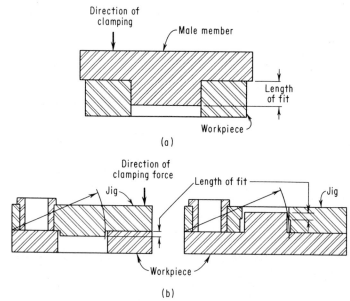

(a)

(b)

FIG. 2-16. Locator fit length.

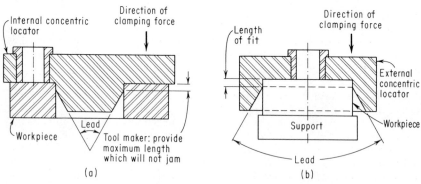

(a)

(b)

FIG. 2-17. Lead on locators for ease of engagement.

If all the other factors are made constant (amount of clearance, size of work), all jamming action may usually be eliminated by sufficiently shortening the length of fit.

In using short-length fits, preliminary engagement is greatly facilitated by providing a lead on one member (Figs. 2-17a and b).

It is not the lead itself which eliminates jamming; the lead merely assists preliminary positioning, allowing the parts to be practically thrown together rather than being carefully positioned to engage. This fact can be readily verified by engaging two close-fitting concentric parts that have ample lead. It will be found that, although the length of fit is long enough, the mating parts will show a strong tendency to jam in a slightly misaligned position. Besides the length of fit, the size of work and amount of clearance will also determine the critical depth before jamming begins.

The length of fit may be solved by construction through marking the tool drawing as shown in Fig. 2-17a. This, however, does not mean that the closeness of fit is to be left to the discretion of the toolmaker, for this factor is definitely controlled by the tool-diameter dimensions specified by the jig designer.

Spherical Internal Locators. A spherical internal locator, if properly proportioned, will not jam because of misalignment.

A sphere has only one dimension, and so, no matter in which direction it is turned, it has no dimension larger or smaller than its diameter and therefore cannot generate a jamming action.

Figure 2-18a shows an example of a simple spherical internal locator incorporated in a drill jig. No matter how misaligned the work and concentric locator, the two will always engage and disengage freely. This type of locator acts as lead for preliminary engagement.

Locators of smaller radius (less wearing surface) can also be used as nonlocking locators, as shown in Fig. 2-18b. Instead of being spherical, the locator can be of any shape containable in a sphere.

Such locators will not jam. The essential difference between these and the spherical type is the wearing surface, or life. Inasmuch as it is rather difficult to machine a spherical surface, this second type will probably cost a little less.

Aligning Shoulders. This is a simple and practical method of minimizing locking action when a close-fitting internal concentric locator is used. The method consists in machining a small groove near the end of the internal locator, as shown in Fig. 2-19.

When the plug has entered into the hole in a misaligned position as shown, it can travel only a very short distance before the work edge of the hole strikes the

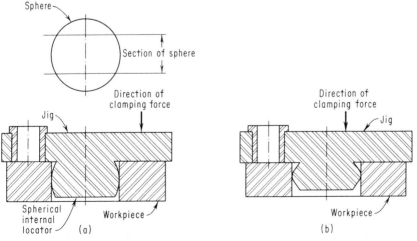

FIG. 2-18. Spherical locators.

shoulder of the plug. To meet the shoulder, the work edge must enter slightly into the locator shoulder groove. This allows the plug to move slightly sideways, and it is thus possible for the opposite edge of the plug to enter into the hole deep enough to pass the critical point at which jamming ordinarily occurs. Once the plug has entered below the depth of this critical point, no jamming can occur and the two members engage freely. On retracting the plug from the hole, the reverse process takes place, allowing the members to disengage freely.

The aligning shoulder can be shown on the tool drawing with a build-to-suit note. The method may easily be made to work very smoothly by trial-fitting the locator to the work.

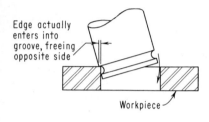

Edge actually enters into groove, freeing opposite side

Workpiece

FIG. 2-19. Locator with an aligning shoulder.

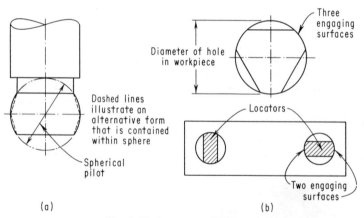

Diameter of hole in workpiece

Three engaging surfaces

Dashed lines illustrate an alternative form that is contained within sphere

Spherical pilot

Locators

Two engaging surfaces

(a)

(b)

FIG. 2-20. Locator modification.

Similar results can be accomplished by a ball-end spherical portion, as shown in Fig. 2-20a, or any form of end that can be enclosed in the sphere.

Cutting the Sides of Concentric Plugs. Jamming of concentric locators can also be minimized by cutting away three sides of the male mating locator, as shown in Fig. 2-20b. The locator has no two engaging points opposite each other; thus, the jamming is lessened though not entirely eliminated.

The same principle can be effectively applied to instances in which two concentric engagements must be made into the same part. Such a case is also illustrated in Fig. 2-20b. The engaging locators are cut away so that each establishes a location that does not conflict with the other locator engagement. For example, the left-hand engagement establishes the vertical relationship, and the right-hand engagement establishes the horizontal relationship. The purpose of such a scheme is to relieve the jamming that would be caused by very small-dimensional location variation between the holes in the work.

Methods for the Concentric Locating of Finished and Rough Workpieces. The most practical methods for concentrically locating rough workpieces may differ basically from the methods used for concentrically locating finished workpieces. For example (Fig. 2-21a), if the locator can enter the smallest cored hole, including surface roughness, etc., the locating method is inaccurate when the same locator engages a casting having the largest cored hole with fairly smooth surfaces. The potential locating error is equivalent to the difference between minimum and maximum casting variation; this holds true of external concentric locators (Fig. 2-21b).

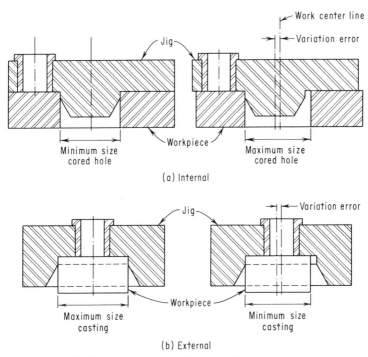

(a) Internal

(b) External

FIG. 2-21. Concentric averaging locating of finished workpieces.

Averaging Method for Locating Rough Parts. For locating rough parts, the averaging method can be used.

Internal concentric averaging locating, as shown in Fig. 2-22a, is achieved by an internal locator which is a truncated cone that will center itself into any diameter within its capacity. The casting variation, reflected in spacing variation between the bushing plate and the workpiece support, coincides with the center line of the drill and does not change the correct relation of drill and workpiece. The jig must be constructed to maintain the bushing plate and workpiece support parallel for all positions of the bushing plate. The locating cone should be long enough for a lead to readily enter the workpiece.

An internal concentric averaging locator can be inverted (Fig. 2-22b).

External Concentric Averaging Locating. The principles for concentric internal locating apply to concentric external locating, as illustrated by Fig. 2-22c and d.

Figure 2-23a shows the workpiece located in a V; workpiece size variation results in its incorrect locating to the drill bushing.

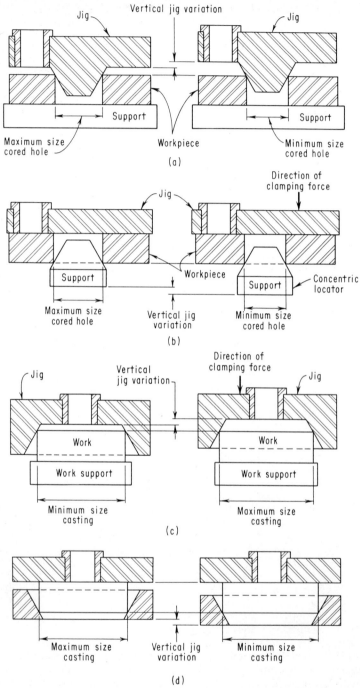

FIG. 2-22. Concentric averaging locating of rough workpieces.

Shown in Fig. 2-23b is an example of a correct averaging locator for the same workpiece.

An irregular-shaped workpiece that requires both concentric and radial location is shown in Fig. 2-24a. The workpiece, finished all over, will not only have to be located concentrically but will also require a radial locator, as shown, to establish radial alignment between its irregular shape and the drill bushing. If it were not for the radial locating block, the workpiece could be turned about the concentric locator and drilled in the correct concentric but in the wrong radial position. There is only one correct spot for the hole to be drilled, and that is at the intersection of the concentric and vertical center lines.

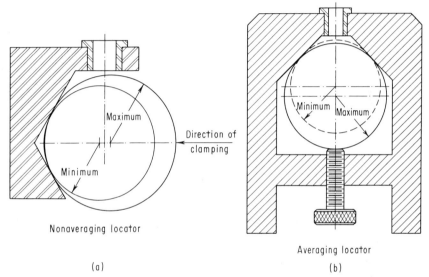

FIG. 2-23. External, averaging concentric location of a cylindrical workpiece.

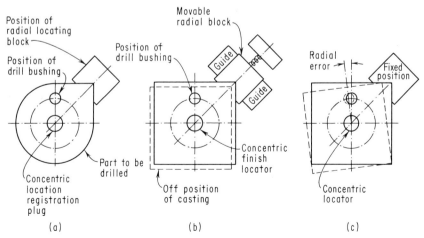

FIG. 2-24. Workpieces requiring concentric and radial locating.

Concentric and Radial Locating of Second-operation Work. The drilling of a rough casting having a machined bore frequently presents problems in location to its rough and smooth surfaces.

Concentric locating to the rough casting body cannot be accurate; it will have to be accomplished in relation to the machined surface.

Radial locating, if required, generally must be true to the irregular rough-cast surfaces.

One jig must simultaneously locate a workpiece with different relations to the two surfaces. Therefore, since these two locations (concentric and radial) are often made to different surfaces (machined and rough), there may be (and usually is) an appreciable variation between the concentric and radial locating points. This variation can be compensated by locating accurately to the machined surface (concentric) and by averaging the radial locating.

An example of averaging radial locating is shown in Fig. 2-24b. A V-shaped radial locating block, mounted between guides, is under spring pressure which keeps the radial locating block in constant contact with the workpiece whether the casting variations are on the low or on the high side.

Whether the locating block is forward or retracted, it is always in a true radial relation to the central pivot point. Any proposed averaging-locator design should be checked with this important question in mind: Is the locator true in both the forward and the retracted position?

An averaging radial locator need not necessarily be spring operated as shown.

A radial locator is fundamentally intended for locating only and not for clamping. If there is no established central locator to prevent the workpiece from shifting, a locator of this type will not average-locate but will force the workpiece out of true concentric position. It correctly functions only when acting against another locator that holds the workpiece in a true central position.

If a nonaveraging radial locator is used (Fig. 2-24c), it is necessary to set the radial locator back far enough to clear maximum chucking and casting variation; otherwise, the parts will jam between the concentric and radial locators. If the fixed radial locator is set back far enough to clear the maximum position, the smallest casting would be able to rotate appreciably and thus vary the radial location of the hole to be drilled.

Use of Extreme Work Edges for Radial Registration. It is ordinarily best to use an extreme edge of the workpiece for radial registration for maximum radial locating accuracy.

Section 3

DESIGN AND MECHANICS
OF CLAMPING DEVICES

By RICHARD SPOOR

Tool Engineer, The Linde Co., Div., Union Carbide Co.

The function of any clamping device is that of applying and maintaining sufficient counteracting holding force to a workpiece to withstand all tooling forces.

Proper clamp design, based upon simplicity with utility, affects total tool and
product costs and permits optimum production, surface finish, and tool life, if
other process conditions are controlled.

Clamp selection is predicated upon analyses of the workpiece, the operation on
it, and the quantity of parts to be produced. Clamp design considerations should
include its location in the fixture to achieve the following purposes:

1. Direct clamping pressure to supported and/or rigid portions of the work so as
   not to distort the workpiece
2. Facilitate easy and/or rapid loading and unloading
3. Maintain required workpiece relation to locators, gages, and tools
4. Provide minimum hazards to operator, workpiece, fixture, and tool before,
   during, and after the work cycle
5. Allow its incorporation as an integral part of the fixture

Clamping Forces in Various Operations. The type and amount of tooling forces
in the various operations requiring clamping of the workpiece must be considered
in clamp design.

Since *milling operations* induce vibrations in the workpiece from components of
cyclic forces as the cutter contacts and leaves the work, clamping arrangements
must be designed to prevent the clamp from loosening under these forces. Large
tooling forces are generally present in milling operations because of the large
metal-removal rate; therefore, strong, carefully located clamps must be used to
hold the workpiece without distorting it.

Planing and *shaping* tool forces are smaller but more uniform than forces present
in milling, and clamping requirements are less exacting with respect to size and
resistance to loosening.

In *drilling* and *tapping*, the clamping force must exceed the torsional force of the
drill or tap.

In *welding*, considerable stresses are created by thermal expansion and contraction of the workpiece and/or the fixture. Clamps must be designed to withstand
these forces, with respect to both cross-section and material selection (high yield
strength), to prevent excessive deflection or failure. Another consideration is that

of the fit between the clamp and other members of the fixture to allow for uniform thermal expansion and contraction of the members. The thermal conductivity of the clamp material selected must also be considered when clamps, besides supplying holding force, are required to dissipate (chill) or retain heat in an area adjacent to a welded joint. Since a clamp sometimes serves as an electrode, such as in flash butt welding, it must have good electrical conductivity. Application requirements influence clamp-material selection in regard to any tendency of the electrode material to weld to the workpiece.

In *soldering* fixtures, since generally less mass and heat input are involved than in welded joints, the forces of thermal expansion and contraction are smaller, permitting clamps to be reduced in size and strength.

In *chemical bonding* and *adhesive joining,* the amount of heat energy generated by chemical action, or otherwise concentrated in a fixture, is generally negligible; and little consideration to the thermal properties of the clamp material need be given.

Workpiece Considerations for Clamp Design. The *configuration* of the workpiece may require contoured clamps or product redesign to add bosses, lugs, etc., as clamp areas for adequate holding; or the workpiece may be held by magnetic, electrostatic, or vacuum devices instead of conventional clamps.

Equalizing clamps, or clamps with very long or short travel, or small but powerful pneumatic or hydraulic clamps may have to be used with workpieces of complex and/or asymmetrical contours.

For large workpieces, one of two clamping methods can be used: (1) a greater number of small clamps or (2) fewer, larger, and stronger clamps. The choice will depend upon which arrangement provides the best holding force combined with minimum clamp operation, design, and fabrication costs.

Surface finish of the workpiece may necessitate clamps incorporating soft or resilient faces of nylon, rubber, plastic, etc., to prevent the defacing of workpieces.

Surface variations, normal for some castings, may dictate equalizing-clamp design to compensate for these and similar irregularities. If surfaces of the clamps contacting the workpiece are subject to appreciable wear, such surfaces should be hardened or equipped with wear inserts.

TYPES OF CLAMPS

All clamps are variations of the following basic types: strap, screw, wedge, cam, toggle, or rack and pinion. Clamping forces can be transmitted by screws, cams, levers, or wedges and by rack-and-pinion, electrostatic, magnetic, or vacuum devices. Actuation can be manual, *e.g.,* with a wrench, key, lever, crank, or it can be automatic, *e.g.,* by means of an air or hydraulic valve or a limit switch, which is tripped by movement of a member of the machine such as the table, ram, etc.

Strap Clamps. A strap clamp, one of the simplest forms of a clamp, is a rectangular beam and subject to the laws of applied mechanics, particularly to the laws of levers and strength of materials.

All strap clamps belong to one of the three classes of levers, illustrated in Fig. 3-1, where F is the fulcrum or clamp rest, W is the force applied to the lever, and P is the clamping force on the workpiece.

In the arrangement shown in view *a,* the fulcrum or clamp rest should be as near as possible to the part. The distance L between the workpiece and the fulcrum should not exceed the distance l between the applied force and the fulcrum.

The class of lever shown in view *b* is the simplest and probably the most commonly used arrangement. Since this arrangement gives the smallest value for the clamping force, the force W should act as close to the workpiece as possible.

If the arrangement of view c is adopted, the part should be as near as possible to the clamp rest.

The simplest of all strap-clamp designs is shown in Fig. 3-2a. The strap bears against the workpiece and a loose fulcrum block, and holding pressure is applied by a nut and a stud. A compression spring between the base and strap keeps the strap up when the nut is loosened. A suitable integral nut-and-handle component, such as a wing nut, a bar handle, a knob, etc., would eliminate a wrench to turn the nut. The design of Fig. 3-2b reduces clamping time, since a separate fulcrum block and its positioning are eliminated. The height of the fulcrum block is fixed, while that of Fig. 3-2c is adjustable.

This clamp is the class of lever shown in Fig. 3-1b.

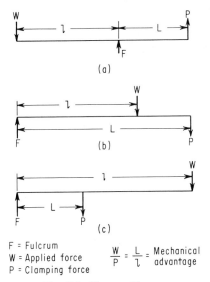

(a)

(b)

(c)

F = Fulcrum
W = Applied force
P = Clamping force

$$\frac{W}{P} = \frac{L}{l} = \text{Mechanical advantage}$$

FIG. 3-1. Classes of levers.

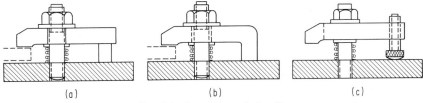

(a)   (b)   (c)

FIG. 3-2. Strap-clamp design.[2]*

Jigs and fixtures may necessitate movable clamps to facilitate insertion and removal of the workpiece. Movable strap clamps can be sliding, swiveling, hinged, or these motions can be combined.

A *sliding* clamp's motion is in one plane onto and off a workpiece.

A *swiveling* clamp moves about the axis of a pivot that is generally at a right angle to the clamping surfaces of the workpiece.

* Superior numbers refer to specific references at the end of this section.

A *hinged* clamp moves about a pivot axis that is located in a plane parallel to the clamping surface of the workpiece.

Slide Clamps. The clamp shown in Fig. 3-3*a* has a slotted fulcrum block which provides both constraint and movement to the strap. Placing the strap clamp between uprights prevents side movement of the strap; engagement of the strap pins in the side slots controls direction and amount of strap travel. Curved side slots allow vertical and horizontal movement of the strap when retracted. These slots can have a dwell portion to permit the strap, when retracted, to remain in that position. Clamping force is applied by the lever-actuated screw which also serves as a handle.

The slotted strap clamp of Fig. 3-3*b* is fastened to the base with a stud, two adjusting nuts, and a pair of mating spherical washers. A compression spring between the strap and the base keeps the assembly under tension. The hand screw assembly is aligned with the workpiece by the guide slot in the base.

A simple cam-actuated sliding clamp is shown in Fig. 3-3*c*. The design of cam clamps is discussed elsewhere in this section.

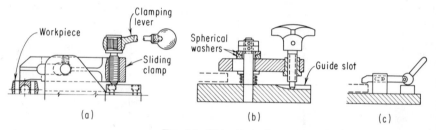

FIG. 3-3. Slide clamps.[2]

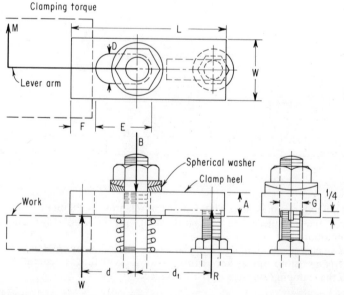

FIG. 3-4. Sliding-clamp design (see Table 3-1 for dimensions). (*The Cincinnati Milling Machine Co.*)

TABLE 3-1. Recommended Dimensions for Strap Clamps*

A	*W*	*L*	*D*	*E*	*F*	*G*
3/4	1 1/2	2 3/4 3 1/2 4 1/2	17/32	1 1/16 1 11/16 2 5/16	5/16	17/32
7/8	1 3/4	4 1/2 5 6 1/2	21/32	1 15/16 2 7/16 3 3/16	3/8	21/32
1	2	4 3/4 6 7 1/2	25/32	2 5/16 2 15/16 3 11/16	7/16	
1 1/2		8 10 12	1 1/32	3 5/8 4 5/8 5 5/8	1/2	25/32

* See Fig. 3-4. Material: SAE 1112 steel, heat-treated.

A commonly used simple sliding-clamp design is shown in Fig. 3-4. Design dimensions recommended are listed in Table 3-1.

Swing Clamps. The fixed-height swing clamp of Fig. 3-5*a* has a strap that bears against the workpiece, with the clamping force applied to the strap between the pivot post and workpiece. The swinging clamps shown in views *b* and *c* apply the clamping force at the center of the strap. One design is removable; the other is secured to the fixture.

The swing clamp of Fig. 3-5*d* is adjustable in height to accommodate workpieces of various thicknesses. It has no separate wrench or key to tighten the screw head, which is the handle for one-hand operation. The strap should be short and of a cross section large enough to resist deflection. The pivot must be large enough to resist the clamping forces.

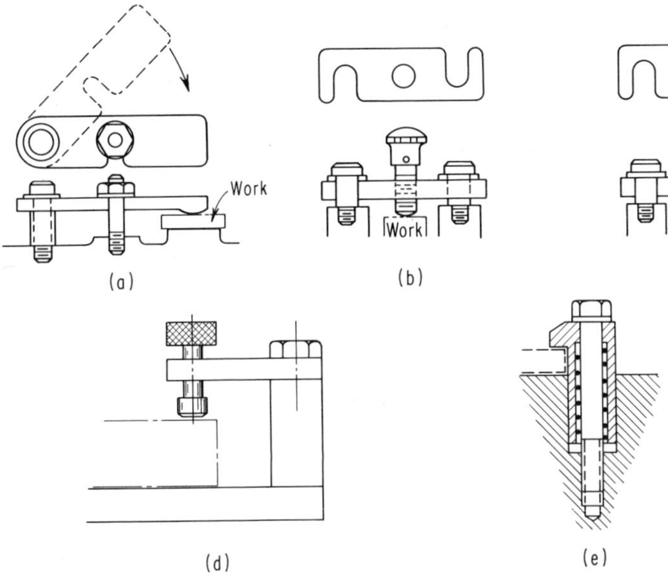

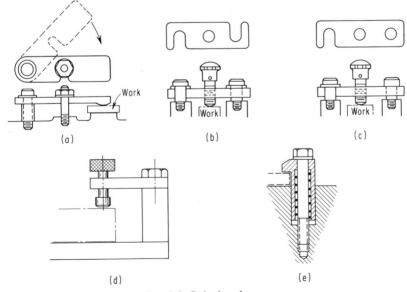

FIG. 3-5. Swinging clamps.

The swing clamp of Fig. 3-5e is effective when space is limited. It is usually cylindrical in shape with an integral lug projecting from one side. Its outside surface is the bearing surface when it is inserted in the fixture base. It is counterbored to hold a compression spring. A cap screw fastens the clamp and spring to the base. The hole in the base and the threads on the screw should be long enough to compensate for variations in workpiece height. With the lug projecting over the workpiece, clamping pressure is applied by tightening the screw. When it is loosened, the spring raises the clamping lug above the workpiece. The clamp is then pivoted around the screw, which allows workpiece removal. This clamp is commercially available.

Hinge Clamps. A hinge type of strap clamp, adjustable for workpiece height, is shown in Fig. 3-6a. Since both the strap and bolt are hinged, they can be rapidly swung to their clamping and load-unloading positions. By rounding the edge of the strap, as shown, less nut travel is required to clear it for the clamping position. A range of workpiece heights can be clamped by adjustment of the clamping stud in the strap.

Figure 3-6b shows an equalizing-hinge type of strap clamp which incorporates a pivoted block in place of the adjustable stud shown in Fig. 3-6a. Clamping pressure, directed to four points on the workpiece, is equalized for slight variations in workpiece height.

A poor clamping condition can result from differences in workpiece and fulcrum-block heights. By interposing a pair (male-female) of spherical washers between the nut and the strap (Fig. 3-7), full bearing surfaces are utilized despite the inclination of the stud caused by the difference in heights of the fulcrum block and workpiece. The angle of inclination that can be tolerated is limited by the clearance between the stud and the ID of the washers. The modification of the strap ends, that

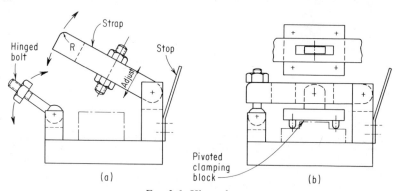

FIG. 3-6. Hinge clamps.

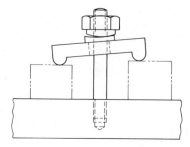

FIG. 3-7. Spherical washers for equalizing clamping forces.

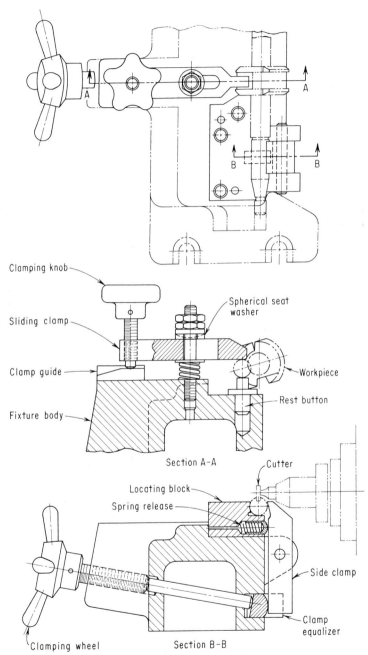

Clamping knob

Spherical seat washer

Sliding clamp

Clamp guide

Workpiece

Fixture body

Rest button

Section A-A

Cutter

Locating block

Spring release

Side clamp

Clamp equalizer

Clamping wheel

Section B-B

FIG. 3-8. Method of clamping a small crankshaft by use of a sliding clamp and equalizing pivoting clamps. (*The Cincinnati Milling Machine Co.*)

of raised and rounded toes, provides more effective clamping than a design having flat strap ends.

The design of Fig. 3-8 includes a sliding strap clamp (section *A-A*) and a pair of equalizing pivoting strap clamps (*B-B*). These clamps, incorporated in a milling fixture, are actuated by a clamping wheel and a clamping knob which are centrally located on the fixture. The pivoting clamp produces a clamping force which tends to seat the workpiece against the locating and supporting surfaces. The clamp is retracted from the workpiece when unclamped by pivoting on the fulcrum. A pivoting clamp takes less space than a sliding clamp. Figure 3-9 illustrates a pivoting clamp actuated by a setscrew.

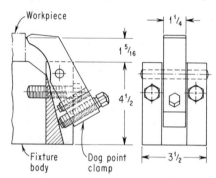

FIG. 3-9. Pivoted strap clamp. (*The Cincinnati Milling Machine Co.*)

Two-way or Multiple Clamps. An advantage of a two-way clamp is that all clamping actuation is done from one central position, usually adjacent to the fixture loading position. If separate clamps are used, the machine operator may be required to reach across the workpiece or travel to the other side of the machine to operate the clamps. Figures 3-8, 3-10, and 3-11 illustrate methods of clamping workpieces at two or more points or of clamping two or more workpieces by centrally actuated clamping devices.

Dimensions of Strap Clamps.[1] Clamping force is generally applied by a screw or threaded rod (stud bolt) in tension or compression or by a pivot pin in double shear. The diameter of the screw and/or the pin and clamp dimensions should be proportioned so that each is of equal strength.

The five cases shown in Figs. 3-12 and 3-13 represent the usual variations of the bar clamp used in tool design. In cases 2 to 5, where both screws and pivot pins are used, the relationship between their diameters is shown.

In Fig. 3-12 the width B, height H, and span L of the clamps are related to the screw diameter D. In cases 1 and 2 the chart gives the effective width only. To find the full width of the clamp, the screw diameter, plus its clearance, must be added to the value of the nomograph.

In cases 4 and 5 (Fig. 3-13), beam proportions are related to the diameter of the pivot pin P.

Nomograph values are based upon these assumptions:

1. Loading of the beam is central.
2. Root area of the screw is 65 per cent of its full diameter area.
3. Pivot pin is in double shear.
4. Ultimate shear strength of the pivot pin is 80 per cent of the ultimate tensile strength of the screw and clamp.

In cases 1, 2, and 3, given the clamping force required, the screw diameter D is easily determined; the span, effective width, and height of the clamp beam are found by multiplying their charted values by D.

Equations used in compiling Fig. 3-12 are:

$$\text{Stress in bolt} = 2W/D^2 \tag{1}$$

$$\text{Stress in beam:} \quad \text{Cases 1 and 2} = WL/4Z \tag{2}$$

$$\text{Case 3} = WL/2Z \tag{3}$$

where W = clamping force exerted by screw
  Z = section modulus of beam = $BH^2/6$

By equating the stress in beam and screw and assuming value of 1 for D, the relationship between D, B, H, and L is established:

$$L = 4\ BH^2/3 \text{ in cases 1 and 2} \tag{4}$$

$$L = 2\ BH^2/3 \text{ in case 3} \tag{5}$$

EXAMPLE 1. Assume that a bar clamp, arranged as in case 1 or case 2 (Fig. 3-12), has a span L of 6 in., and that it is used to clamp a workpiece with force $W/2$ of 2,000 lb.

The material used is machinery steel having an ultimate tensile strength of 60,000

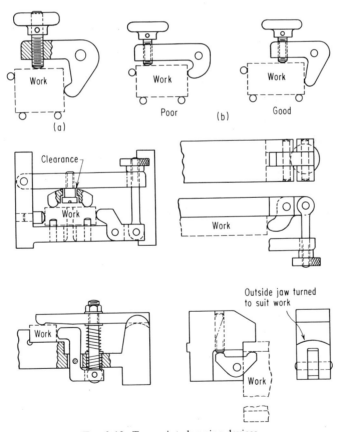

FIG. 3-10. Two-point clamping devices.

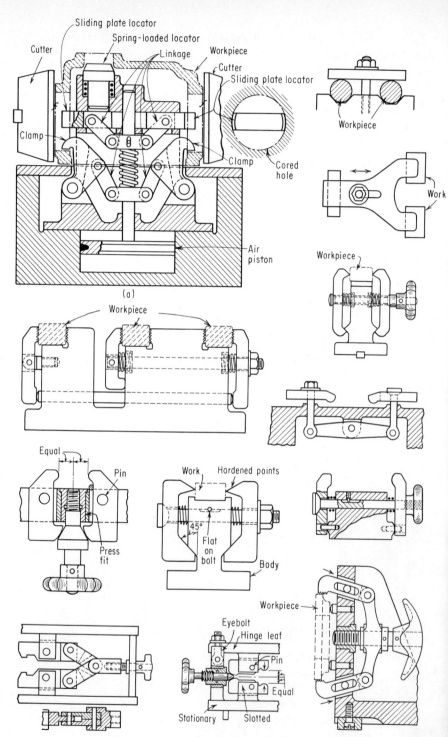

FIG. 3-11. Centrally actuated clamping devices.

3–10

psi. With a factor of safety of 4, the design stress is 15,000 psi. The screw must exert a force W of 4,000 lb. Root area of the screw must be $4,000/15,000 = 0.267$ sq in.

Full area of the bolt is $0.267 \times 100/65 = 0.411$ sq in. A ¾-in. bolt fulfills the requirements.

Span $L = 6$ in., which is 8 times the screw diameter D.

Turn now to Fig. 3-12 and follow the right-hand arrow down to the curve for span = 8; then move along the curve to select suitable height and width factors— say 2 in. high by 1½ in. wide. Multiply these factors by the diameter of bolt D, giving a height of 1½ in. and an effective width of 1⅛ in. If a ¹³⁄₁₆-in. screw hole has been drilled in the bar, this amount is added to the effective width, making the full width 1⅛ in. + ¹³⁄₁₆ = 1¹⁵⁄₁₆, or say 2 in.

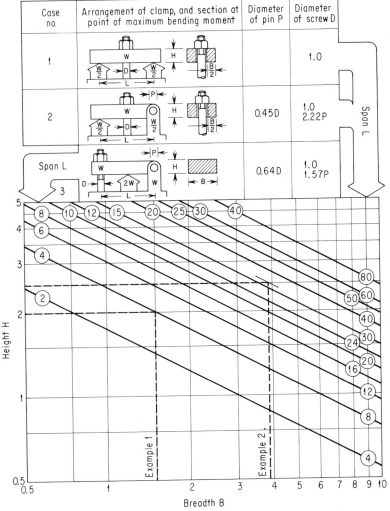

FIG. 3-12. Strap-clamp dimensions related to screw diameter.[1]

The height and width of the beam, therefore, are 1½ × 2 in. at the center.

EXAMPLE 2. Consider now an arrangement, as in case 3 (Fig. 3-12), having a span *L* of 6 in. and a clamping force 2*W* at the workpiece of 2,000 lb, as before. The allowable design stress is again 15,000 psi. In this case, the screw must exert a force of 1,000 lb or half the clamping load.

The full sectional area of the bolt will be (1,000 × 100) ÷ (15,000 × 65) = 0.103 sq in. A ⅜-in. screw will suffice.

By dividing the span, 6 in., by this diameter, we find a span factor of 16.

Follow the left-hand arrow down, and interpolate between the curves for 15 and 20. Choose suitable proportions, such as 2½ × 4, approximately, for height and width.

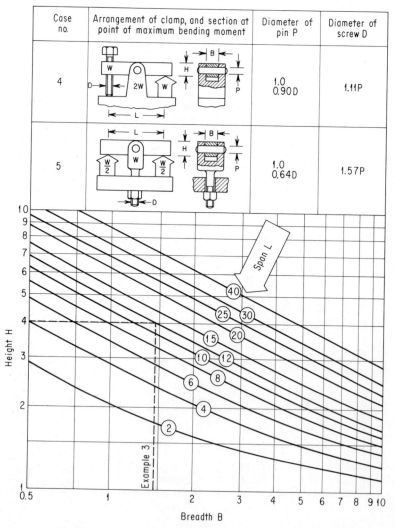

FIG. 3-13. Strap-clamp dimensions related to pin diameter.[1]

These factors, multiplied by the screw diameter, $\frac{3}{8}$, give proportions of $\frac{15}{16} \times 1\frac{1}{2}$ in. Because there is no hole in the center of this beam, its dimensions will be 1 in. deep by $1\frac{1}{2}$ in. wide.

In Fig. 3-13, the proportions of the beam in both cases 4 and 5 are related to the pin diameter. In the diagram, the pin in case 4 carries twice the load of that in case 5; and when related to screw diameter D, it has twice the cross-sectional area of the pin in case 5.

To proportion the beam, the pin diameter in both cases is taken as 1, and the load carried by the pin is assumed to be W.

$$\text{Stress in pin} = 0.8S$$

Where S = allowable stress in beam,

$$\text{Stress in beam } S = \frac{WL}{4Z}$$

When section modulus $Z = \dfrac{(BH^3) - (BP^3)}{6H}$,

$$S = \frac{6WLH}{4\,(BH^3 - BP^3)} \tag{6}$$

By equating stress in beam and pin and assuming a value of 1 for P,

$$L = 0.53B\left(H^2 - \frac{1}{H}\right) \tag{7}$$

It follows that, when the pin diameter has been calculated from the known clamping load and the span of the clamp has been established, division of the latter by the former will give the chart value of span L. Then decide upon suitable chart values of B and H, and these multiplied by the actual pin diameter will give the required dimensions for the beam.

EXAMPLE 3. A beam is loaded, as in case 4 or 5 (Fig. 3-13), with the beam proportions related to the diameter of the pivot pin P.

As before, span L is 6 in., and the clamping load at the workpiece is 2,000 lb. The force exerted at the pivot pin is $2,000 \times 2 = 4,000$ lb, and this load is carried by a pin in double shear with a design stress of 12,000 psi.

Cross section of the pin is $4,000 \div (12,000 \times 2) = 0.167$ sq in.; and its diameter is 0.46 or $\frac{1}{2}$ in.

Span factor is 6 divided by $\frac{1}{2} = 12$.

Follow the curve for span 12 on Fig. 3-13, and select height and width factors, for example, $4 \times 1\frac{1}{2}$.

These factors multiplied by the pin diameter give a beam 2 in. deep by $\frac{3}{4}$ in. wide.

No addition to the height is required to take account of the pivot-pin hole, because this has been included in the nomographs.

Dimensions of Clamp Screws. Clamping forces, commonly transmitted and applied by fixture members having screw threads, such as commercially available bolts, nuts, wheels, etc., have the largest mechanical advantage of all simple machines.

By definition, a screw thread is a circular inclined plane (wedge). References in this section to screw threads are restricted to the Unified thread form.

To induce a clamping force by means of screw threads, one member, either the nut or the screw, must not revolve, while the other member must be free to rotate. Clamping force parallel to the axis of the threads is generated by rotation of one of the members. The amount of axial movement in one revolution is equal to the pitch or lead of a screw or nut having a single thread.

When torque (force × lever arm) is applied, axial movement occurs; but, since both threaded members are in intimate contact, frictional resistance must be overcome by the applied torque, as well as tension resistance of the thread assembly. The clamping force applied to the workpiece must withstand the total tooling forces.

Lengthy formulas for computing screw torque are not exact, since the value of the coefficient of friction cannot be predicted accurately. The values found with the

TABLE 3-2. **Maximum Torque for Screws[4]***

Bolt size	Low-carbon steel	18-8 stainless	Brass	Silicon bronze	Aluminum 2024-T4	316 stainless	Monel
	In.-lb	In.-lb	In.-lb	In.-lb	In.-lb	In.-lb	In.-lb
2-56	2.2	2.5	2.0	2.3	1.4	2.6	2.5
2-64	2.7	3.0	2.5	2.8	1.7	3.2	3.1
3-48	3.5	3.9	3.2	3.6	2.1	4.0	4.0
3-56	4.0	4.4	3.6	4.1	2.4	4.6	4.5
4-40	4.7	5.2	4.3	4.8	2.9	5.5	5.3
4-48	5.9	6.6	5.4	6.1	3.6	6.9	6.7
5-40	6.9	7.7	6.3	7.1	4.2	8.1	7.8
5-44	8.5	9.4	7.7	8.7	5.1	9.8	9.6
6-32	8.7	9.6	7.9	8.9	5.3	10.1	9.8
6-40	10.9	12.1	9.9	11.2	6.6	12.7	12.3
8-32	17.8	19.8	16.2	18.4	10.8	20.7	20.2
8-36	19.8	22.0	18.0	20.4	12.0	23.0	22.4
10-24	20.8	22.8	18.6	21.2	13.8	23.8	25.9
10-32	29.7	31.7	25.9	29.3	19.2	33.1	34.9
¼-20	65.0	75.2	61.5	68.8	45.6	78.8	85.3
¼-28	90.0	94.0	77.0	87.0	57.0	99.0	106.0
⁵⁄₁₆-18	129	132	107	123	80	138	149
⁵⁄₁₆-24	139	142	116	131	86	147	160
⅜-16	212	236	192	219	143	247	266
⅜-24	232	259	212	240	157	271	294
⁷⁄₁₆-14	338	376	317	349	228	393	427
⁷⁄₁₆-20	361	400	327	371	242	418	451
½-13	465	517	422	480	313	542	584
½-20	487	541	443	502	328	565	613
⁹⁄₁₆-12	613	682	558	632	413	713	774
⁹⁄₁₆-18	668	752	615	697	456	787	855
⅝-11	1,000	1,110	907	1,030	715	1,160	1,330
⅝-18	1,140	1,244	1,016	1,154	798	1,301	1,482
¾-10	1,259	1,530	1,249	1,416	980	1,582	1,832
¾-16	1,230	1,490	1,220	1,382	958	1,558	1,790
⅞-9	1,919	2,328	1,905	2,140	1,495	2,430	2,775
⅞-14	1,911	2,318	1,895	2,130	1,490	2,420	2,755
1-8	2,832	3,440	2,815	3,185	2,205	3,595	4,130
1-14	2,562	3,110	2,545	2,885	1,995	3,250	3,730
	Ft-lb	Ft-lb	Ft-lb	Ft-lb	Ft-lb	Ft-lb	Ft-lb
1⅛-7	340	413	337	383	265	432	499
1⅛-12	322	390	318	361	251	408	470
1¼-7	432	523	428	485	336	546	627
1¼-12	396	480	394	447	308	504	575
1½-6	732	888	727	822	570	930	1,064
1½-12	579	703	575	651	450	732	840

* Tests were conducted on dry, or nearly dry, products. Mating parts were wiped clean of chips. Bolt tension was held at a factor somewhat less than the yield point.

following formula [Eq. (8)] will be a close approximation of those calculated with more complicated formulas.

Computing Torque in Screws.[3] The torque T, required on a screw to obtain a clamping force W_{min}, is approximately

$$T = 0.2 d W_{min} \qquad (8)$$

where T = torque, in.-lb

d = nominal screw diam. in.

W = axial clamping force, lb

The torque required to give a clamping force of 1,000 lb on a $\%_{16}$-12 UNC bolt, from Eq. (8),

$$T = 0.2 \times 0.5625 \times 1,000 = 112.5 \text{ in.-lb}$$

To withstand total stress in it the nominal diameter of a screw supplying a clamping force W_{min} is

$$d = 1.355 \frac{W_{min}}{S_t} \qquad (9)$$

where S_t = total shear and tensile stresses, psi.

To arrive at a working or allowable stress for the screw, the ultimate strength of the screw material may be divided by a safety factor of from 6 to 10.

The torque values listed in Table 3-2 are offered as a guide.

Since torque is the product of force × lever arm and many clamping devices are manually operated, it is necessary to know what force can be applied by a physical effort. The strength of individuals varies, but the values listed in Table 3-3 are given as a guide.

The length of the lever arm may be dictated by reasons of space, location,

TABLE 3-3. Results of Strength Tests[3]

Event	Force, lb					Source
	Max.	Mean	Min.	Max. mean	Min. mean	
Grip	166	109	52	3.2	.48	a
	148	95	42	3.3	.44	b
	154	103	52	3.0	.51	c
Right grip..........	183	124	65	2.8	.52	d
Left grip...........	165	113	61	2.7	.54	d
Back lift	568	364	160	3.6	.44	a
	496	314	132	3.8	.42	b
	545	368	191	2.9	.52	c
	541	343	145	3.7	.42	d
Leg lift	1,012	617	322	3.5	.52	d
Arm push..........	464	252	40	11.6	.16	d
Arm pull...........	115	79	33	3.5	.42	d
Average	......	......	......	4.0	.45	

[a] 10,593 employed males, 14–65 years of age.

[b] 1,328 unemployed males, 14–65 years of age.

[c] 1,735 students, 16–40 years of age. Reported by E. P. Cathcart, E. R. Hughes, and J. C. Chalmers, "The Physique of Man in Industry," Industrial Health Research Board, Medical Research Council, London, England, no. 71, 1935.

[d] Averages for 250 men entering college. Reported by F. W. Cozens, Strength Tests as Measures of General Athletic Ability in College Men, *Research Quart. Am. Assoc. Health and Phys. Educ.*, Vol. 11, No. 1, March, 1940.

or other limitations. The lever must be long enough to utilize the minimum force and yet short enough to preclude failure of the clamping device if a large force is applied. The torque for a given-size bolt of any of the materials listed in Table 3-2 should not be exceeded. Hence the designer must consider such values in the table when determining the length of the lever arm.

Cam Clamps. Cam clamps provide rapid and effective clamping forces if properly designed and applied. They are available commercially as standard items.

The surfaces of cams and thrust plates are subject to wear, and most cam clamps tend to shift the thrust plate or workpiece during their clamping and unclamping. They may unclamp as the result of vibrations generated by tool forces. For those reasons, they require some attention by the operator for their proper working.

A cam clamp is a machine member having a curved surface which changes distance with respect to its pivot when rotated. Since the distance between the cam's pivot and the workpiece is fixed, the cam must be rotated to apply a clamping force, directly or indirectly, to the workpiece. A cam's resistance to loosening is dependent upon frictional force between its contact surface and that of the surface against which it bears.

There are two types of cam clamps, the eccentric and the spiral cam.

The swiveling cam-actuated strap clamp of Fig. 3-14 has a strap which pivots around the center post for loading and unloading the workpiece. The spherical washers compensate for slight variations in workpiece height. The one-piece cam and handle is a standard commercial component, also available in variations of the type shown.

The design of Fig. 3-15a can also be swiveled about the eyebolt, but it utilizes a fork cam having two bearing surfaces. The guide rest (Fig. 3-15b) allows the strap to be slid on and off the workpiece but prevents strap rotation. As the handle is turned, the strap clamp of Fig. 3-15c is retracted by pressure of a push pin against a dowel which is press-fit in the strap. The clamp is returned by the compression spring.

Two cams are each rotated by hydraulically actuated rack-and-pinion assemblies, as shown in Fig. 3-16. Return of the clamping and locating arms is assisted by return springs.

A sliding-wedge cam operated by an air cylinder (Fig. 3-17) exerts downward pressure, through spherical washers, on the workpiece. The clamp is released when

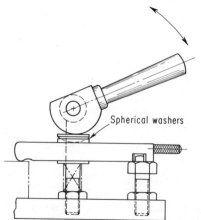

Spherical washers

Fig. 3-14. Swiveling cam-actuated strap clamp.

the air flow, reversed in the cylinder, is directed against the largest end of the piston, ensuring maximum unlocking force to overcome frictional force.

A cam-locking spring keeps the pivoted clamping levers in the clamped position in the design shown in Fig. 3-18. The levers move to their unclamped position only when oil under pressure is directed to the spring-loaded piston. Hydraulic pressure

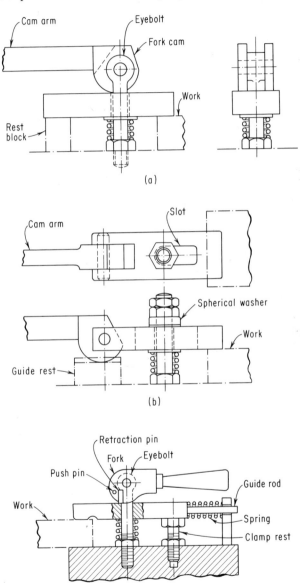

FIG. 3-15. Cam-actuated strap clamps. (*The Cincinnati Milling Machine Co.*)

transmitted to the cam moves it against its spring and permits the pusher pins to move toward each other. The inward movement of the pins allows the two spring-actuated plungers to swing the levers around their hinge pins to their unclamped position. The clamped position is adjusted by the dog-point setscrews bearing against the pusher pins.

Pressure from a cam is transmitted to a sliding wedge (1) in the design of Fig. 3-19 by a connecting link (2). The link is slotted to allow its impact on a pin (3) to aid in releasing the pivoted jaws (4) when the cam handle is rotated clockwise.

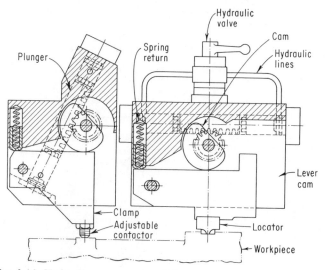

FIG. 3-16. Hydraulic cam actuation. (*The Cincinnati Milling Machine Co.*)

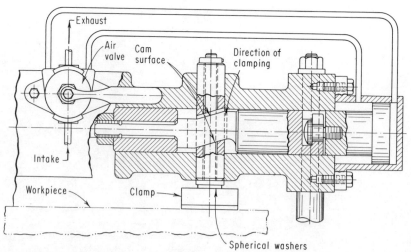

FIG. 3-17. Sliding-wedge cam actuation. (*The Cincinnati Milling Machine Co.*)

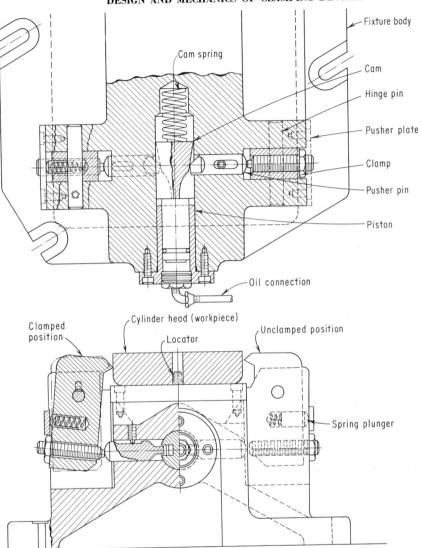

Fixture body

Cam spring

Cam

Hinge pin

Pusher plate

Clamp

Pusher pin

Piston

Oil connection

Cylinder head (workpiece)

Clamped position

Locator

Unclamped position

Spring plunger

FIG. 3-18. Hydraulic cam releasing. (*The Cincinnati Milling Machine Co.*)

Rotation of the cams in the designs of Figs. 3-20 and 3-21 is around axes below the workpieces. The jaws shown in Fig. 3-20 are adapted for round and curved workpieces, while those of Fig. 3-21 hold two workpieces; equalization is secured by a slot in the cam.

The clamp of Fig. 3-22 secures positive release of the workpiece by means of the pin (1) bearing against the lower end of the slotted link as the cam handle (3) is rotated counterclockwise. As the cam is rotated, the equalizing bar (4) is raised, causing the clamps (5) to move upward and away from the workpiece.

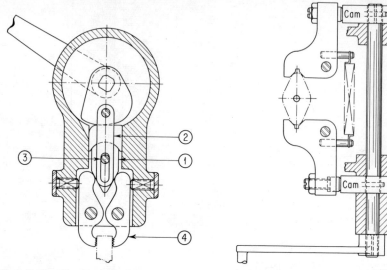

FIG. 3-19. Floating-jaw clamp. (*Special Engineering Service, Inc.*)

FIG. 3-20. Clamping of cylindrical work-pieces. (*Special Engineering Services, Inc.*)

Figures 3-23 and 3-24 illustrate additional applications of cams in clamping arrangements.

Computations for Eccentric-cam Design.[3]   An eccentric cam consists of a circular-cam body which is turned about an eccentric axis (Fig. 3-25). The eccentricity e depends upon the angle through which the cam is rotated (angle of throw) θ and the rise T but not upon the size of the cam radius R.

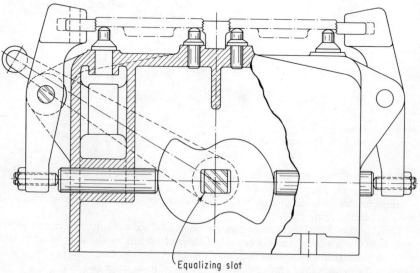

Equalizing slot

FIG. 3-21. Cam clamping of two workpieces. (*Special Engineering Services, Inc.*)

Eccentricity may be calculated from the equation

$$e = \frac{T}{1 - \cos \theta} \qquad (10)$$

and the radius determined by the equation

$$R = e \left(\cos \theta + \frac{\sin \theta}{f} \right) \qquad (11)$$

where f = coefficient of friction for which a value of 0.10 is generally used.

The diameter of the pivot pin, r_s, may be found from the equation

$$r_s = \frac{2}{3} \sqrt{\frac{n}{S_s} + (F_{c\ min} + R_t)} \qquad (12)$$

where

$$n = \frac{F_{c\ max}}{F_{c\ min}} = \frac{R_{t\ max}}{R_{t\ min}} \qquad (13)$$

$F_{c\ max}$ = force applied to cam, lb, max
$F_{c\ min}$ = force applied to cam, lb, min
S_s = working shear stress of the pivot, psi
R_t = force imposed by the cam, lb

The length of the lever arm, L, of an eccentric cam can be found from the relationship

$$L = \frac{R_t[fR + e\,(\sin \theta - f \cos \theta)] + fr_s F_b}{F_c} \qquad (14)$$

where $F_b = R_t + F_c$ approx $\qquad (15)$

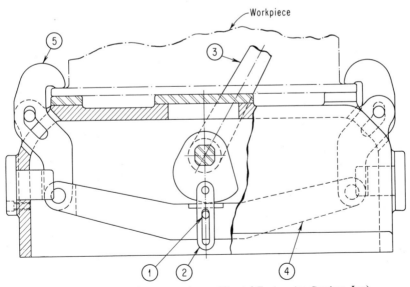

FIG. 3-22. Positive-release cam clamp. (*Special Engineering Services, Inc.*)

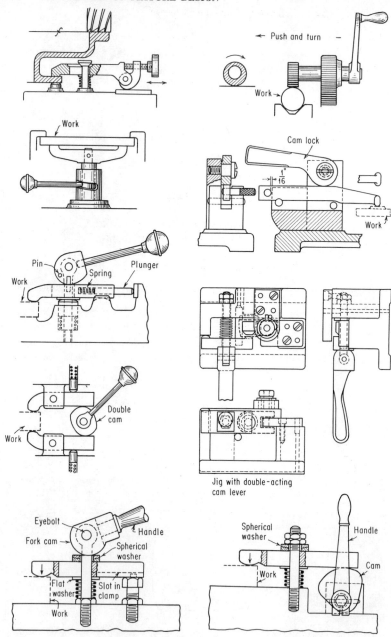

FIG. 3-23. Types of cam-actuated clamps.

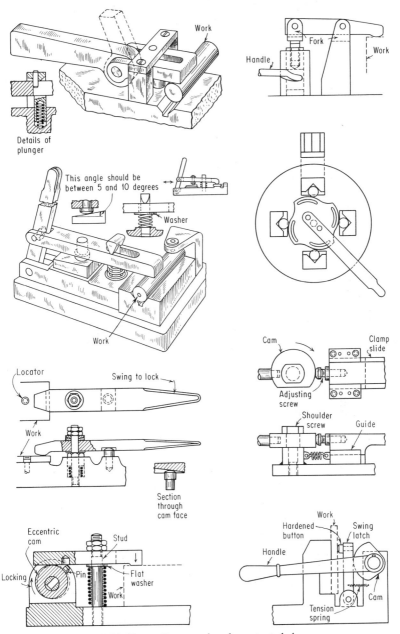

FIG. 3-24. Types of cam- and wedge-actuated clamps.

EXAMPLE 4. Compute the eccentricity, minimum radius, and lever arm of a cam for a throw angle of 90°, a rise of 0.125 in., to impose a force of 900 lb, with a force of 30 to 90 lb applied.

From Eq. (10),

$$e = \frac{0.125}{1 - 0} = 0.125 \text{ in.}$$

From Eq. (11),

$$R = 0.125 \,(0 + 1/0.1) = 1.25 \text{ in.}$$

From Eq. (12),

$$r_s = \frac{2}{3} \sqrt{\frac{3}{10,000} + (30 + 900)} = 0.35 \text{ in.}$$

From Eq. (14),

$$L = \frac{900}{30} \left[0.15 \times 1.25 + 0.125 \,(1 - 0.15 \times 0) \right] + 0.15 \times 0.35 \times 930 = 11 \text{ in.}$$

Computations for Spiral-cam Design.[3] The contour of a spiral cam is based on the spiral of Archimedes. Its locking action is better than that of an eccentric cam. The forces acting on a spiral cam, shown in Fig. 3-26, are the reaction R_t from the workpiece normal to the cam surface; the friction force fR_t; the force F_c applied to the handle; the normal force F_s of the pivot pin on the cam; and its frictional force fF_s. The resultant force of R_t and fR_t is R_a. The resultant of F_s and fF_s is F_b, which is tangent to the friction circle having a radius for practical purposes of fr_s.

EXAMPLE 5. Compute the size of the pin, the minimum radius and lead of the cam, and the length of the lever arm for a spiral cam which will exert 900 lb. The handle will be rotated through 90° with a force of 30 lb min and 90 lb max. The rise

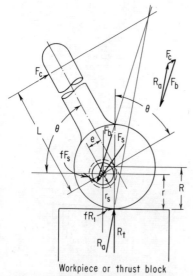

FIG. 3-25. The forces acting on an eccentric cam during engagement. (*The Tool and Manufacturing Engineer.*)

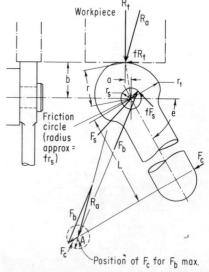

FIG. 3-26. The forces acting on a spiral cam during engagement. (*The Tool and Manufacturing Engineer.*)

of the steel cam, hardened to 400 Brinell, is 0.125 in. The allowable shear stress for the pin is 10,000 psi.

From Eq. (12), the diameter of the pivot pin

$$r_s = \frac{2}{3}\sqrt{\frac{3}{10,000}} + (30 + 900) = 0.35 \text{ in.}$$

The pin's radius is chosen as 0.375 in. (0.750 diam).

The rise from the smallest radius r_1 to the largest radius r of the cam is the lead l of the cam, from the expression

$$r - r_1 = \frac{\theta l}{360} \tag{16}$$

where θ is in degrees
  l is the lead of the cam, in.

From Eq. (16),

$$0.125 \text{ in.} = \frac{90}{360} l$$
$$l = 0.500 \text{ in.}$$

Since, for a self-locking spiral cam, the minimum radius r_1 is

$$r_1 = \frac{l}{2\pi f} \tag{17}$$

where $f = 0.1$
  $r_1 = 1.59 \times 0.500 = 0.80$ in.

Choose a minimum radius of 0.875 in.

The projected area (cam thickness × pin diameter) of the bearing for the pivot pin must be large enough to limit the unit pressure to 3,000 psi, in keeping with accepted practice for bearings for slow speeds and intermittent loads.

The load on the bearing is

$$F_b = R_a + F_{c \max} \tag{18}$$

where $R_a = \frac{nR_t}{\cos T}$

Since $n = 3$
and $f = 0.1 = \tan T$
  $T = 5°45'$
  $\cos T = 0.995$

$$F_{b \max} = \frac{2,700}{0.995} + 90 = 2,714 + 90 = 2,804 \text{ lb}$$

The projected bearing area of the cam is its thickness t multiplied by the ¾ in. diam of the pivot pin.

Since the unit stress on this area should not exceed 3,000 psi,

$$\frac{2,804}{t \times ¾} = 3,000 \text{ psi}$$
$$t = 1.25 \text{ in.}$$

From the following equation and Table 3-4, the length of the cam radius r_1 can be computed:

$$r_1 = \frac{1.1R_t}{Kt} \tag{19}$$

where t = thickness of cam, in.

K = constant, selected from Table 3-4

$$r_1 = \frac{1.1 \times 2,700}{5,530 \times 1.25} = 0.43 \text{ in.}$$

The radius of 0.875 in., established with Eq. (17), is ample to withstand the compressive stress.

The expression for the length L of the lever arm is

$$L = \frac{R_t(l/2\pi) + r_1 f + r_s f_s F_b}{F_c} \tag{20}$$

where F_b is 900 lb and

$$L = \frac{900(0.08 + 0.875 \times 0.1) + (0.375 \times 0.1 \times 900)}{30} = 6.15 \text{ in.}$$

Wedge Clamps. A wedge is a movable inclined plane which provides and should maintain the desired clamping force. The movement of the wedge should not require a large force for actuation. These requirements are controlled by the wedge angle (angle of inclination).

The diagram of Fig. 3-27 shows the forces acting on a wedge at the instant removal begins. It is assumed that the wedge has previously been inserted to exert a clamping force F_2 on the workpiece with a reaction F_1 from the wedge block. F_1 and F_2 act normal to the bearing surfaces. The taper angle of the top of the wedge is α. Two friction forces F_3 and F_4 resist removal of the wedge by pull P. For a coefficient of friction designated by f,

$$F_3 = fF_1$$

and

$$F_4 = fF_2$$

Because the sum of the vertical forces equals zero,

$$F_2 = F_1 \cos \alpha + F_3 \sin \alpha$$
$$= F_1 (\cos \alpha + f \sin \alpha)$$

Also, since the horizontal forces must equal zero,

$$P = F_2 \cos \alpha + F_4 - F_1 \sin \alpha$$
$$= F_1 [2f \cos \alpha + (f^2 - 1) \sin \alpha]$$

Since f is small, f^2 is much smaller and may be neglected, so that

$$P = F_1 (2f \cos \alpha - \sin \alpha) \tag{21}$$

For small values of α, $2f \cos \alpha$ is larger than $\sin \alpha$, and a positive effort is required to extract the wedge. As α is made larger, $\cos \alpha$ decreases and $\sin \alpha$ increases. An angle is reached where P becomes zero, and the wedge no longer stays in place of its own accord. For large angles, P has increasingly negative values, which means there is less and less inclination for the wedge to remain in place. If Eq. (21) is solved for $P = 0$, the result is

$$\tan \alpha = 2f \tag{22}$$

The angle α must have a tangent less than twice the value of the coefficient of friction if the wedge is to stay tight. If the angle is small, the wedge is inclined to stick, and the pull P to remove the wedge becomes very large.

For a coefficient of friction of 0.15, α by Eq. (21) is around 16°. It is almost sure that a taper angle of over 16° will not stay put. But in the presence of oil and other slippery conditions, f may drop below 0.1, for which an angle less than 10° is required. A practical working angle for tapered keys is 7°.

When the wedge angle approaches 16°, the wedge tends to slip; to restrain it, an auxiliary holding force can be applied, as shown in Fig. 3-28. When using an auxiliary closing and holding force on a wedge clamp, the designer must bear in mind that more force is required to open the clamp or retract the wedge than to close the clamp or hold it closed.

The effectiveness of wedge clamping cannot be accurately predetermined, because the coefficient of friction is difficult to evaluate. It depends upon wedge-surface variables, such as the presence of oils or cutting fluids and the surface finish and hardness.

Toggle Clamps. The foggle clamp provides heavy pressure, is quickly operated, and gives complete clearance for loading and unloading the fixture. This type of clamp can accommodate only minor variations in stock thickness and must therefore have a means of adjustment in the clamping end. A C-type toggle clamp is shown in Fig. 3-29a. An adjustment for stock thickness variations is provided by the setscrew in the clamping end. The handle end of the C frame rests on another screw for adjustment of travel beyond dead center. A similar principle is applied on a pusher-type clamp shown in Fig. 3-29b.

A wide variety of sizes and styles of toggle-actuated clamps are commercially

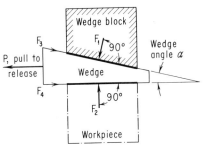

FIG. 3-27. Force diagram for a wedge.

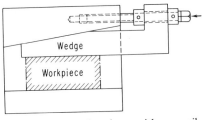

FIG. 3-28. A wedge clamp with an auxiliary holding device.

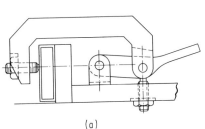

(a)

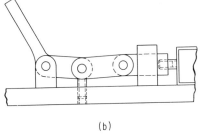

(b)

FIG. 3-29. Toggle clamps: (a) C-frame type; (b) pusher type.

available (see Sec. 15). The manufacturers have evaluated stresses, forces, safety factors, etc., for their designs, so that the ratings for applied and clamping forces in their catalogues preclude excessive deflection of the toggle members.

OTHER CLAMPING MEANS

Vacuum Clamping. This method of clamping is adaptable to holding thin flat sheets or workpieces having contours that can be distorted by conventional clamping forces. The vacuum holding force of nearly 14.7 psi can be uniformly distributed over a surface of the workpiece. The application and amount of the vacuum holding force on the workpiece should result in its distortion only within allowable limits.

In using vacuum clamping, the designer must choose a holding surface that can be effectively sealed. Vacuum chucking is not limited by workpiece material as long as it is not porous. Gaskets, washers, and O rings must also be of nonporous materials.

Spiral grooves, 0.001 in. deep, in the cast-aluminum fixture of Fig. 3-30 distribute the vacuum over the lower surface of the workpiece. Rubber tubing in outside grooves in the fixture is flattened by the weight of the workpiece and forms a seal between it and the fixture.

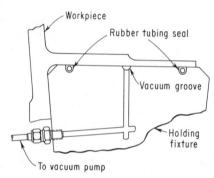

FIG. 3-30. A vacuum chuck. (*The Tool and Manufacturing Engineer.*)

Magnetic Clamping. The holding power of magnetic chucks, of either the permanent magnet or the electromagnet type, is dependent upon the attractive force of the magnets incorporated. The effective force holding the workpiece is dependent upon the amount, direction, and concentration of such forces upon the workpiece. There is considerable variation in the responses of various ferromagnetic materials to a magnetizing force. Variations in holding power of a 36-watt 6-volt chuck (6 by 12 in.) for different positions of steel test blocks are listed in Table 3-4. For cast-iron

TABLE 3-4. Vertical Pull, Lb, Necessary to Remove a 1½- × 6-in. Steel (SAE 1018) Block from 36-watt Electromagnetic Chuck[5]

Block position*	Block thicknesses, in.							
	1½	1	¾	½	⅜	¼	⅛	¹⁄₁₆
A	1,350	1,125	900	450	300	150	50	15
B	1,350	875	700	400	250	175	80	35
C	450	400	375	350	350	325	250	100
D	450	450	450	300	125	60	55	50
E	2,050	1,400	925	700	400	300	150	40
F	2,050	1,650	1,300	825	600	400	200	100

* See Fig. 3-31.

blocks of the same dimensions, the vertical pull required is approximately 60 per cent of that listed for steel test bars.

A chuck of the permanent-magnet type incorporates a series of permanent magnets mounted on a sliding member underneath the working surface of the chuck. A lever, when moved to the ON position, allows the magnetic flux to complete its circuit through the workpiece on the working surface of the chuck, and the part is held by the magnetic force. At the OFF position, the magnets are aligned with a series of nonmagnetic separators, and the magnetic flux passes through the chuck's working surface but not through the workpiece, allowing it to be removed from the chuck.

Electromagnetic chucks activated by direct current are larger and more powerful than those of the permanent-magnet type.

Flux dams, which are bars or plates of nonmagnetic metal, divert magnetic flux (Fig. 3-32) with deep penetration, as shown at *b,* with consequent greater holding power.

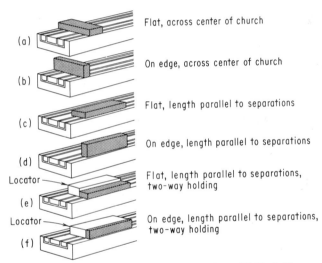

(a) Flat, across center of church

(b) On edge, across center of church

(c) Flat, length parallel to separations

(d) On edge, length parallel to separations

Locator ———
(e) Flat, length parallel to separations, two-way holding

Locator ———
(f) On edge, length parallel to separations, two-way holding

FIG. 3-31. Test-block position for test data of Table 3-4.[5]

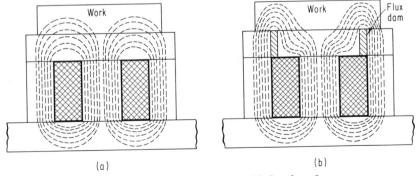

(a)   (b)

FIG. 3-32. Flux concentrations with flux dams.[6]

Thin nonmagnetic workpieces can be clamped under heavier magnetic keeper plates, as shown in Fig. 3-33, for edge-finishing operations. Magnetic force holds the keeper plate against the magnetic locator plate.

The application and release of the holding force of an electromagnetic chuck are instantaneous with the opening and closing of its switch, and its amount may be varied with a rheostat. Auxiliary safety stops can be incorporated to prevent possible workpiece damage and operator injury in the event that the magnetic holding force is accidentally released.

Since workpieces of steel and other ferromagnetic metals and alloys tend to remain somewhat permanently magnetized after they have been held by a magnetic chuck, they may have to be demagnetized before other machining operations. Residual magnetism in the workpiece may limit its function or tightly hold accumulated chips to it.

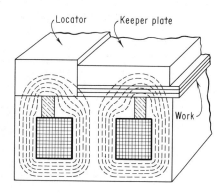

FIG. 3-33. Holding nonmagnetic workpieces.[6]

Electrostatic Clamping. In an electrostatic chuck, the surface of the workpiece is charged with static electricity which is insulated from the chuck's face by a dielectric fluid. Since the static charge on the workpiece is of opposite polarity to that on the chuck's face, the workpiece and chuck face are attracted to each other. This electrostatic force of attraction varies directly as the product of the two charges and inversely as the square of the distances between them. An electrostatic force holds all metals and their alloys, as well as solid nonconducting materials, if their surfaces are coated with a very thin metallic film. No residual magnetism is found in the workpieces clamped by an electrostatic chuck, but they must be dry and clean for its efficient operation.

Chemical Bonding (Adhesive) Clamping. In limited applications, chemical bonding (adhesive joining) of workpieces to fixtures has been successful. The adhesive must be a thin film if close tolerances between workpiece and fixture are required. The designer must consider the curing time of the adhesive, the time needed to remove it from the workpiece, and its resistance to solubility in, or dilution by, coolant and/or cutting fluids. Adhesive clamping is generally restricted to workpieces having flat surfaces and to situations when tooling forces are not large.

Low-melting-point Alloys.[7] Various bismuth alloys that melt at low temperatures and are available commercially can be cast around a workpiece in a split steel flask or mold. After solidification, the casting is cut into two halves, which are machined to adapt them to a chuck, vise, fixture, or other holding device. Before solidification, the surface of the workpiece is coated with a suitable parting agent to facilitate its removal from the halves of the casting.

Fabrication costs of cast jaws are low. Cast jaws are suitable for workpieces having complicated shapes and for low to medium production quantities.

Small or otherwise difficult-to-hold workpieces may be mounted in a low-melting-point alloy for machining. After solidification, the metal containing the workpiece is placed in a chuck or another suitable holding device while the machining operation is performed. The alloy is then melted, freeing the workpiece.

Rack-and-Pinion Clamping. A rack and pinion can be useful in transferring an input force (torque on the pinion) to the rack for clamping at a point remote from the pinion, providing that a holding force is applied to the pinion or rack or that the rack actuates a wedge or cam which is nonreleasing.

Pneumatic and Hydraulic Clamp Actuation. Applications of pneumatic or hydraulic pressures to clamps can be justified because of reduced clamping time; this method is generally used for large production quantities. Pressures are uniform and are controlled by the operator with minimum fatigue.

Pneumatically operated clamps are suitable for high-temperature applications and high cycling rates. A drop in or failure of air pressure can result in inoperative clamps, unless they are designed to prevent their failure.

Hydraulic units are generally smaller and operate at higher pressures than pneumatic units. Oil under pressure is generally provided by an independent unit attached to a machine. When a large number of units are required, the fixture can be more compact, since hydraulic pistons can be incorporated in the fixture body. They are suited for normal temperatures.

Figure 3-34 illustrates the application of air cylinders to clamping devices.

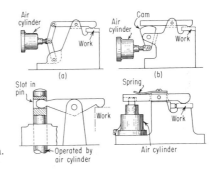

Fig. 3-34. Pneumatic-clamp actuation.

References

1. Tindale, G. R.: Jig Clamp Dimensions, *Am. Machinist,* Nov. 18, 1957.
2. Strasser, F.: Which Clamps Are Best for Jigs and Fixtures? *Iron Age,* Oct. 2, 1958.
3. Doyle, L. E.: The Mechanics of Clamping Devices, *The Tool Engr.,* July-October, 1950.
4. Stevenson, J. A.: Maximum Torque for Screws, *Am. Machinist/Metalworking Manufacturing,* Mar. 21, 1960.
5. Anderson, A.: Low Voltage Magnetic Holding, *Am. Machinist,* May 12, 1952.
6. Suchanek, F.: Magnetic Holding of Ferrous and Nonferrous Materials, presented at the 22d Annual Meeting, ASTME, Philadelphia, Pa., April, 1954.
7. Spoor, Richard: Cast-to-shape Workholders Simplify Tooling Problems, *The Tool Engr.,* October, 1959.

Section 4

DRILL JIGS

By HAROLD J. HARTLIEB*

Sales Engineer, Fidelity Machine Tool Co.

GENERAL CONSIDERATIONS

Cost limitations have a great bearing on design; they may in preliminary planning clearly demonstrate that a drill jig is not economically justified.

A jig borer or a hole-locating machine (requiring no jig) can often produce a limited number of holes within the specified tolerances at less cost than those produced with any other type of drilling machine utilizing a jig which must be amortized over such low production.

Once the tool engineer has established the need for a drill jig on the basis of part quality required, some estimate of design and fabrication costs must be made, since he is rarely permitted to design any tool without costs in mind.

MACHINE AND PROCESS CONSIDERATIONS

For small holes requiring a small, sensitive drill press, the size of the bed and the tooling area will limit jig dimensions.

The drilling of small and/or deep holes will frequently require hand or special feeding. Feed methods are often reflected in jig design, particularly in the type and length of bushings required for a given method.

A radial drill is often used in drilling bulky and/or heavy parts which can be held on the drill table by a large jig, or a smaller and lighter clamp-on jig can be designed to fit around the part area to be drilled.

Multiple-spindle drill heads permit the use of rotary-indexing jigs (Fig. 4-1). Banks of single-spindle machines, with or without multiple-spindle drill heads, may use a single fixture which is transferred from one machine table to another. The jig incorporates the various sizes of drill bushings that are necessary for operations completed by each machine.

As shown in Fig. 4-2, two jigs are used for separate drilling and reaming operations on a part; a six-spindle head is fitted with three drills and three reamers.

A single jig may be designed with bushings to accommodate drills and reamers fitted to a turret drill press, allowing sequential drilling and allied operations as the turret is indexed vertically.

Small air-drill units in locking sleeves can be easily mounted to a jig at various angles (Figs. 4-3 and 4-4) at hole locations.

* Contributing authors: Robert Arva, Industrial Engineer, AMP, Inc.; Nelson Harris, Chief Tool Engineer, New Holland Machine Co.; James Lynch, Supervisor, Tool Design, AMP, Inc.

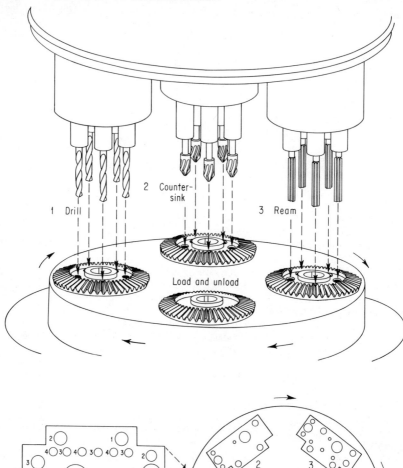

1 Drill   2 Counter-sink   3 Ream

Load and unload

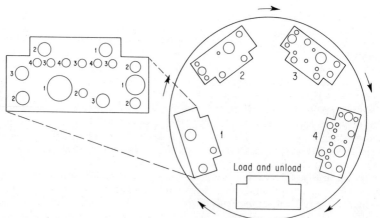

Load and unload

FIG. 4-1. Rotary-indexing jigs.

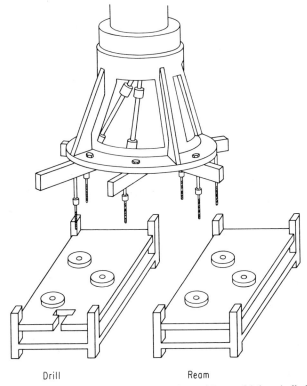

Drill   Ream

FIG. 4-2. Two jigs for simultaneous operations with a multiple-spindle head.

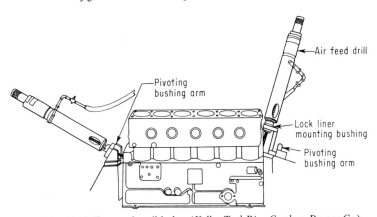

FIG. 4-3. Air-drill setup for oil holes. (*Keller Tool Div., Gardner-Denver Co.*)

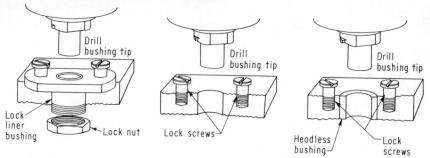

FIG. 4-4. Methods of mounting air drills. (*Keller Tool Div., Gardner-Denver Co.*)

PRODUCT CONSIDERATIONS

Small parts frequently need only simple, inexpensive jigs and, depending somewhat on their shape, may be stacked vertically or in a horizontal row in the jig for multiple or sequential drilling.

Heavy and/or bulky parts, not easily moved by the operator, can be drilled with a clamp-on jig used with a radial drill press or an air drill.

Light workpieces requiring several holes at various angles can be drilled with box or tumble jigs.

Cast or other parts possessing nonuniform and irregular surfaces may require locating, centering, and clamping devices that compensate for dimensional and angular variations.

Stampings of nonsymmetrical or complex contours can fit in nests or cavities in

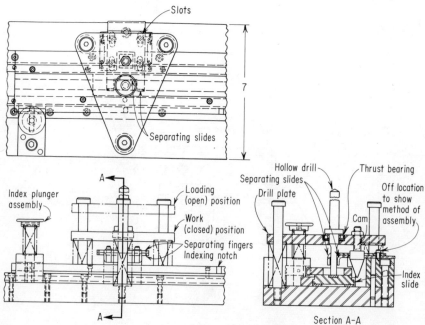

FIG. 4-5. Jig for drilling a rubber channel. (*Standard Products Co.*)

the jig without distortion if the clamping forces are properly directed towards the nests. Flat ferrous stampings can be located by pins in a simple jig held by a magnetic chuck underneath the fixture.

The back of a soft rubber channel is drilled in the indexing fixture of Fig. 4-5. The workpiece is placed in a template mounted on an indexing slide. As the handle of the drill press is pulled down, a cam forces two separating slides apart, pushing the sides of the workpiece out of the way of the descending drill. Pressing on the plunger knob moves the index slide to an indexing notch corresponding to the specified workpiece hole location.

Interchangeable templates with different internotch spacing allow holes to be drilled in workpieces of various sizes at hole locations whose center-to-center distances are the same as the notch spacing (indexing travel).

Parts of other rigid or nonrigid materials having a smooth finish that must be preserved should be held and located with clamps and locators having resilient surfaces and/or points to avoid defacement and distortion of the parts.

The torque required to drill hard materials is seldom a problem in jig design, but the necessary higher thrust values, or the total thrust for multiple drilling, may spring or distort the workpiece. The design should then include support to resist thrust and/or clamps to provide compensating forces. When thrust is reduced by first drilling pilot holes and redrilling them to size, the jig design can include slip bushings and less rigid construction.

When holes are to be drilled at different angles in one or more sides of the workpiece, tumble-jig design is often feasible, particularly if hole locations are

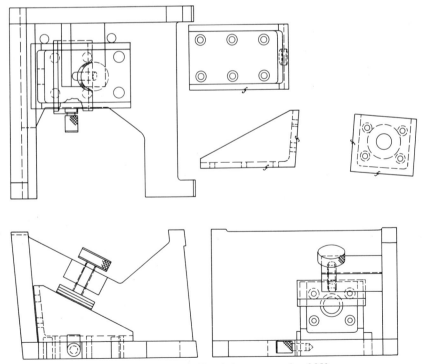

FIG. 4-6. Jig for drilling holes at an angle of 95°.

critical. A single clamping of the part for several drilling operations minimizes hole mislocation, particularly when the locations and angular relations of bushings, jig feet, leaves, etc., are closely controlled.

A tabular analysis of product, operation, machine, operator, and economic considerations for drill-jig planning can be of considerable value to the student designer.

An example of such an analysis is given in Table 4-1 for the part shown in Fig. 4-6.

TABLE 4-1. Typical Preliminary Design Steps for Drill-jig Planning

Product analysis considerations	Effect on jig design
Size, weight	Relatively small; lightweight construction.
Wall thicknesses and general shape provide rigidity	No special supporting and clamping methods are necessary to prevent part distortion.
Surface finish [100]	Clamps, locators, or other details must not incorporate sharp points or edges to mar flat surfaces of part.
Machinability index	Permits metal removal with moderate machining forces.
Angular surface relation (95° ± 15′)	Clamps and locators must not change close angular tolerance.
Surface flatness tolerance (±0.010 in.)	Clamping forces must not alter flatness tolerance.
Normality of hole axes	Clamping and locating must maintain axes normal to respective flat surfaces.
Location (±0.005 in.) and diameter (±0.0156 in.) tolerances on 0.1405-in. holes	Standard drill bushings satisfactory.
Diameter tolerance (+0.001, −0.000 in.) on 0.500-in. hole	Tolerances can be held with drill and ream jig, suitably bushed.
Location tolerance (1.000 ± 0.001 in.) on 0.500-in. hole	Tolerance Cannot be held with single jig. Can be held with a drill jig and a separate jig with a jig ground bushing for reaming. Can be held with a drill jig for rough-drilling all holes and a separate simple holding fixture for finish boring of the 0.500-in. hole.

Maximum possible mislocations, in.:
  1. From true position of liner in jig____0.0005
  2. Due to fit of bushing and liner_____0.0004
  3. Due to fit of reamer and bushing____0.0002
     Total_____0.0011
	Design decision: most accurate results will be obtained with a tumble jig for drilling all holes and a separate holding fixture for boring the 0.500-in. hole.

Operation considerations	Effect on jig design
Operation 1, grinding 2 × 3, 2 × 1¾-in. surfaces, with horizontal disk grinder, according to process sheet	No fixture required. Grinder table provides adequate holding, positioning, and locating facilities.
Operation 2, drilling (10) 0.1405-in.-diam holes and (1) ¹⁵⁄₃₂-in.-diam pilot hole for 0.500-in.-diam hole on Avey number 2 two-spindle drill press, according to process sheet	Torque and feed force allows hand-held tumble-jig design. Clamps must clear drills. Adequate three-point supporting for stability of jig on feet and for normality of hole axes.
Operation 3, bore 0.500-in.-diam hole on Heald Borematic, according to process sheet	Simple holding fixture or vise, not shown; normality of hole axis provided by shims or pins.

Machine considerations	Effect on jig design
Operation 2, Avey number 2 two-spindle drill press, according to process sheet	Tooling area, bed size, and kind of chuck will not limit tumble-jig design.
Operation 3, Heald Borematic, according to process sheet	Simple clamping, positioning, and supporting to ensure $2 \times 1\frac{3}{4}$-in. face at $90°$ to boring bar (this fixture not shown).

Operator considerations*	Effect on jig design
Operation 2, loading, unloading, and fixture handling	Operator loads, unloads, and clamps with lower thumbscrew with left hand; tightens hand knob with right hand. Small tumble jig easily turned for drilling second set of holes.
Operation 3, loading, unloading, and fixture handling	This simple fixture (not shown) will not be handled; unloading, loading, locating, and clamping are simple, nontiring operator motions.

Production considerations	Effect on jig design
200 parts per month, 2,400 per year; possible future production of 8,000 per year	Air clamping, indexing, etc., and various automated designs not justified by production rates and quantity.

Economic evaluation	Effect on jig design
Jig cost, $360 design and make; $0.15 per part, at 2,400 annual rate Boring fixture cost, $146.40 design and make; $0.061 per part, at 2,400 annual rate. Total fixture costs are $506.40; $0.21 per part Operations 2 and 3 costs total $100.65; $0.5032 per part, at 2,400 annual rate	For 2,400 annual production rate, reducing the time to operate the jig and fixture by faster clamping, etc., would not be justified because of increased fixture cost. Setup and run time for both operations is 5.49 min per piece; cost studies show that the cost of timesaving fixture details, such as air cylinder clamping, can be absorbed by the reduction possible just in labor cost to operate the fixtures, when the setup and run time are considerably longer and production is 5 to 10, or more, times the present annual production.

* There are no particular problems of operator and machine safety or operator fatigue.

TEMPLATE JIGS

Template jigs, usually low in cost because of their simple design, are much used as temporary or short-run tooling. It is often more practical to use two or three drill templates in lieu of one drill jig. It is difficult to exactly define a template jig because of the many forms it may take.

The most common template is a single plate with holes, bushed or unbushed, for guiding the drill. The part can be placed on the template, or vice versa, with or without clamping, as shown in Fig. 4-7. The flat part for the jig has two holes that fit the locating pins when the part is positioned on the jig. The workpiece is located from its periphery by pins (view b), or a thumbscrew can replace two pins.

The design of Fig. 4-8 for a cylindrical workpiece has an upper template and a lower locating plate which can be simply clamped together if the part has a tendency to tip over during drilling.

The design of Fig. 4-9 incorporates interchangeable templates, each having various interhole distances. A pin, inserted through a locating hole in the workpiece and through a stop hole in the template, locates the workpiece placed on the template. The sliding guide plates accommodate parts of various sizes.

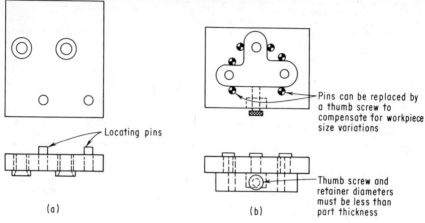

Locating pins

Pins can be replaced by a thumb screw to compensate for workpiece size variations

Thumb screw and retainer diameters must be less than part thickness

(a)   (b)

FIG. 4-7. Template jigs.

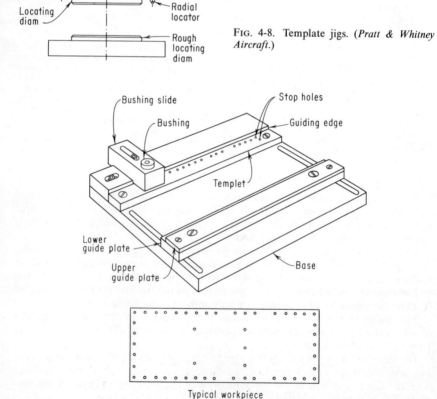

Locating diam

Radial locator

Rough locating diam

FIG. 4-8. Template jigs. (*Pratt & Whitney Aircraft.*)

Bushing slide

Bushing

Stop holes

Guiding edge

Templet

Lower guide plate

Upper guide plate

Base

Typical workpiece

FIG. 4-9. Interchangeable template jig.[3]

PLATE JIGS

A plate jig incorporates a plate, which is generally the main structural member, that carries the drill or liner bushings. Slip bushings of various sizes can be used with liner bushings, allowing a series of drilling and allied operations without relocating or reclamping the workpiece.

The plate jig's general open construction facilitates part loading, locating, and clamping, as well as chip removal. Most plate jigs are inexpensive to design and construct, because they incorporate only a few elementary parts.

The jig shown in Fig. 4-10 has three drill bushings (1) pressed in a plate (5) and two others in a locator block (4). The channel-shaped part is also located by a dowel pin (2) and held by a clamp (3).

The jig of Fig. 4-11 is of open construction since the cross hole to be drilled is at one end of the workpiece which is clamped in a V block. The keyed end of the part is properly aligned with the hole axis by a locating slot and a locating button.

The workpieces (locknuts) shown in Fig. 4-12 were formerly held in a jig designed for drilling three stacked locknuts at a time. Since the flat faces of some of the

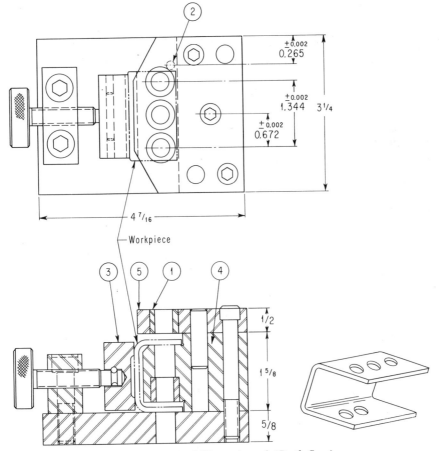

FIG. 4-10. Jig for drilling a channel. (*Barth Corp.*)

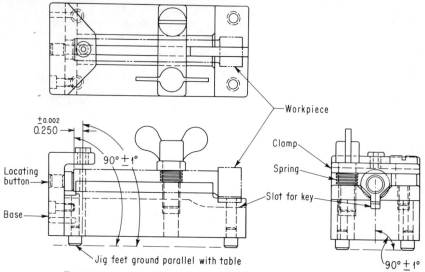

FIG. 4-11. Plate jig for cross-hole drilling. (*ASTME Chapter 100.*)

locknuts were not parallel when stacked together in the jig, holes could not be drilled normal to the faces. A jig to drill one part at a time (Fig. 4-12) superseded the original design and kept jig and drilling costs reasonably low.

The base is fastened to the drill-press table so that drill-bushing A is directly under the drill spindle. The locknut is placed against the lower locating pins, and the cam handle is pushed down, which lowers the bushing plate and allows the upper locating pins to slide over and locate the locknut. The travel X of the slide on the base between the four guide pins is the interhole distance, limited by the stop pins. The stop screw prevents the bushing plate from rising when pressure is applied by the cam, while a spring keeps the plate up when the cam is released and allows loading. A hardened button is pressed into the base and provides a wear surface for the cam.

After the first (rear) hole is drilled, the cam is released and the slide is pulled forward, centering the drill spindle over drill bushing B. Cam pressure is applied, and the second hole is drilled.

A plate jig with standard commercial jig legs is shown in Fig. 4-13. A diamond locator (5) and a round locator (1) engage large holes in an aluminum casting which is clamped against four standard commercial rest buttons (4). A swing-latch clamp swings to the right for loading and unloading. A swivel pad (6) on the end of a knob-and-shoe assembly (3, another commercial item) compensates for variations in the bottom of the casting. Two drill bushings (7) are mounted in a bushing plug (8), which fits in a liner (9).

For accurate drilling, the center lines of the bushings and of the locators are parallel to each other and square to the ends of the jig legs and rest buttons within 0.001 in. TIR. Two 0.136-in. holes are drilled, countersunk, and tapped in the casting with a three-spindle drill press.

Forty-eight holes around the upper flange and eight around the lower flange of a tapered cylinder are drilled with the jig of Fig. 4-14. The flat base or plate (7) supports a center column (6). A bushing-assembly plate (8) carries the upper and lower drill bushings (3, 5), as well as an upper locating ring (1). The workpiece is located on a revolving locating ring (9), and a locating slide (10) is pushed into a locating notch in the workpiece. The bushing-assembly plate is located on a center plug (11) and is accurately oriented to the workpiece by the locating button (12) mounted on the bracket (13) shown in view *d*. The swinging C clamp (4) holds the upper bushing-assembly plate to the center plug. The plate or base rests on, and is indexed by, a rotary table mounted on the base of a radial drill.

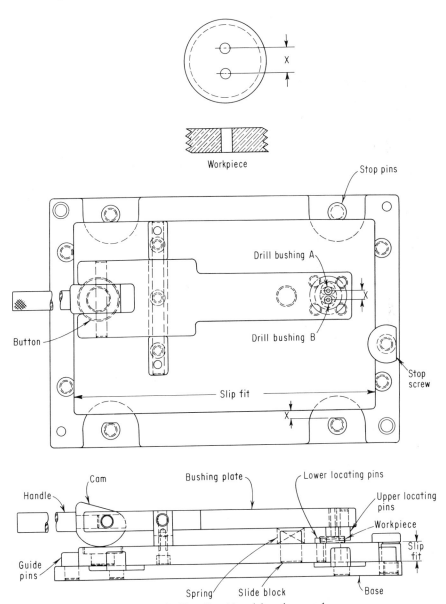

FIG. 4-12. Plate jig with quick-acting cam.[1]

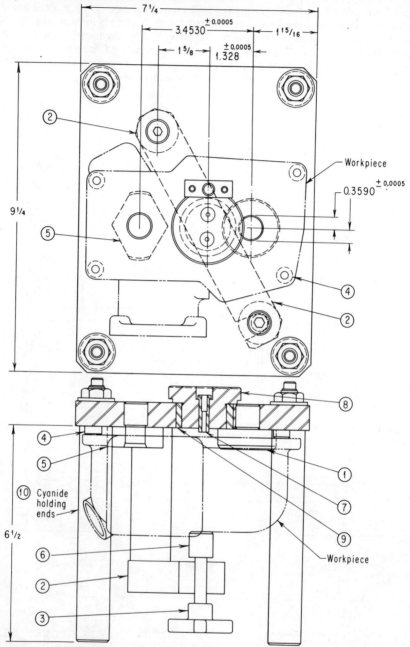

FIG. 4-13. Plate jig for an irregular aluminum casting. (*Thompson Products, Inc.*)

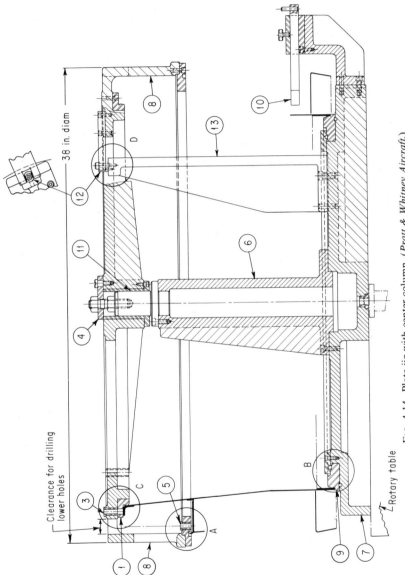

Fig. 4-14. Plate jig with center column. (*Pratt & Whitney Aircraft.*)

Clearance for drilling lower holes

38 in. diam

Rotary table

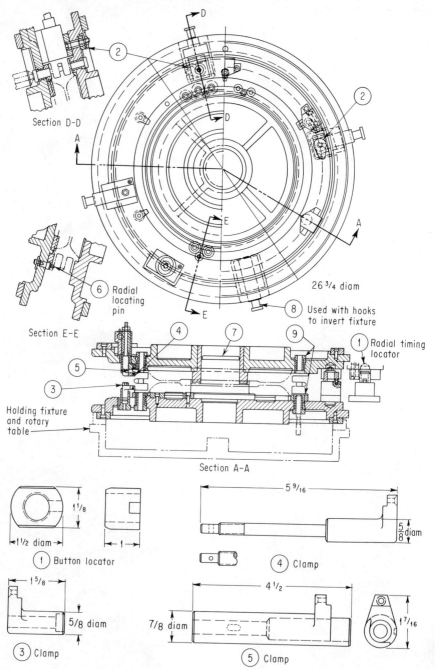

Section D-D

Section E-E

⑥ Radial
locating
pin

26 3/4 diam

⑧ Used with hooks
to invert fixture

① Radial timing
locator

Holding fixture
and rotary
table

Section A-A

① Button locator

1 1/8
1 1/2 diam
1

5 9/16
5/8 diam

④ Clamp

③ Clamp
1 5/8
5/8 diam

4 1/2
7/8 diam
1 7/16

⑤ Clamp

FIG. 4-15. Plate jig for multiple inversion. (*Pratt & Whitney Aircraft.*)

The circular-drill jig of Fig. 4-15 is inverted twice between four drilling operations and then is inverted before finish reaming and chamfering; it is finally inverted for unloading.

The upper and lower halves of the fixture are radially timed (properly located and oriented with each other) by a button locator (1). The halves are held together by six swing washers (2) equally spaced around their circumferences. Six sets of clamps (3, 4, 5) equally spaced around the circular flanges of the workpiece hold it to the upper and bottom halves of the fixture.

The part is located from a hole on one flange by a diamond locator (6) and from the large center hole by a locating plug (7). Thirty-eight holes equally spaced around the workpiece are drilled halfway through, and this operation is repeated after the fixture is turned over. This operational pattern is repeated for successive redrilling, reaming, and chamfering operations with changes of suitable bushings (9). Lugs (8) are used with hooks to invert the fixture.

LEAF JIGS

A leaf jig is generally a small jig incorporating a hinged leaf carrying the bushings and through which clamping pressure is applied. Although a leaf jig can be used for large and/or cumbersome workpieces, most designs are limited in size and weight for easy handling. A leaf jig can be box-like in shape, with four or more sides for drilling holes normal to each side.

Most leaf jigs are easy to load, and their normally open design allows rapid and easy removal of chips and good visibility of the workpiece.

In designing a leaf jig for drilling and reaming, the drill bushings can be located in the leaf and the reamer bushings in the base or vice versa, depending upon the amount of deflection of the leaf that can be tolerated during either operation.

A cylindrical part drilled in the simple leaf jig of Fig. 4-16 is located on a plug and by a pin engaging a hole in an internal flange. A leaf carries a drill bushing and is locked down by a quarter-turn screw to clamp the part.

The clamp of the leaf jig of Fig. 4-17 is one of a company's standard for cam clamps (Fig. 4-18). Locating pins engage the inner holes of the workpiece (Fig. 4-19), and it is held on both sides by two sliding wedge clamps. The workpiece, an assembly of two jaws, is held down by two pressure pads mounted on the leaf. Disk springs and a cam lever supply pressure to the pads while the central pivoting holes in the jaws are reamed. The heads of the pressure pads and the disk

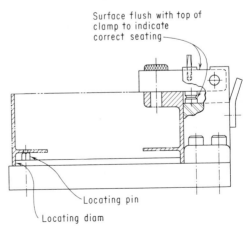

Surface flush with top of clamp to indicate correct seating

Locating pin

Locating diam

FIG. 4-16. Leaf-type drill jig. (*Pratt & Whitney Aircraft.*)

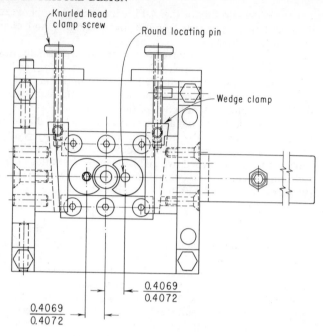

$$\frac{0.4069}{0.4072}$$

$$\frac{0.4069}{0.4072}$$

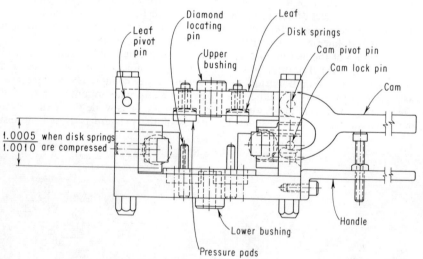

1.0005 when disk springs
1.0010 are compressed

Fig. 4-17. Leaf jig for workpiece-assembly drilling. (*AMP, Inc.*)

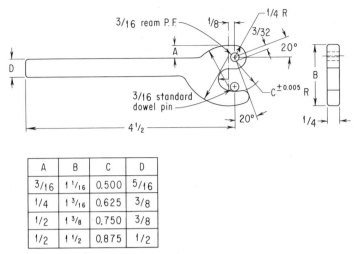

FIG. 4-18. Clamp for jig of Fig. 4-17.

A	B	C	D
3/16	1 1/16	0.500	5/16
1/4	1 3/16	0.625	3/8
1/2	1 3/8	0.750	3/8
1/2	1 1/2	0.875	1/2

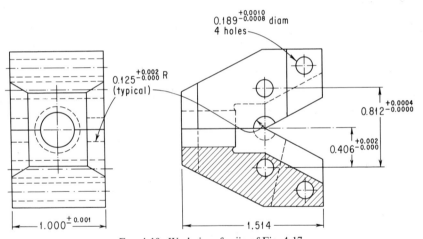

FIG. 4-19. Workpiece for jig of Fig. 4-17.

springs are contained in counterbored holes in the leaf to prevent chip entry and interference with the springs.

Since closely spaced workpiece holes make it impractical to fit standard bushings in either leaf of the jig of Fig. 4-20, each is made of hardened steel with guide holes. The part, clamped by thumbscrew pressure, has a center hole for locating on a stud. A pin locks either leaf in its working position under the spindle, while the other leaf is swung out of the way.

The frame of a snap gage is nested in the bed (6) of the drill jig shown in Fig. 4-21. A clamp (8) is released with a knurled knob (7) which allows a plunger (9) to force the workpiece snugly into the nest. A clamp screw (2) is adjusted to bring a clamp (1) downward on the part.

A knob (10) locks the leaf. The lock assembly has clutch-action teeth (3, 4) which allow only predetermined, constant, spring-loaded pressure on the leaf for minimum distortion. After the *A* holes are drilled, bushings (5) and locator pins are inserted to offset any side thrust produced during the drilling of four other holes, with the drills guided by two sets of bushings (11, 12).

The small jig of Fig. 4-22, which can be called a pan type of jig, incorporates a clamp bolt (1) which holds the flat workpiece (Fig. 4-23) against an L-shaped locator. A leaf (2) carrying the drill bushings is held down against the workpiece by a cam latch (3) which bears against a pin (4) when the latch is pressed down. After loading the jig, the operator uses the handle to place the jig under the drill-press spindle.

The workpiece (a diestock, Fig. 4-23) to be drilled in the jig of Fig. 4-24 is placed between the locating studs. It is also located and held by the spring-loaded plunger. An eyebolt is swung upward into the slot in the leaf, and the hand knob is tightened to bring the locator assembly above the center hole in the diestock. The locator assembly in the leaf enters the central hole in the diestock when the clamp screw of the locator assembly is rotated.

BOX AND TUMBLE JIGS

A box jig, as the name implies, is boxlike in shape, and if it incorporates drill bushings in two or more sides to present them (and the desired work faces) to the drill spindle, it can also be classified as a tumble jig. If such a tumble jig, boxlike in shape, also has a leaf or latch, it can be classified as a leaf jig.

A tumble jig, sometimes called a turnover or a flop-over jig, presents a different face of the work to the drill spindle each time the jig is turned or set on a different side. A plate, box, leaf, or other type of jig can be classified as a tumble jig when it can be turned to successively sit on two or more sides (or legs), each of which is directly opposite the work face.

Since the part is loaded, located, clamped, and unloaded only once in a tumble jig, greater accuracy can often be obtained and less part handling is required than when several separate jigs are used whose number depends upon the number of holes having parallel axes.

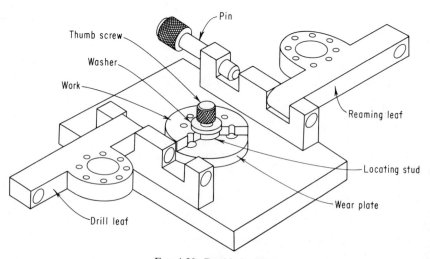

FIG. 4-20. Double-leaf jig.[4]

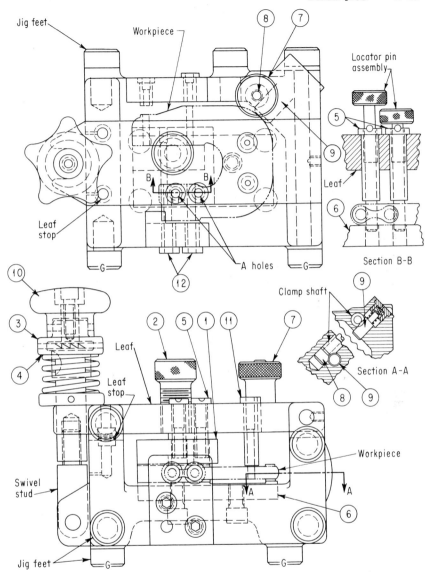

FIG. 4-21. Leaf jig having constant clamping pressure. (*ASTME Chapter 100.*)

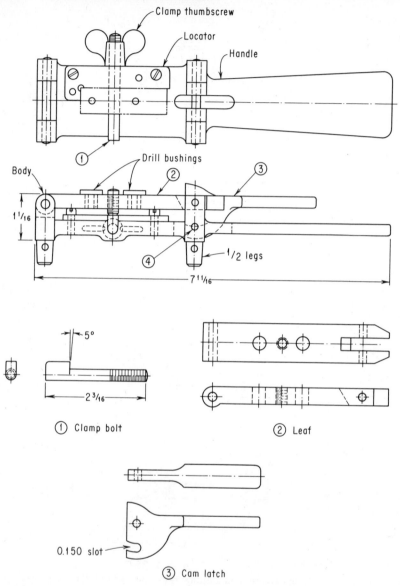

FIG. 4-22. Small leaf or pan-type jig. (*L. S. Starrett Co.*)

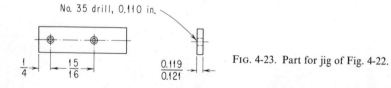

FIG. 4-23. Part for jig of Fig. 4-22.

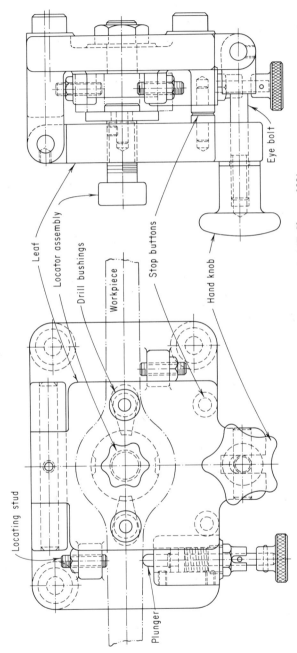

Locating stud

Leaf

Locator assembly

Drill bushings

Workpiece

Stop buttons

Hand knob

Eye bolt

Plunger

FIG. 4-24. Leaf jig for drilling a diestock. (*ASTME Chapter 100.*)

A tumble jig can be more complicated and costly than several simpler types, but its total cost is frequently absorbed by savings in drilling and fixture operation costs. Jig operation time is considerably shortened because bushings are not changed.

The tumble jig of Fig. 4-25, having separate renewable slip bushings for drilling and reaming operations, is modified as shown in Fig. 4-26. Press-fit bushings, costing less than liners and slip-fit bushings, are substituted. The side members are lengthened to provide feet for support when the jig is turned over for the reaming operation. Another design would incorporate four standard commercially available jig feet mounted on top of the side members.

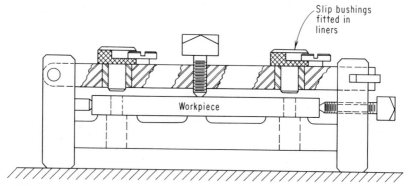

FIG. 4-25. Tumble jig with renewable slip bushings. (*H. J. Gerber, ASTME member-at-large.*)

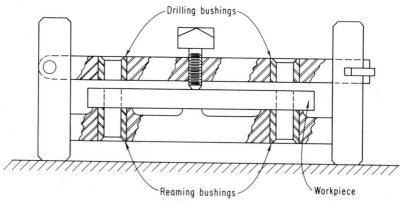

FIG. 4-26. Redesign of the jig of Fig. 4-25. (*H. J. Gerber, ASTME member-at-large.*)

The part (Fig. 4-28) for the drill jig of Fig. 4-27 requires the drilling of four small holes with the close tolerances that are noted on the part drawing. The shaft of the part, ground to 0.0003 in. tolerance, is positioned in Vs whose center line is square and parallel with the feet within 0.0001 in. TIR. To ensure extreme accuracy, tolerances of 0.0001 in. were held for other dimensions, locations, and alignments as shown. Two clamps (7) are mounted to a leaf (4) which pivots around a dowel (2). A hand knob (5) provides clamping pressure through a swing bolt (6). After the first hole is rough-drilled and sized, a locating pin (3) is inserted

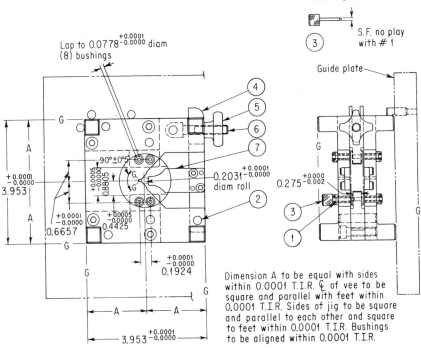

FIG. 4-27. Tumble jig of extreme accuracy. (*International Business Machines Corp.*)

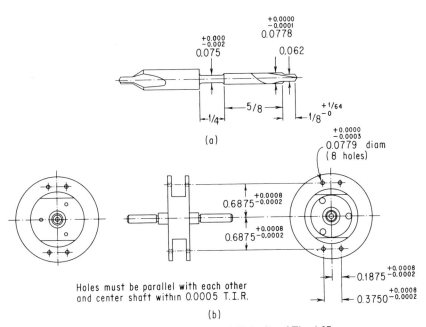

FIG. 4-28. Part and modified drill for jig of Fig. 4-27.

into the carbide bushing (1) (and the drilled hole) to prevent shifting of the workpiece. After the fourth hole is drilled, the tumble jig is turned over and the operation is repeated.

As a further aid to accuracy, a guide plate (Fig. 4-29) is mounted under the drill-press spindle so that the jig can be rigidly held against pins and exactly under the spindle. An indicator checks its squareness with the spindle.

One side of a tumble jig (Fig. 4-30) (opposite the drill bushing for hole A) is machined at a 90° angle to the axis of the bushing. This side serves as a base while drilling hole A; during the drilling of holes B and C, the side opposite each is used as a base.

The jig is bored to a slip fit for a workpiece locating hole, and a hole (1) through one side provides clearance for the stud in the workpiece. This side is flatted on both sides of its center, providing openings (2, 3) for the escape of chips. A bayonet-lock clamp fits into the enlarged locating hole. The slots (4) form cam surfaces which transmit clamping pressure to the workpiece when the hub is turned clockwise with an Allen wrench. Reverse rotation of the hub releases clamping pressure for loading and unloading the jig.

The workpiece shown in Fig. 4-31, a cast pipe having a rectangular bore, is located by a round and a diamond locating pin. Two strap clamps (6) hold it against three rest blocks (5) secured to the bottom of the jig.

A removable bushing carrier plug assembly (1) is pushed through the square cutout in the fixture, and the rectangular end of the wedge rod is slipped into the bore of the pipe. Rotation of a hex nut (7) on the outer end of a wedge rod (2) forces two clamp pins (3) and two steel balls (4) outward against the four flat surfaces of the bore. A pin (12) pressed in the wedge rod prevents its rotation. The assembly is thus clamped firmly in the bore of the pipe to position four guide bushings (8) for drilling four 0.1302-in.-diam holes in the flange of the workpiece.

The tumble jig is turned for drilling and reaming four 0.193-in.-diam holes in the lugs of the workpiece with guide bushings (9) inserted in one side plate of the jig. The jig is then turned for drilling a 0.046-in.-diam hole, as well as tapping, counter-

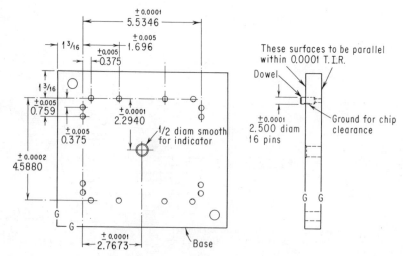

FIG. 4-29. Guide plate for jig of Fig. 4-27.

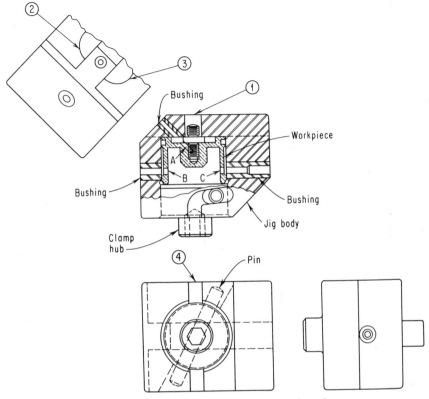

FIG. 4-30. Tumble jig with bayonet-lock clamp.[2]

boring, and countersinking operations on the hole, using suitable removable bushings (10). Twelve rest buttons (11) function as jig feet.

The workpiece, a magnesium casting, is held by three clamps, (1) and (2), in the fixture of Fig. 4-32, during the drilling of three 0.187-in.-diam holes at 109° to the axis of another hole which is drilled and counterbored.

Three locating studs (5, 9, 10) are adjusted and located against ribs of the casting. Three thumbscrews (3, 4) also apply clamping pressure against ribs and the end of the workpiece. The three small bushings (6) guide the 0.187-in.-diam pilot drill, and suitable bushings (7) guide a 0.250-in.-diam drill and a 0.750-in.-diam counterbore. For each of these operations, the jig rests on a separate set of jig feet (8).

PUMP JIGS

Many pump jigs are in use because of the many fine types commercially available (see Sec. 15) and because of their rapid clamping action and design simplicity.

A handle connected to a cam or a rack and pinion moves either a bushing plate or a nest plate, generally vertically, to clamp the workpiece. Parts held in pump jigs have surfaces adaptable to fitting against the surfaces of the bushing plate and

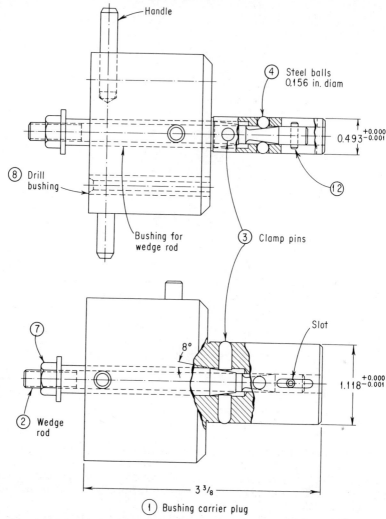

FIG. 4-31. Tumble jig for drilling a rectangular pipe. (*Emerson Electric Mfg. Co.*)

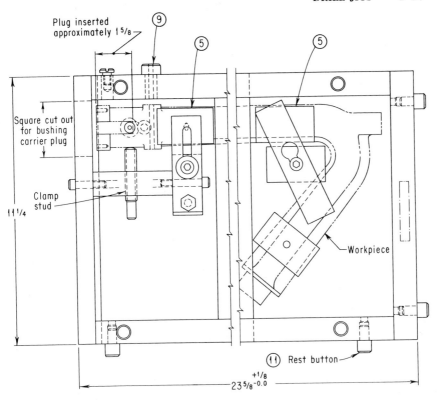

Plug inserted approximately 1 5/8

⑨

⑤

⑤

Square cut out for bushing carrier plug

Clamp stud

11 1/4

Workpiece

⑪ Rest button

Square cut out for bushing carrier plug

23 5/8 +1/8 -0.0

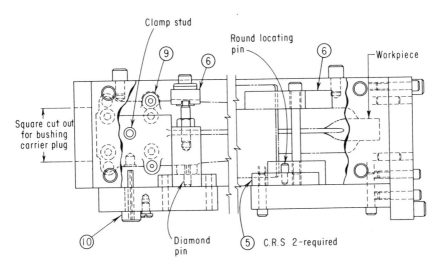

Clamp stud

Round locating pin

⑨

⑥

⑥

Workpiece

Square cut out for bushing carrier plug

⑩

Diamond pin

⑤ C.R.S 2-required

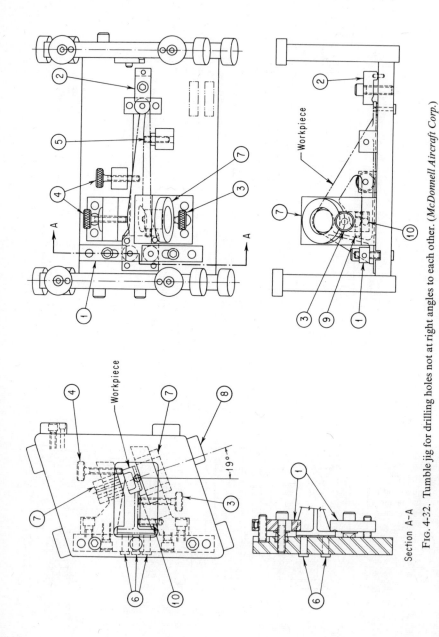

Section A–A

Fig. 4-32. Tumble jig for drilling holes not at right angles to each other. (*McDonnell Aircraft Corp.*)

nest. Generally a pump jig is not adaptable for drilling several holes from various angles at one clamping or for drilling large parts.

The pump jig of Fig. 4-33 has the bottom of the bushing cut away at an angle to allow the bushing to be brought down close to the workpiece for drilling a hole at a 60° angle.

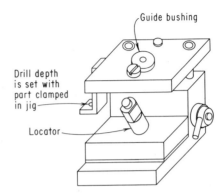

Guide bushing

Drill depth is set with part clamped in jig

Locator

FIG. 4-33. Pump jig for drilling a hole at a 60° angle. (*AMP, Inc.*)

The nest plate (4) of the jig of Fig. 4-34 (with an equalizing spherical surface) moves up to clamp the workpiece against the bushing plate. The part is located by a center locating plug (1) and by two locators (3). Correct locating is provided by an error-proof pin (2) which will interfere with the lug of a workpiece that is incorrectly loaded. Four rest buttons (5) and six drill bushings (6, 7) are press-fit in the bushing plate. A guard (8) protects the spherical surface and mating conical surface from chips and dirt.

JIGS FOR MULTIPLE-HOLE DRILLING

A problem that frequently confronts the tool or process engineer is the question of when to use multiple-spindle operations. Such operations should not be used unless the result is a definite saving. One approach to this problem is to count the total number of holes to be drilled; if they require more than two days of production time per month, single-spindle operations should be specified. On the whole, it is cheaper to let a drill-press operator spend two days a month drilling holes than it is to have special tooling made to do the job in a few hours.

The most important basis for multiple-spindle selection is the quantity of parts required. Estimate production requirements by week, day, and hour. If a part with 4 holes is required at 100 per hour, a single setup with a 4-spindle head and a quick-clamping fixture will do the job. For 300 per hour, the parts may be produced more economically with a 16-spindle head, 4 parts clamped at a time. But for 1,000 per hour, a more elaborate setup would be required, probably with mechanized feed and ejection (Fig. 4-35a, b, c).

If a part requires more holes than is convenient with available equipment, the work might be fixtured on a slide and indexed across the table under a head that drills only one or two rows of holes at a time (Fig. 4-36). However, gearless heads have been built for as many as several hundred spindles, so the total number of holes is not normally a critical problem. Complications more often develop because of too-close center distances, unequal hole sizes, and difficult hole patterns. An analysis of present methods of producing similar parts may help in planning a new setup. If a single deep hole is to be drilled along with several shorter holes that take

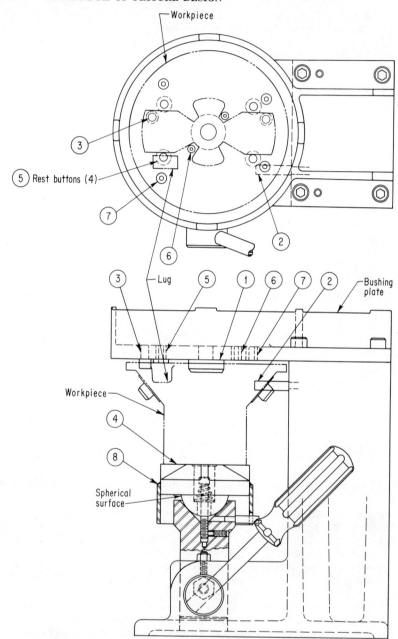

Fɪɢ. 4-34. Pump jig with a spherical nest surface for equalizing. (*Millers Falls Co.*)

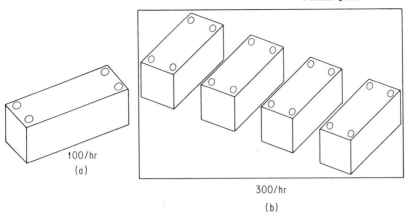

100/hr
(a)

300/hr
(b)

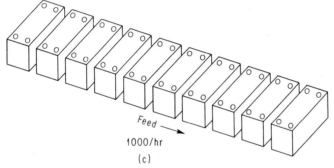

Feed ⟶
1000/hr
(c)

FIG. 4-35. Setups for drilling four holes at various rates.

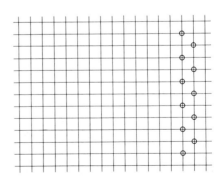

FIG. 4-36. Drilling one or two rows of holes at a time.

Part indexed

less cycle time, the deep hole can be split up between several spindles, each drill starting to cut where the previous drill left off (Fig. 4-37).

When a large number of spindles is available, it is usually practical to operate as many of them as possible to allow shortest cycle time.

For parts that must be drilled in several faces, the simplest kind of fixture is a box or a tumble jig. It holds the part during several operations and keeps the drill bushings in constant alignment with the work. The jig may be simply shifted and tumbled along a long table, stopped by rails or pins, and positioned under a large multispindle head at several stations or under several separate heads, all mounted over the same table (Fig. 4-38).

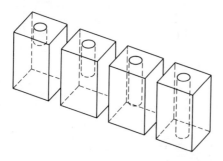

Fig. 4-37. Progressive drilling of five holes at 50 per hr.

Assuming that the same number of spindles are set up to drill a limited number of holes, production can be roughly tripled by moving parts through a straight-line setup. A single large fixture or several smaller ones can be aligned and clamped to the table to hold parts in several different positions. Parts progress through the fixture from station to station, moved and clamped by hand. A completed part is produced at each machine cycle; however, there is lost time between cycles as the operator shifts parts from one location to the next. The total number of spindles may be the same as with a box-jig or moving-fixture setup, but all spindles work at the same time (Fig. 4-38).

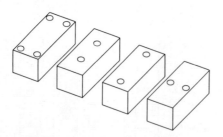

Fig. 4-38. Methods of drilling holes in several faces: (*a*) box jig, 25 per hr; (*b*) straight-line setup, 75 per hr.

Trunnion fixtures allow higher production and reduce the amount of parts handling. The part is clamped once, then indexed around to several stations. Several parts are in the fixture at one time, and a complete part is produced at each machine cycle. Only one clamping and unclamping is required (Fig. 4-39).

Progressive operations such as drilling, counterboring, reaming, and tapping can be set up on a straight-line arrangement under a single head or a number of heads. A single fixture may be moved along rails if all operations are on a single work face, or parts may be shifted progressively from one clamping fixture to the next. In either case, the workpiece must be located exactly at each station so the tools will come down on the center line common to each part. Work may be shifted by hand, but the machine arrangement may be as similar to a mechanized transfer machine as can be justified by the quantity of parts (Fig. 4-40).

Rotary indexing tables increase cycle rate and production output. Fixtures are locked to a rotary table which indexes under power. Proper alignment requires careful setup, but this can be justified by a high output. Work remains clamped until all operations are complete. Clamping and unclamping can be done when the machine is working (Fig. 4-41). Production rates can be compared this way: assume that 50 parts per hour can be made with a manual straight-line arrangement for small parts; a rotary table that clamps 1 part at each station can produce about 200 per hour and attain about 300 per hour with 4 parts clamped at each station.

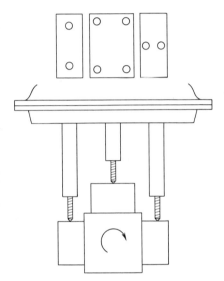

FIG. 4-39. Trunnion fixture; production rate, 100 per hr.

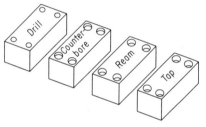

FIG. 4-40. Progressive operations: part and fixture moved to various working positions or stations.

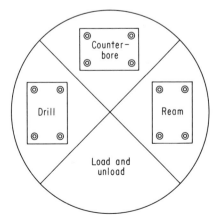

FIG. 4-41. Rotary indexing, 200 per hr.

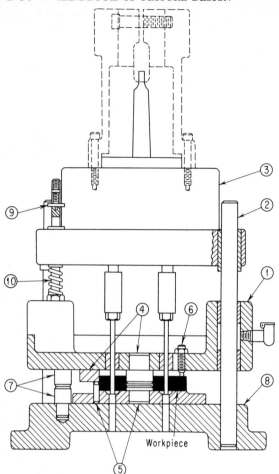

Workpiece

FIG. 4-42. Jig for multiple-spindle drilling.

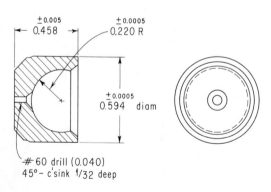

±0.005
0.458

±0.0005
0.220 R

±0.0005
0.594   diam

#60 drill (0.040)
45°– c'sink 1/32 deep

Scale 2:1

FIG. 4-43. Workpiece for jig of Fig. 4-44.

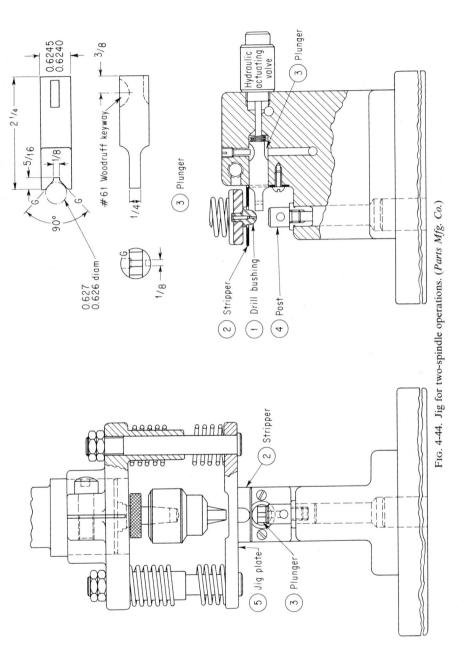

FIG. 4-44. Jig for two-spindle operations. (*Paris Mfg. Co.*)

0.6245
0.6240

3/8

2 1/4

5/16

1/8

#61 Woodruff keyway

1/4

90°

0.627
0.626 diam

G

G

G

1/8

③ Plunger

Hydraulic actuating valve

③ Plunger

② Stripper

① Drill bushing

④ Post

② Stripper

⑤ Jig plate

③ Plunger

The multiple-spindle jig of Fig. 4-42 incorporates a spring-loaded bushing carrier (1) which slides vertically on leader pins (2). As the drill head (3) moves down, upper locators (4) engage the workpiece which had been approximately located by the lower locators (5). Spring plungers (6) clamp the workpiece. Stop pins (7) in the bushing carrier and in the fixture base (8) limit travel of the bushing carrier and maintain it parallel to the top of the workpiece.

When a bushing carrier supplies clamping pressure to irregular parts, it may cause cocking of the parts, necessitating the use of separate clamps mounted on the fixture base.

Cross pins (9) inserted through holes in the holding pins (10) allow the bushing carrier to be lowered for drill changing and sharpening.

The jig of Fig. 4-44 is one of two identical jigs (except for guide bushings) mounted on the bases of hydraulic feed drills. The drilling of a 0.040-in. hole in the workpiece (Fig. 4-43) is done in the jig shown, and the hole is countersunk in the second fixture.

The workpiece is placed on a post (4) and against the V of a plunger (3). The descending drill spindle and jig plate (5) clamp the workpiece under a guide bushing (1) having a spherical surface matching that of the workpiece. A stripper (2) allows the plunger to eject the workpiece after the rapid return of the spindle and jig plate.

The pressure of the workpiece against the plunger, transmitted to the hydraulic actuating valve, starts the rapid descent of the spindle through a hydraulic circuit and slows its rate as the drill passes through the workpiece. The operator feeds both jigs, resulting in the production of 1,320 drilled workpieces per hr and the production of 1,800 countersunk workpieces per hr.

In the fixture of Fig. 4-46, the workpiece (a diestock) is located on a locating stud, and its handle is located against a locating bracket. It is held on the stud by an air cylinder actuating a linked swinging clamp. A lower locating bracket, interchangeable drill bushings, and locating studs allow three holes to be drilled in diestocks of different sizes.

A fragile thin-walled aluminum die casting is located in the tumble jig of Fig. 4-47 by a diamond locating pin (3) and a round locating pin (6) which engage bored holes in the casting. Rotation of the collar screw (5) forces the clamp leaf (9) and two rest buttons (4) down to clamp the casting against the rest block (7). Actuation of a hand knob (8) clamps the end of the workpiece. Two diamond loca-

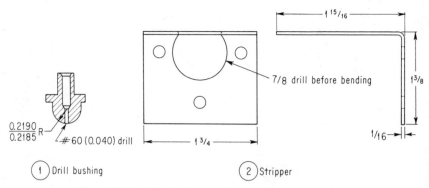

FIG. 4-45. Drill bushing and stripper of the jig of Fig. 4-44.

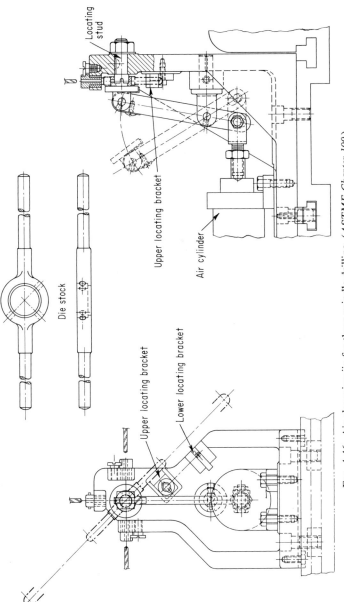

Locating
stud

Upper locating bracket

Air cylinder

Die stock

Upper locating bracket

Lower locating bracket

Fig. 4-46. Air-clamping jig for three-spindle drilling. (*ASTME Chapter 100.*)

4-37

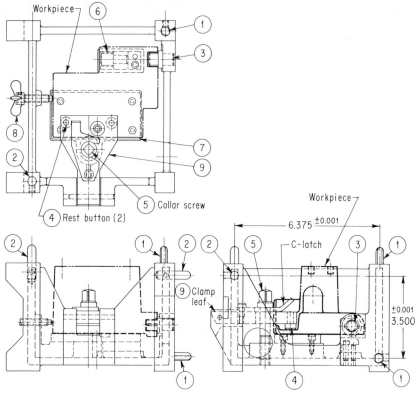

FIG. 4-47. Jig for spindle-to-spindle drilling with interchangeable bushing plates. (*Universal Winding Co.*)

tors (2) and two round locators (1) align the jig with a bushing plate (Fig. 4-48, 1) attached to the drill head. These locators engage bushings (2) in the bushing plate to position the jig under a drill and two reamers guided by a drill bushing (6) and two reamer bushings (7).

After drilling and reaming are completed, the jig is shifted to allow the locators to enter the right-hand bushings in the bushing plate, which positions three reamer bushings (8, 9) under three reamers. Three other similar bushing plates allow the positioning of the tumble jig under three different sets of spindles for drilling, reaming, and tapping operations. The jig is rotated for some of these operations, which are at right angles to each other, and is positioned by the corresponding locators (1, 2). Straight-line spindle-to-spindle production output, using the four bushing plates with the tumble jig, is from 500 to 2,000 workpieces per month.

The shuttle-type drill of Fig. 4-49 incorporates four wheels which run on rails of an auxiliary table clamped to the drill-press table. The table is adjusted until the rails are parallel with the centers of the four spindles. With a handle the operator slides the fixture under the spindles for the sequence of operations shown.

The workpiece, a cast lever (Fig. 4-50), is located and clamped between two cones. Air pressure is applied to one cone for clamping the cored hole of the workpiece through a wedge cam, a clamping lever, and a clamp rod. An adjustable stop prevents rotation of the workpiece around the cones. Production is from 60 to 100 parts per hour.

INDEXING JIGS

Indexing jigs are used in the drilling of holes in a pattern, usually radial. Location for the holes is generally taken from the first hole drilled, from other holes in the part, or from registry with an indexing device incorporated in the jig.

The simple jig of Fig. 4-51 has an angle-iron base incorporating a locating stud (2) on which a bored cylindrical workpiece (1) is placed. It is clamped on the stud with a C washer (4) and a hexagon nut (3). A drill bushing (5) is press-fit in the bushing plate (8). The hexagon nut is loosened after the first hole is drilled; the workpiece is revolved; the index pin (6) is pushed into the hole; and the second of four holes, 90° apart, is drilled after the nut is tightened. A flat spring (7) holds the index pin in place.

Another indexing jig (Fig. 4-52) utilizing an angle plate is of welded construction. A spindle pressed into the jig's pivot point is threaded on one end for the locking wheel. The clamp for holding the workpiece is not shown. The part, bushing plate, and bushings are rotated for drilling holes at various angles, determined by the location of the index holes in the jig and in the angle plate.

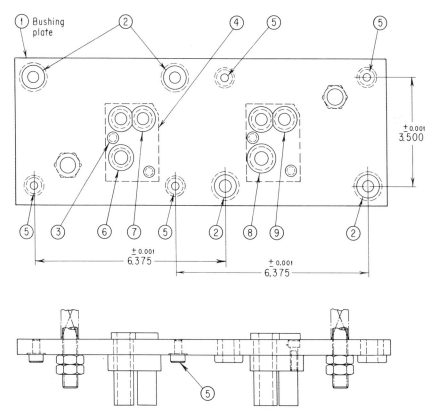

FIG. 4-48. Bushing plate, attached to drill head, used with the jig of Fig. 4-47.

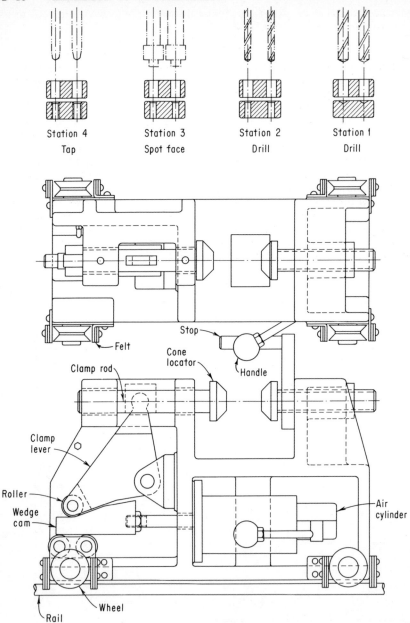

FIG. 4-49. Shuttle jig. (*Textile Machine Works.*)

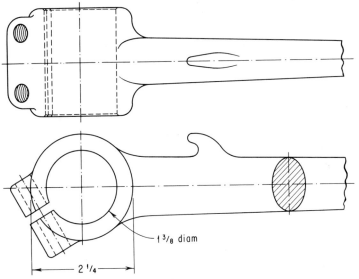

Fig. 4-50. Workpiece for jig of Fig. 4-49.

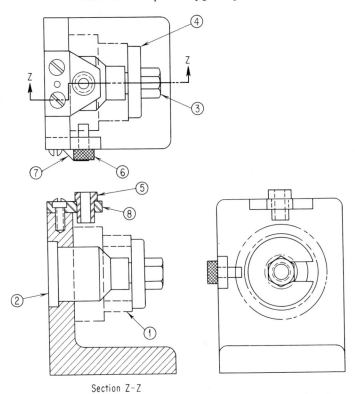

Section Z-Z

Fig. 4-51. Simple indexing jig with a base of standard angle iron.[5]

Figure 4-53 shows an indexing jig that is adaptable for drilling holes radially toward the center of pistons, cylinders, or shafts. The workpiece is held in a locator (6) by a cam-lock clamp (7). Movement of the indexing handle (1) controls the engagement of the index plunger (3), with the 12 bushings (2) equally spaced around an index plate (4). A renewable slip bushing (5) guides the drill. Indexing is accurate, because the tapered index plunger and tapered index bushings allow little if any side thrust and movement of the workpiece.

The workpiece to be drilled in the jig of Fig. 4-54 is held by four clamps (7, 8) and located by a diamond locator (6) and a round locator (9). Drill bushings (2, 3, and 5) guide the bushings after the jig is mounted on the indexing angle plate (Fig. 4-55). The locating plug (1) of the jig fits the 1½-in. hole in the hub of the index plate (Fig. 4-55). A series of bushed holes around the plate are engaged by the index pin. A cover for this pin allows the accuracy of ±0.0002 in. to be utilized.

The jig is held on the angle plate by four socket-head screws which pass through holes in the base of the jig and by two strap clamps (not shown).

ASSEMBLY-DRILLING JIGS

The clamping of subassemblies or mating parts in their positions of assembly in a jig and then drilling holes for rivets, screws, or pins ensure alignment of the assembly holes. The subassemblies can be pinned or screwed together in the same jig; or after drilling, they can be separated and stored for later assembly with no fitting problems.

A Jig for Drilling Rivet Holes. The rivet holes in the parts of an aluminum frame were drilled in the jig of Fig. 4-56. A master block (1) is machined to fit the inside of the assembly and to position the gussets. The gussets are held in place against the block with two strap clamps (2) and knurled nuts (3). Two pins (4) allow movement of the clamps in one direction only. One edge of the bracket rests on a locating button (5), and a locating pin (6) vertically positions the bracket. A knurled-head screw (7) clamps the bracket and incorporates a fiber plug (8) to prevent marring. Bushing blocks (9, 10, 11, 12) incorporate bushings for guiding the drills. Knurled-head screws (13) provide additional clamping pressure against the bracket and gus-

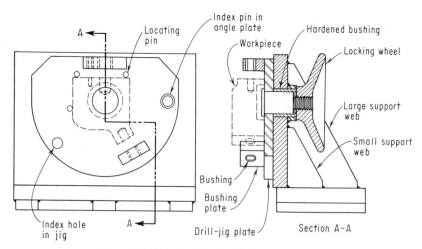

FIG. 4-52. Indexing jig of welded construction.[6]

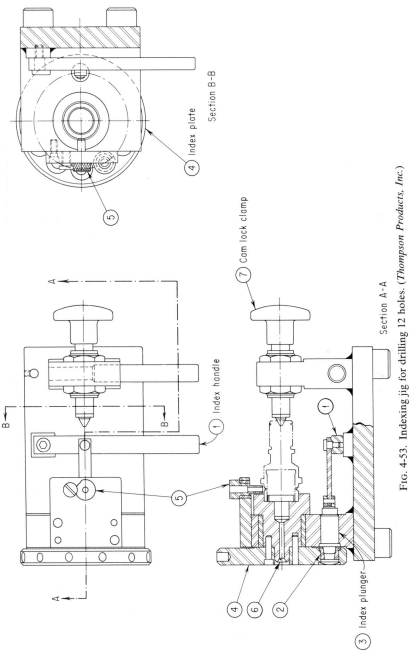

Section B-B

④ Index plate

⑤

⑦ Cam lock clamp

Section A-A

① Index handle

⑤

④ ⑥ ②

③ Index plunger

FIG. 4-53. Indexing jig for drilling 12 holes. (*Thompson Products, Inc.*)

4–43

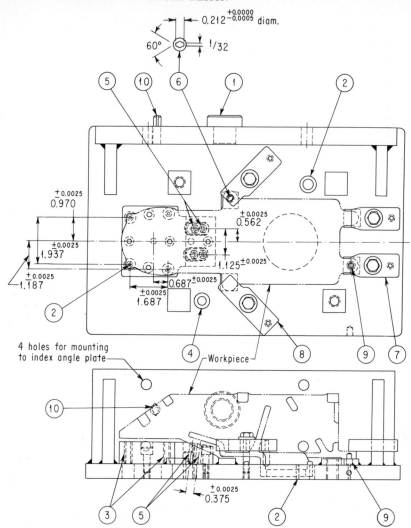

FIG. 4-54. Jig used with an indexing angle plate of Fig. 4-55. (*International Business Machines Corp.*)

sets. Locating pins (14) vertically position the support. The jig is supported by pins (15) and a support block (16). The parts are removed from the jig for later riveting.

A Drill, Ream, and Pin Jig. Two cams and two arms are slip-fit on the shaft (Fig. 4-57) before the shaft is held by V locators (1, 2, 3) incorporated in the jig of Fig. 4-58. A pin (4) positions the two cams by engaging the 0.3145-in. slot and by engaging square bushings (5), 0.314 by 0.324 in., and is held by a clamp (6). The arms are clamped in position as shown in sections *A-A* and *B-B*.

After the holes are drilled and reamed, four pins are inserted and driven lightly before the assembly is removed from the jig.

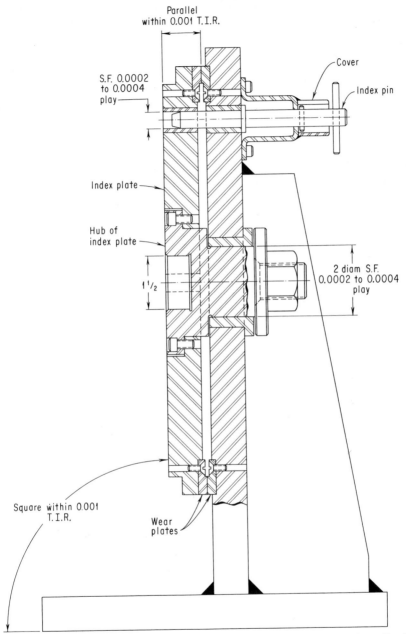

Parallel
within 0.001 T.I.R.

Cover

Index pin

S.F. 0.0002
to 0.0004
play

Index plate

Hub of
index plate

$1\frac{1}{2}$

2 diam S.F.
0.0002 to 0.0004
play

Square within 0.001
T.I.R.

Wear
plates

FIG. 4-55. Indexing angle plate for jig of Fig. 4-54. (*International Business Machines Corp.*)

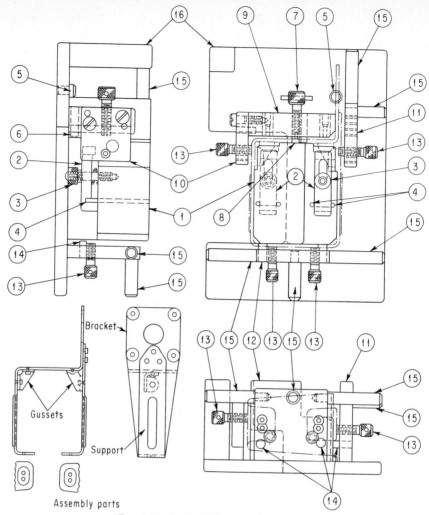

Bracket

Gussets

Support

Assembly parts

FIG. 4-56. Jig for drilling subassemblies.[7]

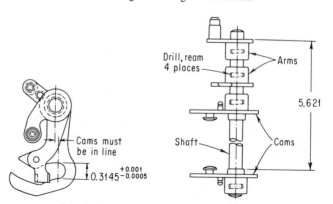

Drill, ream
4 places

Arms

Shaft

Cams

Cams must
be in line

$0.3145^{+0.001}_{-0.0005}$

5.621

FIG. 4-57. Workpieces for the jig of Fig. 4-58.

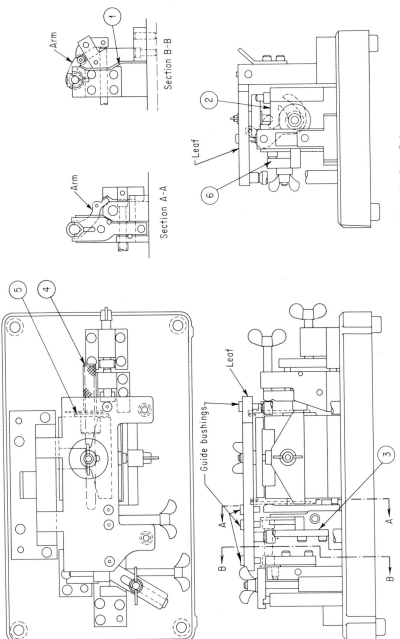

FIG. 4-58. Jig for drilling, reaming, and pinning. (*Burroughs Adding Machine Co.*)

HANDBOOK OF FIXTURE DESIGN

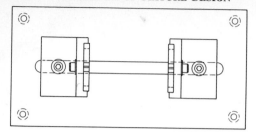

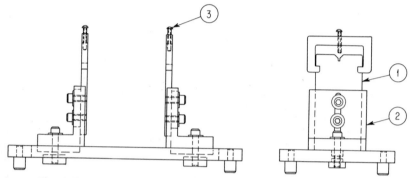

FIG. 4-59. Drill-and-pin jig for shafts and gears. (*Norden Instruments, Inc.*)

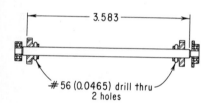

FIG. 4-60. Workpieces for jig of Fig. 4-59.

A Drill and Pin Jig. The jig of Fig. 4-59, although simple in design, can accommodate various shaft lengths to be pinned to gears. The slotted holders (2) allow the center distance between the V blocks (1) to be set up with gage blocks. The gears to be pinned to a shaft 3.583 in. long have been spot-drilled before they have been placed in the V blocks of the jig. Two clamping screws (3) which hold the shaft in the Vs are of brass to prevent marring the stainless steel shaft.

References

1. Newton, R. W.: Jig for Drilling Spanner-wrench Holes, *Machinery,* March, 1951.
2. Newton, R. W.: Jig Designed for Rapid Drilling of Air-valve Part, *Machinery,* September, 1950.
3. Austin, L. H.: Interchangeable Templets Diversify Drill Jig, *Am. Machinst,* Mar. 1, 1954.
4. Bower, C. T.: "Drop-leaf" Fixture Helps Drill, Ream Closely Spaced Holes, *Am. Machinist,* Nov. 21, 1955.
5. Rush, F. L.: Drill Jig for Uniformly Spaced Radial Holes, *Machinery,* September, 1957.
6. Frommer, H. G.: Rotating Fixture on Angle Plate Indexes Parts for Drilling, *Am. Machinist,* Dec. 1, 1949.
7. Newton, R. W.: Jig Designed to Drill Sub-assemblies, *Machinery,* July, 1951.

Section 5

BORING FIXTURES

By ASTME BOOKS STAFF

All or nearly all of the considerations in the design of jigs and fixtures used with machine tools for all types of metal-cutting operations (see Sec. 1) must also be considered in the design of fixtures for boring operations.

Some considerations or conditions unique to boring-fixture design are:

1. Since some types of boring are performed on boring machines that allow the adjustment of the machine table or of the boring bar, it may be advantageous to provide indicating surfaces and holes in the fixture.

2. While master plates, measuring bars, or other devices for alignment and positioning of the bar with respect to the fixture and workpiece holes may or may not be integral with the fixture, they are frequently designed by the fixture designer.

3. Allowances should be made for bar travel and boring-tool adjustment without interference with the fixture.

4. When the fixture is designed to support the bar, hardened stationary bushings or frictionless bearings should be incorporated to minimize vibration and whip in the bar for best accuracy of hole size and location.

5. If the fixture designer is also responsible for bar design, the surfaces of the bar contacting the bearings in a fixture should be chrome-plated or hardened for minimum wear.

A Vertical Jig-boring Fixture. The locating surfaces of the rest blocks (5) of the fixture of Fig. 5-1 are ground parallel to and 0.812 ± 0.0002 in. from the center of the indicating hole, which is 1.875 ± 0.0002 in. from the center of the round locating pin.

The bottom of the indicating groove in the upright (6) is ground parallel to its outside edges within 0.0002 in. TIR and square to the bottom of the base (7) of the fixture within 0.0005 in. TIR.

The fixture is placed on a vertical jig borer; and with its probe in the indicating hole, the indicator is brought to zero. The fixture is also oriented on the jig-borer table with the probe bearing against the indicating edge of the fixture.

The workpiece is located by a round locating pin (1) and a diamond pin (2) which are spring-loaded for firm seating in workpiece holes and slide-in bushings (3). A keeper plate (4) bearing against a flat on the diamond pin prevents its rotation.

A clearance of ½₂ in. between the shoulder of the diamond pin and its bushing is allowed for variations in the locating holes in the part.

The left-hand clamp straddles the part to rigidly hold the workpiece, while the wide right-hand clamp exerts pressure directly over finished pads on the mounting surface.

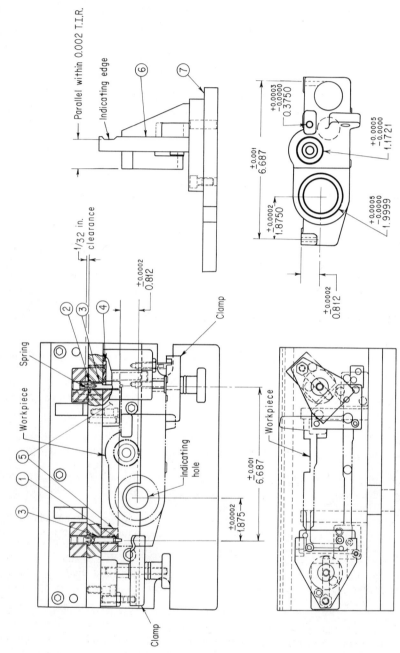

Fig. 5-1. Fixture for vertical jig boring. (*International Business Machines Corp.*)

A Fixture for Boring 15 Holes. Twelve 0.0928-in. holes (*B* holes) and three 0.5000-in. holes (*A*, *S*1, and *S*2 holes) are bored in the workpiece, a casting, of Fig. 5-2*a*. The workpiece is placed on rest plates (8, 9, 10) in the fixture of Fig. 5-2*b*, and a diamond locating pin (3) is pushed into the locating hole in the side of the casting.

A keeper plate (4) bears against a flat on the side of this pin to prevent its rotation in a bushing (6).

A tapered locating pin (1) is inserted through the *S*2 hole in the casting and into a bushing (5) in a post (13). Three cam clamps (7), pressing directly on three pads on the part, are tightened; the tapered pin is removed; and the *S*2 hole is finish-bored. This pin is replaced by a slightly larger one (2), and all other holes in the

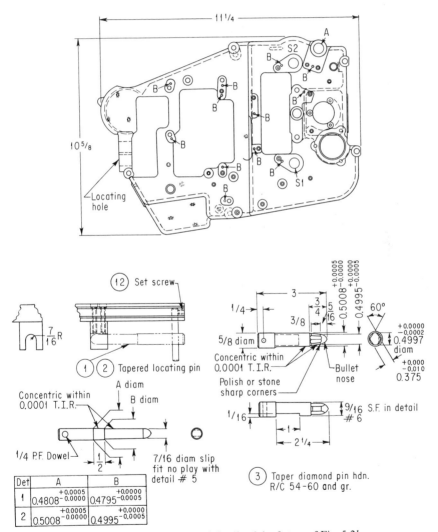

Fig. 5-2*a*. Workpiece for and details of the fixture of Fig. 5-2*b*.

casting are bored. The tapered pins snugly fit the hole in the workpiece and accurately locate it.

An indicating edge is ground in the back of the base (11) for orientation of the fixture on the table of a jig borer.

For storage, one tapered pin is left in its bushing (5), and a setscrew (12) secures the other pin to the fixture.

A Double-purpose Fixture. The fixture of Fig. 5-3 holds the casting of Fig. 5-2a for additional boring operations on a jig mill; and for milling certain surfaces, two cutter set blocks (4) are provided.

Tapered locating pins (1, 2) are inserted in locating holes in the workpiece which is clamped against rest buttons (7) and rest plates (8, 9) by clamps (3, 5, 6).

The fixture is correctly positioned on the table of a jig mill by a straight key (11), an eccentric key (10), a locating pin (12), and an indicator properly contacting the ID of the indicating hole bushing (13).

A Fixture for Boring and Fly-cutting. Four locating blocks (2) of the fixture of Fig. 5-4b engage the central hole in the workpiece shown in Fig. 5-4a, while a dia-

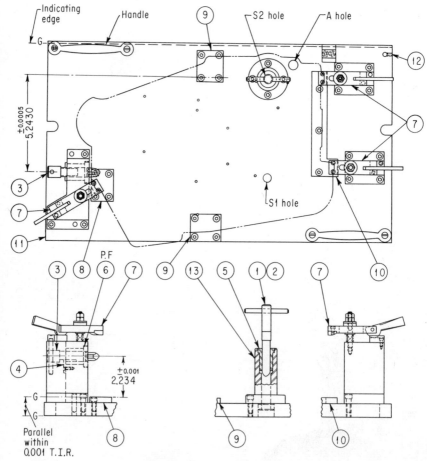

FIG. 5-2b. Fixture for a jig borer. (*International Business Machines Corp.*)

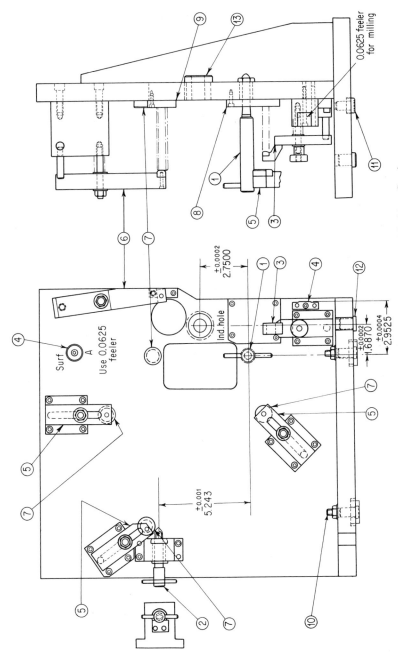

FIG. 5-3. Fixture for a jig mill. (*International Business Machines Corp.*)

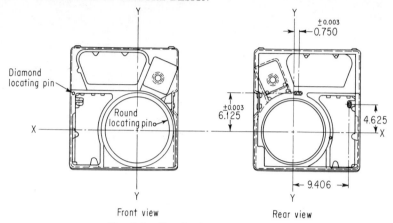

FIG. 5-4a. Part for fixture of Fig. 5-4b.

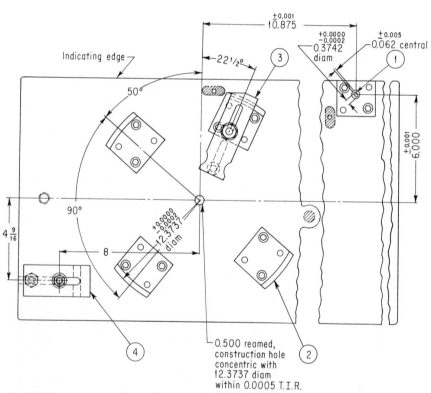

FIG. 5-4b. Fixture for boring and fly-cutting five pads. (*International Business Machines Corp.*)

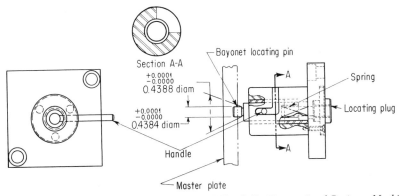

FIG. 5-5a. Centering fixture for boring fixture of Fig. 5-5b. (*International Business Machines Corp.*)

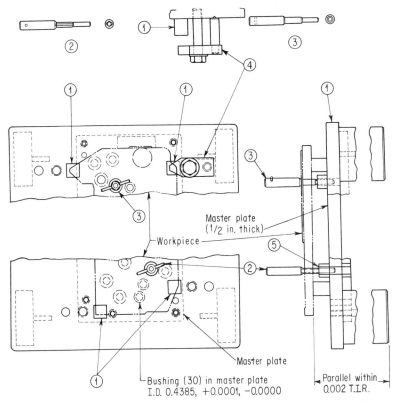

FIG. 5-5b. Boring fixture and master plate. (*International Business Machines Corp.*)

mond locating pin (1) engages a hole on the front surface of the casting. Two slid-ing strap clamps (3, 4) hold the workpiece, a casting, on the relieved edges of the locating blocks. The location of all parts of the fixture is established from the cen-tral construction (reference) hole.

Boring with a Master Plate. The centering fixture of Fig. 5-5*a* is positioned with its locating plug and bolted to the table of a small, vertical boring machine. The boring fixture of Fig. 5-5*b* has a master plate with 30 holes for registration with the bayonet-type locating pin projecting upwards from the centering fixture. Moving the fixture and plate over the centering fixture is a fast method of exactly position-ing the fixture and workpiece and permits the holes, which are held to a tolerance of 0.0005 in., to be bored at locations corresponding to the accurate hole layout of the master plate.

The workpiece is placed on four rest blocks (1) and is located by a round locating pin (3) and a diamond locating pin (2) which are pushed through holes in the work-piece and into bushings (5). Four strap clamps (4) hold the workpiece against the rest blocks.

A Fixture for Horizontal Boring. The workpiece, a casting to be bored in the fixture of Fig. 5-6, is located on two diamond pins (3, 7) and by a spring-loaded

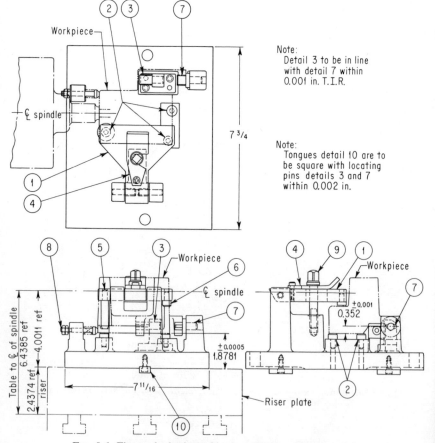

FIG. 5-6. Fixture for horizontal boring. (*Universal Winding Co.*)

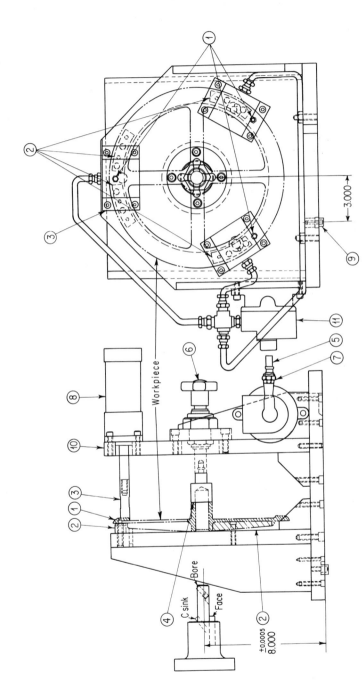

FIG. 5-7. Fixture for combined boring, facing, and countersinking. (*The Maytag Co.*)

pin (8). It rests on three rest buttons (2). A pin (5) and a rest button (6) press-fit in a swing-latch clamp (1) contact the top and bottom of the casting.

Clamping pressure is applied at these points by a collar screw (9) after a C clamp is swung under it.

Two fixture keys (10) align the fixture on a riser plate fastened to the table of a double-end boring machine.

A Fixture for Boring, Countersinking, and Facing. The fixture of Fig. 5-7 incorporates locating pins (1) which engage three of the eight holes in the outer rim of the workpiece, a ribbed aluminum spider; the pins also establish concentricity of the hole to be bored (of 0.002 in.) with these holes.

The relieved end (4) of a cam-lock clamp assembly (6) clamps the hub against a locating plate (2). Distortion of the workpiece from thrust and torque of the boring tool is prevented by this clamp and also by three air-actuated clamps (3) which are aligned with the supporting pads.

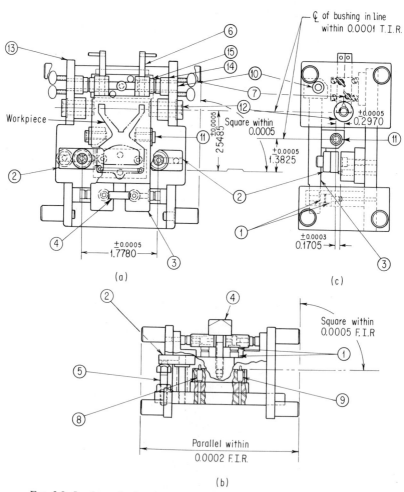

FIG. 5-8. Leaf-type boring fixture. (*International Business Machines Corp.*)

The handle (7) of the air valve (11) controls three double-acting air cylinders (8) which, together with the hand clamp (6), permit rapid clamping and release of the work.

The rapidity and ease of clamping, loading, and unloading and the boring, countersinking, and facing by one pass of the boring quill permit fast and economical machining of large production quantities.

Fixture keys (9) align the fixture with the table of a boring machine, which is necessary to produce holes with a size tolerance of $+0.000$, -0.001 in.

The air valve with its Aro speed connector (5) and piping is mounted on the fixture to allow its easy removal as a unit from the boring-machine table.

A Leaf Boring Fixture. A leaf type of fixture (Fig. 5-8) incorporates two independently sliding V jaws (6) to compensate for casting variations in the workpiece. The leaf (3), carrying two drill bushings (11), applies no clamping pressure to the workpiece to force the bushings out of alignment. The workpiece is placed on a round locating pin (8) and a diamond pin (9) and is held by the sliding jaws, which are clamped by four thumbscrews (7).

A quarter-turn screw (4) holds the leaf against two clamps (2) which hold the workpiece. The heels of two spring-loaded strap clamps (2) rest on two clamp rests (5) and are held by socket-head cap screws.

Extra-long bushings (11, 12) for piloting the reamers for boring two holes in the workpiece are jig-ground to size after they are in place in the fixture.

Two bushings (14) that are press-fit in the two uprights (13) and two others (15) press-fit in the leaf function as bearings for the leaf hinge pin (10).

Four small jig feet (1) function as rest buttons for the leaf.

It takes a drilling machine 12 min to bore the four holes.

A Fixture for Boring a Thin-walled Aluminum Casting. To avoid distortion of the thin walls of the aluminum workpiece of Fig. 5-10a, clamping pressure is exerted on its exterior projecting portions rather than across its major diameter. The workpiece, a die casting, is located in a shaped block (1) and clamped by a bolt (2) and a handwheel (3), as shown in Fig. 5-10b. After positioning the cast-

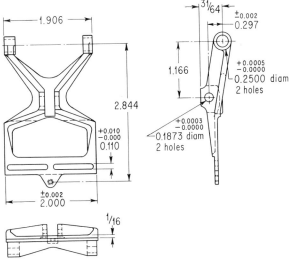

Fig. 5-9. Workpiece for fixture of Fig. 5-8.

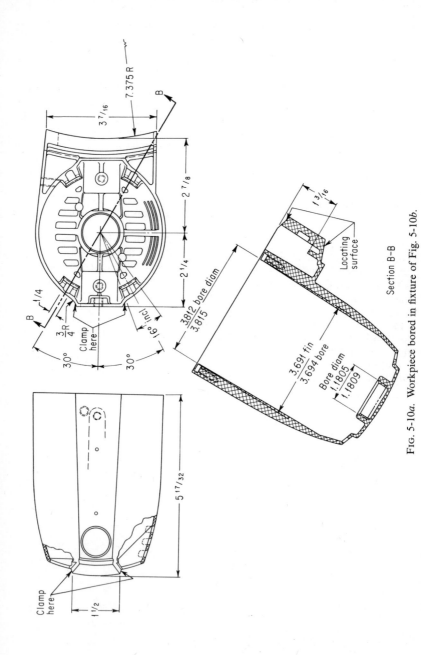

FIG. 5-10a. Workpiece bored in fixture of Fig. 5-10b.

Section B-B

Locating surface

$3\frac{7}{16}$

7.375 R

B

$2\frac{7}{8}$

$2\frac{1}{4}$

$\frac{3.812}{3.815}$ bore diam

$\frac{1}{4}$

$\frac{3}{4}$ R

B

30°

Clamp here

30°

16.9 incl.

$1\frac{3}{16}$

$\frac{3.691}{3.694}$ fin bore

Bore diam $\frac{1.1805}{1.1809}$

$5\frac{17}{32}$

Clamp here

$1\frac{1}{2}$

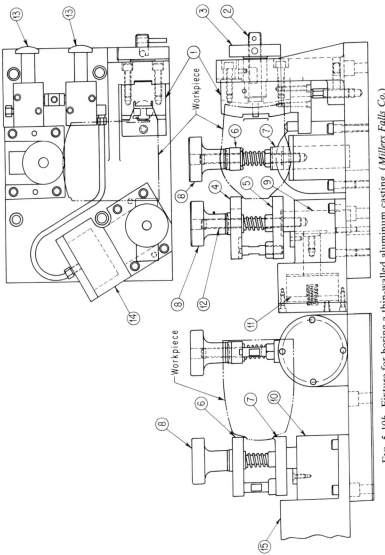

Fig. 5-10b. Fixture for boring a thin-walled aluminum casting. (*Millers Falls Co.*)

ing, floating clamps (4, 5, 6, 7) are tightened by rotating hand knobs (8). These two clamp assemblies, mounted on clamp posts (9) and (10) respectively, are free to move vertically, until air pressure is applied to the pistons of two air cylinders (14, 15).

When push-pull air valves (13) are opened, the rod ends of the pistons (11) press against the clamp posts, providing solid support to the workpiece held in the clamp assemblies.

After boring is completed, the air valves are opened, and the floating clamps are loosed and rotated for unloading.

A Horizontal Bushed Boring Fixture. If the distance from the spindle face to the workpiece hole to be bored is more than five times the hole diameter, it is recommended that the end of the boring bar be piloted as shown in Fig. 5-11.

Two stop blocks and two diamond locating pins locate the workpiece on the fixture base. A leaf clamp holds it on the base, which is keyed to the machine table. A pilot bushing is mounted in an upright member which is held square to the face of the spindle.

A Fixture with Two Split Bushings. The workpiece, made of 1035 steel tubing (Fig. 5-12), is held by suitable clamps (not shown) on the locating pads. The chrome-plated boring bar rotates in two bushings tapered at each end but having

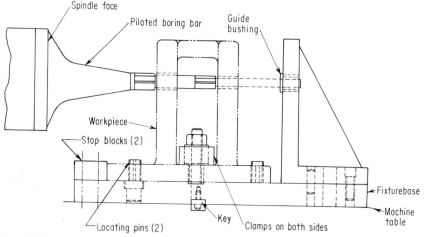

FIG. 5-11. A boring fixture with single-boring bar bushing. (*Ex-Cell-O Machinery Sales Co.*)

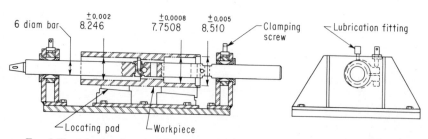

FIG. 5-12. A boring fixture with two split bushings. (*LeTourneau-Westinghouse Co.*)

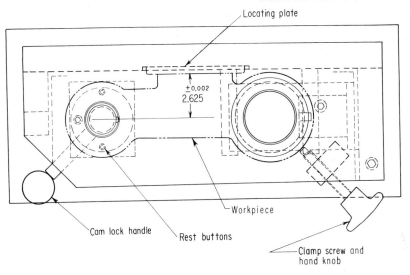

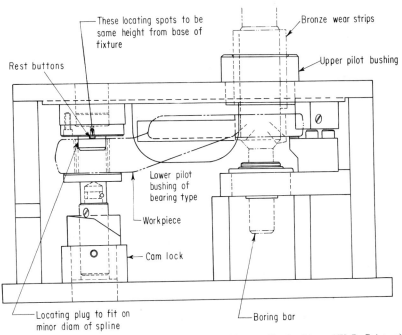

Fig. 5-13. A vertical-boring fixture with upper and lower pilot bushings. (*W. D. Bristow.*)

a straight bore approximately 1½ in. long. The split halves of the bushings are squeezed around the bar by clamps fitted around the OD of each bushing, securing minimum bar runout and a bore finish of 125 microinches.

A Boring Fixture with Upper and Lower Pilot Bushings. The workpiece shown in Fig. 5-13 is located by a plug fitting on its splined end, and it is clamped against the vertical locating plate by the clamp screw and hand knob. A cam-lock clamp handle is rotated to hold the splined end of the workpiece up against the rest buttons.

The boring bar has hard bronze wear strips and is piloted in the upper bushing. The lower roller-bearing bushing accommodates and pilots the lower end of the boring bar.

Section 6

LATHE FIXTURES

By LATHE FIXTURES COMMITTEE*

Holding the workpiece for lathe operations is given comparatively little thought because standard chucks are available for all machines. However, the lack of sufficient attention to certain basic principles can lead to difficulties.

There are five essential rules that should be followed in order to hold a workpiece satisfactorily. These are:[1][†]

1. Grip the rotating workpiece to resist torsional forces.
2. Locate the workpiece on critical surfaces which are areas from which all or major dimensional and angular tolerances are taken.
3. Provide adequate support for frail sections or sections under pressures from the lathe tools.
4. Reduce loading or unloading time to justify reduced total cost per part for the quantity of parts to be produced.
5. If machining is done at high spindle speeds, solve the special problems these speeds may cause.

Gripping the Workpiece. Gripping should be done on the largest workpiece diameter; wherever possible the gripping diameter should be larger than the diameter being machined.

The moments of force (torque) around the center of these diameters are proportional to the length of their lever arms (radii) and can provide a mechanical advantage for the gripping member over the cutting tools.

The workpiece must be gripped on a section which must remain rigid during and after machining. An example of this is the fixturing of a multiple-grooved V-belt sheave shown in Fig. 6-1. The sheave was located on a stub mandrel and clamped with a draw rod (1), ring (2), and C washer (3) against three support pads (4).

Clamping the rim of the sheave between three support pads and a clamping ring normally should keep the workpiece securely gripped during the OD turning and

---

* The members of the committee are: Joseph Benedict, Prod. Tool Engineer, The DoAll Co.; E. Cairelli, Tool Engineer, Wilson-Jones Co.; Glenn Haley, Chief Draftsman, Scully-Jones & Co.; E. C. Helmke, Chief Engineer, Gisholt Machine Co.; R. C. Kristufek, Asst. Head, Quality Control, Borg & Beck Div., Borg-Warner Corp.; D. E. Ostergaard, Chief Engineer, The Ostergaard Co.; Robert Quilici, Tool Engineer, Scully-Jones & Co.; John Sepanek, Chief Engineer, Speed-O-Print Corp.; G. H. Sheppard, Director of Research, The DoAll Co.; E. T. Swenson, Section Chief, Tool Design, Western Electric Co., Inc.; Stanley Snorek, Dept. Chief, Tool Design, Western Electric Co., Inc., Secretary; and M. A. Romano, Chief Engineer, Craft Manufacturing Co., Chairman.

† Superior numbers refer to specific references listed at the end of this section.

grooving operation. However, the sheave slipped during the grooving operation, damaging the finished sides and frequently damaging the grooving tools.

Slipping did not occur until after at least three grooves had been cut; the rim of the sheave, which before grooving had formed a rigid gripping surface, became resilient after the cut. Larger air-clamping forces distorted the previously cut grooves. A solid pin locating in one of the cored holes in the web of the sheave provided a satisfactory driver for the sheave.

Magnetic and vacuum holding devices can withstand comparatively small cutting forces. Magnetic devices hold ferromagnetic workpiece materials only and, in attracting the chips, may interfere with their disposal. Vacuum-operated devices can be used on any material provided the contour of the workpiece allows a suitable area to be sealed off with Neoprene sealing rings so that atmospheric pressure will exert sufficient holding force.

Locating the Workpiece. Satisfactory lathe operations on the workpiece also require that the workpiece be suitably located. Often the location must be taken from a rough bore, and a spring-loaded tapered plug similar to that shown in Fig. 6-1 may be used. The plug is tapered and is free to move axially in the fixture body, thus compensating for variations in the rough hole. Standard or special chuck jaws, machined or ground, depending upon whether they are soft or hard, may be used for locating and gripping on a previously machined diameter.

Locating the workpiece axially in the chuck requires suitable supports which can be either adjustable or of a fixed height. In many instances, the locating surface can be a step on the chuck jaws. It is advisable to avoid the use of surfaces on the chuck jaws for locating the work axially, because these surfaces must move with the opening and closing of the jaws. If the location is to be taken from a rough surface, this jaw motion frequently causes undesirable axial motion of the workpiece while it is being chucked.

Location should be taken from three surfaces, and these surfaces should be kept as small as possible for minimum cleaning. On special fixtures using a ring for locating the workpiece axially, the ring should be relieved to reduce the contact area to three small areas, thereby providing three-point location in one plane and reducing the amount of surface requiring cleaning.

For ease of loading the workpiece, locating pins and studs should have tapered

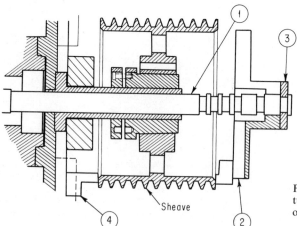

FIG. 6-1. Lathe fixture for turning OD and grooving operation.

Sheave

pilots and locating surfaces that are as short as possible. If two locating pins are required, one must be diamond shaped with its narrow width placed to accommodate allowable variations in the location of the two locating holes in the workpiece. To reduce handling time, ejectors may be incorporated to remove the workpiece from the locating pins.

Thin Workpieces. Fragile workpieces or sections under heavy cutting pressure require support. If locating is from a previously machined surface and support is required at particular points, adjustable supports may be provided in addition to the separate or critical locating and supporting surfaces.

Certain parts are so fragile that they can only be successfully located radially with the very lightest of pressure. These parts must be held with clamps designed to hold the workpiece in an unstressed position during machining.

Frail workpieces can present vibration problems due to cutting stress. Neoprene-lined dampening rings, pressure pads, or spring-actuated plungers can dampen induced vibrations.

Problems Introduced by High Speeds. The new cutting materials and machine tools with higher spindle speeds present some problems to the fixture designer.

Vibration in the rotating assembly may originate in the machine itself, the chuck or fixture, the jaws, the bolts holding the chuck or fixture to the spindle, the bolts holding the jaws to the fixture bases, or the workpiece. Vibrations originating in the machine or chuck may be dampened or reduced by the machine-tool or chuck manufacturer or by the machine repair department.

The bolts that hold the chucks and fixtures to the machine spindle and the chuck jaws to the jaw bases may vary somewhat in weight and should be brought to the same weight to decrease or prevent vibratory forces, particularly when the chuck or fixture is frequently removed. Special chuck jaws should be of the same weight to minimize torsional vibrations therein.

Irregularly shaped workpieces must be counterweighted for the same reason. Size variations in a run of castings or forgings preclude exact imbalance correction for each workpiece with one counterweight.

Individual corrections should be made for each of the above named sources of vibration so that when a changeover is made from one holding device to another or from one workpiece to another, the source of any new vibration can be easily found.

Centrifugal forces may cause workpiece distortion and lowered chucking pressure in the ordinary lever-operated power chuck.

This loss of chucking force is not always serious since most pneumatic or hydraulic cylinders have more capacity than is actually required. However, when chucking a frail part, loss in chucking force with high spindle speed becomes important because the necessary increase in chucking pressure to overcome centrifugal force may distort the workpiece when it is not revolving. In cases of this kind, a power chuck having a self-locking type of operating mechanism is required.

LATHE CHUCKS

A chuck is a device mounted on the spindle nose of a machine tool. It has jaws for holding workpieces or cutting tools, usually the former.

There are five types of chucks standardized by the American Standards Association.[2] They are:

An Independent Chuck. This chuck is one in which each individual work-holding jaw is moved to or from the workpiece by a screw without disturbing the position of any other jaw.

A Self-centering Chuck. This chuck is one in which all jaws move to or away from the workpiece and are maintained on one common center.

A Combination Chuck. This is a chuck in which are combined the features of both the independent and self-centering chucks. The work-holding jaws may be moved collectively as in the self-centering chuck and/or individually adjusted as in an independent chuck.

A Wrench-operated Chuck. This is a chuck in which the jaws are opened or closed with a wrench which may be either hand- or power-operated. This chuck is available in independent, self-centering, and combination designs.

A Drawbar Operated Chuck. This chuck is one in which the jaws are opened or closed by an operating bar or tube located on the central axis of the chuck and extending through the spindle of the machine tool on which the chuck is mounted. The operating bar is usually actuated by a pneumatic cylinder, a hydraulic cylinder, or other power sources located at the rear end of the spindle. This chuck is available in a self-centering and combination design.

Chucks for use on engine, toolroom, turret, and automatic lathes fit the American Standard spindle noses of ASA B5.9-1960.[3] The dimensions of these chucks are listed in the American Standard ASA B5.8-1954, R 1959.[2] These chucks are made in four classes for four different types of duty. The nominal size, actual diameter, and dimension from the chuck center to the cross slot on the master jaw are given in Table 6-1.

Class I chucks are medium-duty wrench-operated chucks with the tongue-and-groove type of master jaws for use on engine lathes and for other applications where the service is not severe. These chucks may be two-, three-, or four-jaw chucks and may be of the independent, self-centering, or combination type. Dimensions for the top jaw are given in Table 6-2.

Class II chucks are heavy-duty wrench-operated or drawbar-operated chucks with master jaws of the tongue-and-groove type for use on turret lathes and for other applications where the service is severe. The wrench-operated chucks may be either hand-operated or power-operated. The drawbar-operated chucks are actuated by an air or a hydraulic cylinder or by other means. These chucks may be two-, three-, or four-jaw chucks and may be of the independent, self-centering, or combination type. Dimensions for the top jaw are given in Table 6-2.

Class III chucks are heavy-duty wrench-operated or drawbar-operated chucks

TABLE 6-1. Sizes of Standard Chucks[2]*

Nominal size	OD	Dimension A†		
		Class I	Class II	Class II‡
6	$6\frac{1}{2}$	$2\frac{5}{16}$	$2\frac{5}{16}$	$2\frac{7}{16}$
8	$8\frac{1}{4}$	$2\frac{15}{16}$	$2\frac{15}{16}$	$3\frac{1}{16}$
10	10	$3\frac{11}{16}$	$3\frac{11}{16}$	$3\frac{13}{16}$
12	12	$4\frac{3}{8}$	$4\frac{3}{8}$	$4\frac{1}{2}$
15	15	$5\frac{1}{2}$	$5\frac{1}{2}$	$5\frac{5}{8}$
18	18	$5\frac{1}{2}$	$5\frac{1}{2}$	$5\frac{5}{8}$
21	21	$5\frac{1}{2}$	7	$7\frac{1}{8}$
24	24	7	7	$7\frac{1}{8}$
28	28	9		
32	32	11		
36	36	13		

* All dimensions in inches.
† See Fig. 6-2.
‡ Class II drawbar-operated chucks.

with master jaws of the serrated type. The top jaws may be set at various locations along the face of the master jaw. The tops of the master jaws are below the face of the chuck bodies on wrench-operated chucks and may be either above or below the face of the bodies on drawbar-operated chucks. These chucks may be three- or four-jaw chucks and may be of the independent or self-centering type.

Class IV chucks are two-jaw chucks of the self-centering type with master jaws of the slip-jaw type.

Chucks for First Operations. For initial operations on rough castings, forgings, or bar stock, self-centering three-jaw chucks may be used provided the part is round, nearly so, or has a contour conveniently reached at three equally spaced points. This type of chuck is capable of gripping quickly and of equally distributing stock allowances in relation to the gripped surfaces. In addition, chucking pressures are distributed equally within the master-jaw bearings.

For economy, serrated top jaws with compensating gripping surfaces may be used on a variety of jobs, but special top jaws should be fitted for unusual contours, for increased gripping pressure, or to hold frail workpieces.

With a given total chucking pressure, the pressure per unit area is inversely proportional to the gripping surface of the chuck jaw. When it is desired to increase the gripping power, the gripping surface of the jaw should be as narrow as workpiece conditions permit. Chuck jaws that are wider than necessary may contact the workpiece at directly opposing points and thus not center properly, as shown in Fig. 6-4.

The four-jaw independent chuck is useful for many applications, although its

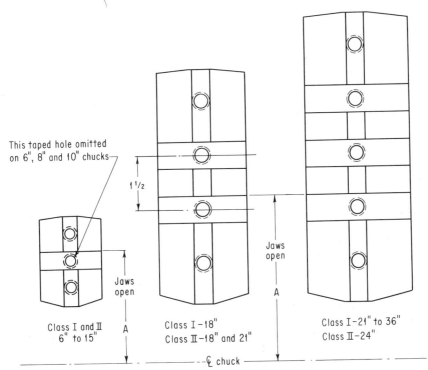

FIG. 6-2. Master jaws for Class I and II chucks.[2]

TABLE 6-2. Dimensions of Top Jaws for Chucks[2] (See Fig. 6-3)

Dimension	Nominal size					
	6	8	10	12	15†	18-36† 15-24‡
A	2⅝	3⅛	3¾	4 5/16	5	5
B	1½	1¾	2⅛	2½	3	3
C	⅝	¾	⅞	1	1⅛	1⅛
D	½	⅝	1 1/16	⅞	1⅛	1⅛
E†	1 3/32	1 3/32	1 7/32	1 7/32	2 1/32	2 5/32
F†	1 9/32	1 9/32	2 5/32	2 5/32	2 9/32	1 15/32
E‡	1 5/32	1 7/32	2 1/32	2 1/32	. . . . . .	2 5/32
F‡	2 1/32	2 5/32	2 9/32	2 9/32	. . . . . .	1 15/32

* All dimensions in inches. Tolerances ±1/64 in.
† For Class I chucks.
‡ For Class II chucks.

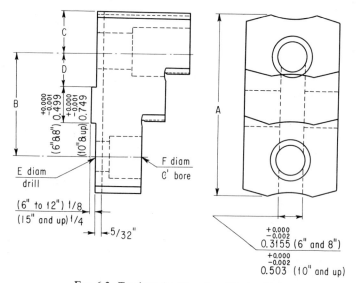

FIG. 6-3. Top jaws for Class I and II chucks.[2]

operation is slower than the self-centering two- or three-jaw chuck. It is most economical on jobs where chucking time is a minor consideration. Also, it may grip many irregular workpieces not easily held in other types of chucks or overhanging workpieces requiring high gripping pressures. Problems involving unequal machining-stock distribution are easily resolved with the four-jaw chuck.

The two-jaw combination chuck is designed to handle irregular workpieces not having three equally spaced areas suitable for chucking with a three-jaw chuck; or it is to be used when excess travel in opening and closing of the jaws in a three-jaw chuck would be required for loading and unloading the workpiece. The two-jaw chuck will not truly equalize stock allowances as will the three-jaw chuck; however, the two-jaw equalization is acceptable for some types of work. Valve bodies, pipe fittings, and miscellaneous hardware items are typical workpieces generally suited to the two-jaw chuck.

For long workpieces, auxiliary holding fixtures may be used in conjunction with three- and four-jaw chucks. This type of fixture incorporates a fabricated or cast housing, bolted to the chuck face and extending beyond the jaws, in which two or more adjusting screws are placed which bear against the overhanging workpiece to provide additional support. These fixtures are particularly useful when the only available surfaces on the workpiece against which support can be applied are rough and irregular in shape. To support or locate on a round, smooth surface, or on a machined circumference of the extended area of the workpiece, a steady rest is useful.

Chucks for Second Operations. Second-operation holding devices, though not usually required to compensate for large stock variations, must still grip tightly and must frequently grip concentrically with the surfaces to be machined.

The four-jaw chuck, though slow in operation, is economical and offers a means both of gripping tightly and of truing up surfaces on both sides of the workpiece.

When the concentricity between the sides is not critical, the three-jaw self-centering chuck with standard jaws is faster operating than the four-jaw chuck. Closer concentricity of a three-jaw chuck is gained if its soft top jaws are bored true, with the chuck under pressure, to suit the diameter being gripped. If the three-jaw chuck is manually operated, the same scroll pinion must be used at all times when opening and closing the chuck jaws. Commercially available adjustable top jaws can be substituted for the plain top jaws, thereby eliminating the need for boring the jaws in place on the machine.

If concentricity and squareness must be held to very close tolerances throughout the run, adjustable chucks are available. These chucks have the usual pinion and scroll for clamping the workpiece but have an additional feature which, after a workpiece is gripped, allows a dial indicator to be positioned against it and the chuck to be rotated slowly by hand to the lowest reading. With a wrench, adjusting screws are turned in the chuck body which centers the workpiece perfectly. Depending upon the condition of the machine spindle bearings, concentricity within 0.0002 in. TIR is possible if the same scroll pinion is used every time to load and unload the chuck.

The combination chuck is also adapted for second operations to hold the work squarely and to close concentrically. When workpieces of an irregular or off-center shape are to be machined, the jaws of the combination chuck are individually adjusted to their proper eccentric position, and the work is then gripped or released by simultaneously moving all the jaws.

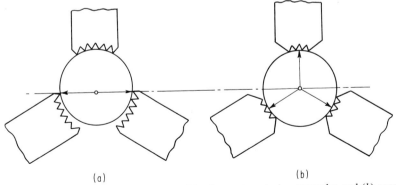

(a)   (b)

FIG. 6-4. Chuck-jaw conditions: (a) too wide, thus not centering properly; and (b) correct width for specific pressure and good centralization.

Another holding device obtaining extremely accurate concentricity and square-ness is the diaphragm chuck shown in Fig. 6-5. This chuck uses a flexing diaphragm to open and close in gripping jaws. The chucks are equipped with interchangeable and adjustable dovetail jaws. The user can change the jaws, make a permanent setup on a diaphragm and change the diaphragm assembly; or he can make cen-tralizing locators, nests, or cages to adapt this type of chuck for different workpieces.

For chucking gears, an interchangeable diaphragm assembly with master jaws can be used with gear cages, as illustrated in Fig. 6-6. The master jaws are ground to a nominal diameter; by changing cages which are designed for specific parts, any gear within the chuck's range can be processed. The gears, whether spur or helical, are located from the pitch diameter, assuring concentricity between the pitch circle and bore. For bevel gears, the chuck must incorporate fingers or clamps which pull the gears toward the chuck.

Standard Jaws vs. Special Jaws. The application of special jaws can often result in reducing the number of chucking operations required with standard jaws. Fig-ure 6-7a shows special jaws, designed to fit the draft angle of the hub, which pro-vide a solid grip for removing stock from the large end of the workpiece. For the second operation, special soft jaws grip the circular surface, which is almost twice the diameter of the surface to be machined, and maintain a desirable relationship between the driving and cutting torques. Figure 6-7b illustrates the application of

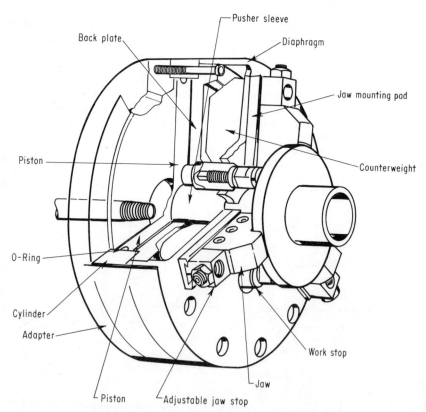

FIG. 6-5. Diaphragm chuck. (*N. A. Woodworth Co.*)

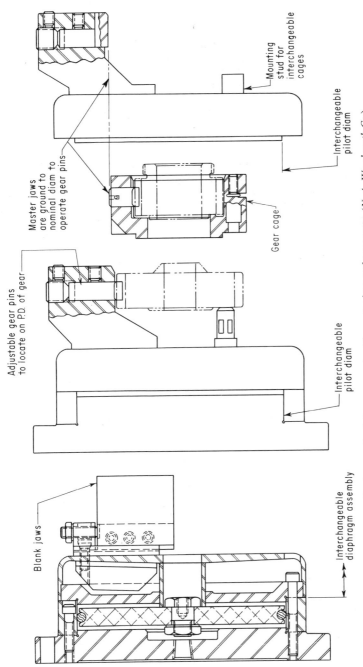

Master jaws
are ground to
nominal diam to
operate gear pins

Mounting
stud for
interchangeable
cages

Interchangeable
pilot diam

Gear cage

Adjustable gear pins
to locate on P.D. of gear

Interchangeable
pilot diam

Blank jaws

Interchangeable
diaphragm assembly

Fig. 6-6. A diaphragm chuck for gear work with master jaw and gear cage. (*N. A. Woodworth Co.*)

6–9

standard jaws requiring an additional chucking because they will not fit the draft angle of the hub.

TOP-JAW APPLICATIONS

To produce screw-machine box-tool bodies, a manufacturer of such tools uses special top jaws for a 12-in. Class II power chuck to properly locate and turn the shanks and face the backs of the bodies in the lathe. The general contour of the box-tool body is suitable for gripping in a three-jaw rather than in a four-jaw chuck.

Figure 6-8 shows the chuck top jaws used for gripping and properly locating the shank in relation to the body contour. The jaws' lengths are measured from the tongue, and two of the jaws have construction holes for measuring and machining purposes.

The working face of jaw *A* makes a 15° angle with the sides of the jaw and has small straight serrations for better gripping, but it has no pad against which the workpiece can be rested. Jaw *B* has its working face square with the sides and incorporates serrations and a step against which the part rests. Jaw *C* has its serrated working face at an angle with the sides, and one end of its step is cut away to permit jaws *A* and *B* to come close together. The jaws are made of tool steel, hardened and ground.

Top Jaws with Inserts. For boring the inside and facing the outer faces of the flanges of ball bearing cages, an automatic lathe with an air-operated chuck holds

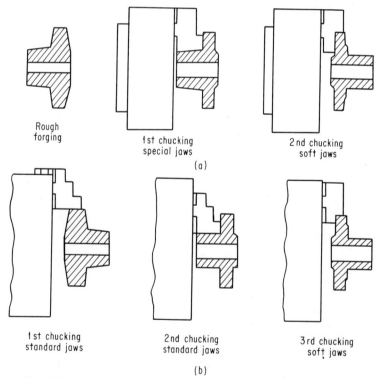

Rough forging

1st chucking special jaws

2nd chucking soft jaws

(a)

1st chucking standard jaws

2nd chucking standard jaws

3rd chucking soft jaws

(b)

Fig. 6-7. Application of chuck jaws: (*a*) special jaws; (*b*) standard jaws.

and drives cages. The top jaws (1) shown in Fig. 6-9 are machined to accommodate a set of hardened-steel inserts (2) which can be replaced for similar parts of different dimensions. Cone-pointed setscrews (3) slightly penetrate the workpiece to ensure its driving, while the smooth-faced jaw inserts act only as a centering device. Air pressure to the chuck is reduced to avoid distortion of the thin-walled bearing cage. The small conical impressions in the workpiece are not objectionable.

When the design of the workpiece permits or the operation requires additional gripping pressure, the face of the inserts may be serrated with a square or diamond pattern.

Equalizing Top Jaws. The chuck jaws of Fig. 6-10 grip a tractor rear-wheel hub during turning, boring, and facing. These operations require that the large flanged end of the workpiece be nearest to the chuck face, with the smaller end extending

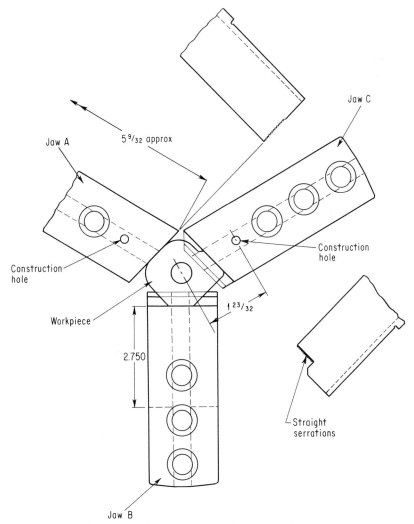

FIG. 6-8. Top jaws for gripping screw-machine box-tool body. (*Boyar-Schultz Corp.*)

toward the cutting tools, and that both ends be centered for concentricity. These locating requirements are met by providing a hinged block (1, 2) on jaws *A* and *B* respectively, with the contact point below the center of the hinge pin on the block on jaw *A* and approximately centrally spaced about the hinge pin in the block of jaw *B*. When loading the workpiece into the chuck, the blocks are swung outward; but when in place, the gripping pressure holds them securely without any other locking means. The inserts have serrations on their working faces and are hardened and ground. The top jaws are also hardened and ground. A rotary pilot pushing (3) is mounted in the chuck to guide the boring bar.

An Adjustable-and-compensating Top Jaw. Figure 6-11 shows an adjustable-and-compensating jaw assembly for holding a very large, frail steel forging while the ID and one face of it are machined. This jaw was used on a special six-jaw 42-in.-diam chuck but can be used on three- or four-jaw chucks of smaller diameters as well.

The jaw consists of the faceplate (1) which is machined to fasten to the master jaw (2) of the chuck. Mounted to this faceplate are two separate pivoting sub-bases (3) to which two clamping or top jaws (4) are mounted and which pivot about the stud (5).

The pivoting action compensates for variations in the diameter of the forging, and once the forging is securely held in the jaws, the pivoting sub-base is locked in place with clamp screws (6). The top jaws are provided with circular inserts (7) threaded with a suitable right-hand thread to form serrations that grip the workpiece. Any tendency of the part to slip in the chuck causes it to be pulled inward and against the locating surface (8) of the top jaws by the serrations.

Three keyways (9) and a T slot (10) are machined in the sub-base plate for each top jaw, so that workpieces of various diameters can be held with one set of jaws. To release the workpiece after machining, the locking screws (6) must first be loosened; and to limit the outward travel of each set of jaws, stops (11) are screwed to the chuck face which engage each end of the base plates (1) in the outward direction. For durability, almost all the parts are made of high-strength steels, heat-treated, and ground for accuracy.

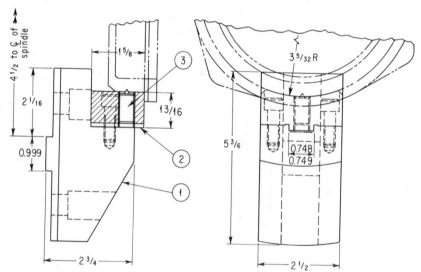

FIG. 6-9. Top jaw with hardened inserts. (*International Harvester Co.*)

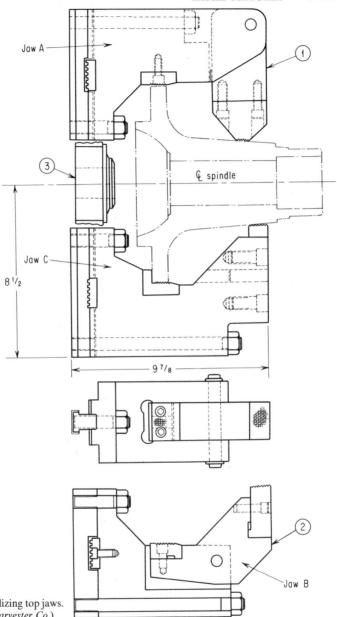

Jaw A

①

③

₵ spindle

Jaw C

8 ¹/₂

9 ⁷/₈

②

Jaw B

FIG. 6-10. Equalizing top jaws.
(*International Harvester Co.*)

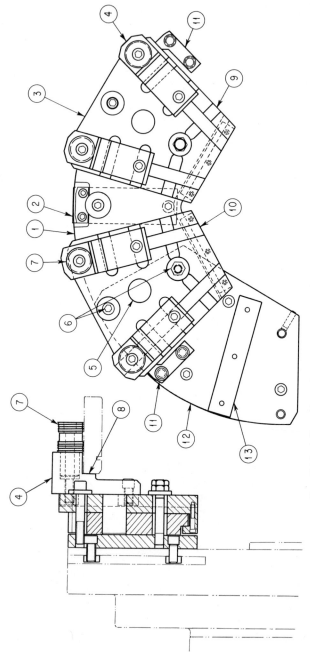

FIG. 6-11. Adjustable-and-compensating top jaws. (*Gisholt Machine Co.*)

To stabilize the top-jaw assembly, spacer plates (12) with two wear plates (13) are fastened to the chuck face.

Compensating Jaws as Work Drivers. Figure 6-12 shows a simple compensating-jaw design used with a standard three-jaw air chuck for gripping on the rough OD of the shank of special drill blanks. Since all work, including rough and finished machining and grinding of the drill blanks, must be done between centers, a system of compensating jaws is required to grip and drive the workpieces.

A conventional male center (1) is mounted in an adapter in the chuck body, and a female center (2) is mounted in the lathe tailstock.

Incorporated in the top jaw (3) is a pivoted insert (4). This method of clamping minimizes distortion in the workpiece and supports it near the work area.

SPECIAL CHUCKS

Special chucks may be used when the gripping action of the jaws is not suitable, when additional clamping or locating features are required, when a smaller chuck is required, or when the distance from the spindle nose to the workpiece must be reduced.

A Spring-actuated Chuck. The fixture of Fig. 6-13 is designed to locate and hold torque-converter housings in a multiple-station, vertical-index type of machine while turning and grinding the 1.9367- to 1.9380-in.-diam hub concentric and square with the 12.835-in. diam within 0.005 in. TIR, and while milling 0.690-in.-wide tangs equally spaced within 0.008 in. The fixture is actuated by spring pressure only, with air being used solely for unclamping; this is necessitated by the fact that the fixtures are mounted on an indexing work table.

At the loading station, a push bar (1) is actuated by a pneumatic cylinder located at this station to bear against a cam block (2) and a sleeve (3). At the top of its stroke, the push rod has opened or unclamped the fixture. The part is loaded onto the fixture or chuck, located from its 12.835-in. ID, and rested on the surface near its periphery. The push bar, working off the pneumatic cylinder, is retracted.

The following sequence of programmed motions then occurs: to locate, round out, dampen, and clamp the part prior to its indexing around to the work stations.

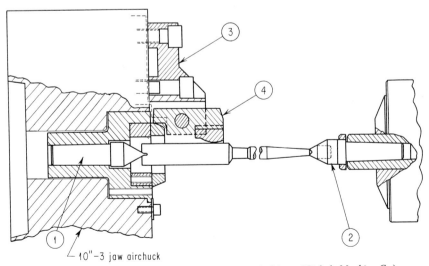

10"–3 jaw airchuck

FIG. 6-12. Compensating top jaws used as a work driver. (*Gisholt Machine Co.*)

Compression springs (4) exert a downward pressure on the cam block. As this block moves down, six pins (5) are expanded to centralize and round out the housing, engaging it at the 12.835-in. ID. Simultaneously, the drawbar (6), working off a spring (7), pulls down and expands the Neoprene washer (8) in the ID of the hub. This washer dampens or erases any vibrations which may result from the machining or grinding operations. As the pins (5) round out the housing and reach the end of their travel, the cam block likewise reaches the end of its travel. At this point six support pins (9) have been brought to bear and locked by means of a cam block (10), and fingers (11) below the housing support the area around the hub during machining.

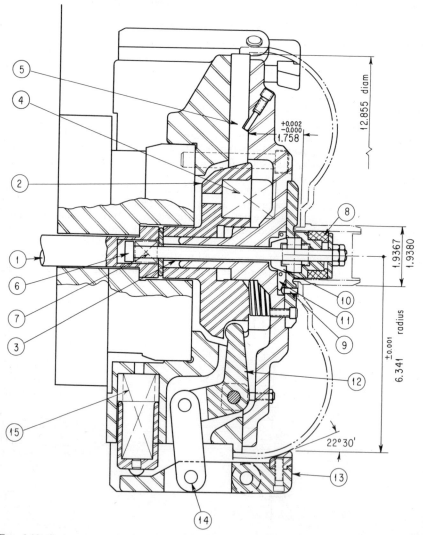

FIG. 6-13. Spring-actuated chuck for a vertical multiple-station indexing machine. (*Borg and Beck Div., Borg-Warner Corp.*)

The downward movement of the cam block (2) releases a linkage (12), allowing three jaw assemblies (13) to pivot about a fulcrum pin (14). With pressure exerted on the jaws by springs (15), the workpiece is clamped on the outside. The part has thus been located and clamped ready for machining. Pressure from a push rod and an air cylinder reverses the train of motions and releases or unclamps the chuck for unloading.

Top Jaws for Centering Sheet-metal Part. Figure 6-14 shows a three-jaw chuck used to grip and drive a sheet-metal part while it is centered on a cone arbor fastened to the chuck face.

One-third of a circular plate (1) is fastened to the top jaws (2) to support the

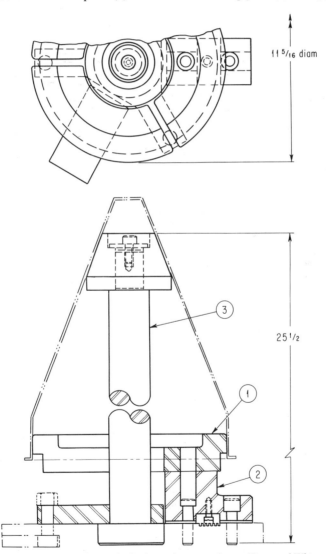

FIG. 6-14. Top jaws for centering and gripping a sheet-metal part. (*Pratt and Whitney Aircraft.*)

workpiece at its large end while turning and facing its flange. The outboard end of
the part is centered and supported by a cone-arbor assembly (3) during the facing
of the small end.

A Centralizing Chuck for Pressure Plates. The chuck shown in Fig. 6-15 for
machining pressure plates for automotive clutches centralizes and pulls the workpiece back against rest buttons and then clamps the workpiece prior to its being
faced, bored, and chamfered. The air-actuated chuck employs six jaws (1) to clamp
the workpiece against three fixed adjustable rest buttons (2) to locate and support
it in a parallel plane.

The workpiece has three lugs nesting into recesses in the chuck body which act
as positive drivers.

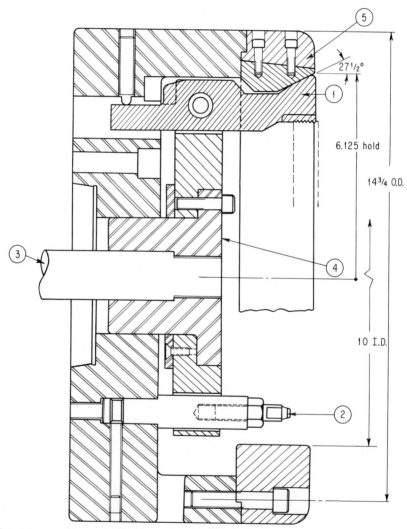

FIG. 6-15. Special chucks for automotive-clutch pressure plates. (*Borg and Beck Div., Borg-
Warner Corp.*)

Actuation of the air cylinder coupled to the chuck by the drawbar (3) starts the retraction of the jaw-carrier assembly (4). The jaws (1), on being retracted into the chuck, ride with their back edges on hardened cam blocks (5). The cam blocks direct the motions of the jaws to clamp on the OD of the workpiece while pulling it firmly against the rest buttons. The jaws are hard-faced, serrated, and ground to the same angle as the draft angle on the OD of the cast-iron workpiece.

The chuck can accommodate similar parts having different diameters and thicknesses by changing the jaws and by adjusting the stop pins. The chuck can also be adapted to clamp on the ID of parts to facilitate machining of the OD.

Boring a Frail Workpiece. Figure 6-16 shows a chuck that locates and holds a very frail workpiece for the contour boring of its full inside contour.

A three-jaw universal chuck incorporates top jaws to center and drive the small end of the workpiece. To locate it longitudinally, a shoulder is provided in the jaws (1). To support the workpiece fully, a contoured ring, or a work support (2), is screwed onto a longitudinally adjustable carrier (3); this carrier compensates for slight variations in the outside contoured surface and over-all length of the

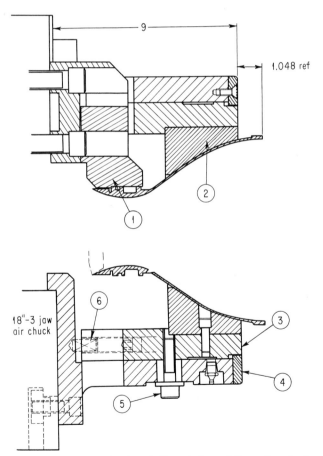

FIG. 6-16. Chuck for holding frail workpiece while contour-boring the entire internal surface. (*Gisholt Machine Co.*)

workpiece. A carrier-ring housing (4), machined to bridge over the chuck jaws and to rigidly support and drive the work support, is screwed to the chuck face.

In operation, screws (5) are released, the workpiece is forced against the locating area (1) in the top jaws, and the jaws are tightened. In forcing the part forward, the work-supporting ring seats itself against the contour of the workpiece and moves along with it against the tension exerted by a spring (6) and is locked in this position by the screws.

A Compensating Jaw Spring Chuck. The rectangular compensating-jaw spring chuck of Fig. 6-17 is used for boring and facing a vacuum-tube part of a turret lathe. The compensating feature distinguishes its design from that of other spring chucks. It is important that the part be bored centrally in relation to the four small drilled holes in the part. Since the location of these holes may vary in relation to the periphery of the part, the usual spring chuck, which centralizes the part in respect to its periphery, would not meet the requirements.

A chuck body (1) mounted on the spindle nose of the machine carries on its front end a spider (2) serving three purposes:

1. Driving the chuck by means of a key (3)
2. Acting as a rest plate, thereby positioning the part longitudinally
3. By means of a round pin (4) and a diamond-shaped pin (5) locating the part laterally on two of the drilled holes with respect to the center of the work spindle

The chuck closing sleeve (6) departs from the usual collet-chuck design in that the front end is allowed a predetermined amount of float in the chuck body, and the back end is tapered slightly to permit it to pivot inside the spindle. Within the closing sleeve, the spring chuck is carried in the usual manner, except that its four jaws project through openings in the spider to grip the part on its periphery. Variations in the positions of the locating holes in the part with respect to the four sides require the chuck and sleeve assembly to be slightly eccentric with the machine spindle at the gripping end and to pivot from the rear end of the chuck sleeve. The taper and float of the sleeve within the chuck cap permit this deviation from nor-

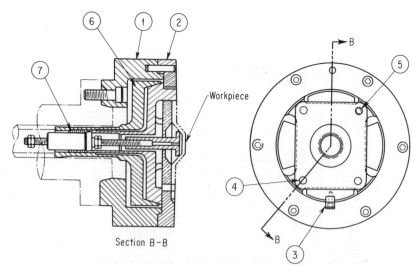

Section B-B

FIG. 6-17. Rectangular compensating-jaw spring chuck. (*Western Electric Co., Inc.*)

mal position. Nevertheless, since the part is resting on the spider, instead of being seated within the tilted chuck, it may be machined square and true.

After machining operations on the part have been completed, a heavy spring (7) between the spring chuck and the chuck closing sleeve moves the closing sleeve backward, permitting the chuck to open and release its grip on the part. The spring ejector, an adaptation of a standard ejector assembly, then removes the part.

The next part to be processed is then loaded manually over the two locating pins and held flat against the spider by a pressure bar in the turret while the chuck is closed.

A Manually Actuated Spring Chuck. A simple chuck (Fig. 6-18) for accurately chucking and maintaining concentricity in internal-boring or grinding and facing operations consists of a body (1), a split collet (2), and a closing screw (3). While the fixture illustrated was especially designed for the workpiece illustrated, the principle may be applied to other work which must be chucked on the OD and, at the same time, must be accurately positioned.

The body is made of machine steel which is pack-hardened and ground on the ID, back, and inside face. It may be machined for mounting on a faceplate or spindle-nose adapter. The collet is made of tool steel that is spring-tempered, with the OD and ID ground to fit respectively the ID of the body and the OD of the workpiece.

To operate, the part is placed in the collet and the screw is tightened, springing the collet against the work. While the part shown has a large center hole which permits access to the screw for tightening with a wrench, the same effect can be obtained by using a drawbar through the spindle of the machine when chucking a part without a center hole.

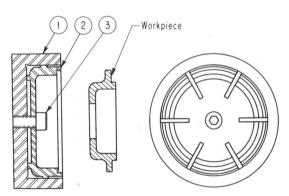

FIG. 6-18. Manually actuated spring chuck.

A Chuck for Glass Parts. The chuck of Fig. 6-19 provides means for gripping and driving rectangular or elliptical objects of glass, such as the bulb of a cathode-ray tube, to maintain them centrally in relation to the axis of the lathe. With or without alterations, this chuck could be the answer to some holding and driving problems presented by metallic workpieces.

The chuck comprises a circular supporting plate or body (1) having a central opening enabling it to be secured over a dish-shaped hub (2) for attaching to the lathe spindle and for forming a vacuum chamber (3) for partially holding an object during chucking.

An annular recess of rectangular section in the chuck body nests three concentric rings (4, 5, 6) which are free to rotate. The cover plate (7) encloses the rings and carries four slides (8) which move the chuck jaws (9).

The outer ring (4) and the inner ring (6) contain two arcuate eccentric slots, 180° apart, which extend a distance of 20 to 25° and have ample lead pitch to accommodate workpieces of different sizes.

The outer and inner rings are connected and driven by the center ring (5) by means of toggle levers (10) which either pivot on a pin pressed into the center ring or are held in a circular recess in the ring. The extremities of the levers fit into circular recesses in the rings (4, 6), having clearance to allow the levers to pivot through an angle of about 20°.

Each of the slides (8) supporting the jaws carries a pin which extends through radial slots in the cover plate (11) into and to follow the arcuate slots.

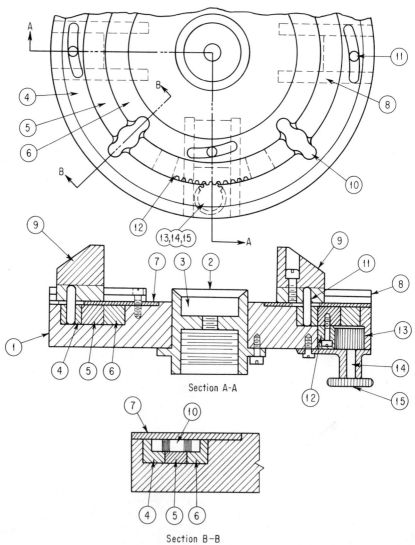

Fig. 6-19. Chuck for gripping objects of glass. (*U.S. Patent* 2,780,470.)

Attached to the underside of the driving ring (5) is a rack (12) which engages a pinion (13) keyed to a shaft (14) that is actuated by a knurled knob (15). Means are provided for locking the knob at any position of rest.

A Vacuum Chuck for Sheet Stock. The vacuum chuck of Fig. 6-20 holds sheet stock of various thicknesses for turning, facing, and counterboring. The unit has three components: the vacuum pump and motor, the rotary joint, and the chuck.

In operation, a workpiece is held against the chuck, and a vacuum is drawn behind the part. Assuming the efficiency of the device to be 75 per cent, a 6-in.-diam workpiece is held with a force of 300 lb. As the workpiece area increases, the holding force increases.

Materials as thin as 0.005 in. are held by using a flat disk for backup. Six to eight ¼-in.-diam holes are drilled per square inch of the auxiliary disk area to expose the workpiece to the vaccum.

The chuck is machined from a linen-based, laminated phenolic plate 2 in. thick. It is bored and threaded to fit the lathe spindle. After mounting the plate, the chuck is finish-turned, faced, and grooved to receive rubber sealing rings. A hole is drilled from the outside to the inside diameter and sealed at the outer end. Holes connecting the single radial hole are drilled between each pair of sealing rings.

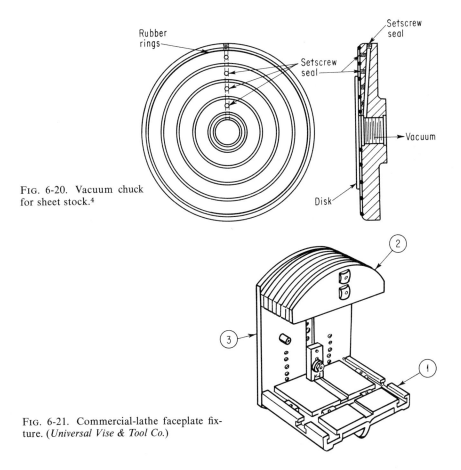

FIG. 6-20. Vacuum chuck for sheet stock.[4]

FIG. 6-21. Commercial-lathe faceplate fixture. (*Universal Vise & Tool Co.*)

Connecting holes are tapped so they can be sealed as necessary to ensure a vacuum behind the workpiece. Rubber rings are cemented in the grooves.

Machining of thin contoured parts may be accomplished with vacuum chucks made to fit the contour of the workpiece.

FACEPLATE FIXTURES

A lathe faceplate fixture, usually fastened to the lathe faceplate, incorporates conventional fixture-clamping and locating devices for holding a workpiece for lathe operations.

A shallow counterbore in the lathe faceplate receives a fixture back plug to locate the lathe fixture on the lathe-spindle center line. The fixture is secured to the faceplate by cap screws inserted through the fixture into tapped holes in the faceplate or by T bolts inserted into T slots in the faceplate. For more accurate positioning of the fixture on the lathe-spindle center line, circular-fixture base plates

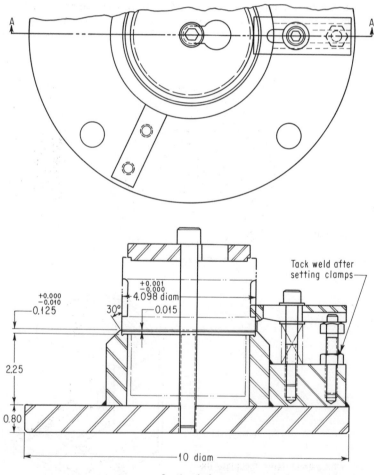

Section A-A

FIG. 6-22. Faceplate fixture to turn, bore, and tap a cylindrical part. (*McDonnell Aircraft Corp.*)

having indicating grooves or other accurately machined surfaces are used (see Figs. 6-22 and 6-26).

On high-speed lathes, the fixture, with a workpiece in place, should be dynamically balanced as accurately as possible. For low-speed operations, a reasonably exact static balancing is satisfactory. Balancing of the fixture with the workpiece in place helps to reduce vibration.

Commercial Faceplate Fixtures. Figure 6-21 illustrates a commercially available faceplate fixture for general use. The position of the worktable (1) is adjustable to suit workpiece requirements. The workpiece may be clamped to the table through the T slots. Adjustable counterweights (2) are provided to ensure proper balance in operation. The base plate (3) is fastened to the lathe faceplate by cap screws inserted through the faceplate slots into tapped holes provided.

Faceplate Fixture for Threading and Boring. The fixture of Fig. 6-22 locates and internally holds a cylindrical part for turning the OD, which is then clamped on the outside while boring and threading the ID.

To eliminate the need of two fixtures, two clamping arrangements are supplied for one basic fixture. Each set of clamps is removed before the other set is used.

The 4.098-in.-diam bore is used as an indicating surface to position the fixture accurately on the lathe-spindle center line.

Boring Two Holes in Two Operations. The fixture shown in Fig. 6-23 locates and clamps a casting for accurately boring holes at two places by moving the holding part of the fixture to another spot on the faceplate. The casting is located on the sub-base plate (1) by a diamond pin (2) and a round pin (3). The sub-base plate is fastened to the base (4) by cap screws. As illustrated, the fixture is set up for boring hole *A* of the workpiece. To bore hole *B*, the sub-base plate containing the locating pins and clamps is moved to the right to another set of mounting holes. Dowel pins (5) pressed into the sub-base plate accurately position the plate by engaging bushed holes in the base plate.

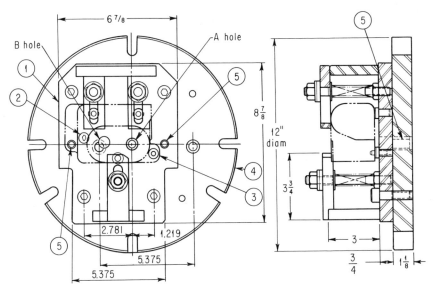

FIG. 6-23. Fixture for boring two holes in different locations in two operations. (*Boyar-Schultz Corp.*)

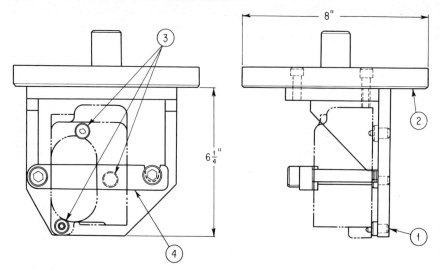

FIG. 6-24. Right-angle faceplate fixture. (*Boyar-Schultz Corp.*)

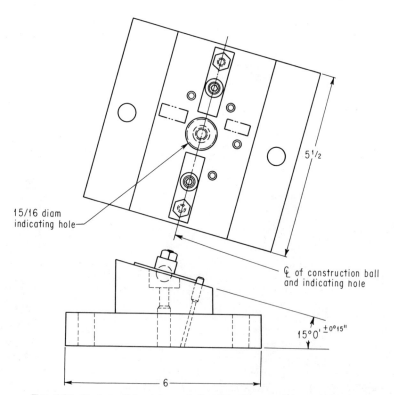

15/16 diam
indicating hole

¢ of construction ball
and indicating hole

FIG. 6-25. Boring a thin part on a lathe. (*The Emerson Electric Mfg. Co.*)

A **Right-angle Faceplate Fixture.** The fixture of Fig. 6-24 is used for boring a hole in the end of the part of Fig. 6-23. Locating pins engaging the same workpiece holes utilized in the fixture of Fig. 6-23 are mounted in a right-angle bracket (1) which is fastened to a base plate (2). The part is supported on three rest buttons (3) and clamped by a strap clamp (4). Clamping pressure is applied within the triangular area described by the three supporting points.

Boring a Thin Part in a Lathe. Figure 6-25 illustrates a simple fixture for holding a part in a lathe while boring a hole at a 15° angle to the face of a flat plate $1^{13}/_{16}$ in. square and $^1/_{16}$ in. thick.

The fixture is of welded construction using standard strap clamps to hold the part. Three dowel pins position the part and a fourth pin prevents rotation of the part if it slips under insufficient clamping pressure. A $^{15}/_{16}$-in.-diam hole in the center of the fixture is used as an indicating surface to properly position the fixture on the spindle center line.

A Fixture for a Micrometer Stop Body. Figure 6-26a illustrates a fixture that holds and locates a workpiece while four operations are performed in a horizontal turret lathe. The workpiece, shown in Fig. 6-26b, is a small casting. Surfaces (1) to (5) were finished in a prior operation, and a hole (6) was previously drilled and tapped.

The fixture has a cast-iron faceplate (1) for mounting on the headstock of a turret lathe. A locator (2) made of CRS, machined, hardened, and ground, mates to workpiece surfaces (2), (3), (5). A screw (5) engages the tapped hole (6) in the workpiece and draws the workpiece down to the nesting element. An upper block (3), also hardened and ground CRS, guides a profiled jaw (4) which clamps the top of the workpiece by rotation of a jackscrew (6). The fixture parts are attached to the faceplate with cap screws, and their location and alignment are ensured by dowels.

The nested workpiece is drilled, counterbored, tapped, and faced at the surfaces respectively numbered (7), (8), (9), and (10).

Chucking Threaded Workpieces. It is sometimes necessary or desirable to chuck a workpiece on a threaded portion of the part. If such a workpiece has a hexagonal or some other flat-sided surface, it can easily be unscrewed with a wrench at the conclusion of the operation. A wrench is generally necessary to break the seal formed between the work and the chuck face by the pressure of the cutting tools. If the part to be machined is round with no flat surfaces, or if the surfaces are not to be marked or damaged, the chuck must be designed so that this seal can be broken without using a wrench.

The chuck illustrated in Fig. 6-27a is used for holding a symmetrical piston by means of an internal thread while machining the opposite end of the part. The chuck seen in Fig. 6-27b is employed for holding a bushing by means of an external thread while finish-boring the work. An entirely different approach is necessary in designing chucks to hold workpieces by external threads than is required for those that hold by internal threads.

The chuck of view a consists of a body which is internally threaded to fit the spindle nose of a screw machine. A stud is threaded on one end to fit the workpiece and has a left-hand thread on the opposite end to fit a plate. The stud is a slip fit in a hardened bushing, which is pressed into the chuck body.

For better accuracy in locating the work, a hardened cover, which is screwed and doweled to the chuck body, is machined to fit the bead on the face of the piston. A handle, screwed into the plate, can be moved through an angle of 60° in a clearance slot provided in the chuck body. The handle is pushed against the forward end of the slot before a piece is screwed on the chuck; and after the machining operation is completed, it is pushed to the other end of the slot. This rotates the plate on the stud, thereby breaking the seal between the piston and the cover.

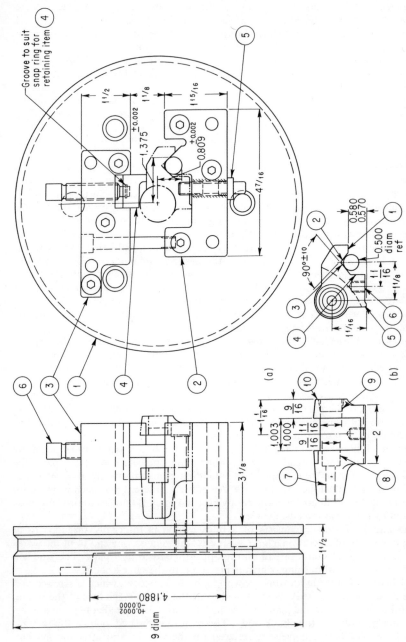

FIG. 6-26. (*a*) Fixture for multiple operations in a horizontal turret lathe; (*b*) workpiece for fixture of (*a*). (*Rockwell Mfg. Co.*)

A hole drilled radially in the periphery of the chuck body provides a means for mounting and removing the chuck from the machine spindle with a spanner wrench.

The chuck of view *b* consists of a body which is threaded to fit a master-chuck adapter. A nut, screwed on the chuck body, is internally threaded to fit the workpiece. The outside of the nut is slotted for a spanner wrench. A loose plug is a slip fit in the nut and rests against the face of the body. A recess is provided in the center of the plug to clear the boring tool.

In chucking, the work is screwed against this plug. After the machining operation, a slight turn of the nut will break the seal formed between the work and the plug. Flats or pin-spanner wrench holes are provided on the chuck body for wrenching it on or off the adapter.

These chucks can be designed to fit a large variety of workpieces and can be used on many types of machines. They are economical to make and yet provide a quick and accurate means to hold work.

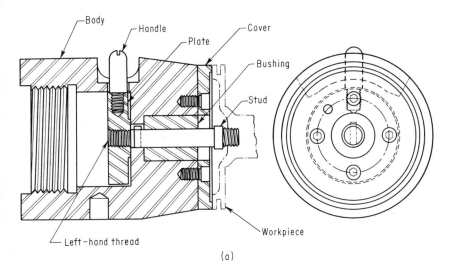

(a)

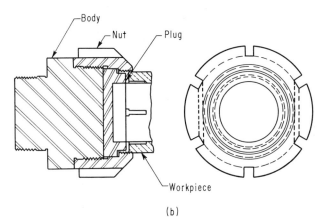

(b)

Fig. 6-27. Chucks for holding workpiece by threaded portions. (*Machinery.*)

A Pull-back Type of Clamp Fixture. A pull-back fixture (Fig. 6-28), with air-operated clamps, clamps comparatively frail parts in a lathe after locating them radially on locating pins (1).

Six clamping fingers (2), each three of which are supported in a self-compensating manner in the two spiders shown (3, 4), draw the workpiece firmly against the locating pads (5) to properly clamp it laterally. Compensation is accomplished by two Neoprene rings (6, 7) at the centers of the spiders and by bronze spherical seats (8) on the clamping-finger pins (9).

The cam tracks (10) in the pins rotate the clamping fingers out of position for loading and unloading the work. To keep the mechanism clean and to provide a bearing (11) for the end of the drawtube (12), a cover (13) is provided.

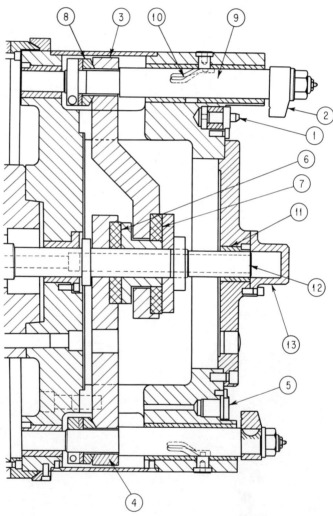

FIG. 6-28. Special air-clamping fixture with compensating clamps. (*Gisholt Machine Co.*)

A Fixture with a Plastic Nest. Figure 6-29 illustrates a fixture incorporating a cast plastic workpiece nest. The fixture base (1), 13-in.-diam by 1-in.-thick HRS, is tapped and drilled for mounting to the faceplate of a lathe. The cast-epoxy nest (2) is attached to the fixture base by a socket-head cap screw and three press-fit dowels. Two of the dowels (3) extend above the nest to serve as radial locators for the workpiece. Two clamps (4) slide in and are tightened to hold the workpiece in the nest. The smooth center hole in the fixture base is an indicating hole for centering during setup.

A Fixture with Reversible Clamps. Figure 6-30 illustrates a method of holding thin circular workpieces.

The base of the fixture (1) is a circular 16½-in.-diam HRS plate. The base is machined for mounting to a lathe faceplate and has symmetrically located

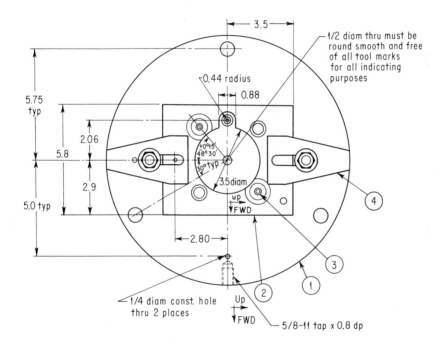

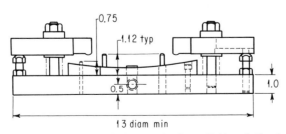

FIG. 6-29. Fixture with cast-plastic nest. (*McDonnell Aircraft Corp.*)

tapped holes for the mounting of the other fixture elements. A $1\frac{1}{8} \times$ 12-in.-diam HRS plate (2), profiled to the contour of the workpiece, is the workpiece nest. Four clamps (3) are located 90° apart around the perimeter of the base. The clamps have contoured pads (4) which mate to and bear on the nested workpiece. Two sets of clamp bolt holes (5, 6) are drilled and tapped in the base. The clamps can be mounted to bear on the workpiece from a location beyond the OD of the workpiece, as shown. In this position, the ID of the workpiece is accessible for finishing. With the clamps mounted in the inner set of holes, the OD of the workpiece is accessible.

A Faceplate Fixture for Turning an OD. Figure 6-31 illustrates a fixture of welded construction that holds a light workpiece for turning its OD.

The fixture base (1) is $1\frac{1}{4}$-in.-thick HRS. Minor fixture elements (2 to 6), also of HRS, are machined and welded to the base, and the assembly is then normalized. The minor elements are tapped and drilled to receive threaded studs (7) which with jam nuts are used as adjustable workpiece locators. Three studs (8) with jam nuts are threaded into the base and also function as adjustable locators.

A triangular CRS plate (9) with three adjustable studs (10) is mounted on two pins (11, 12) that are pressed into the fixture base. At both points of contact with the pins, the triangular plate is chamfered on both sides to leave a land of $\frac{1}{16}$ in. The larger pin (12) protrudes approximately $2\frac{1}{16}$ in. farther from the base than the other pin (11). A CRS block (13) is placed on the large pin and is locked in that position by a drill-rod key (14). To prevent loss, the key is attached to the block with a flexible cable. An adjustable threaded stud (15) bears on the center of the triangular plate. The adjustable studs in the triangular plate bear on the workpiece at the points where it is supported by three locators (8).

The fixture base has a 1-in.-diam indicating hole for centering the fixture on the lathe faceplate.

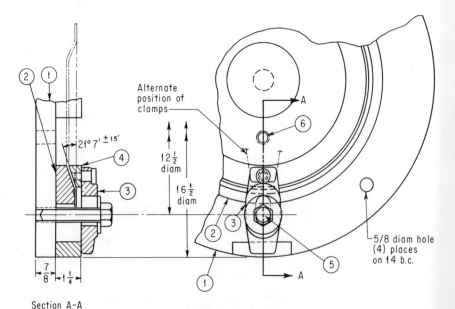

Section A–A

FIG. 6-30. Fixture for alternately boring ID and OD of thin workpieces. (*The Martin Co.*)

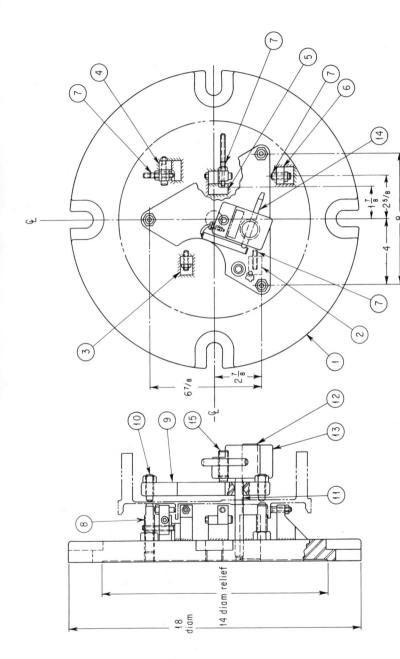

Fig. 6-31. Faceplate fixture for holding a drum while turning its OD. (*The Emerson Electric Mfg. Co.*)

COMMERCIAL COLLETS

The spring collet is the simplest device developed for holding work in lathes and screw machines. It is the universal chucking device used in both hand and automatic machines when parts are turned from bar stock. A collet consists of a hollow cylindrical sleeve partially slotted along its length to provide a spring-type closing action which firmly grips the bar. The external tapered portion on the forward end closes the collet when it contacts a mating taper in the machine spindle or in a cap fastened to the spindle end. The slots vary in number, depending primarily on the cross-sectional shape of the stock being clamped. For cylindrical work, three slots are most effective, since this permits the collet to grip the bar on three equally spaced portions of its periphery. Collects with two slots are not recommended, since the two halves do not consistently register accurately and tend to grip the bar only at the opposite ends of a single diameter; in addition, the spring action is stiff, requiring considerable force to close the collet. For positive and accurate gripping of smooth workpieces, the bore of the collet should not vary more than 0.002 in. from the size of the workpieces. When this condition exists, eccentricity will vary from 0.001 in. TIR for ⅛-in.-diam work at a distance of 1 in. from the face of the collet to 0.002 in. TIR for 1⅛-in.-diam work 2 in. from the collet.

For more positive gripping action on workpieces with rough surfaces, such as hot-rolled steel or castings, collets with serrated inner bores are practical when the resulting deformation of the gripped surface is not objectionable.

Spring collets are of two principal types, differentiated by the method used for closing them: drawback or push-out. The drawback collet (Fig. 6-32a) is threaded onto the end of the drawtube in the machine spindle. It is closed by retracting the tube to draw the collet backward into the tapered hood on the end of the spindle. This type is not in extensive use today and is usually used on older machines and toolroom lathes. It is not recommended for operations where accurate control is required of the length of workpiece projecting beyond the collet, since the retractile closing action pulls the work back toward the spindle of the machine. This action causes variations in the length of stock fed out in first-operation work, and a facing operation is necessary to secure accurate lengths.

The push-out collet (Fig. 6-32b) is closed by pushing it into the tapered hood on the spindle end. The forward closing action pushes the bar stock firmly against the external stop, resulting in accurate feed-out. Consequently, this type of collet is recommended for first-operation work.

The stationary collet, Fig. 6-32c, is a variation of the push-out type. It is closed by a sliding sleeve operated by the push-out mechanism. Since the collet does not move longitudinally, there is no movement of the work during the closing operation. This type is recommended for both first- and second-operation work. Owing to the radial clearances necessary between machine spindle, sleeve, and collet, the stationary collet is not entirely suitable when close concentricity must be maintained between the portion of the work in the collet and the surfaces to be machined.

The rubber flexing collet (Fig. 6-32d) consists of flat steel jaws molded in a matrix of synthetic rubber. It is closed by sliding a tapered sleeve over the mating taper of the collet. The bearing surface of the steel jaws, longer than the gripping surface of the standard spring collet, provides a parallel gripping action throughout the entire range of the collet. Since the rubber provides the flexing necessary for closing, the steel jaws can be held to maximum hardness and, consequently, have a longer life than the spring collet. Each size of collet has a range of approximately 0.050 in. or about 10 or more times that of a standard steel collet.

Master collets (Fig. 6-32e) with interchangeable pads are similar in type and operation to one-piece collets. A recess in the forward end holds a set of pads

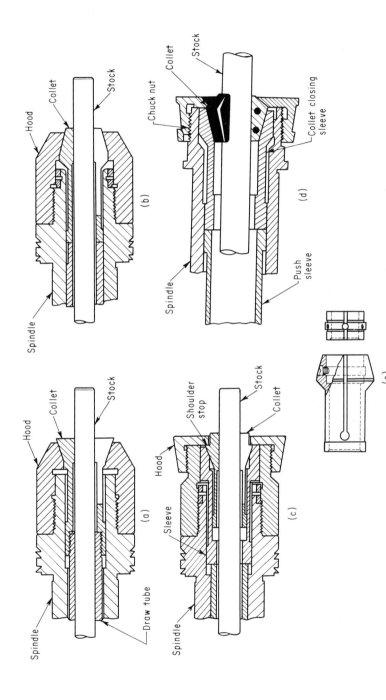

FIG. 6-32. Commercial collets: (a) drawback type; (b) push-out type; (c) stationary type with closing sleeve; (d) rubber collet; and (e) master collet.

shaped to accommodate the work. The number of pads in a set varies with the type of collet and the shape of the stock. One master collet, plus a suitable number of pads, fits all sizes and shapes of stock within the range of a particular machine. Pads are usually made or hardened steel and are available with smooth or serrated gripping surfaces; the latter hold more securely but tend to mar the gripped surface and are more suitable for holding rough work such as hot-rolled steel or the outside surface on the workpiece that will be completely refinished. Pads of softer materials such as bronze, brass, or fiber are suitable when scoring of the work is objectionable. Master collets are more expensive than the solid type, but the pads are relatively cheap; consequently, one master collet with several sets of pads costs less than the same number of spring collets required for the same range of work.

The collet chuck of Fig. 6-33a, available in a wide range of sizes, is an attachment fastened to the spindle of a lathe and holds a slotted spring collet. It is used primarily on toolroom lathes and for low production work. Tightening of the handwheel moves the operating sleeve back against the collet and closes it to grip the work. Collet chucks of the handwheel type are also available for use with rubberflex chucks. A faster-operating version substitutes a hand lever for the handwheel. The lever moves a closing collar which actuates a series of cam levers that force the collet into the tapered closing ring. This collet can be closed and opened without stopping rotation of the machine spindle. A specialized version (Fig. 6-33b) uses a steel spring collet with opposed closing tapers and with two sets of spring slots, each slotted from opposite ends. It is closed by a tapered sleeve moving toward the machine spindle and also forcing it against a companion sleeve. The sleeves, in closing the collet at both ends, provide a uniform and parallel action, ensuring close concentricity of work and spindle.

Extra-capacity collets grip workpieces of larger sizes than can be accommodated by standard collets. They are usually used only for second-operation work. Figure 6-34a shows a typical extra-capacity collet of the drawback type. The back end fits the spindle of the machine and is threaded to receive the drawbar which retracts to close the collet. The oversize gripping portion has tapered closing surfaces that fit a mating taper in the closing ring pressed into its hood which is threaded on the machine spindle. Also illustrated are stationary locating stops for accurately locat-

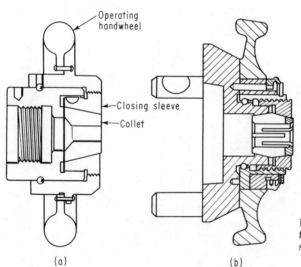

FIG. 6-33. Collet chucks for mounting on a lathe-spindle nose.

(a)   (b)

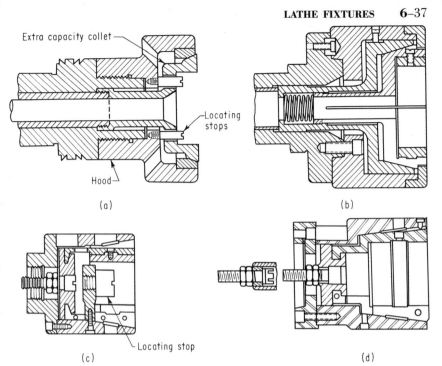

Fig. 6-34. Extra-capacity collet chucks.

ing the part longitudinally as the collet and work are drawn back during the closing operation.

Figure 6-34b shows an extra-capacity collet of the stationary type which is closed by the forward movement of a sleeve actuated by the push-out mechanism in the machine. The collet is similar to a master collet since it is arranged to hold interchangeable pads. Collet and closing sleeve are contained in a cylindrical retainer fastened to the spindle nose of the machine. To retain the collet, a ring-shaped hood is threaded to the forward end of the retainer.

Figure 6-34c shows a skeleton collet for second-operation work in turret lathes. It is a drawback type of three-sectional master collet mounted in a cylindrical housing which is threaded on the spindle and cored out for chip disposal. Closing is usually done by an air cylinder which permits a longer than usual closing stroke, and it is consequently suitable for holding rough work which varies considerably in diameter. As shown, this collet can be arranged with a fixed stop to locate the workpiece longitudinally.

Another type of collet chuck for turret lathes (Fig. 6-34d) operates on the drawbar principle and incorporates a three-section split collet to which sets of pads are fastened with machine screws and accommodates various sizes of workpieces. It has a housing which holds the collet segments. The offset portion at the rear of the collet segments fits into the groove of a cylindrical yoke fastened to the drawtube. The matching tapers on the inside of the housing and outer periphery of the collet segments provide parallel closing action when the drawtube retracts. Coiled springs are used to separate the collet segments and to keep them from collapsing in the open position. The housing is fastened to an adapter ring that fits the spindle nose of the machine.

A stop collet is used for holding and locating individual workpieces for second-operation work. It consists essentially of a standard spring collet in which is mounted a cylindrical stop. Separate workpieces are fed into the collet from the front; its contact with the stop provides proper longitudinal positioning for machining. Two basic types are available:

1. The *solid stop* (Fig. 6-35a) is threaded into a body mounted in the back end of the collet and secured by a locknut; longitudinal adjustment for varying operating conditions is easily effected by turning the threaded stop in or out. This type is used when workpieces are loaded and unloaded manually.

2. The *spring-ejector stop* (Fig. 6-35b) is one in which the stop is affixed to a plunger arranged to slide axially within the body. Longitudinal positioning occurs when the loaded part pushes the stop backward until a shoulder on the plunger contacts the body, simultaneously compressing a spring behind the plunger. Opening the collet upon completion of the operation releases the spring which ejects the finished part. This type of stop is suitable for operations requiring automatic loading and ejection of workpieces.

Various types of solid and spring-ejector stops are available.

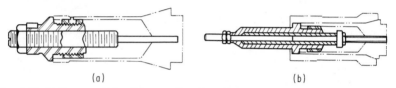

(a)   (b)

FIG. 6-35. Collet stops: (*a*) solid stop; (*b*) spring-ejector stop. (*Brown & Sharpe Mfg. Co.*)

SPECIAL COLLETS

The wide variety and complexity of turned parts often require holding means beyond the capability of commercial collets and chucking devices. Illustrated herein are examples of specially designed single-purpose collets intended to hold complex parts.

Special Collet Stops. Figure 6-36 shows a spring-ejector stop collet designed specially to accommodate one particular workpiece. It requires no adjustment as do the adjustable general purpose stop collets available commercially, and its use for repetitive high-production work reduces machine setup time. The stop body is fastened to the back of the standard collet with two opposed pins. The body projects into the collet to allow its forward face to position the workpiece for the turning operation. With the workpiece loaded in the collet, the spring plunger recedes completely into the stop body. For effective ejection of the workpiece, the spring plunger normally travels within $\frac{1}{32}$ in. of the face of the collet.

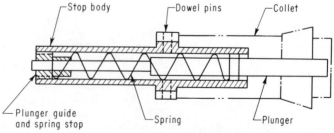

FIG. 6-36. Stop and ejector assembly for screw-machine collet. (*Western Electric Co., Inc.*)

Figure 6-37 shows a stop collet for second-operation work on long parts when the portion of the part extending into the machine spindle is longer than the collet. It consists of a standard spring collet and a tubular body fastened to the collet with flat-head cap screws. A cylindrical plug fastened to the rear of the tubular body holds a setscrew that longitudinally positions the long workpiece. The diameter of the stop body is a close fit in the machine spindle near the collet and near the other end of the tube to reduce whipping of the collet and workpiece during the turning operation. To load this stop collet into a hand screw machine without removing the turret, the collet and body are disassembled; the body is loaded from the back of the spindle and then assembled to the collet which is loaded from the front. The long workpieces are loaded through two diametrically opposed unused tool positions in the machine turret.

Gripping Small-headed Parts. A duplex collet arrangement for gripping the body (0.375 in. diam) of a workpiece for turning its small end while the large (0.562 in. diam) head at the opposite end is cleared within the collet is shown in Fig. 6-38. This special collet opens to permit automatic loading of the workpiece with the large head entering first. This collet is designed for use in a five-spindle machine.

In operation, the outer collet grips the inner collet which in turn grips the body diameter of the workpiece. The inner collet is bored to clear the large diameter of the workpiece. The outer collet is operated by the machine's drawback-collet closing mechanism and the inner collet by the stock-feed mechanism. When the outer collet is opened, the inner collet is fed out until its gripping end is completely outside the outer collet. In this position, the inner collet springs open to accept the workpiece, with its large-head end first, from a loading tool in the machine turret. The advancing workpiece contacts the spring ejector and stop, which move inward and reinsert the inner collet into the outer collet. The workpiece and loading tool maintain pressure until the drawback mechanism closes the outer collet to complete the clamping.

Three equally spaced slots in the inner collet provide the free, spring type of opening action required. The gripping end is a three-pronged spider which fits mating slots in the outer collet, permitting rotation of both collets as a unit.

The outer collet is similar to a conventional drawback type of spring collet. The gripping portion is slotted for the inner collet and also for a key which prevents rotation of the collets in the wear sleeve mounted in the machine spindle. The forward end of the outer collet tube is tapped to receive the outer collet. The inner end is fastened to the collet-tube thrust ring which is actuated by the drawbar mechanism of the machine.

The inner collet tube is tapped to receive the inner collet, and the opposite end is mounted in a thrust bearing fastened to the stock-feeding mechanism.

The stock stop is screwed to an extension rod which bears against a spring-loaded ejector. The extension rod and the spring ejector have tungsten-carbide bearing surfaces to reduce wear.

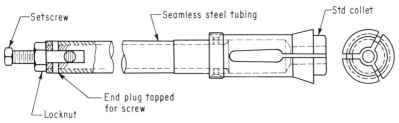

FIG. 6-37. Spring collet and stop for long workpiece. (*Western Electric Co., Inc.*)

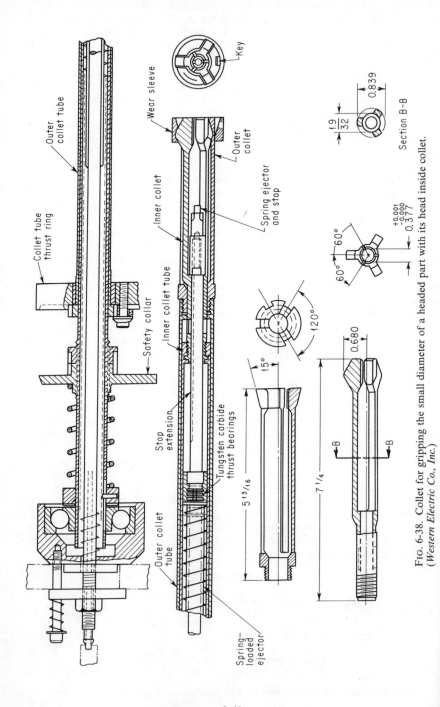

Fig. 6-38. Collet for gripping the small diameter of a headed part with its head inside collet. (*Western Electric Co., Inc.*)

A safety feature of the design is that which retracts the inner collet if a workpiece has been loaded into the machine. Without a workpiece to push the inner collet into the outer collet, the inner collet could be gripped while projecting beyond the spindle. To prevent this, a safety collar is threaded to the inner collet tube and secured with a locknut. During the backward movement of the drawbar mechanism which closes the outer collet, the collet-tube thrust ring contacts the safety collar, thus retracting the inner collet tube and moving the empty inner collet into the outer collet.

A Collet Bushing for Small-diameter Stock. Small sizes of nonmetallic bar stock such as hard rubber are usually difficult to load into production machines because of their tendency to bend or whip away from the hole in the collet. To overcome this, a collet and bushing assembly with a special feed finger (Fig. 6-39) can be used. A bushing pressed into the rear of a standard collet guides the stock into the gripping portion of the collet. The long slotted feed finger carries the stock forward to the end of the bushing bore where a conical projection opens the feed finger, releases its grip, and permits the stock to continue feeding through the collet. The hole in the bushing is 0.002 in. larger than the bar stock and must be concentric with the hole in the collet. The forward end of the feed finger is slotted to provide a spring action to grip the stock.

A Collet for Metal Powder Parts. The special collet of Fig. 6-40 holds a fragile metal powder ring while facing one end and chamfering the edges of both its ID and OD. It securely grips parts which vary $\frac{1}{32}$ in. in diameter, without crushing those of maximum size. The nose is removed from the end of the spindle of an automatic screw machine, and the collet is positioned longitudinally by a tubular extension fastened to the collet.

The collet (1) is a modified drawback type with ten equally spaced slots to provide a uniform gripping action around the entire periphery of the fragile workpiece. The back end is threaded to receive an extension tube (2) which has

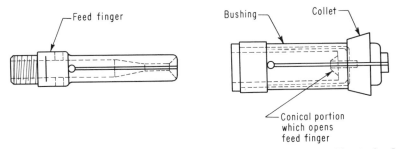

FIG. 6-39. Collet bushing and feed finger for small-diameter stock. (*Western Electric Co., Inc.*)

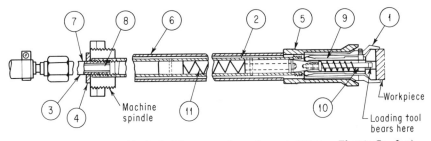

FIG. 6-40. Collet assembly for holding a metal powder part. (*Western Electric Co., Inc.*)

a threaded connection to another tubular extension (3). The body diameter of the extension is less than the threaded portion of the tube (2) and provides a shoulder which restricts longitudinal travel of a collar (4). This collar normally bears against the back end of the machine spindle to longitudinally position the collet. The collet is closed by moving the collet closing sleeve (5) forward to engage mating tapers on the inner bore of the sleeve and outer portion of the collet. The sleeve is actuated by the standard collet-closing tube (6) of the machine. To prevent crushing maximum-diameter workpieces, the collet can be moved slightly forward by the action of the closing sleeve against the pressure of a spring (7) behind the collar.

Also threaded into the back end of the extension is a tube (8) which has a hose connection permitting air to be blown through the spindle to clear the collet of chips. Located within the collet, but not fastened to it, is a stop (9) which keeps the workpiece from shifting longitudinally under pressure of the turning operation. The back end has four longitudinal slots similar to those in a collet to permit the stop to be locked in position by bearing against two tapered surfaces, one on the back of the bore of the collet and the other on the spring plunger (10). A spring (11) forces the plunger forward through a hole in the workpiece to complete the locking action. Positioning the workpiece is controlled by a loading tool which inserts it into the collet where it bears against the stop. Simultaneously the loading tool bears against the forward end of the plunger, locking the stop in position when the collet is closed. Variation in the longitudinal position of the collet due to variation in workpiece diameters is compensated by the spring.

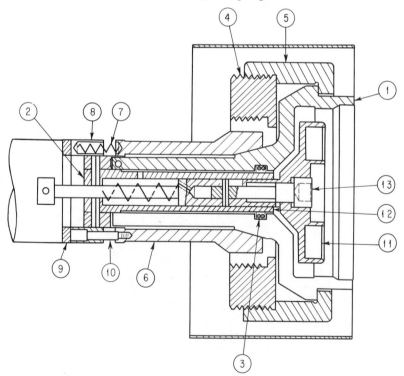

FIG. 6-41. Oversize collet for a fragile part. (*Western Electric Co., Inc.*)

An Oversize Collet for a Fragile Part. A special oversize collet for holding a fragile die-cast frame during a series of facing and turning operations in an automatic screw machine is illustrated in Fig. 6-41. The workpiece is manually placed into a loading tool which inserts it into the collet. This is a stationary collet closed by a sliding sleeve. To prevent crushing of the fragile workpiece, the closing action is controlled by a coupling spring between the sliding sleeve and the collet-closing mechanism of the machine. Upon reaching a predetermined gripping pressure, further advance of the closing mechanism is prevented by compression of the coupling spring.

The collet is made of four individual pieces and does not follow conventional design. The gripping portion consists of three equal segments (1) pinned to a

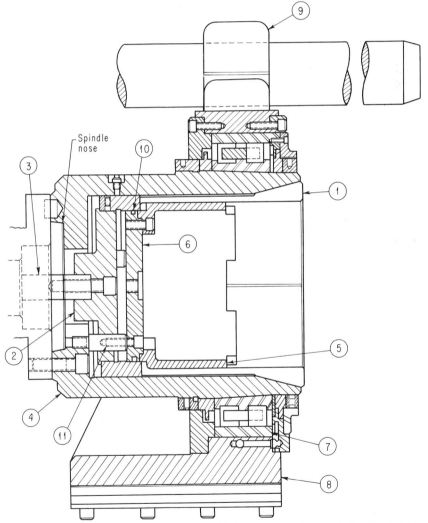

FIG. 6-42. Collet chuck for turning bottle molds in an automatic turret lathe. (*Gisholt Machine Co.*)

retaining yoke (2) which permits the segments to open and close for workpiece gripping and ejection. A torsion spring (3) prevents the collet sections from collapsing inwardly when empty. An adapter (4) and a hood (5) replace the standard machine hood and retain the collet in the spindle. The closing sleeve (6) closes the collet when moved forward by the collet-closing mechanism in the machine spindle. The coupling spring which controls the gripping pressure of the collet consists of twelve springs (7) mounted in a retainer (8). It is backed up by a wear plate (9). Both retainer and plate move forward as a unit to close the collet when actuated by the collet-closing tube in the machine spindle. Three retaining screws (10) fasten the retainer to the sleeve. The spring-actuated stop (11) is recessed to clear projecting lugs on the workpiece. The stop recedes into the collet as the loading tool inserts the workpiece and provides longitudinal positioning when it contacts the forward edge of the stop body (12). The body is pinned to the yoke (2) which also holds the collet segments. When the collet opens, the workpiece is partially ejected by a spring behind the stop. Final ejection is accomplished by an ejector (13) through the action of a compression spring moving the workpiece forward far enough to eject it from the recesses in the stop.

A Collet for Bottle Molds. A collet chuck used in an automatic turret lathe for turning ring-neck molds used in the bottle-mold industry is shown in Fig. 6-42. This collet is a large drawback type fastened to the face of the machine spindle and supported by an outboard bearing. The collet (1) is made in six squal sections which are threaded to a base plate (2) that is fastened to a drawbar (3). The collet assembly is contained in a housing (4) secured to the spindle and fitted to the spindle nose to ensure concentricity. A cylindrical sleeve (5) fits inside the collet and is fastened to a bumper plate (6); this assembly is used as an end stop for positioning the workpiece and is held in place by three screws in the studs (11) which are threaded into the housing. A felt ring (10) impregnated with graphite acts as a bearing between the stationary bumper plate and the collet. Support at the outer end of the collet chuck is provided by a bearing (7) fitted to the collet housing and supported in the saddle (8) which is mounted on the ways of the lathe. The saddle is supported at its upper end by the overhead bar in a bearing (9). The bearing is lubricated by a gravity oil line from the headstock oil reservoir.

A Hydraulically Actuated Collet Chuck. Figure 6-43 illustrates an externally operated hydraulic collet chuck designed to take full advantage of the bore size of the machine spindle. The collet consists of a pad adapter (1), the three sections of which are held apart by springs, and of three sectional pads (2), in sizes and shapes to suit the bar stock, that are fastened to the pad adapter. The pad adapter is retained in the hood (3) by a ring (4), and the entire mechanism is mounted in a body (5) fastened to the spindle nose of the machine. Collet closing and opening takes place through the action of three levers (5) pivoted in the body. The levers are operated by the tapered inner bore of a cylindrical slider wedge (6) fitted around the chuck body and which is arranged to move axially through the action of a pivoted fork (7) whose opposite end is actuated by a hydraulic cylinder (8). This is a single-action cylinder whose return stroke is actuated by a spring. The cylinder and fork are contained in a cast housing fastened to the head of the machine.

LATHE MANDRELS

Mandrels, or shafts for holding work to be machined, are of two types, plain and expanding.

Plain mandrels have a taper of about 0.010 in. per ft and are forced into the work. Because of possible wear when driving mandrels on and off workpieces, they are generally suitable for low production only.

Expanding mandrels for locating and in many cases for driving from the bore of a workpiece can be of many designs. The stationary-collet type of mandrel is usually most satisfactory and most efficient. Since there is no movement between the collet and the workpiece, compared with plain mandrels, they are much less subject to wear and have less tendency to damage the bore of the workpiece. Expanding mandrels have been made with Neoprene disks expanded by an air cylinder

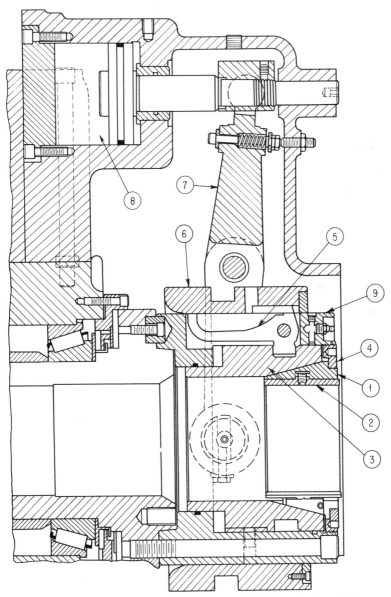

FIG. 6-43. Hydraulically actuated collet chuck. (*Gisholt Machine Co.*)

and a draw rod. Unless the machining cut is very light, they are not very satisfactory.

Expanding pin mandrels are used for chucking rough bores of shells and similar items. With the ends of the pins serrated and hardened, these work very well. Wherever possible, expanding mandrels should be provided with a positive driver to help drive the workpiece. Locating shoulders and pins must be incorporated to locate the workpiece longitudinally in the machine.

COMMERCIAL MANDRELS

A Split-sleeve Expanding Mandrel. This type of mandrel has a tapered arbor and a split sleeve having an internal taper matching that of the arbor. These mandrels have an accuracy of 0.0002 to 0.0005 in. A single mallet blow on the large end of the arbor shown in Fig. 6-44 expands the sleeve through wedge action against the bore or inside surface of the workpiece. A similar blow on the small end of the arbor releases the part from the sleeve.

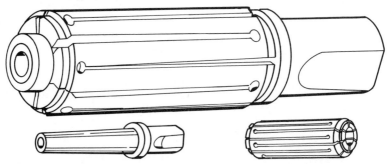

FIG. 6-44.   Between-center-type split-sleeve expanding mandrel. (*Western Tool & Mfg. Co., Inc.*)

The mandrel of Fig. 6-45 is designed for mounting on a lathe spindle or faceplate. It is operated by a drawbar which pulls the sleeve along the taper, which expands to hold the workpiece on its inside surface.

The mandrel shown in Fig. 6-46 has a taper at each end of the sleeve to expand the sleeve and hold the workpiece. These mandrels are also available with a flange for drawbar operation or for drawbar cantilever locknut operation.

A Hydraulically Actuated Expanding Sleeve Mandrel. This type is expanded by a self-contained hydraulic system which creates true, accurate centering with an equalized gripping force. By turning the actuating screw, the piston is moved for-

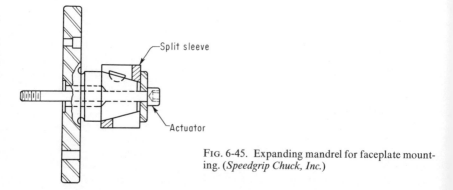

FIG. 6-45.   Expanding mandrel for faceplate mounting. (*Speedgrip Chuck, Inc.*)

ward, and the hydraulic fluid is forced from the piston chamber up through the port and into the space between the expanding sleeve and the mandrel body. A single mandrel can be designed to expand in several different sizes of bores of a workpiece or different workpieces. Figure 6-47 shows a center type of mandrel which can also be supplied with a flange for faceplate mounting.

A Roller-actuated Expanding Sleeve Mandrel. This mandrel (Fig. 6-48) is expanded by turning the actuating cone clockwise. The spiral motion of the rollers, held in a cage at an angle to the center line, forces the cone toward a positive stop as though it were threaded. A wedging action between the tapers expands the sleeve. This tool can be used for turning and similar operations on a lathe, as well as for grinding and inspection. The mandrel shown has a flange for faceplate mounting but can be designed to mount between centers on a lathe or grinder. Figure 6-49 shows the same type of construction for clamping on an external surface.

An Expanding Mandrel for Internal Gears. The mandrel shown in Fig. 6-50 will locate on or near the pitch diameter of an internal gear or spline. The splined

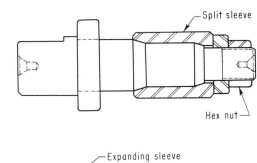

FIG. 6-46. Mandrel with sleeve expanded by two tapers. (*Erickson Tool Co.*)

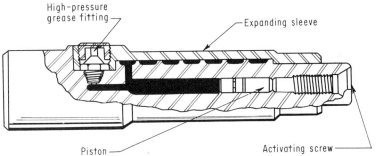

FIG. 6-47. Hydraulically actuated expanding-sleeve mandrel. (*A. &. C. Engineering Co.*)

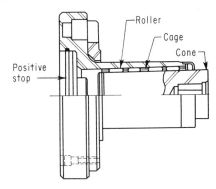

FIG. 6-48. Roller-actuated expanding-sleeve mandrel. (*Scully-Jones & Co.*)

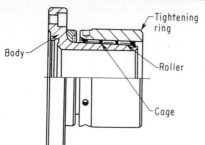

FIG. 6-49. Roller-actuated mandrel for clamping on the outside surface of a work-piece. (*Scully-Jones & Co.*)

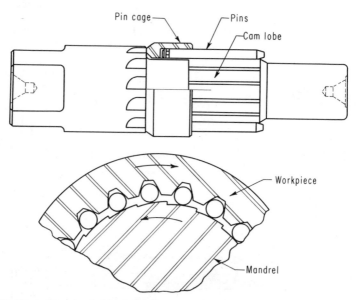

FIG. 6-50. Expanding mandrel for internal gears, splines, and serrations. (*Scully-Jones & Co.*)

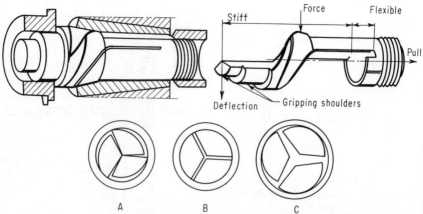

FIG. 6-51. Collet-type mandrel which grips on inside surfaces. (*E. Westberg Corp.*)

part is slipped over the pins and rotated. The pins move along cam lobes gripping the part on or near the pitch diameter. The pins can also be moved outward, and they are accurately located on the periphery of the expanding sleeve. These mandrels can be designed for faceplate or between-centers mounting.

A Collet-type Mandrel. The mandrel of Fig. 6-51 is a reversed collet, *i.e.*, a collet which grips the workpiece from the inside surfaces. It has all the advantages of a collet. It has one member which grips and releases the inside of the workpiece with the same action as a collet which grips and releases the outside of a part. When its stiff fingers are twisted half a turn between the taper and the mandrel portion, a reversal of the gripping motion occurs. Since the motion is now outward, the mandrel portion opens and grips the workpiece from the inside. The gripping force increases as the pull on the collet mandrel increases. Mandrels are ground to an accuracy of less than 0.001 in. runout.

In view *A*, the mandrel is collapsed. In view *B*, it is expanded to the same diameter as originally ground. View *C* shows the mandrel expanded to a diameter greater than that ground, which is not to exceed $\frac{1}{32}$ in. At this position the high points run true.

This mandrel may be used on any lathe that uses a collet. Diameters range from $\frac{1}{2}$ to 4 in.

A Mandrel for Machining Cams. The machining of cams, throws, and other eccentric parts is facilitated by the mandrel shown in Fig. 6-52. Workpieces are reamed to fit the mandrel and have broached keyways to hold them in position. Centers are machined in the end of the mandrel and the end collar according to the eccentricity required. The parts are held on the mandrel by the lockout. The pins through the end collar are a close fit into the slot in the mandrel.

It is possible to machine parts of different eccentricity by changing to different centers, and the mandrel can be made long enough so that several cams can be machined at the same time.

A Precision Expanding Mandrel. To eliminate the need for an excessive number of similar tools, a mandrel with adjustable jaws, similar to that shown in Fig. 6-53, can be used to obtain a greater bore and bearing range.

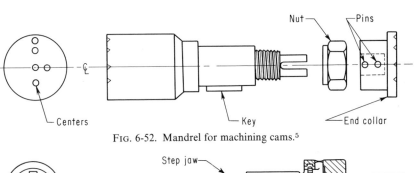

FIG. 6-52. Mandrel for machining cams.[5]

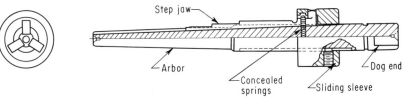

FIG. 6-53. Parallel sliding-jaw mandrel.[6]

Principal components of this mandrel are the three sliding jaws, the retaining springs, the tapered mandrel, and the sliding-lock sleeve. When the workpiece is located on the jaws, the sleeve and parallel jaws slide up inclined planes on the mandrel until the part is firmly retained. The sleeve is then locked by the setscrew to retain the jaws and part during the machining operation. The jaws slide in a groove in the arbor to keep them parallel.

A Mandrel for Large-diameter Rings. Precision between-center turning or cylindrical grinding of the OD of large-diameter rings can be done with the mandrel illustrated in Fig. 6-54.

A round blank of the proper size is bored and fitted to a central shaft, and the two are welded together. After stress relieving, the weldment is center-drilled and finished to the required diameter for a snug fit in the workpiece.

The layout of the four chordal slots is made, but before they are machined, the holes for taper pins and setscrews are drilled, taper-reamed, and tapped. The setscrews should be located near the outer end of the slot for effective clamping.

When the setscrews are tightened against the standard taper pins in the tapered holes, the segments between the slots will expand outward and tightly grip the workpiece. To release the workpiece, the setscrews are backed off and the small end of the hardened taper pin rapped with a mallet.

On some jobs, the taper pins and setscrews may be replaced with standard taper-pipe plugs.

A Mandrel for Threaded Parts. One of the main problems in doing secondary work on internally threaded parts is to hold the work securely and concentric with the threads and to permit its easy removal from the work holder.

The surface of the OD of the part shown in Fig. 6-55 is polished and will not allow the use of a gripping device which might mar it. The mandrel is of soft tool steel and turned to fit the taper in the lathe spindle. It is finish-turned; its threads are chased; and a shoulder is faced, against which the workpiece bears after it is screwed on the mandrel. The threaded end is slit along the center line and a hole for a setscrew drilled and tapped through one side. A cup-point setscrew seats against a steel ball to open and close the mandrel.

A Differential Expanding Mandrel. When hollow castings having stepped bores are machined on the exterior, it is often essential that uniform wall thicknesses be maintained. One way of locating a casting internally with a differential expanding type of mandrel is illustrated in Fig. 6-56. Two sets of locating members contact the interior walls of the casting. They operate independently of one another and adjust themselves automatically to size variations and steps in the bore.

The mandrel body is a solid-steel cylinder with recesses bored in each end to

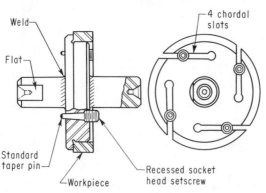

FIG. 6-54. Mandrel for large-diameter rings.[7]

accommodate expansion cones. Each cone has right-hand threads along about half of its straight length for engagement with a corresponding internal thread in the mandrel recess. A cylindrical guide portion on each cone ensures positive radial location. The cones are case-hardened, and their outer ends are center-drilled for mounting between lathe centers. Flats are machined on the projecting ends for engaging with a wrench.

Three hardened-steel disks form the expanding members which engage the interior walls of the component. The disks slide without clearance in radial slots machined in the mandrel body. They are pushed outward by the expansion cones. The disks are prevented from falling out of the slots when the mandrel is unloaded by a ring of spring wire which passes through a small hole drilled through each disk.

Disk-shaped locators have the advantage of ease in manufacture. Even in the maximum expansion position, they are adequately supported by the mandrel body. The grip of the disks on the work surface is sufficient to prevent the work from slipping under heavy turning cuts.

In use, the lathe driving dog is attached to one of the expansion cones. The rotary driving action will tend to tighten the cone and force out the locating members to press firmly on the interior walls of the castings. The drag of the tailstock center on the right-hand expansion cone has a similar tightening effect.

Since the gripping members expand independently, they adapt themselves readily to internal surfaces. When gripping such a workpiece, there is a tendency for heavy cutting-tool pressure to slide the workpiece axially. This effect can be minimized by providing some positive form of stop for the workpiece. This might be a sleeve slipped over the mandrel and bearing at the left-hand end on the driving dog.

A Ball Expanding Mandrel. A ball expanding mandrel (Fig. 6-57) provides a positive centralizing method of registering accurately through the center of a part, regardless of variations in size or taper in its bore.

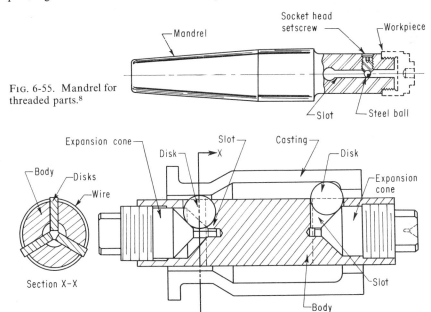

FIG. 6-55. Mandrel for threaded parts.[8]

FIG. 6-56. Expanding mandrel for stepped bores.[9]

It is well adapted for locating in two bores of different sizes, provided the space between bores can accommodate the cylindrical cones and that the diameters of the radially spaced balls and of one cylindrical cone correspond to those of the workpiece bores.

The cones have a register diameter at each end having a minimum diametrical clearance which allows a sliding fit. The precision balls are retained in cages that are located without any linear error.

As the cones are drawn together by the drawbolt, the balls are forced outward. As one set of balls engages the bore of the part, additional tightening moves the other set until they have engaged the part. The part is automatically centralized at both ends in relation to the center line of the bore(s) of the part. It is recommended that the ball cages and cylindrical cones be hardened to prevent indentation and wear.

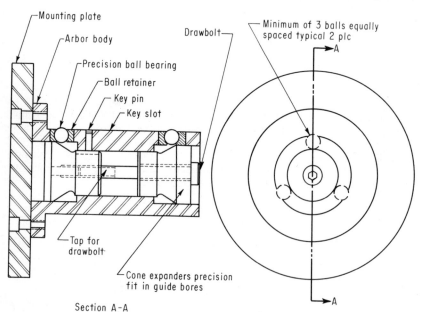

Section A-A

Fig. 6-57. Double expanding arbor compensates for variation in bore diameter. (*Commercial Air Products, Inc.*)

References

1. Helmke, E. C.: Hold That Workpiece, or How to Apply 5 Basic Rules in Chucking Work for Turning and Boring, *Tooling and Production,* July, 1957.
2. "Chucks and Chuck Jaws," American Standard ASA B5.8-1954, R 1959, American Standards Association, New York.
3. "Spindle Noses for Toolroom Lathes, Engine Lathes, Turret Lathes, and Automatic Lathes," American Standard ASA B5.9-1960, American Standards Association, New York.
4. Vacuum Faceplate Holds Sheet Stock, *The Tool Engr.,* February, 1955.
5. Spicer, Charles: Mandrel for Machining Cams, *The Tool Engr.,* January, 1958.
6. Precision Expanding Mandrels, *The Tool Engr.,* September, 1958.
7. Gerber, H. J.: Precision Mandrel for Large Rings, *The Tool Engr.,* December, 1954.
8. Brown, George W.: Mandrel for Threaded Parts, *The Tool Engr.,* August, 1959.
9. Bower, C. T.: Differential Expanding Mandrel, *The Tool Engr.,* May, 1956.

Section 7

MILLING FIXTURES

By MARIO MARTELLOTTI

Development Engineer, The Cincinnati Milling Machine Co.

Many milling operations are performed without a fixture by clamping the workpiece on the milling-machine table, especially when few parts are to be machined. For production jobs when the number of parts being machined is large enough to justify the cost, a fixture is used for holding and locating the work. Quantity alone is not the only criterion for determining the application of a fixture; required workpiece accuracy and shape may dictate its use, although only a few parts may be machined.

A fixture, like any other piece of shop equipment, must justify its use by contributing to the reduction in the cost of a milling operation for which it was designed. Fixtures are sometimes very complicated and expensive units, but on the other hand they may be rather simple modifications of the familiar milling-machine vise.

The design of a fixture should not be started without necessary data concerning the milling machine with which the fixture will be used, including the dimensions of the milling-machine table, center-to-center distance, and dimensions of T slots; the range of vertical, longitudinal, and transverse table travel; the power capacity and speed and feed ranges. On what type of milling machine is the fixture to be used, vertical or horizontal? Can the design of the fixture be simplified by selecting another type of milling machine on which the job will run?

A fixture should be designed for as many milling operations as possible on a part.

Gaging or setting surfaces are required for locating the cutter in relation to the work and the fixture and to ensure that the cut is within the specified tolerance limits.

Clearance space should be provided to allow cutter change without disturbing the setup.

The workpiece area to be milled should always be located within the area determined by the supporting points, or the supporting points should be under the area to be milled.

Fixtures used in milling operations may be any of the following types or combinations:

Milling-machine vises may be used for holding relatively small parts.

Temporary fixtures may be built up with commercial parts such as clamps, T bolts, locators and stops, and standard milling-machine attachments, using the table of the milling machine as the base of the fixture (see Sec. 15). Temporary setups are generally used in the toolroom or when few parts of a special nature are to be milled which would not justify the cost of a permanent fixture.

Permanent fixtures are made when the number of parts in production is large enough to warrant the cost of the fixture.

Fixtures are sometimes classified in accordance with the type of operation performed on the work, such as slotting, straddle milling, face milling, form milling, etc. A more comprehensive classification identifies their design features such as: hand clamping, power clamping, automatic, center type, pilot or stud type, V block, stationary, cradle type, rotary, drum, indexing, oscillating, rise and fall, transfer, built in, universal contour or profile, etc.

ESTIMATES

The estimate is the tool engineer's analysis of a milling operation. It provides a sound basis for the selection of (1) the method of milling, (2) the machine for the job, (3) the type of fixture most suitable for the job, and (4) the milling cutters, for milling at the lowest net cost per piece.

The factors considered in estimating a milling job are:

1. Size, strength, rigidity, and the locating surfaces of the part
2. Operation to be performed, such as form milling, thread milling, facing, slotting, straddle milling, etc.
3. Required finish and accuracy of the milled surface
4. Stock to be removed and machinability of the workpiece material
5. Number of parts to be milled and rate of production
6. Milling method, type, size, and capacity of the milling machine
7. Type and design of the fixture
8. Cutter design and material

A preliminary study should be made of the various methods of milling and of the different machines that could do the milling operation, together with the proposed types of fixture.

For each method tentatively selected, a series of analyses are made to obtain estimated time per piece and production rates.

The placing of the workpiece on the table in relation to the milling cutter identifies, and is descriptive of, the method of milling. Some of the most generally used methods are single piece, string, abreast, reciprocal, progressive, index, and their combinations (Fig. 7-1).

Single-piece milling is that in which one part, held in a fixture or directly on the machine table, is milled during each machine cycle.

In *string milling,* two or more parts are placed in a row parallel to the feeding movement of the table. They are milled in consecutive order as the machine is cycled. The parts may be in contact with each other or spaced closely and clamped.

With the *abreast* method, two or more parts are placed in a row at right angles to the direction of table feed, *i.e.,* side by side in front of their individual cutters.

Reciprocal milling is the method in which both the right- and left-hand ends of the machine table are provided with fixtures. While milling the part in one fixture, the operator unloads and loads the other fixture.

Progressive milling is that method which performs two or more similar or different operations either simultaneously or successively on separate parts on the same machine. Parts are progressively moved from one fixture station to the next until all intended operations are performed.

Index milling includes one or more operations on one or more workpieces which are indexed to the next position during the operating cycle of the machine. This type of milling may use rotary fixtures.

In analyzing the methods of milling, the estimated milling time may be determined by the following equations.

$$t = \frac{L + A + O_1 + O_2}{F} \qquad (1)$$

where t = time required to complete cut, min
L = length of surface to mill
A = cutter approach
O_1, O_2 = overtravel of cutter at end and start of cut, in. (see Fig. 7-2)
F = feed rate, in. per min

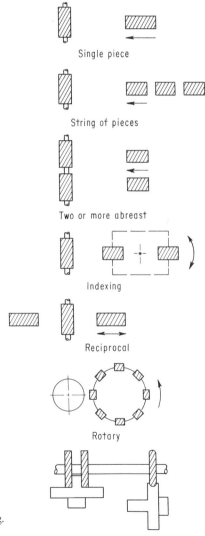

Single piece

String of pieces

Two or more abreast

Indexing

Reciprocal

Rotary

Progressive

FIG. 7-1. Methods of milling.

In peripheral milling (Fig. 7-2a), the cutter approach may be determined by

$$A = \sqrt{H(D - H)} \qquad (2)$$

where H = depth of cut, in.

   D = diameter of cutter, in.

In face milling, with the cutter centered on the center line of the workpiece (Fig. 7-2b),

$$A = \frac{D}{2}\left[1 - \sqrt{1 - \left(\frac{W}{D}\right)^2}\right] \qquad (3)$$

For a face-milling cutter off center on amount M, the cutter approach is

$$A = \frac{D}{2}\left[1 - \sqrt{1 - \left(\frac{W + 2M}{D}\right)^2}\right] \qquad (4)$$

The time for milling a group of pieces by the string method would be expressed as

$$t = \frac{nw + (n - 1)s + A + O}{F} \qquad (5)$$

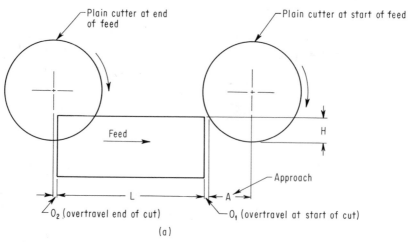

(a)

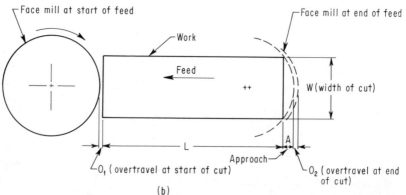

(b)

Fig. 7-2. Cutter approach and overtravel in (a) peripheral milling and (b) face milling.

where n = number of pieces in a row
   w = length of milled surface of each piece, in.
   s = space between two pieces, in.

Milling time is at a minimum when the space between the parts is zero. If this cannot be arranged, the alternative is to make the space as narrow as possible. The increase in milling time resulting from spaced parts in a row can in part be minimized by adding rows abreast; this will decrease the milling time in inverse relation to the number of rows abreast.

In all cases, the idle machine time, including the time spent in placing the workpiece near the cutter, the time required to return the workpiece or cutter to the starting position after milling, and time spent in loading and unloading, must be added to the milling time to arrive at a cycle time.

MILLING-FIXTURE DESIGN

Fixtures consist of essential elements which may vary in shape and arrangement as required by the nature of the workpiece but are identical in the duty which they perform. The essential elements of a milling fixture are shown in Fig. 7-3.

The relative position between the workpiece and cutters may be determined by means of a gage or properly located setting surfaces. The setting surfaces may be incorporated in the fixture and are either fixed or removable. When the setting surface is located so that it would be in the path of the cutter, provision is usually made either to remove the gage or to set it down or over a certain distance from the cutter to avoid interference. A feeler gage of proper thickness is then provided for gaging the position of the cutter.

Figure 7-4 illustrates the use of an 0.0625-in.-thick feeler gage between the setup gage and cutter. The use of a straightedge to establish the relationship between cutter and setup gage is shown in Fig. 7-5. A removable setting gage is shown in Fig. 7-6. The gage is positioned by the central locating plug on the fixture and a small pin, which are the means of locating the workpiece on the fixture.

Vise Jaws. A commonly used work-holding device for milling is the plain or universal vise (Fig. 7-7). Provision is made for attaching special jaw inserts to the fixed and movable vise jaws.

Self-adjusting vise jaws for simultaneously holding three cylindrical workpieces are illustrated in Fig. 7-8. The fixed jaw (1) has three vertical 90° V grooves. The

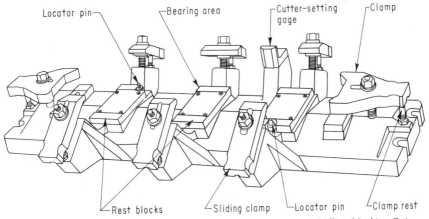

FIG. 7-3. Essential elements of a milling fixture. (*The Cincinnati Milling Machine Co.*)

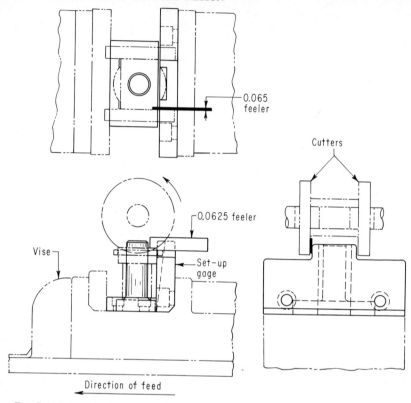

FIG. 7-4. Setup gage incorporated in a vise jaw. (*The Cincinnati Milling Machine Co.*)

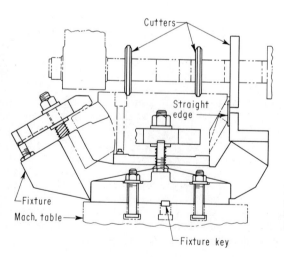

FIG. 7-5. Using a straightedge for setting fixture-cutter relationship. (*The Cincinnati Milling Machine Co.*)

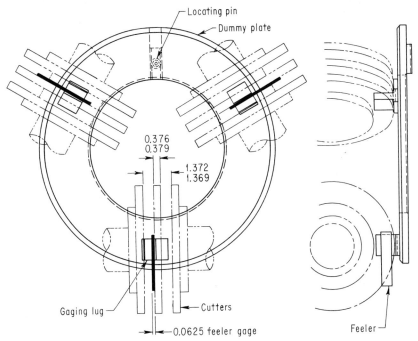

FIG. 7-6. Removable cutter-setting gage. (*The Cincinnati Milling Machine Co.*)

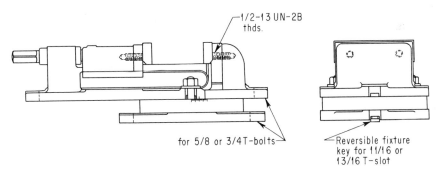

FIG. 7-7. Universal milling-machine vise. (*The Cincinnati Milling Machine Co.*)

movable jaw (2) has three horizontal plungers (3) opposite the V grooves, and on closing the vise, each workpiece is clamped in one of the V grooves by a plunger. The variation in part diameter is compensated automatically by a lateral adjustment of the angle-faced plungers (4). Vertical pins (5) transmit motion from plunger to plunger.

Figure 7-9 illustrates three methods of holding round stock in vise jaws. View *a* shows a set of jaws with equalizers for holding four headed parts. Two spring-loaded equalizers (1) are in one jaw while four Vs are in the second jaw.

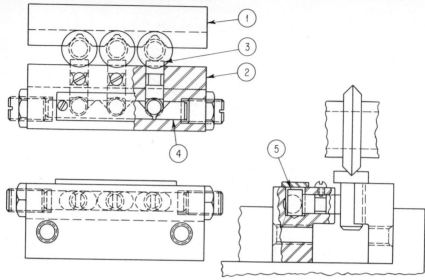

FIG. 7-8. Self-adjusting vise jaws for multiple parts.[1]

In Fig. 7-9*b* is shown a set of jaws for holding two cylindrical parts while milling the circular grooves. The part is positioned vertically and supported by the pin (2).

The jaws of view *c* are used to hold two ¼-in.-diam shafts while milling a slot in the end. The shafts are supported on a ledge of one jaw (3) and clamped by beveled surfaces (similar to a dovetail) in both jaws. An end stop block (5) locates and supports the parts while being milled.

All of these jaws were made of tool steel, hardened and ground. For low-production items, the jaws may be made of low-carbon steel, either case-hardened or in the soft state.

Small castings and forgings may also be held in special vise jaws. Figure 7-10 shows a set of vise jaws having an equalizing bar (1) for holding a part in a horizontal V slot at one end and at the other end in a vertical V slot and against a rest button (2).

Figure 7-11 illustrates a set of vise jaws for holding a valve body for a straddle-milling operation on its hexagon-shaped portion. Since the surface being milled is off center of the gripping surface, the surface beneath the cut rests in a V slot. A locator (1) is provided to locate the part to the cutters.

A Fixture for Mounting-pad Milling. The first operation in the machining of many parts is the milling of the reference surface used in subsequent operations. Figure 7-12 shows the fixture for the first operation on a small casting. One adjustable (2) and three fixed (1) rest pins support the areas to be milled in this fixture. The part is held against two locators (3) by a thumbscrew (4). The cutting force is opposed by the stop (5) while the clamp (6) holds the workpiece against the stop. Hold-down clamping is accomplished by the clamp assembly (7) bearing on a cutout in the center tongue. A cutter set block (8) is provided to establish the cutter position.

A Milling Fixture for Four Operations. To reduce tooling costs on low-production items, it is often desirable to use one fixture for more than one operation. The fixture shown in Fig. 7-13 is used for operations involving plain, straddle, and three face milling operations.

The fixture is designed for down milling in the first operation, with the thrust against the solid locator (1). The workpiece is located on two round locators (1, 2) which fit the 1.024-in.-diam end holes. One of the locators (2) also serves as a clamp. Equalizing clamps (3) with a compression spring between them are guided by gibs (4) and are used for the first and second operations on the part.

When milling the 15° surface, the fixture is set crosswise on the machine table

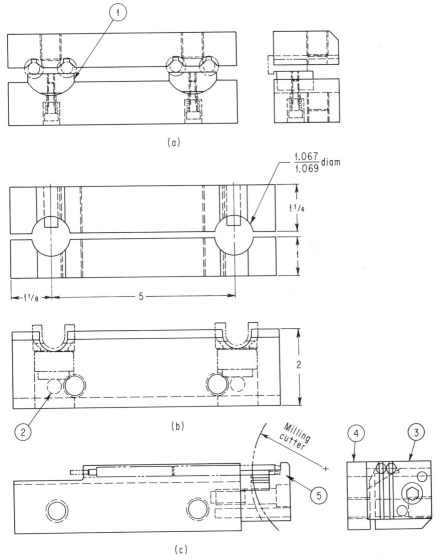

Fig. 7-9. Vise jaws for holding round stock. (*American Standard Controls Div.*)

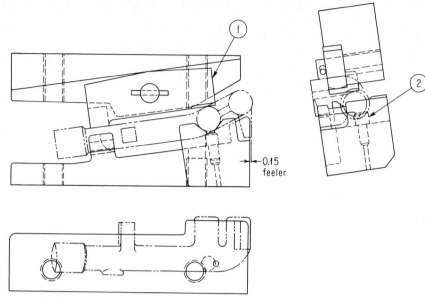

Fig. 7-10.   Vise jaws for a small casting. (*American Standard Controls Div.*)

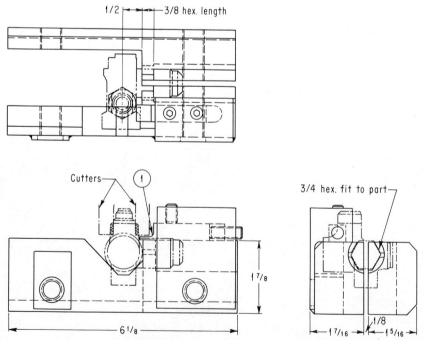

Fig. 7-11.   Vise jaws for straddle-milling valve body. (*American Standard Controls Div.*)

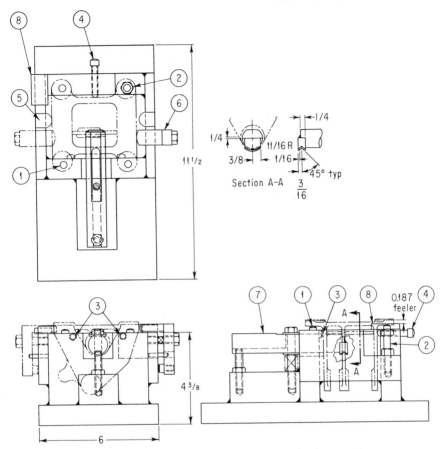

FIG. 7-12. First-operation milling fixture for an aluminum casting.

and is tilted to a 15° angle. It is aligned on the machine table T slot with a fixture key. Tilting of the fixture allows side milling of the 15° surface in a plane normal to the machine table. The vertical setting of the milling cutter is done by using a 0.062-in. feeler on the surface provided. Lateral positioning is accomplished by using a 1-in.-gage block and a straightedge.

For milling the 23° surface, a third position of the fixture is provided. The fixture rests on the surface of the main base crosswise on the machine table located by a fixture key. A second pair of jaws (5, 6) replaces previously used jaws (3). This operation may be performed on a horizontal milling machine using an arbor-mounted side-milling cutter or with an end mill in a vertical machine.

A First-operation Fixture for a Mounting Bracket. The fixture (Fig. 7-14) for milling the mounting pads of a small casting uses a sight gage (1) to position the part prior to machining. Three adjustable jackscrews (2) position and support the workpiece. The spring-loaded support pin (3) is locked by the thumbscrew (4), thereby providing direct support beneath two of the milled surfaces. Downward clamping force is applied with the clamp plate (5).

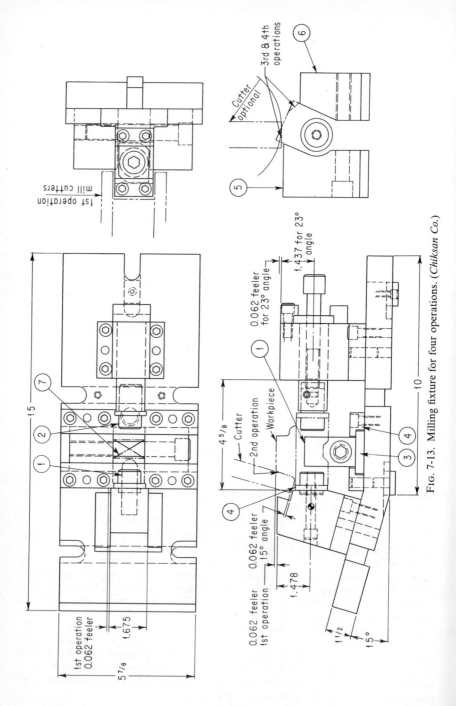

Fig. 7-13. Milling fixture for four operations. (*Chiksan Co.*)

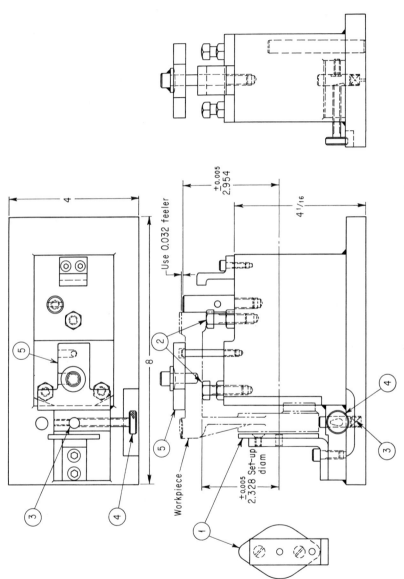

FIG. 7-14. Milling fixture for mounting bracket. (*Koehler Aircraft Co.*)

Use 0.032 feeler

2.954 ±0.005

4 1/16

2.328 Set-up diam ±0.005

Workpiece

A Fixture for Milling a Compound Angle. The fixture of Fig. 7-15 is used in milling a compound angle on the end of a right- and left-hand bracket. The part is positioned sidewise by the two-point locator (1) and endwise by another locator (2). A tapered block (3) supports the end of the clamp (4) and forces it to hold the part against the side locator (1). An adjustable jackscrew (5) provides support for the milled surface.

For construction and inspection purposes, two 0.875-in.-diam holes and two 0.500-in.-diam construction balls (6) are incorporated in the fixture. The cutter is positioned by a set block (7) and a 0.050-in.-thick feeler gage.

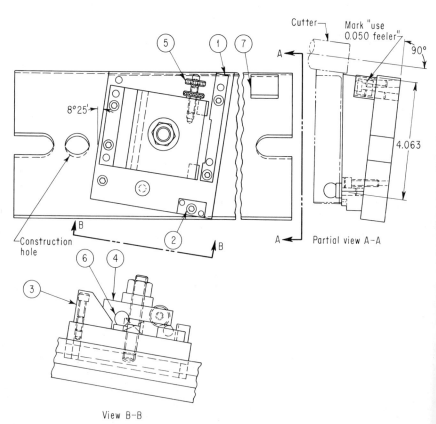

Fig. 7-15. Milling fixture for compound angle. (*The Emerson Electric Mfg. Co.*)

Milling a 0.315-in. Slot. Figure 7-16 illustrates a fixture for milling a 0.315-in.-wide slot in an aluminum forging. The part is located by two flatted or diamond pins (1). These pins are held in place by a ball detent (2). A ⅛-in.-diam rod brazed to the strap clamp (3) fits in a groove to hold the part down during the milling operation. A set block (4) and a 0.050-in.-thick feeler set the cutter to the workpiece. Two blocks (5) fastened to the base plate (6) position the workpiece.

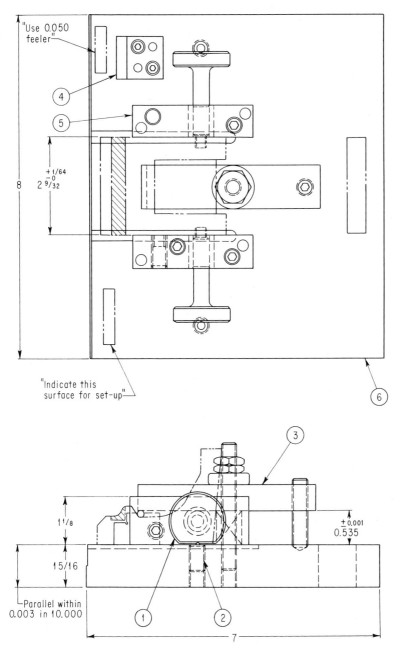

FIG. 7-16. Milling fixture for 0.315-in.-wide slot. (*The Emerson Electric Mfg. Co.*)

Fixtures for Milling Plain and Micrometer Stop Bodies. The fixture of Fig. 7-17 has two female centers that locate one of two parts, a plain stop body or a micrometer stop body, from bosses while milling a V groove and adjacent surfaces. One female center (1) is fixed and is press-fitted into the stand (2). The opposite end of this locator along with two ¼-in.-diam dowel pins locates a removable cutter-set gage (3) which sets the cutter for either of the two parts milled on this fixture. The end of the locator (1) is threaded to receive a standard hexagon nut to hold the set gage in place.

An adjustable female-center locator (4) has a threaded end which screws into a fixed nut (5). The center is rotated by a machine handle which advances or retracts it to accommodate either part between centers.

The parts are located laterally by a locator (6) which has two sloping surfaces. One surface is used to locate the plain stop body. The locator is reversed, positioning the other sloping surface for locating the micrometer stop body. A thumbscrew (7) holds the parts against this locator.

Since the V groove is $^{15}/_{16}$ in. from the center of the boss in the plain stop unit and 1⅛ in. from the center of the boss on the micrometer stop unit, the setting gage (3) is reversible on the fixture for setting the cutter for either part.

The subsequent milling operations on the two stop bodies are not similar; therefore different fixtures are required.

The second operation on the plain stop body finish-mills and chamfers one end at a time with the fixture of Fig. 7-18. The stop body is located from the surface milled in the first operation.

The cutter is guided in a liner bushing and a drill bushing (which functions as a stop collar). The vertical adjustment of the part is made by a dog-point setscrew (1). The cutting tool consists of a holder for a two-lip end mill which mills to center and for two brazed carbide tips for the chamfering operation.

The second operation on the micrometer stop body is the milling of the 1-in.-wide slot. A fixture for this operation is shown in Fig. 7-19.

The part is located on an inverted V-rest surface (1) and a flat-rest surface (2) from the previously milled V groove and adjacent flat surfaces. A hand screw (3) threaded into a hole in the part locates the piece sidewise and holds it in position.

A strap clamp (4) with a cutter-clearance slot has a V-shaped centralizing groove in the toe. Its heel has a sloping surface engaging a mating surface on a heel support (5) adjustable for height. A clamping wheel (6) pulls down and in on the workpiece, seating it on the V rest and pressing it against the flat rest surface. Compression springs (7) support the clamp in the unclamped position. Another compression spring (8) holds the clamp away from the workpiece for loading and unloading.

A separately mounted cutter-setting gage (9) is incorporated.

Milling a Small Triangular Part. The size and shape of the part shown in Fig. 7-20a presented difficult handling and machining problems. The stock for this part is $^3/_{16} \times ^3/_8$-in. alloy-steel bars sawed into 12-in. lengths. These bars are ground on both sides to a thickness of 0.140 ($+0.003$, -0.001) in. and milled on one edge to a width of 0.337 in.

In the next operation, four bars are clamped into the fixture shown in Fig. 7-20b and machined to size while maintaining the 25° angle and the 0.140, 0.300, and 0.374-in. dimensions.

A $5 \times \frac{1}{2} \times 1$-in. side-milling cutter and a $6 \times \frac{1}{16} \times 1$-in. metal slitting saw with side chip clearance are used for cutting the workpiece.

The workpieces are placed in four V grooves in the block (1) and up against a locator (2). Two strap clamps (3) hold the part for milling and cutting off.

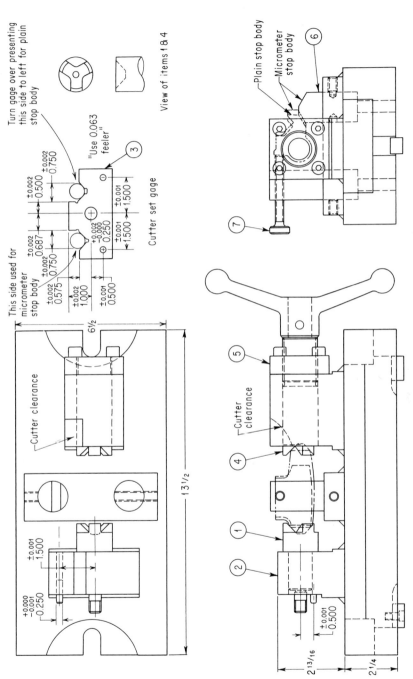

Turn gage over presenting this side to left for plain stop body

This side used for micrometer stop body

View of items 1 & 4

"Use 0.063 feeler"

Cutter set gage

Cutter clearance

Cutter clearance

Plain stop body

Micrometer stop body

Fig. 7-17. V-way milling fixture for stop bodies. (*Rockwell Mfg. Co.*)

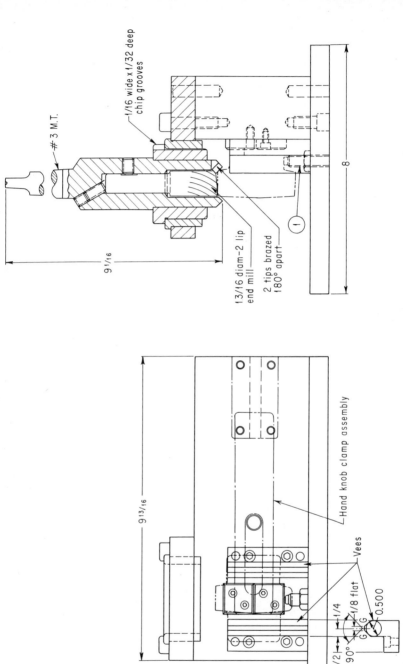

#3 M.T.

1/16 wide x 1/32 deep chip grooves

9 1/16

1 3/16 diam—2 lip end mill

2 tips brazed 180° apart

8

9 13/16

Hand knob clamp assembly

Vees

1/4

1/8 flat

0.500

1/2

90°

G G G

FIG. 7-18. Fixture for end-milling and chamfering stop body. (*Rockwell Mfg. Co.*)

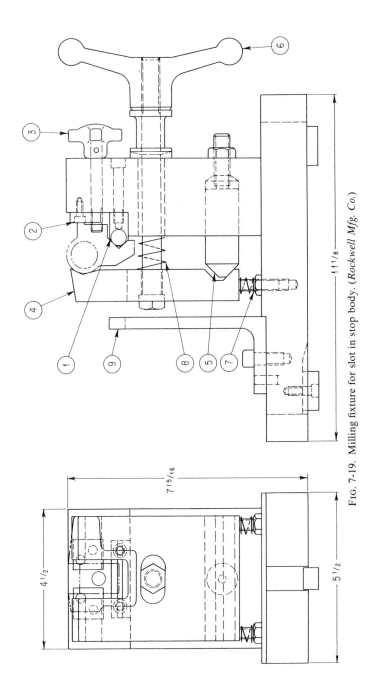

Fig. 7-19. Milling fixture for slot in stop body. (*Rockwell Mfg. Co.*)

7–19

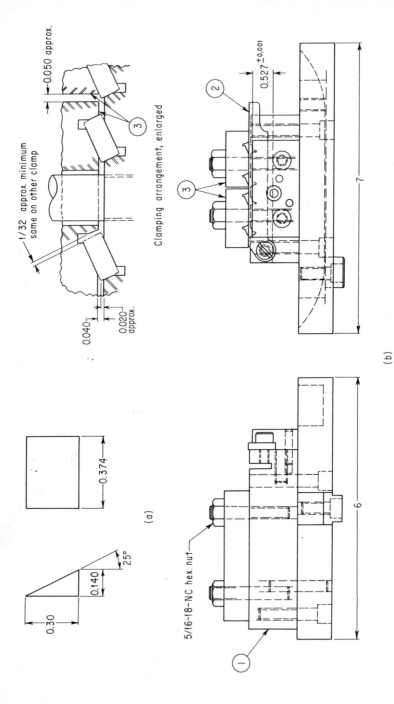

0.050 approx.

1/32 approx. minimum
same on other clamp

③

③

Clamping arrangement, enlarged

0.040

0.020
approx.

②

0.527 ±0.001

③

7

(b)

0.374

(a)

25°

0.140

0.30

5/16-18-NC hex. nut

6

①

Fig. 7-20. Milling fixture for small triangular-shaped part. (*U.S. Naval Gun Factory.*)

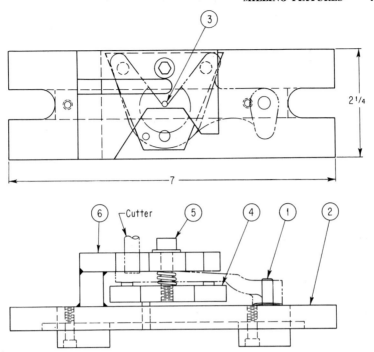

FIG. 7-21. End-milling a slot in an aluminum die casting. (*Allen Gauge & Tool Co.*)

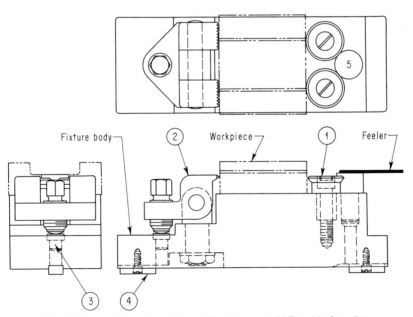

FIG. 7-22. Straddle-milling fixture. (*The Cincinnati Milling Machine Co.*)

Milling a Groove in Aluminum Casting. The fixture of Fig. 7-21 is for end-milling a groove in an aluminum die-cast part. Since the cutting pressure is small, it is permissible to perform the operation against the clamp.

The part is placed over the locating pin (1) which is pressed into the base plate (2) and against the smaller pin (3). The clamp (4) is tightened against the part by a socket-head cap screw (5). A slot in the top plate (6) of the welded fixture base gives the milling cutter access to the work area.

Straddle Milling a Block. In the fixture of Fig. 7-22 the width of the rest surface is slightly less than that of the workpiece. Two locators (1) of the wedge type easily locate the workpiece sidewise by approximately centering it on the rest surface.

In order not to interfere with the cutters that mill the top surface, the clamp (2) is of the bell-crank type. A square-head setscrew applies pressure to the clamp. A hardened rest button (3), placed beneath the setscrew, prevents indentation of the fixture base at that point. The fixture is located on the machine table by two fixture keys (4).

In setting up the operation, the fixture is centralized between the straddle-milling cutters. The depth of the groove in the top surface of the workpiece is set with the set block (5) and a feeler gage of appropriate thickness.

Straddle and Slot Milling Round Stock. Two different rods (Fig. 7-24) are held abreast in the fixture of Fig. 7-23 for milling a tang (straddle milling) in one rod (*a*) and a slot in the second rod (*b*). After milling the slot, workpiece *b* is located

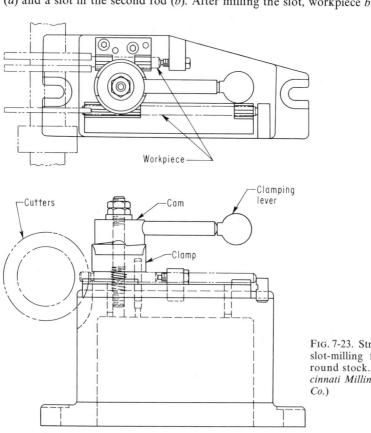

Fig. 7-23. Straddle- and slot-milling fixture for round stock. (*The Cincinnati Milling Machine Co.*)

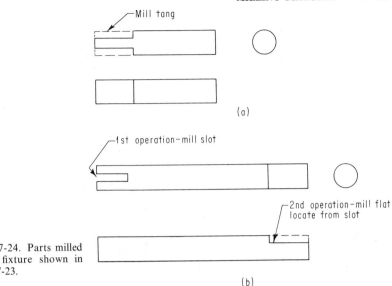

Mill tang

(a)

1st operation—mill slot

2nd operation—mill flat
locate from slot

Fig. 7-24. Parts milled with fixture shown in Fig. 7-23.

(b)

from the slot in another fixture (not shown) to mill the flat. The two fixtures are mounted on the table of the same milling machine and are located at the left and right of the spindle respectively. Thus three milling operations are performed progressively using abreast, single, and reciprocal methods of milling.

Progressively Milling a Gearbox Casting. The five surfaces of a gearbox casting are machined on a planer type of milling machine, using a face-milling cutter in the fixture of Fig. 7-25. The five surfaces are machined in one machine cycle. The part is progressively moved from left to right by the operator during the machine cycle.

The fixture base plate is hot-rolled steel $1\frac{1}{2} \times 15 \times 56\frac{1}{2}$ in. The clamp assemblies and locators for each position of the workpiece are attached to the base plate with cap screws and dowels.

Milling a Contoured Slot. The workpieces were machined to the dimensions necessary for locating them in the fixture of Fig. 7-26. This includes the spline hole which locates on the straight locators (1), the 0.187-in.-diam hole for the diamond locators (2), and the surface which rests on the side of the fixture.

The fixture, of welded construction and of extremely simple design, is very efficiently arranged so that the cutter cuts continuously from the beginning of the action in station 1 to its end in station 2. One workpiece is completed for each cutter cycle by this progressive-milling method.

Operation 1 mills a slot 0.187 (+0.005, −0.000) in. wide with the workpiece located in station 1.

Operation 2 mills the continuation of the slot cut in operation 1 with the workpiece located in station 2 from the same holes and surface used in locating it in station 1. This locating method ensures that the blended slotted surfaces will be cut with greater accuracy than would be possible by changing the locating points. Each part is clamped by a single retractable strap clamp with an integral heel support. Both clamps are kept in a slanting position and prevented from falling into a vertical position by guide pins (3). These pins hold the clamps in position when they are unclamped and retracted, thus minimizing clamp operation time. This

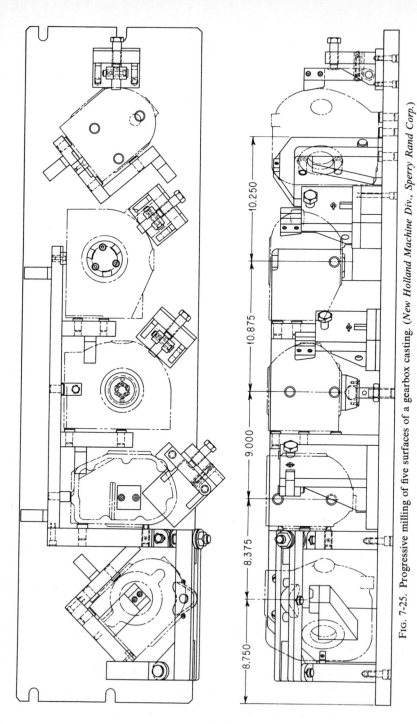

FIG. 7-25. Progressive milling of five surfaces of a gearbox casting. (*New Holland Machine Div., Sperry Rand Corp.*)

method accomplishes the same result as the conventional design of a slot in the underside of a strap clamp engaging the heel support, and it costs less.

The setting of the cutter for height and side position is made by using a 0.125-in. feeler gage with set blocks (4, 5) for the height and side or cross positions. Another set block (6) sets fixture longitudinal travel with a 0.750-in. feeler gage.

Reciprocal Milling of Slots. Two fixtures of identical design are used for this operation (Fig. 7-27). To speed up clamping and unclamping of the parts, the clamps are operated hydraulically. The fixture has a V block (2) as rest and locating surfaces for the cylindrical shape of the workpiece. The part is placed vertically in the fixture and rests in a nest pad (1). It is clamped against a V block by a V clamp (3) actuated by a crank (4). A crank is rotated by a push rod (5) which receives its motion through a wedge cam (6) operated by a hydraulic cylinder (7). A spring (8) pushes on the crank and retracts it when the hydraulic pressure is released.

The wedge-type cam holds the clamp in position without the assistance of the hydraulic pressure, because its angle is smaller than the friction angle of the sliding surfaces of the push rod and the wedge cam. There are three identical stations abreast in each fixture.

The setting gage is shown at (9). Two gaging surfaces are used; the vertical surface is used for setting the cutter transversely and the horizontal surface is used for setting it vertically.

Abreast Milling Long Thin Parts. A simple but efficient fixture for abreast milling of two tool-steel strips is shown in Fig. 7-28.

A 11½° angular surface to be milled along the edge of the workpiece is suited to abreast milling.

The fixture is made up of few parts and is efficient because two pieces are milled at a time. The handling of two parts instead of one requires slightly more time, while clamping time remains the same.

The four clamping bolts (1 to 4), which are operated individually, could by a slight modification be tightened in pairs, thus reducing the clamping time. To further reduce clamping time, each bolt could be provided with an air cylinder for simultaneous clamping and unclamping.

The endwise location of the parts is accomplished by pushing the parts against the stop pins (5). The rest surfaces (6, 7) extend the full length of the workpiece.

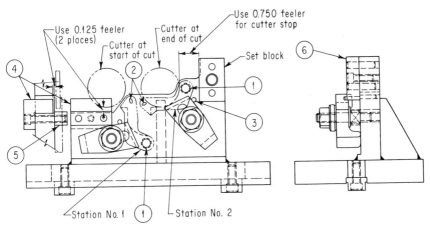

FIG. 7-26. Fixture for milling slots in alloy-steel arm. (*U.S. Naval Ordnance Plant.*)

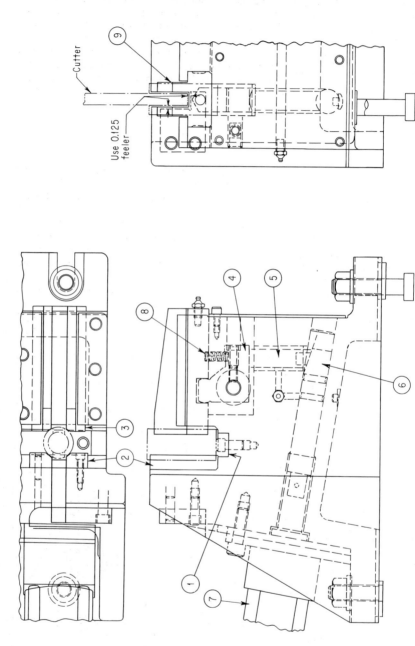

Cutter

Use 0.125
feeler

FIG. 7-27. Three-station abreast slot milling a cylindrical part. (*The Cincinnati Milling Machine Co.*)

7–26

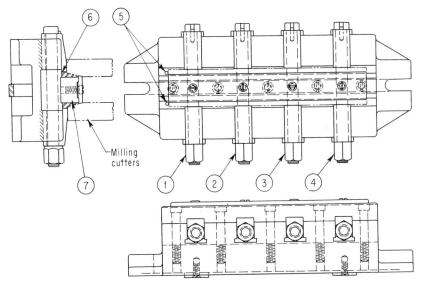

Milling
cutters

FIG. 7-28. Fixture for abreast milling of two strips. (*The L. S. Starrett Co.*)

Straddle Milling a Lever Arm. Figure 7-29 illustrates the holding of an offset lever arm while straddle-milling one end. The part is located by a pin (1) and a stop plate (2). The part is held against the stop by a hand screw (3). A spring-loaded back-up pin (4) is locked during the milling operation by the hand screw (5). Two straps clamp the part to the fixture.

Straddle Milling Nonrigid Flanges. The fixture of Fig. 7-30 is designed to support the nonrigid flanges of an aluminum casting while straddle- and face-milling bosses on the flanges. Predrilled holes position the part which bears on surfaces milled in the fixture of Fig. 7-12.

Tapered slots in a plate (1) hold the flanges against screw clamps (2). The balanced cutting action of the straddle-milling cutters holds the center flange during the cutting. The wide clamps (3) with two bearing points hold the casting against the support pads (4). A cutter-set block (5) at the end of the fixture positions the cutters.

A Face-milling Fixture with Equalizers. The milling fixture of Fig. 7-31 incorporates equalizing supports and clamps which maintain location and rigid support necessary for the successful milling of the part.

The supports are of two types, the positive and the spring-actuated adjustable type. Since three points establish a plane, three supports are required to locate a workpiece in a plane parallel to, or on the flat surface of, a fixture. Positive location in one plane is achieved with two fixed supports (1) and two equalizing adjustable supports (2). The latter are connected by a pivot bar with the result that should one be depressed, the other must rise.

At the ends of the workpiece, adjustable spring-loaded supports (3) prevent the part from being distorted by tool pressure. After the part has been located and clamped, these supports are locked in position with hand screws (4).

The part is located centrally on the fixture by eight diamond-shaped locating pins (5) which enter holes in the part. These pins permit a small amount of mislocation in a longitudinal direction but little or no variation in crosswise hole spacing.

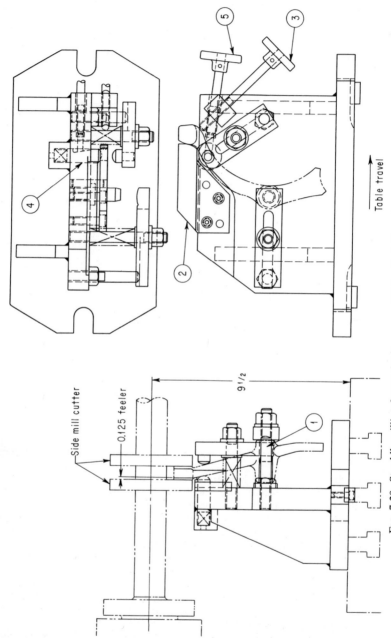

Side mill cutter

0.125 feeler

9¹/₂

Table travel

FIG. 7-29. Straddle-milling fixture for lever arm. (*Fisher Body Div., General Motors Corp.*)

7–28

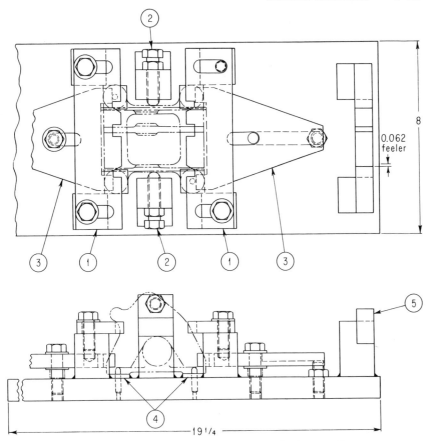

FIG. 7-30. Milling of nonrigid flanges on an aluminum casting.

Two sets of equalizing clamps (6) on each side of the part are attached to clamping levers (7) by shoulder screws. Each pair of clamps is connected by a shaft having right-hand threads on one end and left-hand threads on the other, providing independent clamping.

A cutter set block (not shown) is incorporated in one block containing the end supports.

Fixture keys are provided for aligning the fixture on the machine table, as are slots for T bolts to hold the fixture on the table.

Automatic Clamping-and-unloading Fixture. The fixture of Fig. 7-32 is of the automatic clamping-and-unloading type operated by hand. It consists of a base (1) and a trolley assembly (2) riding in guides within the fixture. One guide or gib (3) has a cam surface. The opposite (6) gib is wedge-shaped and can be moved to adjust the fit and to contact pressure of the rollers (4) mounted to the trolley. The trolley is in two parts hinged at A and separated at B by a compression spring (5) which opens the square opening between the two members of the trolley.

As the trolley travels from left to right, the part is clamped in the square opening for milling. When it is moved farther to the right, the two jaws formed by the trolley members are opened by the spring, releasing their grip on the part, which

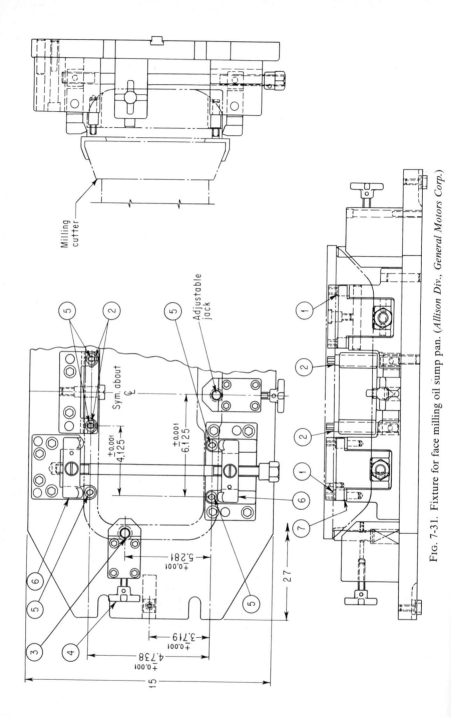

Milling cutter

Adjustable jack

Sym. about ℄

$4.125^{+0.001}_{0.000}$

$6.125^{+0.001}_{0.000}$

$5.281^{+0.001}_{0.000}$

$3.719^{+0.001}_{0.000}$

$4.738^{+0.001}_{0.000}$

27

15

Fig. 7-31. Fixture for face milling oil sump pan. (*Allison Div., General Motors Corp.*)

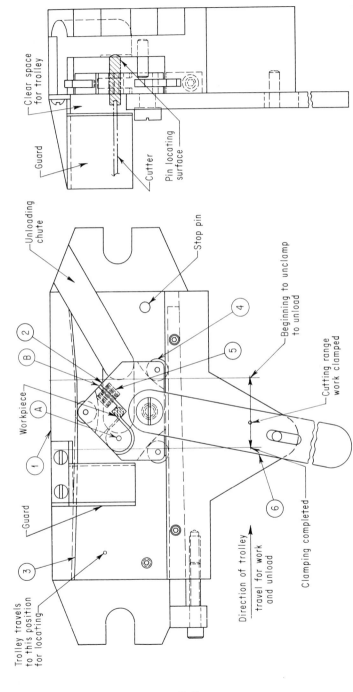

Clear space for trolley

Guard

Cutter

Pin locating surface

Unloading chute

Stop pin

Beginning to unclamp to unload

Cutting range work clamped

Workpiece

Guard

Clamping completed

Direction of trolley travel for work and unload

Trolley travels to this position for locating

Ⓑ

Ⓐ

①

②

③

④

⑤

⑥

Fig. 7-32. Manually operated automatic clamping and unloading of part for milling. (*Goodyear Tire & Rubber Co.*)

7–31

drops into the chute. Small variations in the diameter of the part are equalized by the spring.

The loading position of the trolley fixture is at the extreme left, where the distance between the gib surfaces for the rollers is greater than when it is in position for milling. As the trolley is moved toward the cutter to the right, this distance becomes smaller and finally remains constant through the travel of the trolley during the cutting stroke.

Movement of the trolley is controlled by a lever (6) which is under control of the operator. The milling-machine table is stationary and is used only to locate the fixture in proper position. Milling occurs during movement of the trolley.

Milling a Small Aluminum Part. Figure 7-33 shows a fixture used on a small horizontal mill. The base of the fixture (1) is keyed and bolted to the machine table. Four milling cutters are mounted on the machine arbor. The machine table is traversed parallel to the arbor to align the fixture with the cutters; then it is locked in place for the milling operation.

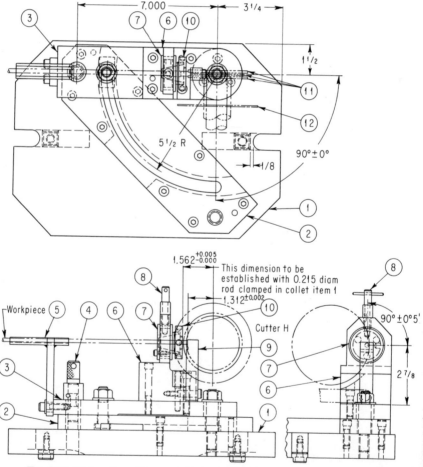

FIG. 7-33. Fixture for milling a small aluminum part. (*U.S. Naval Gun Factory.*)

The workpiece shown in Fig. 7-34 is a 0.170-in. cube with two slots milled in one face. Round-bar stock is clamped in the fixture and fed into a gang of three milling cutters. The two outer cutters straddle the bar to cut two parallel flats. The inner cutter produces a slot in the face of the workpiece midway between the flats. The workpiece is manually rotated 90° and again presented to the cutters. The second pass results in two parallel flats and a slot, all perpendicular to the cuts of the first pass. The fixture is again retracted from the cutting position, the upper element swiveled 90°, and the part cut off from the bar stock by a fourth milling cutter.

The fixture base (1) is a 1¼-in. low-carbon steel plate. A CRS locating plate (2) with a circular track is bolted and doweled to the base. A CRS swivel plate (3) is attached to the fixture base by a hex nut, washer, and stud around which the swivel plate pivots. A T bolt fastened to the swivel plate rides in the machined circular track of the locating plate and limits the travel of the swivel plate to 90°. A pin (4) locks the swivel plate in position at either end of its travel. A feed track (5) bolted to the swivel plate provides for initial alignment of the bar stock. Actual alignment to the milling cutters is dependent on a base (6), a collet assembly (7), and key (8). The bar stock is fed through the collet until it encounters a stop block (9). The collet locknut (10) is tightened to grasp and center the stock. With the stop block rotated out of the way, the machine table is traversed, presenting the bar to the three milling cutters (11). The table is retracted, the key is pulled up, and the collet is rotated 90° where it is again engaged by the key for the second milling operation. The cutoff milling cutter (12) is used after the swivel plate has been indexed and locked in its second position.

PROFILE-MILLING FIXTURES

Profile milling in two or three dimensions can be accurately done with relatively inexperienced operators whether the workpiece is flat, uniformly curved, cylindrical, spherical, or irregular in shape. Some of the machines can be used to reduce, enlarge, reverse, or invert the shape of the master at a part to master ratio of 1 to 1, or any other ratio within the limits of the machine.

In addition to a work-holding fixture, profile milling requires a master or model which guides the cutter in its path through tracer-finger contact with the master or model. For short-run setups, inexpensive masters of wood, brass, aluminum, plastics, or even cardboard may be used. The accuracy of the finished part depends upon the precision of the master. In machines using a ratio of 1 to 1, the accuracy of the part depends directly upon the accuracy of the master. When a reduction ratio is used, *i.e.,* the master is larger than the finished part, the accuracy or error is inversely proportional to the reduction ratio. For example, an error of 0.010 in. in the master would be reduced to 0.001 in. when employing a reduction ratio of 10 to 1.

When designing profile-milling masters, the designer must remember that the

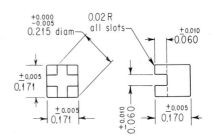

Fig. 7-34. Part made in fixture of Fig. 7-33.
(*U.S. Naval Gun Factory.*)

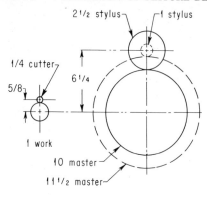

FIG. 7-35. Diagram showing relationship of cutter to stylus and work to master for profile milling.

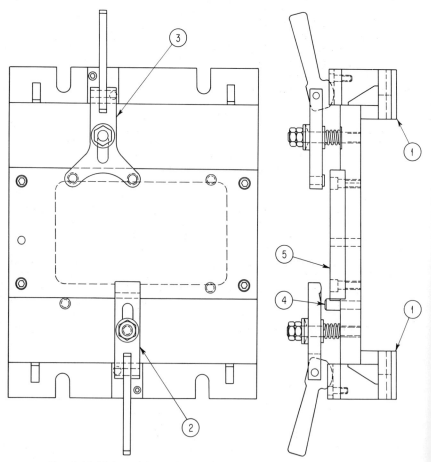

FIG. 7-36. Universal fixture for profile milling. (*Geo. Gorton Machine Co.*)

center line of the cutter follows the path of the center line of the tracer stylus. Figure 7-35 illustrates a 1-in.-diam workpiece being machined with a ¼-in.-diam cutter on a machine having a 10 to 1 reduction ratio. The path of the cutter center line describes a circle of 0.625 in. radius; therefore the stylus center line must follow a path having a radius of 6.25 in. The radius of the master depends upon the radius of the stylus. For a 1-in.-diam stylus (½ in. radius), the radius of the master would be 6.25 − 0.50 or 5.75 in. (11½ in. diam). The tracing stylus can be oversize for rough or semifinish cuts, leaving a small amount of stock on the workpiece until the finish cut is taken with a true proportional size of stylus. The diameter of the cutter limits the size of inside diameters or fillet radii which can be cut. The radius of the cutter is the minimum fillet radius that may be milled.

A technique used to reduce setup time is to key the work-holding fixture to a T slot on the work table and key the master fixture to a T slot on the copy table so that the angular or parallel location, whichever the case may be, is correct. In addition, setup holes are incorporated in the fixture and in the master or its fixture so that the machine operator may install a tracing stylus in the chuck of the work spindle as well as in the tracing stylus position; then the operator moves the work-holding fixture until the styli in the cutter spindle and tracing spindle are in the corresponding holes of the respective fixtures.

Workpieces of approximately the same size may be held in adapters in a universal fixture such as that shown in Fig. 7-36. This base fixture is positioned on the machine table by fixture keys (1) and held down by T bolts in the slots shown. Two cam-actuated clamps (2, 3) hold the blank which is positioned against the stop pins (4) and centralized on the adapter plate (5). The stop pins are in the adapter plate and located to suit the particular part.

Figure 7-37 shows an adapter plate with the outline of the blank and finished part. The cam clamps of the base fixture hold the blank while holes for the clamp

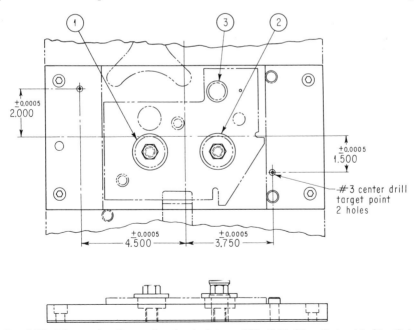

FIG. 7-37. Adapter plate for part locating in fixture of Fig. 7-36. (*Geo. Gorton Machine Co.*)

screws (1, 2) and the locating pin (3) are drilled. Two holes are drilled with a No. 3 center drill as a target point for coordinating the profile master.

A fixture for locating the profile master on the copy table is shown in Fig. 7-38. The fixture keys (1) align the fixture with the table T slots. The profile master is shown in Fig. 7-39. The master plate (1) is profiled to the shape of the workpiece and has holes and center-drill points for locating internal cutouts. The base plate (2) has dowel and cap-screw holes for locating and attaching to the master fixture. Two target points in the same location as on the adapter plate in Fig. 7-37 are provided for positioning.

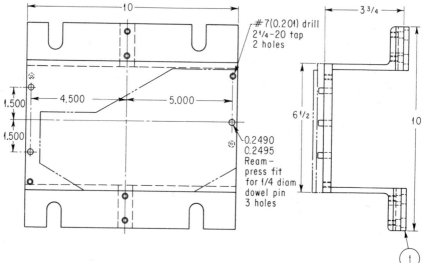

FIG. 7-38. Fixture for holding master profile template. (*Geo. Gorton Machine Co.*)

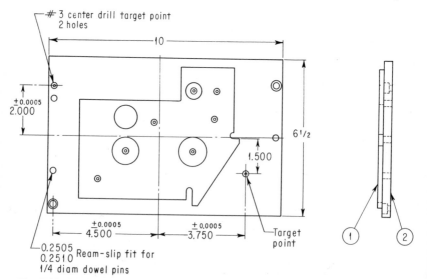

FIG. 7-39. Profile master for use in the fixture of Fig. 7-36. (*Geo. Gorton Machine Co.*)

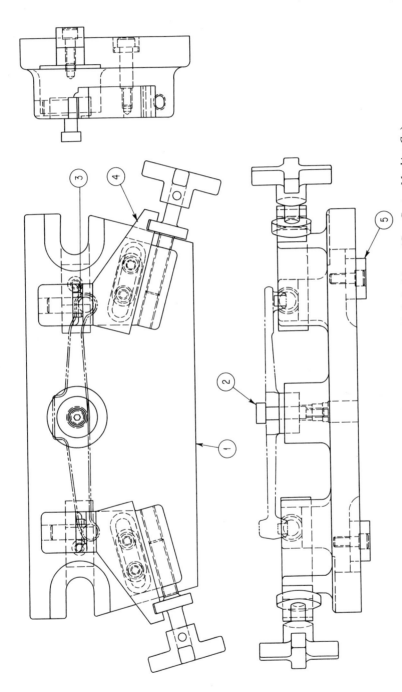

Fig. 7-40. Milling fixture to mill outside contour of belt-feed lever. (*Geo. Gorton Machine Co.*)

A fixture for milling the outside contour of a belt-feed lever is shown in Fig. 7-40. The fixture base (1) is a semisteel casting. The part is centrally located by a shoulder screw (2), and each end is clamped against a rest button (3) by a sliding clamp (4). The fixture is located on the machine table by fixture keys (5). The cutter spindle is coordinated with the tracer spindle by placing the stylus in the hole for the shoulder screw. Since the rest buttons and the supporting surface at the center are hardened, they have been relieved to clear the profile cutter. Figure 7-41 illustrates the profile master.

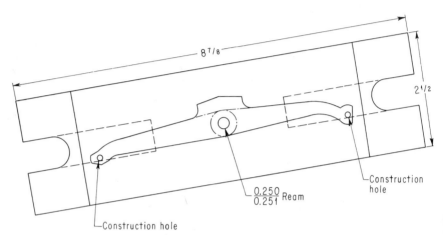

Fig. 7-41. Profile master used in the fixture of Fig. 7-40. (*Geo. Gorton Machine Co.*)

Profile Milling a Textile Machine Pawl. The parts are first located on the right-hand side of the fixture shown in Fig. 7-42 for milling clearance on the back side of the pawl.

The part is placed over the locating pin (1) and clamped with the hand screw (2) against the stop (3) until the top clamps are tightened. The hand screw is then loosened and revolved 120° to provide a clear path for the cutter. The thin cross section of the part does not provide enough rigidity, making two clamps necessary. To provide additional support, two spring-loaded pins (5) are located within each clamp (4). These support pins are locked by two vertical pins (6) through the thick washer (7) beneath the clamping nut (8).

After the parts are finished on the right-hand side of the fixture, they are placed over a pin (9) on the left-hand side to finish the cam side. A hand screw (10), which forces the part against a stop pin (11), provides temporary clamping until the top clamp (12) is tightened. The hand screw is rotated 90° to clear the cutter. The top clamp also has spring-loaded back-up pins to provide additional support.

The base of the fixture is cast iron, and the pawls rest on tool steel blocks, hardened and ground.

Milling a Slot in a Bearing Half. The simple hand-operated fixture of Fig. 7-43 holds half a bronze bearing for the milling of a slot at an 80° angular distance.

The workpiece is located on its ID by a half-round locator, while round rest pads locate its edges and end.

A hinged half-round clamp (6), made in two parts, clamps the workpiece at both ends. The space between the clamps, lined with nylon strips (5) to prevent damage to the workpiece, allows for milling-cutter travel. The strap clamp (7) applies pres-

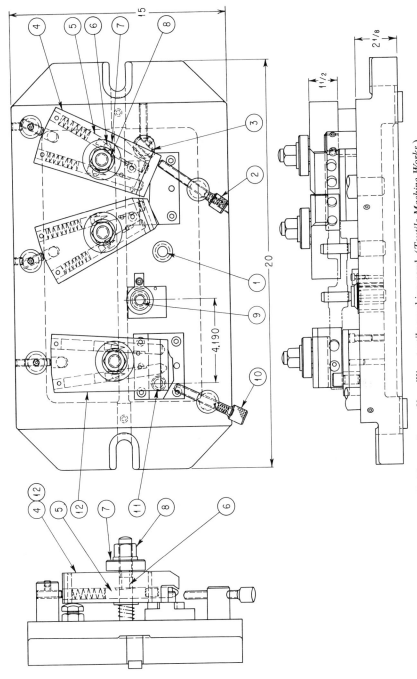

Fɪɢ. 7-42. Fixture for profile-milling textile-machine pawl. (*Textile Machine Works.*)

7–39

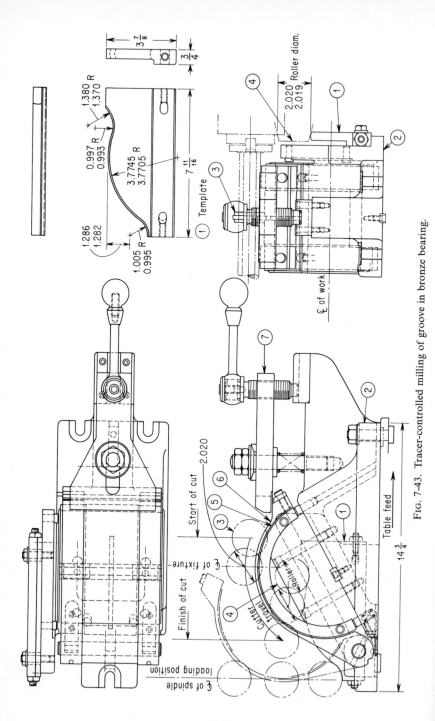

FIG. 7-43. Tracer-controlled milling of groove in bronze bearing.

3 7/8

3/4

1.380 R
1.370

0.997 R
0.993

3.7745 R
3.7705

7 11/16

1.286
1.282

1.005 R
0.995

① Template

2.020 Roller diam.
2.019

℄ of work

2.020

Start of cut

℄ of fixture

Finish of cut

Roller

Cutter

Table feed

14 3/4

℄ of spindle

loading position

7–40

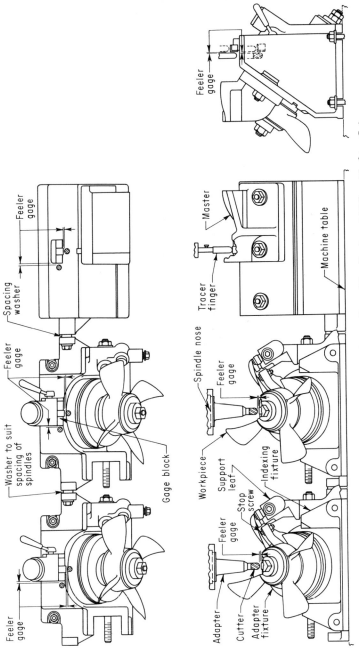

FIG. 7-44. Fixture for profile milling of propellers. (*The Cincinnati Milling Machine Co.*)

sure to the two lined clamps and, for loading and unloading, is rotated and retracted. It is held open by spring pressure.

A cam or template (1) attached to the fixture body (2) guides the milling cutter (3) by means of a roller follower (4) mounted on the spindle carrier of the machine.

The relations shown of the cutter, rollers, and fixture and the locating and clamping areas are good layout practice and check the final design and details.

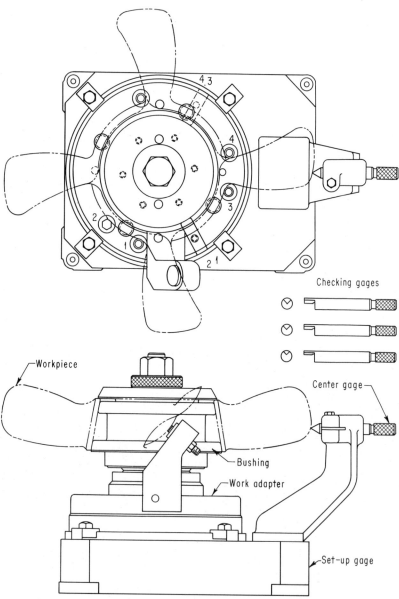

Checking gages

Center gage

Workpiece

Bushing

Work adapter

Set-up gage

FIG. 7-45. Setup gage for fixture of Fig. 7-44. (*The Cincinnati Milling Machine Co.*)

Profile Milling of Propellers. Two propellers are milled simultaneously in the fixture of Fig. 7-44, thus halving the milling time.

Each propeller is held in a separate fixture for alignment of each fixture under its own milling-cutter spindle and of the master to the tracer finger. After alignment, the three fixtures are bolted together. Spacing washers of suitable thickness maintain alignment for this and recurrent setups.

The workpiece is located on its hub diameter and against a locating screw and a supporting jack for each blade to be milled. Each blade is located against a stop screw and a leaf support. Each blade is indexed in a special four-station indexing fixture that approximately locates it horizontally. To align each fixture vertically, transversely, and longitudinally with its corresponding machine spindle, setting surfaces are provided on the top of each fixture and the master bracket. An aligning bar and a special setup tracer finger of the same diameter as the aligning bar are inserted between the machine spindles and tracer bracket.

If the milling operation is composed of a roughing and a finishing cut, a different tracer finger will be required for each type of cut. Corresponding sets of feeler gages will be required for the vertical setting but not for the transverse and longitudinal settings. These settings remain unaltered for either type of cut, because control of stock removal depends on the vertical relation of the cutter to the tracer finger.

To locate the propellers properly in the fixtures, a separate setup gage and a work adapter which fits both the setup gage and the fixture are required. The setup gage (Fig. 7-45) consists of a base and a circular table that is positioned on the base by means of dowel pins at four different stations (1 to 4). The table is held in the selected station by hook clamps.

Stations 1 and 2 are used when milling the face and back of a forward propeller, and stations 3 and 4 are used when milling the face and back of an aft propeller.

Mounted on the base of the setup gage is a bracket which holds four different plug gages. Their probe ends conform to the required settings of the propeller. These gages are characterized by the distance which the gaging point deviates from its center line. The center gage (shown in position in the fixture) sets the propeller. The others are checking gages which determine whether the stock removed from each blade is within the required limits.

The propellers are held on four work adapters required for roughing and finishing cuts on the aft and forward propellers. Each adapter has two bushings, one for roughing and the other for the finish-milling operation, and will fit in both the setup gage and the fixture.

After locating the selected adapter with the proper bushing in the setup gage, a propeller forging is placed in the adapter. The stop screw in the adapter is then adjusted until the tip of the propeller blade lines up with the gaging point in the setup gage and is then locked.

At this point the work adapter is transferred to the fixture. The propeller is repositioned in the adapter, relocated against the stop screw, and clamped in position by the large nut on the fixture stud. A leaf support is then swung into position (Fig. 7-44) for additional support of the blade. The same procedure is followed for setting the work adapter in the second fixture.

Reference

1. Andrews, C.: Vise Jaws Self-adjusting for Multiple Parts, *Machinery*, October, 1958.

Section 8

SAWING FIXTURES

By JOSEPH BENEDICT
Tool Engineer, The DoAll Co.

In contemplating the fixturing of any bandsaw, the tooling engineer should understand some of the basic principles embodied in the design of the basic band machine.

The vertical band machine is employed for straight cuts, contour cuts, or any form of outline. The tolerances can, in most applications, be held to ±0.003 in., plus the saw scratch depth. A closer tolerance can be obtained by use of a continuous band file or of an abrasive polishing band.

There are two basic types of machines, the vertical for straight and contour cuts and the horizontal for straight and angular cutoffs.

Figure 8-1 illustrates the holding forces created by the downward thrust of the saw band and the inward forces of the table feed. In many operations, this feature eliminates need for clamps. The long continuous band of cutting teeth provides a uniform force holding the part down on the worktable.

In any exploratory survey considering the use of tooling, the following factors should be thoroughly investigated prior to adapting the tooling to the bandsaw.

1. Type of material being cut
2. Size, shape, hardness, and weight of the product

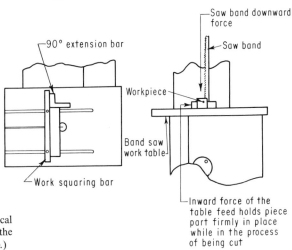

FIG. 8-1. Forces on a vertical bandsaw which help hold the workpiece. (*The DoAll Co.*)

8–1

3. Suitable locating surfaces or process holes to control dimensional tolerances
4. Thorough check of the product to see whether standard bandsaw fixturing can be used or if special fixturing should be considered

The above factors all contribute to determining the bandsaw tooth pitch, surface feet per minute, feed force, and size of machine necessary to economically perform the job. Figure 8-2 shows the minimum radius that can be cut by each width of saw band.

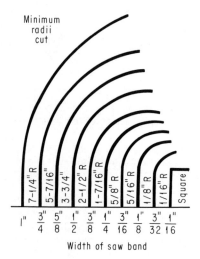

FIG. 8-2. Relationship of bandsaw width to minimum-radius cut. (*The DoAll Co.*)

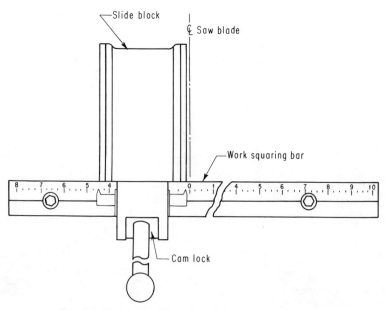

FIG. 8-3. Universal calibrated work fixture. (*The DoAll Co.*)

If a product is to be fed manually into the machine, tooling can be of a simple design and very easy to build. This type of tooling with the bandsaw has successfully proved its application on extensive production runs.

In mass production where automation is required, fixturing would be comparable to any of the standard automatic machining or workpiece-feeding mechanisms.

VERTICAL BANDSAW FIXTURES

The standard attachments of the bandsaw can be adapted to maintain good production rates on both straight and contoured cuts. Special fixtures may be necessitated by a locating surface or some controlling dimension that must be held relative to a construction hole, process area, or other workpiece feature.

Standard Attachments. There are several standard attachments for bandsaws.

The universal calibrated work fixture (Fig. 8-3) has a work squaring bar with a cam-lock locating stop which provides dimensional control for straight cuts to the right and left of the blade.

The mitering attachment (Fig. 8-4) may be adjusted from 0 to 90°. The work can be fed manually or by the power-feeding device.

Circle cutting on the bandsaw can easily be accomplished with the standard at-

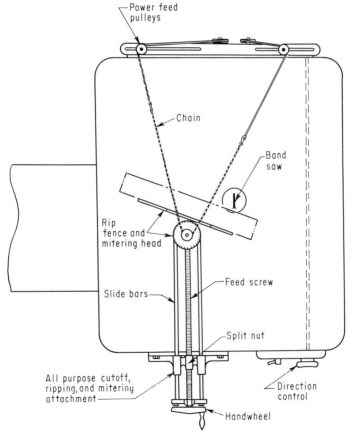

FIG. 8-4. Mitering attachment for a vertical bandsaw. (*The DoAll Co.*)

tachment shown in Fig. 8-5. This attachment is normally used in conjunction with the chain and hydraulic feed unit; however, it can be manually fed.

Figures 8-6 and 8-7 show a workpiece being sawed while held by a workholder. Power feeding is shown in Fig. 8-6 and manual feeding in Fig. 8-7.

Sawing Fixtures. Whenever a fixture is needed because of the characteristics of the workpiece, or possibly of the production rate, a single or a multiple type of fixture can be provided.

In many applications, fixtures can be manufactured of steel or aluminum. There are applications in which a wood or plastic fixture base plate is suitable to supply the necessary holding power or the support required while cutting the product. Clamps are unnecessary on most fixtures because of the downward force of the band. If the operation involves stack cutting, it is advisable to clamp the stacked workpieces to the fixture base plate. Adjustable jackscrews can be used when the

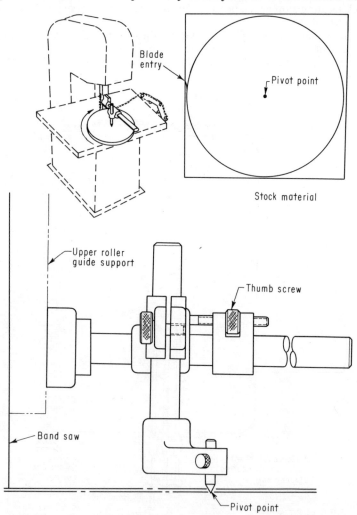

FIG. 8-5. Standard circle-cutting attachment. (*The DoAll Co.*)

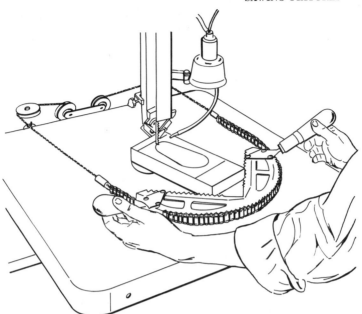

Fig. 8-6. Contour sawing with power feed. (*The DoAll Co.*)

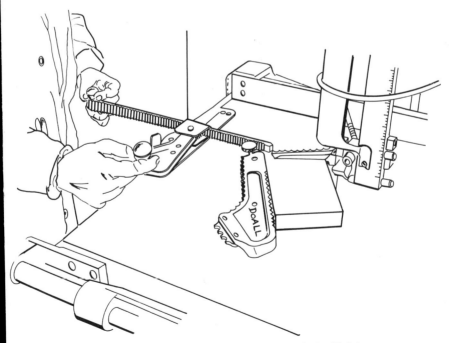

Fig. 8-7. Contour sawing with manual feed. (*The DoAll Co.*)

workpiece requires outboard support. Many variations of clamping can be adapted, depending on the stock that is to be cut. Quick-action toggle clamps are usually preferred, but for some fixtures cam locks are more suitable. Each fixture design should be determined from the stocks' characteristics and the volume of production.

The holding of cylindrical and similar-shaped workpieces is shown in Fig. 8-8. The workpiece rests on the machine table while being positioned by bevel-edged blocks. Strap clamps and long hold-down bolts are used to clamp the workpiece to the table.

Figure 8-9 illustrates a simple, quick-loading fixture for making a saw cut through the lug of a bronze casting. The base plate is made of low-carbon steel. The locator may be made of low-carbon steel, left soft or carburized and hardened, or of tool steel and heat-treated, depending upon production requirements. The

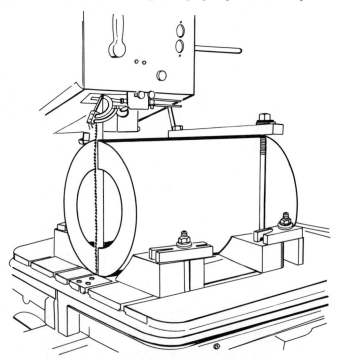

Fɪɢ. 8-8. Holding cylindrical workpieces. (*The DoAll Co.*)

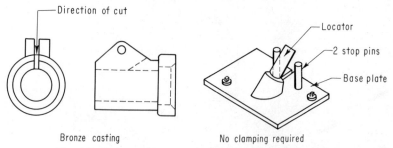

Fɪɢ. 8-9. Fixture for sawing a bronze casting. (*The DoAll Co.*)

two stop pins may be of cold-rolled steel or drill rod pressed into the base plate. Standard T bolts can be used to secure the fixture to the machine table.

A simple indexing fixture such as that shown in Fig. 8-10 may be used for applications when equally spaced slots are needed around the periphery of a product.

The fixture consists of a base plate, a locator and pivot post, and an index pin. Any suitable material can be used for the base plate. The locator is made of drill rod. The index pin is either spring-loaded or screw-actuated. The relationship of the index pin to the saw cut establishes the number of slots around the periphery.

In operation, the workpiece is placed over the locator and the first cut made. The workpiece is then rotated to the second slot position, the index pin inserted into the first slot, and the second slotting operation performed. The process is repeated for cutting the remaining slots. Depending upon the thickness of the workpiece, more than one part can be cut at one time.

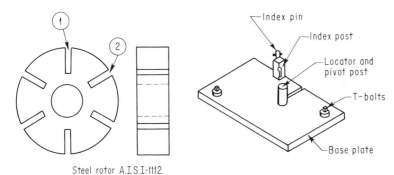

Steel rotor A.I.S.I.-1112

FIG. 8-10. Manually indexed saw fixture. (*The DoAll Co.*)

An indexing fixture for cutting a cylindrical workpiece into equal segments is shown in Fig. 8-11. A center post (2) is screwed into a tapped hole in the base plate (1). The locating sleeve (3) is held to the center post by a shoulder screw (4). For ease of rotation, a bronze sleeve bearing and a ball thrust bearing are used in the assembly. The base of the sleeve has four chamfered holes positioned 90° apart around the periphery and serves as an index plate. A spring-loaded pin locator (5) enters the holes in the index plate to correctly position the workpiece to the saw blade.

A square cavity in the top of the locating sleeve provides a flat clamping surface. A toggle clamp (6) holds the workpiece to the fixture while the cuts are made.

Sawing operations may be performed using automatically indexed and fed fixtures. These units can be independently operated or synchronized with the machine's hydraulic power unit. If an air-actuated cylinder is the source of power for the fixture, an electrical cycle control can be designed and timed with the hydraulic power unit. The table feed would operate alternately with any fixture mechanism. With an 80-psi air supply, a 2- or 3-in. cylinder usually will supply enough force to energize the index or transfer mechanisms.

Figure 8-12 illustrates an air-operated indexing fixture whose action is coordinated with the machine-table movement. With this and similar fixturing, loading and unloading systems are incorporated to achieve automatic operation.

A fixture for a series of four cutting operations on a workpiece with minimum handling is shown in Fig. 8-13. The fixture consists of a base plate, a transfer plate, and an index plate. The part locator also serves as a pivot pin for the index plate. A keyway in the workpiece locates it radially.

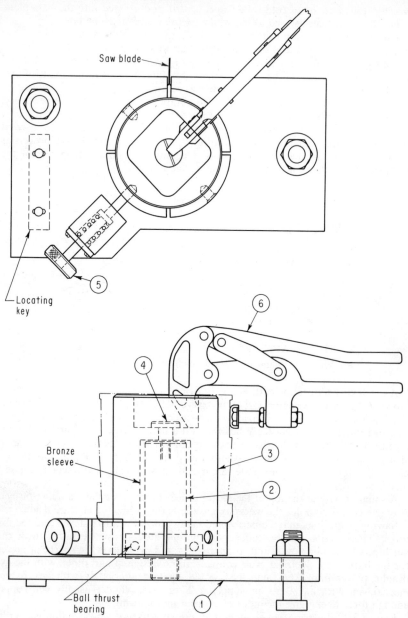

Saw blade

Locating
key

Bronze
sleeve

Ball thrust
bearing

FIG. 8-11. Fixture for sawing cylinder into circular segments. (*The DoAll Co.*)

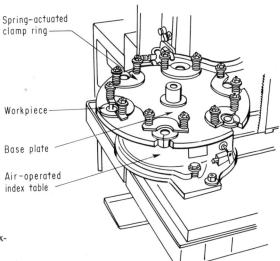

Spring–actuated clamp ring

Workpiece

Base plate

Air–operated index table

Fig. 8-12. Air-operated indexing fixture. (*The DoAll Co.*)

The transfer plate is located and guided by a gib and is positioned by a pin. The travel of the transfer plate is determined by the distance of the saw cuts from each other. The index plate and pin position the workpiece radially.

A fixture for holding a workpiece while making three cuts in a workpiece without removing it from the fixture is shown in Fig. 8-14. The fixture consists of a base plate, a round locator, a positive stop, a clamping device, and a spacer block.

In operation, the universal calibrated work fixture of Fig. 8-3 is placed on the machine table. The right-angle extension bar is set to saw cut 2 with the fixture base of Fig. 8-14 against the extension bar. The spacer bar is placed between the fixture and extension bar for cut 1. The fixture is rotated 180° and located against the extension bar, and the third cut is made. The fixture is designed so that the distance from cut 2 to the edge of the fixture is the same as from cut 3 to the opposite edge; thus the position of the extension bar need not be changed.

Figure 8-15 illustrates the use of power feed in generating a contoured slot. The fixture is mounted on a saw table with automatic infeed and retraction. Two cuts are required in the production sequence. A shuttle plate moves the workpiece to the starting position of each cut. A pivoting plate rotates the workpiece during the second cut.

The CRS base plate is profiled, drilled, and tapped as required. A shuttle plate (2) secured to a pivot plate (3) by gibs (4) is moved to the saw blade by an air cylinder. A locating block (5) and a nest (6) support the workpiece against the pressure of two clamping cylinders (7). The pivot plate (3) is revolved by the pivoting cylinder (9) about the axis, which is fixed by the pivot shoulder screw (8). Adjustable stops (10) limit shuttle and pivoting motion.

The saw table cycles in and out during the straight cut. The shuttle plate moves the workpiece to the starting point of the second cut. The infeed and retraction cycle for the second cut is coordinated with the rotation of the pivoted plate to cut to the required contour.

The air-actuated fixture of Fig. 8-16 was designed to obtain a maximum production rate with minimum operator attention. This fixture is completely automatic in operation except for the loading of each stack of five bars. The air cyl-

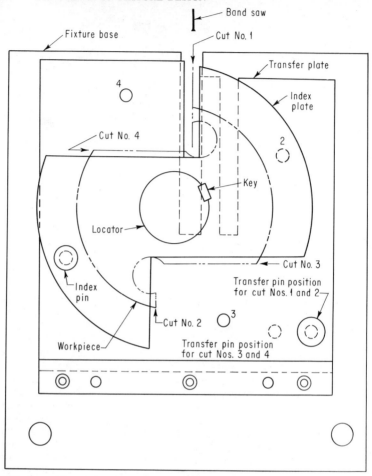

FIG. 8-13. Saw with an index plate and transfer plate for making four saw cuts. (*The DoAll Co.*)

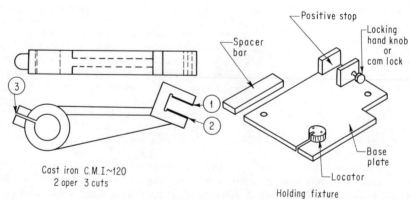

FIG. 8-14. Fixture for making three saw cuts in one setup. (*The DoAll Co.*)

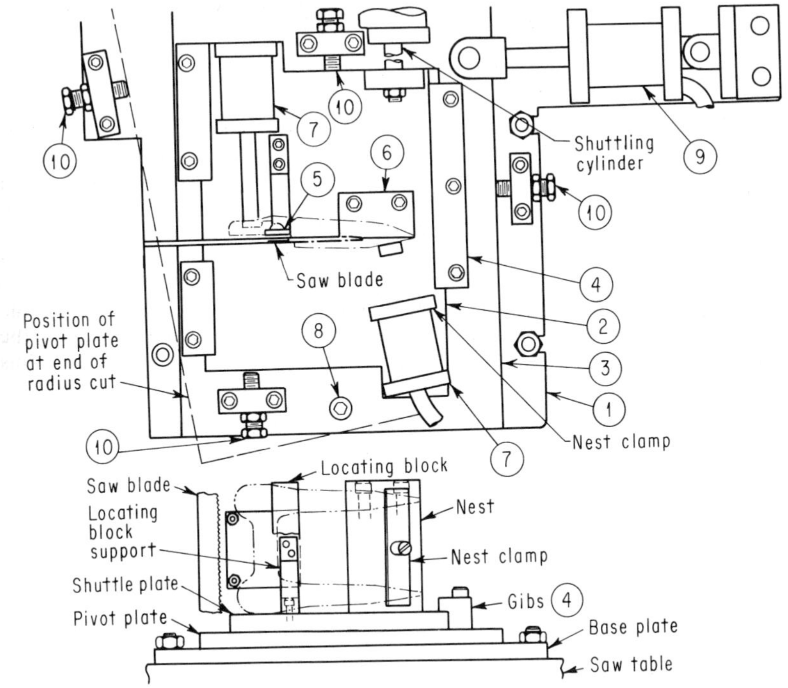

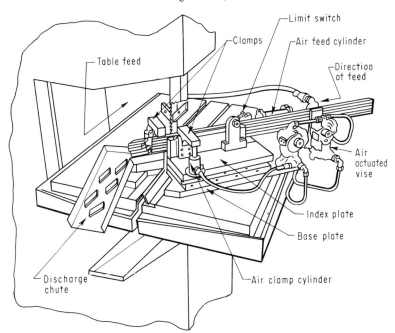

Shuttling cylinder

Saw blade

Position of pivot plate at end of radius cut

Nest clamp

Saw blade
Locating block support
Shuttle plate
Pivot plate
Locating block
Nest
Nest clamp
Gibs (4)
Base plate
Saw table

FIG. 8-15. Slotting fixture. (*The DoAll Co.*)

Limit switch
Clamps
Air feed cylinder
Table feed
Direction of feed
Air actuated vise
Index plate
Base plate
Discharge chute
Air clamp cylinder

FIG. 8-16. Air-operated feeding and clamping devices on a bar-stock-sawing fixture. (*The DoAll Co.*)

inder actuating the stock-feeding mechanism is synchronized with the table feed by solenoid controlled valves.

In operation, the bar stock is pushed into the fixture with the index table in the forward position. The air-actuated clamps and vise are closed for the first cut. The clamps are released, the index table is moved back, and the clamp on the table closes while the air-actuated vise releases its grip on the bars. The clamp ahead of the saw does not close until the index table returns to the forward position. This allows the cutoff pieces to be pushed ahead by the advancing bar stock.

The principle of the circle-cutting attachment of Fig. 8-5 is used in the fixture of Fig. 8-17. Two pivot points are provided. With the pivot plate on the 2⅛-in.-radius point, the workpiece edge is partially cut. The workpiece is then inverted, and the opposite edge is partially cut to the same radius. The pivot plate is moved to the 1-in.-radius point, and the workpiece is again inverted. The resultant 1-in.-radius

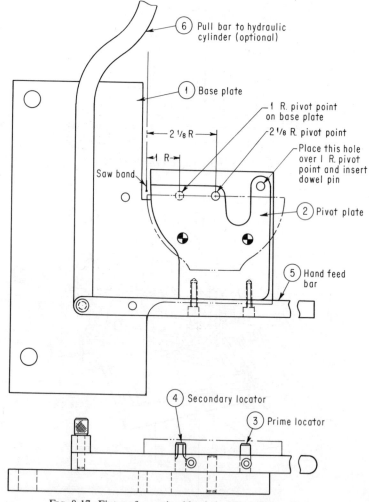

FIG. 8-17. Fixture for cutting blended radii. (*The DoAll Co.*)

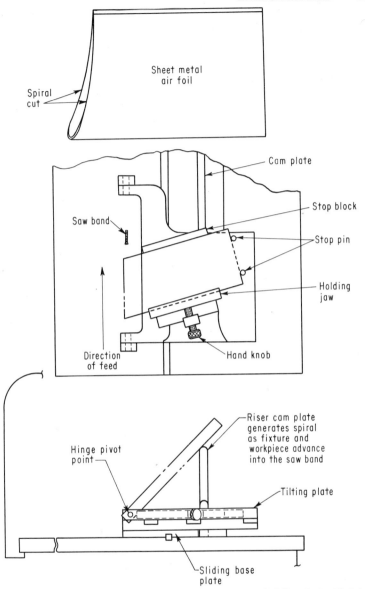

Sheet metal
air foil

Spiral
cut

Cam plate

Stop block

Saw band

Stop pin

Holding
jaw

Direction
of feed

Hand knob

Riser cam plate
generates spiral
as fixture and
workpiece advance
into the saw band

Hinge pivot
point

Tilting plate

Sliding base
plate

FIG. 8-18. Pivoting-plate fixture cuts spiral surface on an air foil. (*The DoAll Co.*)

cut blends into the partial 2⅛-in.-radius cut. One last inversion of the workpiece permits finishing of the opposite edge.

The fixture base plate (1) is drilled for mounting to a saw table and has two bored holes fixing the pivot points. The pivot plate (2) has two locating pins (3, 4) which fix the location of the workpiece. A hand-feed bar (5) permits manual operation, and an optional pull bar (6) is provided for hydraulic actuation. The 2⅛-in.-

radius pivot pin is pressed into the base plate. A dowel pin is inserted into the 1-in.-radius point for the second portion of the production sequence and is removed when the pivot plate is returned to the 2⅛-in. pivot point.

The locating pins can be replaced with longer pins to permit the stacking of parts during the operation.

A Contour-cutting Fixture. The geometry of a product and the production rate are two of the factors to consider in designing contour-cutting fixtures for the bandsaw. Another important factor is that the position of the pivot point controls the contour of the part. The center line of the fixture's pivot point must be at 90° or parallel to the leading edge of the band's cutting edge. Any variation from this location will result in an undesired workpiece contour. It will also cause binding and scoring of the bandsaw. Figure 8-5 illustrates the cutting of circles with cylindrical sides at 90° angles to the base and with the pivot point at a 90° angle to the bandsaw. If the sides were to be tapered, the part would be pivoted along and parallel to the bandsaw, as well as having a pivot point at a 90° angle to the band.

The fixture of Fig. 8-18 produces a spiral surface with a bandsaw. A hinged pivot point is located on the true center line of the saw. The vertex of the tilting plane is always on the center line of the hinge pin. A vertical plate cam rotates the tilting plate a specified number of degrees for each inch of forward movement; this action produces the desired spiral.

HORIZONTAL BANDSAW FIXTURES

The fixturing of the horizontal bandsaw is usually limited to straight cuts on mill or structural shapes. Although many variations of straight cuts can be obtained, a

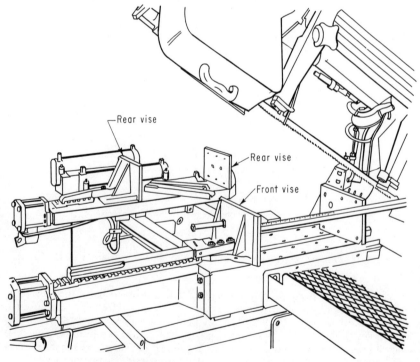

FIG. 8-19. Clamping arrangement on a horizontal bandsaw. (*The DoAll Co.*)

standard vise is used for most applications. Fixtures and other holding devices may be designed to accommodate special conditions.

Special jaws may be used on standard vises to firmly grip round, hexagonal, or irregularly shaped bar stock. Should the workpiece be other than a mill shape, such as a forging or a casting, automatic feeding and transfer fixtures can be designed.

Figure 8-19 illustrates a horizontal bandsawing machine with an automatic stock-feeding device. The workpiece is gripped by the rear vise which moves forward to the cutting position. Both vises grip the work at this position and during the cutting operation. Roller supports assist in feeding the work.

The clamping of round or tubular stock is shown in Fig. 8-20. An air cylinder pressing on the top of the stock holds it securely between the vise jaws.

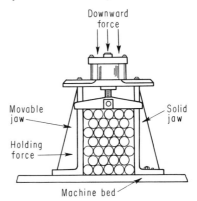

FIG. 8-20. Horizontal bandsaw fixture for stack-cutting bar stock. (*The DoAll Co.*)

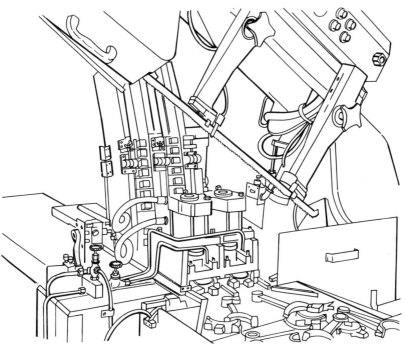

FIG. 8-21. Automatic splitting of connecting rods on a horizontal bandsaw. (*The DoAll Co.*)

Workpieces are manually loaded into two vertical-loading chutes, as shown in Fig. 8-21. The automatic fixture moves two pieces per stroke into the cutting position, where the ends of the two workpieces are split by the saw. The workpieces are held down by air cylinders during the sawing operation.

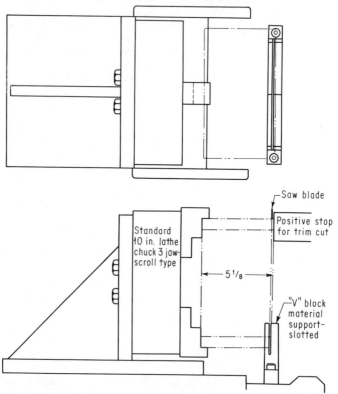

FIG. 8-22. Sawing fixture incorporating standard-lathe chuck. (*The DoAll Co.*)

A standard three-jaw lathe chuck to hold 9-in.-diam tubing for slicing off sections is shown in Fig. 8-22. The chuck is mounted on an angle plate. The stock is brought to the machine in pieces 5⅛ in. long, clamped by the chuck jaws, and the fixture is manually advanced to a positive stop. The machine makes a trim cut to finish the rough end of the raw stock, retracts the saw blade, advances the fixture 0.945 in., and then cuts through the stock, repeating the cycle until five pieces are cut. The 0.045-in. saw kerf will result in pieces approximately 0.900 in. wide. The stock remaining in the chuck is manually reversed and the final cut made.

A V block slotted to clear the saw blade supports the stock against the downward force of the saw blade.

Section 9
BROACHING FIXTURES

By WALTER D. BRISTOW*

Tool Designer, Caterpillar Tractor Co.

For successful broaching, all elements of the broached surface must remain parallel with the broach axis; there must be no obstructions in the plane of the broached surfaces; and the walls of the part being broached must be sufficiently heavy or adequately supported to withstand the pressures of the operation. Compliance with these prerequisites makes broaching-fixture design more exacting and difficult than the design of many other types of fixtures.

The broaching-fixture designer should have a layout of each broaching machine in his plant, similar to those shown later in this section. Over this layout, the designer can make a sketch showing the important parts of the fixture, the workpiece, the broach bar, the machine elements related to the setup, and the necessary accessories such as pullers, broach-bar ends, retrievers, etc. From this layout, the fixture designer can determine the clearances necessary for the broach bar or broach-bar holder.

Because of the high pressures involved in the broaching operation, the workpiece should be supported by fixed stops (positive locking cams or wedges with locking angles), never directly by air or hydraulic pressure. Pneumatic or hydraulic cylinders or machine-table devices should be used only to move clamps or back-up devices into position.

To estimate the broaching force or pull in pounds, the following formulas may be used:

For round broaches

$$P = K\pi DTC \tag{1}$$

For surface broaching

$$P = KLTC \tag{2}$$

For spline broaches

$$P = KSWTC \tag{3}$$

* The author gratefully acknowledges the contributions of the members of Peoria Chapter No. 31, ASTME: Edmond E. Canfield, Tool Designer, Hyster Co.; Walter Fischbacher, Planning Manager, Le Tourneau Westinghouse Corp.; Howard Poland, Tool Design Supervisor, Le Tourneau–Westinghouse Corp.; Caterpillar Tractor Co.: Don Frantz, Tool Designer; Gunter K. Gersbach, Staff Engineer; Otto E. Gunthner, Supervisor Tool Design; Carl A. Holmer, Chief Tool Designer; Gerald H. Ohrt, Tool Designer; Walter J. Peters, Tool Designer; Kenneth E. Starr, Mfg. Development; Leslie B. Wilson, Tool Designer.

where P = broaching pressure or pull required, lb

$\quad K$ = a constant taken from Table 9-1

$\quad D$ = finished diameter of hole, in.

$\quad T$ = number of teeth cutting at one time

$\quad C$ = stock removed per tooth; on round and spline broaches, one-half the difference of two succeeding tooth diameters

$\quad L$ = length of contact of each cutting edge, in.

$\quad S$ = number of splines

$\quad W$ = width of spline, in.

TABLE 9-1. Constants K for Determining Broaching Forces *

Aluminum	50,000
Cast iron	350,000
Bronze	350,000
Mild steel	450,000
Steel castings	450,000
SAE 1010 to 2512	450,000
SAE 3115 to 4615	550,000
SAE 4820, 8620, 8622	550,000
SAE 5120 to 6195	600,000

* For application in Eqs. (1) to (3).

FIXTURE DESIGN FOR BROACHING KEYWAYS

Keyways are successfully broached on both horizontal and vertical machines. The horizontal machine uses a conventional broach bar requiring one or two passes to complete the keyway. Some of the vertical machines use a special cutter bar which is automatically reciprocated and fed into the required keyway depth. The complexity of the fixtures required to hold the part usually reflect the intricacy of the part.

A fixture for cutting keyways is often a simple plate, plug, or horn which establishes the correct position of the workpiece in relation to the broach bar and machine faceplate.

Keyway Broaching Fixture Layout. A layout related to the machine, broach bar, fixture, and workpiece is shown in Fig. 9-1. Table 9-2 gives the dimensions for standard keyway broaches.

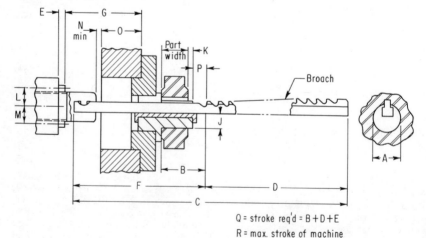

Q = stroke req'd = B + D + E

R = max. stroke of machine

Fig. 9-1. Layout for keyway-broaching machine.

TABLE 9-2. Dimensions for Standard Keyway Broaches*

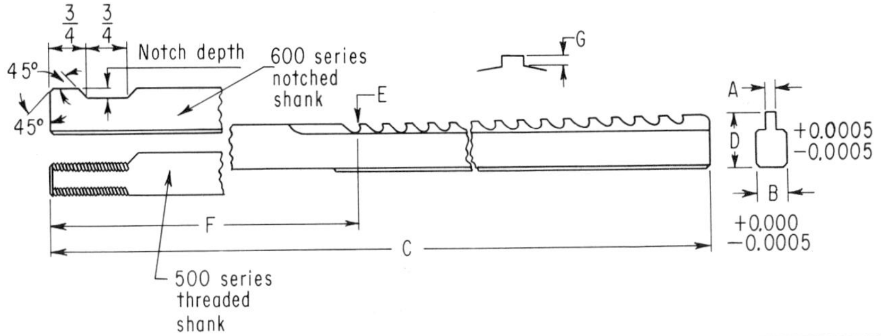

Broach number†	Min. hole size	Min. length cut	Max. length cut	A‡ Nom. dim.	A‡ Dec. dim.	B, width of back	C, total length	D, height last tooth	E, height starting tooth	F, length of shank	G, key-way depth¶	No. of cuts	Thread size, 500 series	Notch depth, 600 series
01	3/8	3/8	1 1/4	1/16	0.0635	0.1552	20	0.313	0.271	7 13/16	0.042	1	1/4-20	1/16
02	7/16	1/2	1 1/2	3/32	0.0948	0.1865	24	0.367	0.309	8 1/4	0.058	1	5/16-18	1/16
03	5/8	5/8	2 1/2	3/32	0.0948	0.249	33	0.491	0.433	10	0.058	1	3/8-16	1/16
04	1/2	1/2	1 1/2	1/8	0.126	0.249	30	0.438	0.364	9	0.074	1	3/8-16	1/16
05	7/8	5/8	2 1/2	1/8	0.126	0.3115	36	0.594	0.520	10	0.074	1	1/2-13	1/8
06	19/32	1/2	1 1/2	5/32	0.1572	0.249	30	0.525	0.436	9	0.089	1	3/8-16	1/8
07	23/32	5/8	2 1/2	5/32	0.1572	0.3115	33	0.625	0.536	10	0.089	1	1/2-13	1/8
08	11/16	5/8	2 1/2	3/16	0.1885	0.374	36	0.581	0.476	10	0.105	1	1/2-13	1/8
09	15/16	11/16	3 1/2	3/16	0.1885	0.374	36	0.796	0.691	10 11/16	0.105	1	1/2-13	1/8
10	11/16	5/8	2 1/2	7/32	0.2198	0.374	33	0.557	0.437	10	0.120	1	1/2-13	1/8
11	15/16	11/16	3 1/2	7/32	0.2198	0.374	42	0.813	0.693	11 1/16	0.120	1	1/2-13	1/8
12	11/16	5/8	2 1/2	1/4	0.251	0.374	36	0.612	0.476	10	0.136	1	1/2-13	1/8
13	1	11/16	4	1/4	0.251	0.499	45	0.877	0.741	11 13/16	0.136	1	5/8-11	1/8
14	1 7/16	7/8	6	1/4	0.251	0.624	51	1.250	1.114	13 1/2	0.136	1	3/4-10	7/32
15	7/8	11/16	4	9/32	0.2828	0.499	42	0.716	0.564	11 5/8	0.152	1	5/8-11	1/8
16	1 1/4	7/8	6	9/32	0.2828	0.499	51	1.093	0.941	13 1/2	0.152	1	5/8-11	3/16
17	1	11/16	4	5/16	0.314	0.499	45	0.908	0.741	11 13/16	0.167	1	5/8-11	1/8
18	1 5/16	7/8	6	5/16	0.314	0.499	51	1.158	0.991	13 1/2	0.167	1	5/8-11	3/16
19	1 1/16	11/16	4	3/8	0.3765	0.499	45	0.938	0.739	11 13/16	0.199	1	5/8-11	1/8
20	1 5/16	7/8	6	3/8	0.3765	0.499	54	1.189	0.990	13 1/2	0.199	1	5/8-11	3/16
21	1 9/16	11/16	4	7/16	0.439	0.624	48	1.390	1.160	12	0.230	1	3/4-10	7/32
22	2	1	8	7/16	0.439	0.624	48	1.611	1.496	15 5/8	0.230	2	3/4-10	7/32
23	1 1/2	11/16	4	1/2	0.5015	0.624	48	1.312	1.051	12	0.261	1	3/4-10	7/32
24	1 1/2	1	8	1/2	0.5015	0.624	48	1.377	1.246	16 1/2	0.261	2	3/4-10	7/32
25	1 3/4	11/16	4	9/16	0.5645	0.6865	54	1.438	1.146	11 13/16	0.292	1	1-8	7/32
26	1 5/8	1	8	9/16	0.5645	0.6865	51	1.391	1.245	16	0.292	2	1-8	7/32
27	2 1/4	1 1/8	12	9/16	0.5645	0.874	60	1.641	1.495	20	0.292	2	1-8	7/32
28	1 7/8	11/16	4	5/8	0.627	0.749	60	1.625	1.301	12 3/16	0.324	1	1-8	7/32
29	2 1/2	1	8	5/8	0.627	0.874	54	1.657	1.495	16 3/8	0.324	2	1-8	7/32
30	2 1/4	1 1/8	12	5/8	0.627	0.874	57	1.657	1.495	20	0.324	2	1-8	7/32
31	1 7/8	11/16	4	3/4	0.752	0.874	60	1.625	1.239	12 3/16	0.386	1	1-8	7/32
32	2	1	8	3/4	0.752	0.999	60	1.688	1.495	16 1/4	0.386	2	1 1/4-7	7/32
33	2 1/4	1 1/8	12	3/4	0.752	0.999	57	1.688	1.560	20	0.386	3	1 1/4-7	7/32
34	2 1/4	11/16	4	7/8	0.877	1.124	63	1.875	1.426	12 3/8	0.449	1	1 1/4-7	7/32
35	2 1/4	1	8	7/8	0.877	1.124	63	1.719	1.494	15 3/4	0.449	2	1 1/4-7	7/32
36	2 1/4	1 1/8	12	7/8	0.877	1.124	63	1.719	1.569	20	0.449	3	1 1/4-7	7/32
37	2 1/4	5/8	2 1/2	1	1.002	1.249	63	1.750	1.239	10 1/2	0.511	1	1 1/2-6	7/32
38	2 1/4	7/8	6	1	1.002	1.249	63	1.750	1.494	14 1/4	0.511	2	1 1/2-6	7/32
39	2 1/4	1 1/8	12	1	1.002	1.249	60	1.750	1.580	20	0.511	3	1 1/2-6	7/32

* All dimensions are in inches.
† Add prefix 5 for threaded shank and 6 for notched shank.
‡ Tolerance is ±0.0002 in. for numbers 01 to 24 inclusive, ±0.0003 in. for the remainder.
¶ Keyway depth at side of slot is indicated. See Table 9-3 for allowances along center line.

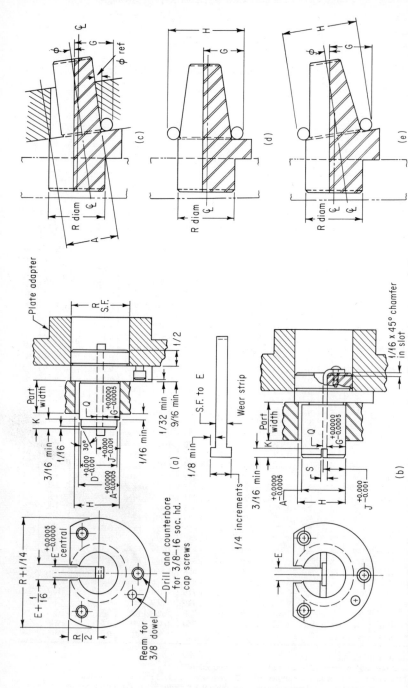

Fig. 9-2. Keyway broaching horns: (*a*) horn design with wear strips over ⅛ in. thick; (*b*) horn design with wear strips under ⅛ in. thick; (*c*) horn for angular keyway; (*d*) horn for keyway parallel to center line in tapered hole; (*e*) horn for keyway parallel to taper in tapered hole.

Dimensions G, L, M, O, and R are obtained from the machine or machine specifications. Dimension E, the amount of stroke lost by the setup or the distance the forward stop is set back from its maximum forward position, will vary according to broach shank length, part thickness, fixture thickness, etc.

Dimension P depends upon the method of loading the part of the fixture. If the part is slipped over the broach, P must be not less than the part width. If the broach shank is fed through the part after it is on the fixture, then P is ½ in. minimum. If the broach has a loading step, dimension P may be a minimum of ½ in.

Dimension L-M is the adjustment of the sliding head on the ram face above and below the ram center line. This feature reduces the need for the center line of the horn to be below the center line of the ram or faceplate mounting hole.

The required stroke Q of the machine equals $B + D + E$, which should equal not more than the maximum machine stroke minus 1 in.

The minimum hole size given in Table 9-2 allows the part to pass over the last tooth on the broach bar. If the hole in the workpiece is smaller than this dimension, the plug will be fragile and difficult to make.

If the keyway must be broached in more than one pass, a shim or a thicker wear strip is placed under the broach, and the pull head is adjusted upwards to level the broach bar.

Keyway Broaching Horns. The broaching of keyways and other internal shapes commonly requires the use of horns to hold the broach in correct relationship to the work. Since the hole through the machine faceplate has a large diameter, the fixture horns are mounted to a faceplate adapter. This adapter has an extension on one side to fit the hole in the machine faceplate and a through hole to accommodate the fixture plug. The adapter is cap-screwed and dowel-pinned to the machine but easily removed for other adapters.

Figure 9-2 illustrates the design of fixture horns for broaching keyways. To minimize wear on the broach bar and to adjust the depth of the keyway after broach sharpening, a wear strip is used. This wear strip may be of heat-treated steel for maximum wear resistance or of a hard bronze, although chips may become embedded in the bronze strip making it unsatisfactory. View a of Fig. 9-2 shows the design of wear strips over ⅛ in. thick and view b of those under ⅛ in. thick. The minimum thickness of a wear strip is about 0.050 in. A wear strip is not used when the slot would make the plug too thin.

The best material for fixture plugs is a nondeforming tool steel. The guide slot is machined to size before hardening, necessitating grinding only on diameters and the faces of the mounting flange.

Recommended dimensions and specifications for the design of Fig. 9-2 are:

$A = $ low limit of part

$H = $ height of keyway on part (see Fig. 9-3 and Table 9-3)

$D = A - 0.003$ (do not use lead when tolerance on hole is over 0.001 in.)

$E = 0.001$ in. over high limit of broach-bar width

$F = 1.5\ (A - J)$ or ¼ in. min when A is under 1 in.

            ½ in. min when A is 1 to 2 in.

            ¾ in. min when A is over 2 in.

$G = J - Q$

$J = H$ minus height of last tooth (D of Table 9-2) minus 0.002 in.

$Q = $ ⅛ in. min, ¼ when possible

$R = $ snug-fit in hole in faceplate adapter

$S = $ next fraction over wear-strip thickness

$U = $ No. 8-32 screw or larger when possible

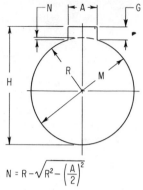

$$N = R - \sqrt{R^2 - \left(\frac{A}{2}\right)^2}$$

$$H = M + G - N$$

FIG. 9-3. Calculating keyway height.

TABLE 9-3. Chord Rise N for Calculating Keyway Depths*†

M diameter	Key width A												
	1/16	3/32	1/8	5/32	3/16	7/32	1/4	5/16	3/8	7/16	1/2	5/8	3/4
1/4	0.004	0.009	0.016										
3/8	0.003	0.006	0.011	0.017	0.025								
1/2	0.002	0.004	0.008	0.013	0.018	0.025	0.032						
5/8	0.001	0.003	0.006	0.010	0.014	0.019	0.025	0.041					
3/4	0.001	0.003	0.005	0.008	0.012	0.016	0.022	0.034	0.051				
7/8	0.001	0.002	0.004	0.007	0.010	0.014	0.017	0.028	0.042	0.058			
1	0.001	0.002	0.004	0.006	0.009	0.012	0.015	0.024	0.036	0.050	0.067		
1 1/8	.....	0.002	0.003	0.005	0.008	0.011	0.013	0.021	0.032	0.044	0.058	0.095	
1 1/4	.....	0.002	0.003	0.005	0.007	0.010	0.012	0.019	0.029	0.039	0.052	0.084	0.125
1 1/2	.....	0.001	0.002	0.004	0.006	0.008	0.011	0.016	0.024	0.032	0.042	0.068	0.100
1 3/4	.....	0.001	0.002	0.003	0.005	0.007	0.009	0.014	0.020	0.027	0.038	0.059	0.084
2	.....	0.001	0.002	0.003	0.004	0.006	0.008	0.012	0.017	0.024	0.031	0.050	0.073
2 1/4	.....	.....	0.002	0.003	0.004	0.005	0.007	0.010	0.015	0.021	0.028	0.044	0.065
2 1/2	.....	.....	0.002	0.003	0.004	0.005	0.006	0.009	0.014	0.019	0.025	0.040	0.057
2 3/4	.....	.....	.....	0.002	0.003	0.004	0.005	0.008	0.013	0.017	0.023	0.036	0.052
3	.....	.....	.....	0.002	0.003	0.004	0.005	0.008	0.011	0.016	0.021	0.033	0.046
3 1/4	.....	.....	.....	0.001	0.002	0.003	0.004	0.007	0.011	0.014	0.019	0.030	0.044
3 1/2	.....	.....	.....	.....	0.002	0.003	0.004	0.007	0.010	0.013	0.018	0.027	0.041
3 3/4	.....	.....	.....	.....	0.001	0.002	0.004	0.006	0.009	0.012	0.016	0.026	0.037
4	.....	.....	.....	.....	.....	0.002	0.004	0.006	0.009	0.012	0.016	0.025	0.035

* All dimensions are in inches.
† See Fig. 9-3.

Horns for Keyways in Angular and Tapered Holes. Keyway broaching horns may be required for keyways not parallel to the part center line or in parts having tapered bores. Figure 9-2c illustrates a horn for an angular keyway in a straight hole. View d shows a horn for a keyway parallel to the center line of a tapered hole. View e shows a horn for broaching a keyway parallel to the side of a tapered hole.

To eliminate the difficulties in making a horn of the type shown in Fig. 9-2c and e, the angle of inclination can be incorporated in the adapter plate (see Fig. 9-4a).

Dimensions for tapered plugs can be calculated from the following equations (see Fig. 9-4b):

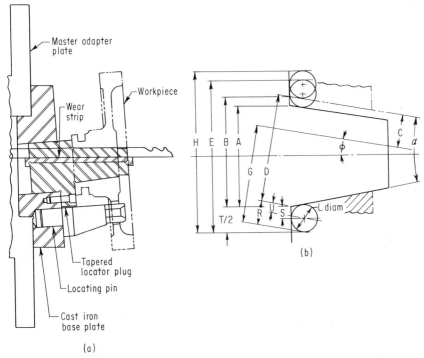

FIG. 9-4. (*a*) Adapter for angular keyway broaching; (*b*) dimensions for tapered horns.

$$H = B + T \qquad\qquad (4)$$
$$E = A + T \qquad\qquad (5)$$
$$T = 2S + L \qquad\qquad (6)$$
$$S = \frac{L}{2} \ \tan \ \frac{90 - \phi}{2} \qquad\qquad (7)$$
$$C + G = D + R \qquad\qquad (8)$$
$$D = B \cos \phi \qquad\qquad (9)$$
$$R = \frac{L}{2} + S \cos \phi - \frac{L}{2} \sin \phi \qquad\qquad (10)$$

where α = included angle for a given taper per foot (TPF)
$\phi = \alpha/2$; $\tan \phi = \text{TPF}/24$
H = dimensions over pins at large end of taper, in.
B = dimension from bottom of taper to top of keyway at large end, high limit, in.
A = diameter of taper at large end, in.
L = diameter of gage pins, in.
E = dimension over pins for large end of taper, in.
C = height of broach bar plus wear-strip thickness, in.
G = height over lower pin to bottom of broach-guide slot, in.

Off-center Locating Horns. Horns (Fig. 9-5) are used for broaching keyways in large holes having radii greater than the outward adjustment of the broach in the

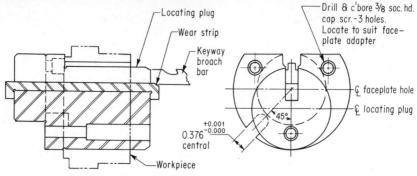

FIG. 9-5. Off-center keyway-fixture horn.

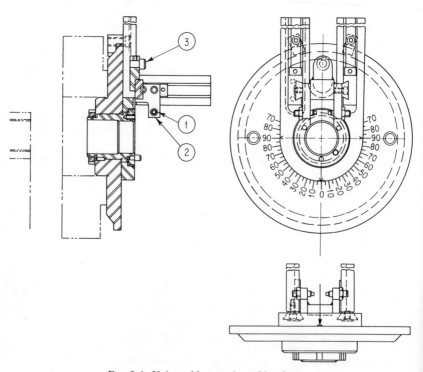

FIG. 9-6. Universal keyway-broaching fixture.

sliding head on the machine ram. The horn serves to orient the workpiece so that the keyway is approximately at the ram center line.

The diameter of the mounting flange should be large enough for adequate support of the workpiece during broaching.

Both the locating plug and wear strip should be made of tool steel, hardened for toughness and wear resistance.

Broaching Keyways in Thin Parts. Parts with a thickness of less than the minimum required for a keyway broach bar may be stacked on a plug to obtain the required thickness. To prevent the loading of more parts on the plug than originally planned, the K dimension of Fig. 9-2a and b may be increased approximately ¼ in. and tapered.

The tolerances on the bores of the thin parts should be ±0.001 in., or less, to minimize part movement.

Universal Keyway Broaching Fixture. A broaching fixture with radial location accurate to ½° is shown in Fig. 9-6. This fixture was designed for low-production runs of special equipment levers having keyway location tolerances of ±1°.

Setscrews (1) in the locating block (2) are adjustable to suit the thickness of the levers. The blocks holding the screws are adjusted away from the faceplate and the locating plug to suit lever width and length.

A removable locating pin (3) is provided for parts having a hole suitable for radial location of the keyway.

The locating plugs used in this fixture are similar to those shown in Figs. 9-2 and 9-5.

Broaching and Marking a Timing Gear. Figure 9-7 shows a fixture for broaching a keyway in a gear with previously cut teeth and also for marking the gear in line with the keyway and at a 90° angle to the keyway.

The fixture base is cast iron with a pilot diameter to suit the machine faceplate. The center hole is bored for a fixture plug similar to those shown in Fig. 9-2. An adjustable stop (7) supports the gear opposite each marking device (3), which is a standard steel stamp mounted in a swinging holder and held by a dog-point setscrew (4).

The locating pin, made of hardened and ground SAE 8645 steel, is piloted on each end in a bushing (1) to advance and lock it in position during the broaching operation. The fixture plug (5) incorporates a wear strip (6).

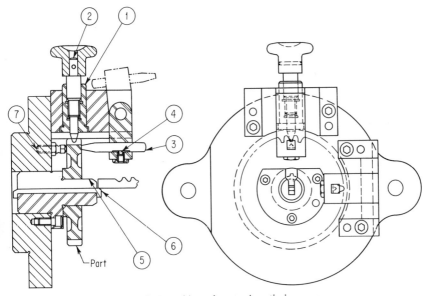

FIG. 9-7. Broaching a keyway in a timing gear.

Indexing Fixture for Broaching Serrations. Figure 9-8 illustrates a fixture for broaching splines, serrations, etc., in a straight hole. This fixture is probably not practical for small-diameter holes if a machine with capacity for pulling full round spline-broach bars is available.

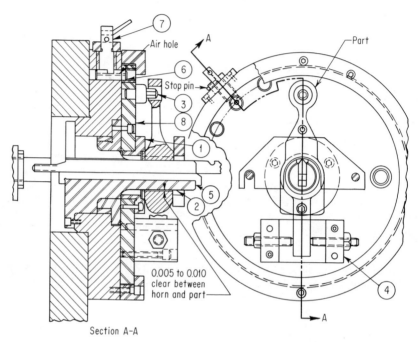

Section A-A

FIG. 9-8. Hand-indexing fixture for broaching splines and serrations.

The fixture has a locator (1), a broach guide (2), and a small locating pin (3) for locating the workpiece from previously machined holes. Adjustable stops may be used instead of the locating pin to position the part from a lever arm. The index-plate detent pin (6) is actuated by a hand-operated eccentric pin (7).

The broach guide, the index plate (8), and the locating plate may be changed for broaching other parts.

The external locating diameter is specified, since a clearance of 0.010 to 0.020 in. is required between the broach guide and bore of the workpiece.

Tilting Table Fixture with Indexing. Figure 9-9 shows a tilting-table fixture, incorporating an indexing mechanism for use on a vertical keyseating machine. The fixture is mounted on the horizontal table (1) of the machine and clears the machine vertical column (2). The column supports and guides the arm (3) to which the cutting tool (4) is attached.

With a workpiece bearing directly on the table, the tool path and resultant cut are perpendicular to the bearing surface. The tilting table (5) permits generation of splines, gear teeth, etc., at an angle to the bearing surface. The index plate (6) establishes the position of the generated characteristic on the ID of the workpiece. The support column (7) must be of sufficient cross-sectional area to with-

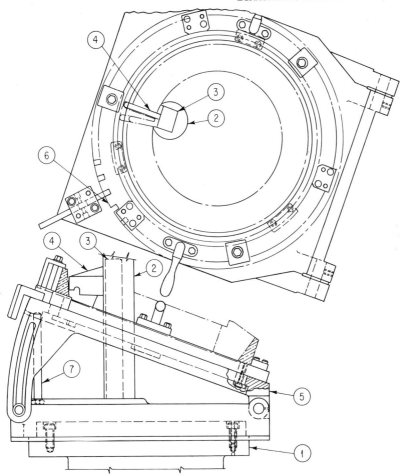

FIG. 9-9. Tilting-table fixture with indexing arrangements. (*Mitts and Merrill.*)

stand operation pressures without deflection. Extra index plates are provided for various workpieces.

In-line Indexing Fixture. Figure 9-10 illustrates a fixture for broaching one keyway in two holes and two wide keyways in four holes in a workpiece. The part is located on two horns, one fixed (1) and the other (2) pivoted to allow for variation in the distance between the holes. The fixture is mounted on rollers (3) for indexing between each of the six stations. The fixture moves on an overhead rail from station to station and is held on the bottom by keeper plates (4). The index plunger (5) is held in indexing slots by a weighted handle (6). Felt wipers (7) remove dirt and chips from the overhead rail.

BROACHING INTERNAL FORMS

This type of broaching is similar to keyway broaching inasmuch as the broach bar is guided by a slot in the fixture.

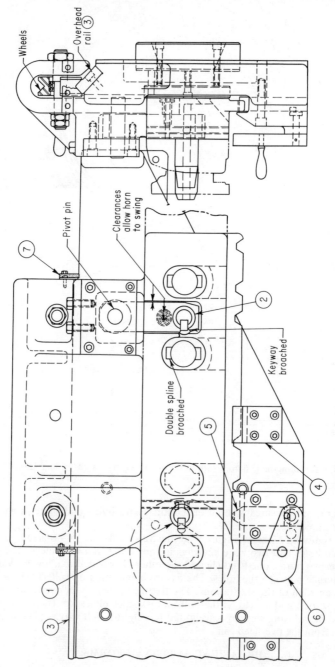

Wheels

Overhead rail ③

Pivot pin

Clearances allow horn to swing

Double spline broached

Keyway broached

Fig. 9-10. Trolley-type fixture for broaching keyways. (*Continental Tool Works, Div. of Ex-Cell-O Corp.*)

Broaching an Irregular Hole. The fixture of Fig. 9-11 is used to broach four internal surfaces in an irregular hole in a forging. The broach bar is guided by two keys to produce broached surfaces concentric to the finish-turned diameters of the workpiece. A close fit between the counterbore of the workpiece and the fixture plug holds the workpiece concentric with the axis of the bar.

Guide keys in this type of fixture have a sliding fit in the grooves of the broach bar. The guide keys assure alignment of the broach bar and pull head and guide the bar to offset the drift experienced in horizontal internal broaching. A similar application would be that of symmetrically elongating a hole on each side of its center line.

Because of an unequal amount of stock on each surface, it was necessary to clamp the workpiece securely before broaching. A positioning gage (7) is used to equalize the stock removal as much as possible.

The fixture consists of a base plate (1), a large hollow plug (2) with guide strips (3), a workpiece locator (4), a straddle clamp (5), and a cam (6) to actuate the straddle clamp.

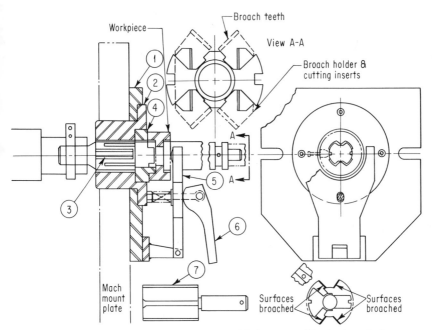

FIG. 9-11. Horizontal broaching fixture with keys to guide the broach bar.

Surface Broaching Internal Pads. Figure 9-12 shows a fixture for broaching three pads on a casting in three passes. The workpiece is supported on a mandrel and positioned by an index pin (2) through holes in its periphery. A back-up cam (3) presses the part against the index pin to dampen any tendency to chatter, and a cam-actuated bottom-support pin (4) takes up any clearance between the part bore and the mandrel.

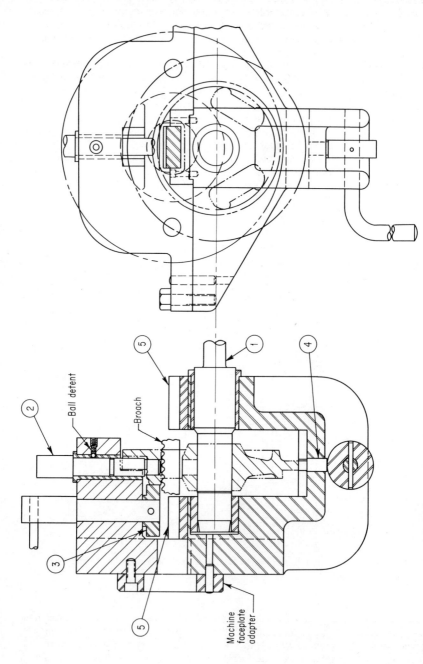

Ball detent

Broach

Machine
faceplate
adapter

FIG. 9-12. Fixture for broaching three internal pads. (*National Broach and Machine Co.*)

9–14

The broach bar is guided and supported by two hardened and ground steel guides (5). Since the broach bar is not supported beneath the cut, the bar must be thick enough to resist deflection between the front and rear guides.

The fixture is made of two castings with press-fit bushings for the workpiece, support mandrel, and index pin.

A Cam-locking Fixture for Internal Broaching. Figure 9-13 illustrates a fixture for broaching a door-closing cylinder. The cylinder is approximately 4⅛ in. long,

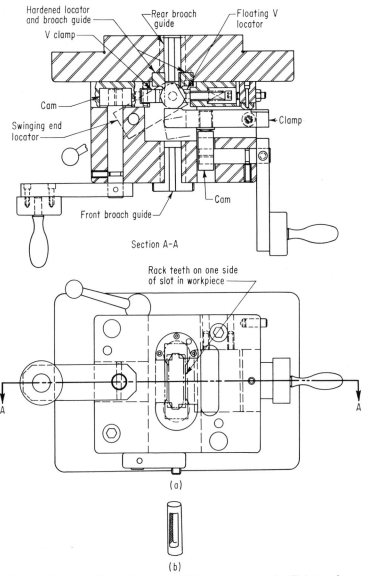

FIG. 9-13. (a) Fixture for broaching part with internal gear rack; (b) internal gear rack broached. (*National Broach & Machine Co.*)

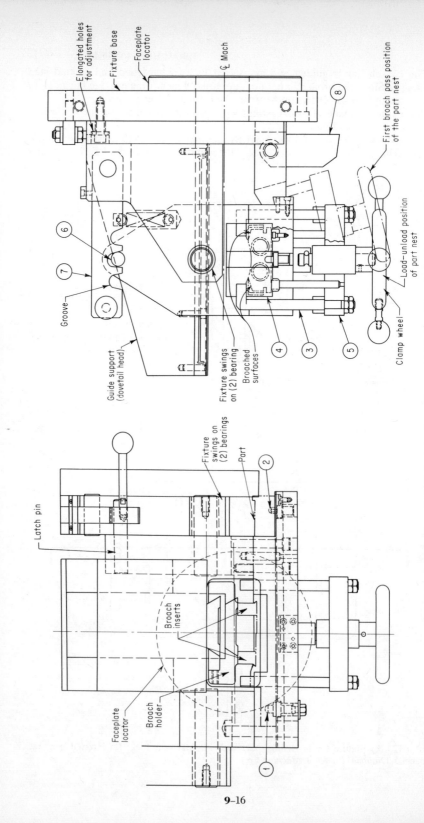

Fixture base

Faceplate locator

Elongated holes for adjustment

First broach pass position of the part nest

¢ Mach

Load-unload position of part nest

Clamp wheel

Groove

Guide support (dovetail head)

Fixture swings on (2) bearing

Broached surfaces

Fixture swings on (2) bearings

Part

Latch pin

Broach inserts

Faceplate locator

Broach holder

Fig. 9-14. Indexing broaching fixture for dovetail grooves. (*National Broach and Machine Co.*)

1⅞ in. diam, with the slot 3¼ by 1 in. Three surfaces of the slot are broached. One side becomes a rack, and each end is finished to size. The rack is broached first; then ribs on the broach bar engage the rack teeth to act as a guide while the top and bottom surfaces are finished.

The workpiece is placed in the fixture through a slot at the top; it rests, for end-wise location, on a swinging locator. A small flat on each side of the slot bears against hardened locators which also serve as broach guides. A cam-actuated clamp holds the part against these locators. The part is centrally located by a pair of V blocks, one of which is actuated by a cam for clamping purposes. Weights are incorporated in the operating handles of these cams to assist in keeping them in locked position.

When the broaching is complete, the clamps are released; and the end locator swings aside, allowing the part to fall out of the bottom of the fixture.

SURFACE BROACHING ON A HORIZONTAL BROACHING MACHINE

With proper fixturing and broach support, surface as well as internal broaching may be done on a horizontal machine.

Indexing Fixture for Dovetails. Figure 9-14 illustrates a fixture which holds and guides the broach-bar holder with a dovetail guide. The workpiece is located by a round pin (1) and a diamond-shaped pin (2); it is clamped by four hook pins (3) pulled through the base of the part nest (4) by a plate and central screw assembly (5) with a handwheel. The operation on the part is the broaching of two sets of dovetailed grooves whose bottom surfaces are at an included angle of 152°. The broaching is done in two passes of the broach bar.

The fixture pivots through 28° and is held in each position by a pin (6) nesting in a grooved, spring-loaded latch bar (7). Back-up bars (8) swing in and out of position for each pass. Bottom- and side-adjusting screws move the broach-bar guide for initial adjustments.

The broach-insert holder (Fig. 9-15) is made of SAE 8645 steel. The inserts are of high-speed steel, hardened and ground. The positioning of the finishing teeth is accomplished by an adjusting wedge. The roughing and semifinishing inserts are positioned by placing shim stock between them and the holder.

Double Station Corner Broaching Fixture. The part broached in the fixture of Fig. 9-16 is a small casting requiring the inside of each corner to be finished. The fixture has two slots for identical broach-insert holders pulled by a two-station pull head for broaching two parts at each pass.

Two cams (1) clamp the piece through the plunger assemblies (2) and a V block (3). The plunger-assembly retainer is cap-screwed and keyed with vertical and horizontal keys to the base casting.

The broach holder is guided by a slotted bar which has been hardened and ground for a minimum clearance of 0.001 in. between the broach holder and slot. Top guide strips (5) are used as a part nest, as well as to retain the broach holder (6) in the guide slots. Broach inserts (4) are fastened to the broach holder.

HORIZONTAL BROACHING OF ROUNDS, SPLINES, AND SIMILAR FORMS

In this type of broaching, the broach bar is not usually guided or supported by the fixture. For support it must depend upon the pull head, the workpiece, or the rear carrier if the machine is equipped with one. Rear carriers were originally added to broaching machines to support the finish-tooth ends of heavy broach bars but can be used to great advantage to support light bars for better alignment. A rear carrier will not eliminate all the sag of a broach bar due to the weight of the bar or part.

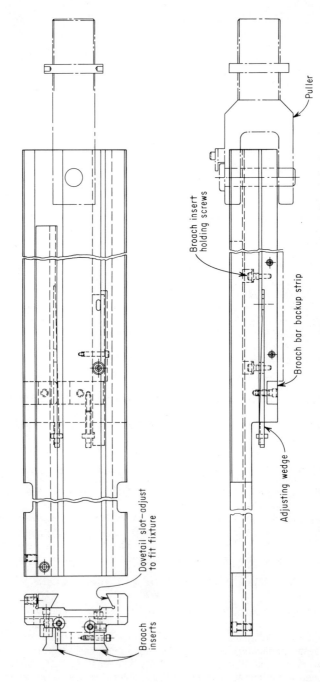

Dovetail slot—adjust to fit fixture

Broach inserts

Broach insert holding screws

Broach bar backup strip

Adjusting wedge

Puller

FIG. 9-15. Broach holder used with the fixture of Fig. 9-14. (*National Broach and Machine Co.*)

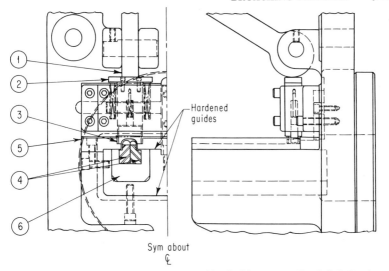

FIG. 9-16. Double-station fixture for broaching inside corners. (*Ex-Cell-O Corp.*)

For machines without a rear carrier, it is preferable to design fixtures with work-piece supports or centering devices. Supported or centered parts are usually started on the broaching operation in better alignment than can be accomplished by depending on the operator to level the bar by eye.

Universal Fixtures for Round or Spline Broaching. When parts of various sizes are to be broached by one broach machine, it is often desirable to have a minimum number of faceplate adapters with replaceable bronze bushings and hardened pressure plates similar to those shown in Fig. 9-17. The faceplate adapter may be of cast iron or low-carbon steel with a pilot turned to fit the hole in the machine faceplate. Holes are drilled and counterbored for attaching this plate to the machine.

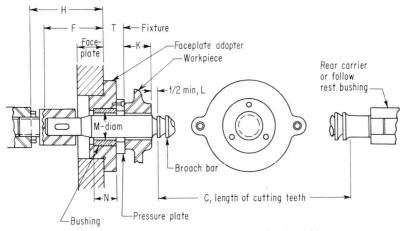

FIG. 9-17. Universal fixture for round or spline broaching.

A hole is bored in the center of the faceplate adapter, as shown in the illustration, to receive the bronze bushing. The number of adapters made will depend upon the maximum desirable wall thickness of the bushing. Holes are tapped in the adapter plate for mounting the pressure plate.

The pressure plate, usually hardened and ground, holds the bushing in place and acts as a bearing surface for the workpiece. The hole through the pressure plate should be from $\frac{1}{16}$ to $\frac{1}{18}$ in. larger than the hole to be broached.

The hole through the bronze bushing should only be a few thousandths of an inch larger than the broached hole. This bushing is always soft to prevent damage to the broach teeth in case they accidentally contact it or if the broach bar is returned through the bushing.

Pot Type of Fixture for Locating on OD of Part. The fixture shown in Fig. 9-18 centers the part and supports the broach bar while the hole is being broached. This type of fixture may be used for more than one part if the individual parts are too short to be broached separately.

This fixture consists of a base plate (1), a bushing (2), a pressure plate (3), a locating ring (4), and if necessary, a clamp assembly (5). The parts (2, 3, 4) are interchangeable as a group or individually, depending upon the part requirements.

Thin parts must be securely clamped to prevent chips from lodging between them, a cause of faulty parts. It has been found that a series of $\frac{1}{8}$-in.-thick parts moved so much when not clamped that a spline broach produced a nearly round hole in the parts.

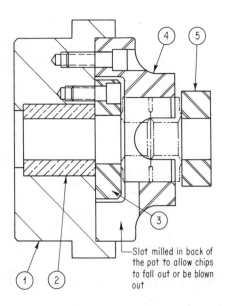

—Slot milled in back of the pot to allow chips to fall out or be blown out

FIG. 9-18. Pot-type internal-broaching fixture.

Fixture for Broaching 0.156-in.-thick Parts. This type of broaching requires that the combined height of stacked parts broached at one time be not less than twice the pitch of the broach-bar teeth plus $\frac{1}{16}$ in. Locating of the parts by their periphery is preferred, but they can be located by the front pilot section of the broach bar and clamped securely before the broaching cycle starts.

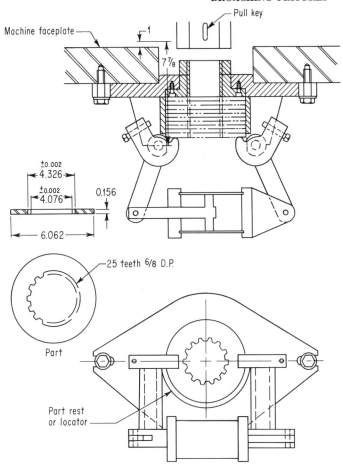

FIG. 9-19. Fixture for clamping thin parts with an air cylinder. (*Le Tourneau-Westinghouse Co.*)

The fixture shown in Fig. 9-19 holds nine parts 0.156 in. thick and 6.062 in. diam while broaching an internal spline. The parts rest in a semicircular locator and are held in position by air-actuated clamps.

Positioning Type of Spline Broaching Fixture. Figure 9-20 illustrates a horizontal broaching fixture for broaching a splined hole with a specified relationship to a reference point, in this case a hole in the web of the part.

The basic fixture is similar to that shown in Fig. 9-17, but with the addition of a diamond-shaped locating pin and two blocks used to position the broach pull head. The broach bar was designed for correct relationship between the flats on the pull end and one spline. The pull head has flats ground on the outer sleeve which establish its proper relationship with the inside locator. It is not necessary for the pull head to reenter the positioning blocks after each stroke, but only occasionally to recheck its position.

To operate the fixture successfully, it was necessary to hold the distance between the faces of the hub and flange to 0.250 in. (+0.004, −0.000 in.). Rest buttons un-

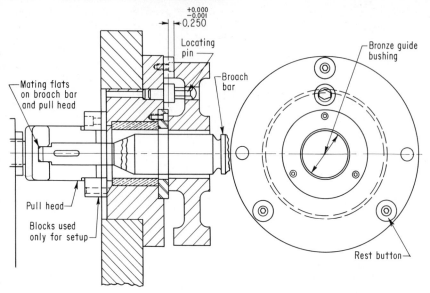

FIG. 9-20. Horizontal broaching fixture with positive workpiece positioning to a tooth of a spline.

der the flange hold the gear-face runout to a minimum. Because of broach-bar drift, the part should be finish-turned and the gear teeth cut after broaching.

Spline Broaching Fixture with Lead Bar. Figure 9-21 illustrates the layout of a spiral or helical spline-broaching fixture with a lead bar. In broaching internal spiral or helical splines, the arrangement of the teeth on the broach, when brought to bear on a smooth bore, causes a turning moment. For helix angles of less than 5°, a ball-bearing fixture bushing which permits the workpiece to rotate as the

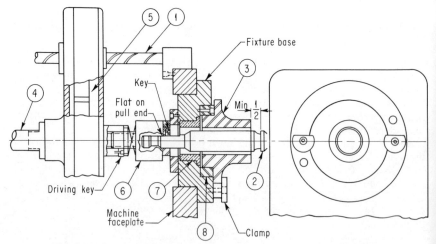

FIG. 9-21. Layout of spiral broaching fixture showing lead-bar attachment.

broach passes through is satisfactory. An alternate method uses a swivel-type puller permitting the broach to rotate as it is pulled through the workpiece. Although the turning moment exists at larger helix angles, better quality can be achieved by controlling the rotation of the broach as it is pulled through the workpiece.

The lead bar (1) has a spiral groove machined at the required helix angle. As the broach (2) is pulled through the workpiece (3) by the piston rod (4), the gearbox (5) moves on the stationary lead bar, causing rotation of the gear train which is keyed to the spiral groove. The gear keyed to the lead bar rotates a mating gear on a shaft keyed to the broach puller (6). The broach has a machined flat which mates with the puller. Broach rotation is therefore a positive duplication of the lead-bar groove.

The machined fixture base has a bronze bushing (7) to prevent contact with and possible damage to the broach. An expendable ring (8) serves as a workpiece nest and as a thrust plate.

Automatic Spline Broaching. Figure 9-22 illustrates the fixturing of a horizontal broaching machine which automatically cuts internal splines in gear blanks.

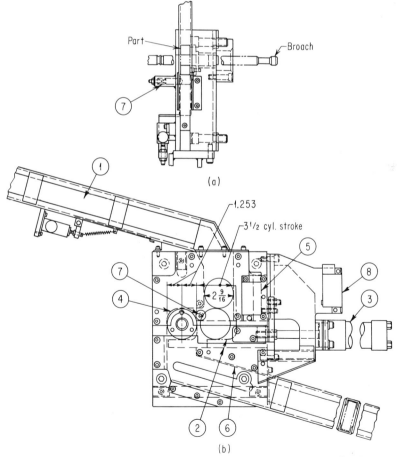

FIG. 9-22. Automatic spline broaching of gear blanks. (*Detroit Broach Co.*)

The workpiece, 0.840 in. wide and having an OD of 2%6 in. with a concentric
15⁄16-in.-diam bore, rolls down an inclined loading chute (1) and drops to the loading platform (2). A hydraulic cylinder (3) moves the platform to the broaching
position and clamps the workpiece between the platform and the broaching nest
(4). The platform, at the completion of the loading stroke, actuates a limit switch
(5) which starts the broaching cycle. An automatic toolholder advances the broach
through the bore to engage the broach puller, and the broach is pulled through the
part. The loading platform returns to its initial position under the chute while the
finished part drops to and rolls down the disposal chute (6).

A workpiece dropping to the loading platform is kept from prematurely entering the nest or disposal chute by a spring detent (7).

The platform on completing its retraction contacts a second limit switch (8) to
initiate the return of the broach from the pulling head to the tool-handling mechanism. An interlock prevents platform motion during broach return.

The machine cycle, including loading, broaching, part disposal, and return of
the broach, is completed in eight seconds.

The loading and unloading chutes and the fixture-mounting brackets are weldments. Working surfaces, including the loading platform and workpiece nest, are
hardened tool steel.

VERTICAL BROACHING

Vertical broaching can be divided into three general categories: pull down, push
down, and pull up, depending upon the method of holding the broach and direction of applied force. Both internal and external, or surface, broaching operations
are performed on vertical machines.

The machine layout will provide the fixture designer with dimensions necessary
to develop the size of the fixture elements. The travel of the machine elements is of
particular significance in that the broach length must be specified therefrom. The
broach must clear the workpiece at the extreme upward and downward positions,
and the first broach tooth must clear the workpiece before the stroke begins.

Pull Down Internal Broaching Fixtures. A general arrangement and some of
the design considerations involved in pull-down broaching are shown in Fig. 9-23.
The fixture has a loading table (1) which is manually alternated between the load
and work positions.

The loaded table is placed in the work position, and the shank of the broach (2)
is passed through the workpiece. The puller (3) engages the broach and pulls
it through and clear of the workpiece. With the loading table returned to the outward position, the puller travels upward to return the broach to the retriever (4).
The upward travel of the broach puller causes a release ring (5) to contact a ring
(6) which releases the broach to the retriever head.

Although a spring-detent type of retriever head is shown, the use of this type
with heavy broach bars is not advised.

When designing fixtures for vertical pull-down internal-broaching operations, the
designer must make sure that the first broach tooth clears the workpiece with the
puller engaged.

Vertical Broaching with a Fixture Guided Broach Bar. Figure 9-24 illustrates a
pull-down type of broaching fixture for generating internal helical splines.

The workpiece is a flanged, circular member with a number of concentric internal and external diameters. The flange face is machined perpendicular to the center line of the diameters. Short helical splines, broached in the inside of the workpiece, are concentric with the various diameters and perpendicular to the machined
face of the flange.

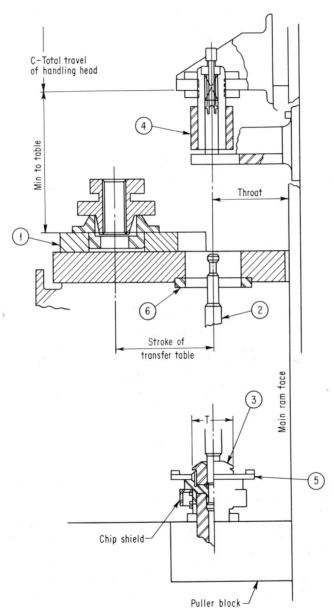

FIG. 9-23. Transfer-type pull-down broaching fixture.

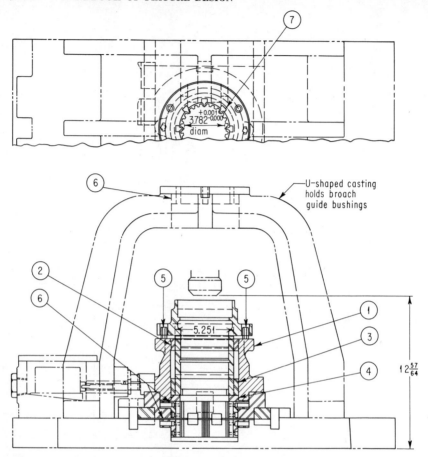

FIG. 9-24. Pull-down type of fixture with fixture-guided broach bar. (*Colonial Broach Co.*)

An alternate method of first broaching the spline and then machining the diameters and face was considered and rejected because of the relative shortness of the splines.

A machined circular collar (1) and three bushings (2, 3, 4) hold the workpiece. Correct radial location is assured by locating from mounting holes in the flange of the workpiece with pin locators (5).

The broach bar is guided by three bushings (6), one above and two below the workpiece. The lower bushings also absorb part of the thrust load. Each bushing has eight equally spaced identical broach-guide inserts (7). The inserts are ground after assembly in the bushings.

Surface Broaching a Universal Joint Yoke. A vertical pull down broaching fixture for holding a universal-joint yoke while finishing the inner faces is shown in Fig. 9-25. The workpiece is placed over the loading pin (1) while in the vertical position, then rotated to the horizontal position. The lower portion of the pin is threaded to receive a stop collar (2) and locknut (3). The threads provide an adjust-

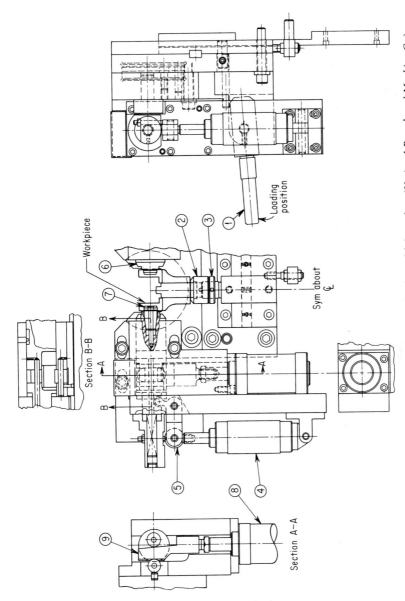

Fıg. 9-25. Pull-down broaching fixture for inside faces of universal-joint yokes. (*National Broach and Machine Co.*)

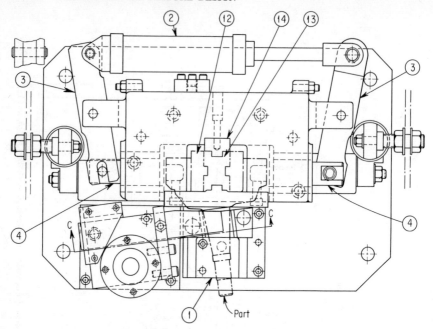

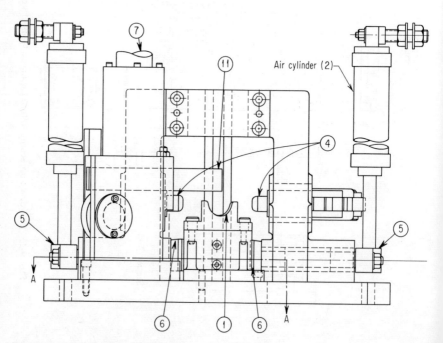

FIG. 9-26. Air cylinder locating and clamping fixture (*continued on facing page*). (*National Broach and Machine Co.*)

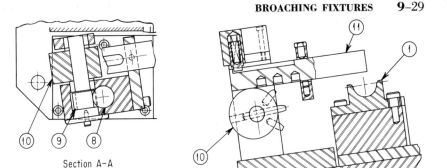

Section A-A

Section C-C

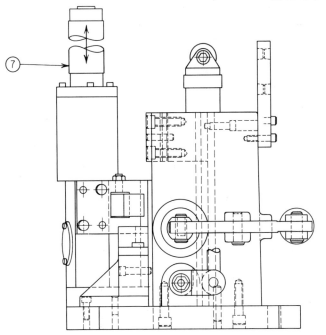

Fig. 9-26 (*continued*). Air cylinder locating and clamping fixture. (*National Broach and Machine Co.*)

ment for positioning the yoke. Different lengths of stop collars may be used for different yokes.

Two air cylinders (4), through levers (5), move plunger assemblies (6) which support and back up the workpiece. Locating pins (7) have a taper fit in each plunger to facilitate interchangeability. The slightly tapered face of the locating pin facilitates guiding it into the hole in the yoke. Two other air cylinders (8) move wedges (9) which lock the plunger assemblies, thus preventing their movement during the broaching operation.

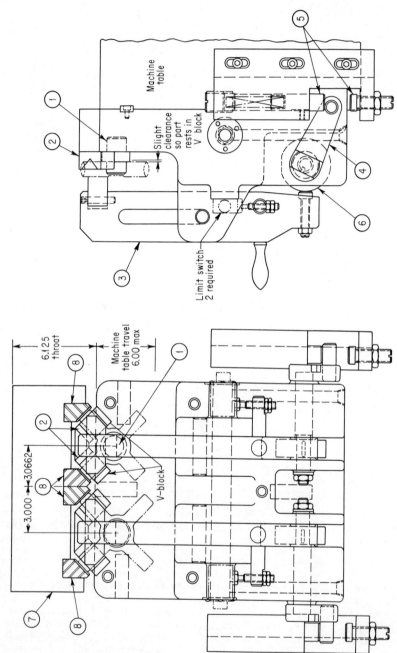

Machine table

Slight clearance so part rests in V block

Limit switch 2 required

6.125 throat

Machine table travel 6.00 max

3.000 — 3.0662

V-block

Fig. 9-27. Vertical broach fixture with transfer table clamping. (*Ford Motor Co.*)

In the broach holder, not shown, are two roughing broaches with shear-type teeth, two finishing broaches with straight teeth, and two broach inserts for finishing the fillet and adjoining surface.

Vertical Surface Broaching Fixture with Air Clamping. Figure 9-26 illustrates a vertical pull-down broaching fixture with air-actuated locating and clamping.

The workpiece, a fork-shaped wheel spindle, has two inside faces that are surface-broached. The spindle is placed in a circular nest (1). An air cylinder (2) moves two pivoted arms (3) to insert two locating pins (4) into two holes in the arms of the workpiece. Two air cylinders move lever arms (5) to rotate cams (6) which contact the workpiece for support during broaching.

An air cylinder (7) actuates a rack (8) which revolves a gear (9) and cam (10). This cam has three pins pressed into it which fit in three holes in the clamp bar (11). The initial movement of the cam moves the clamp bar over the workpiece. Continued cam rotation applies pressure to the underside of the pivoted clamp bar which clamps the workpiece in the nest.

A vertical passage through the center of the fixture contains the broach bars (12), the broach holder (13), and two fixture-mounted bar guides (14).

Vertical Broaching Fixture with Automatic Clamping. Figure 9-27 illustrates a fixture for broaching to length the legs of spider-shaped forgings.

Two workpieces are placed on round locators (1) with the legs of the workpieces resting in V blocks (2). The V blocks are movable to compensate for variations in the forgings. Clamps (3) are manually pushed forward over the workpieces. At the forward position of the clamps, a limit switch is actuated to start the machine cycle. As the machine table on which the fixture is mounted moves from the loading position to the broaching position, cam levers (4) are rotated by actuating stops (5), causing cams (6) to bear on the underside of the pivoted clamps, which in turn bear down on the workpieces. The actuating stops mounted on the machine frame are adjustable and spring-loaded to compensate for overtravel of the fixture and ensure clamping action.

The broach holder (7) retains and orients four broach bars (8), ensuring their perpendicularity to the broached surfaces of the workpieces. The outward travel of the machine table after the broaching cycle again causes rotation of the cam levers, allowing manual retraction of the clamps for workpiece removal or reorientation. Two machine cycles are required to complete two workpieces.

Two Station Rotary Indexing Vertical Push Broaching Fixture. Figure 9-28 illustrates a two-station rotary-index vertical broaching fixture. Five workpieces are manually loaded in slots (1); then the fixture is manually indexed, placing the workpieces in the broaching position. A stationary block (2) attached to the machine frame ensures proper positioning and support of the workpieces during the broaching operation. The second station of the fixture is loaded during the first-station broaching operation. As the fixture is again manually indexed, ejectors (3) strip the finished workpieces from the slots. During the broaching cycle, the fixture is locked in position by a spring-loaded plunger (4). The plunger is manually retracted to permit rotation of the fixture dial but must engage and enter the fixture to trip an adjacent limit switch which completes the circuit initiating the broaching cycle.

Vertical Push Broaching Fixture for Concave Slots. A vertical fixture for broaching curved slots around the perimeter of an adapter nozzle is illustrated in Fig. 9-29.

The saucer-shaped workpiece is placed in a counterbored locator (1). A manually actuated cam clamp (2) with a swiveling plate (3) holds the workpiece. After the slot is broached, the workpiece is rotated to align the slot with a manually actuated index plunger (4), and the next slot is broached.

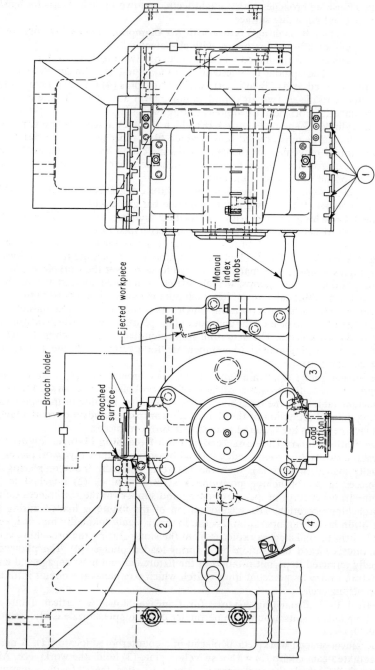

FIG. 9-28. Two-station rotary-indexing vertical broach fixture. (*Ex-Cell-O Corp.*)

Broach holder

Broached surface

Ejected workpiece

Manual index knobs

Load station

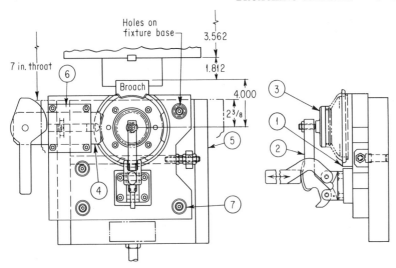

Holes on
fixture base

7 in. throat
Broach

FIG. 9-29. Vertical form broaching fixture. (*Apex Broach Co., Inc.*)

The fixture is mounted on a dovetail subplate (5) for adjustment with the machine throat and is centered with the broach bar by adjustment of a stud (6). Fixture-base mounting holes (7) are drilled oversize to permit adjustment.

The fixture base and subplate are made of machine steel. The locator (1) and the index-plunger housing (6) are made of SAE 6145 steel. The index plunger is of hardened and ground oil-hardening tool steel.

Vertical Straddle Broaching Fixture. Figure 9-30 illustrates a two-station fixture for straddle broaching the crank and pin bosses of a connecting rod. The workpiece (1) is held and centered by fixture members (2) that bear on the sides of the web section. Web clamping is accomplished by positioning the workpiece and then turning the handwheel jackscrew (3). Clamping in the vertical plane is accomplished by turning the handle (4) to revolve the cam (5) which presses the pivoted clamp bar (6) down on the workpiece. A weight on the handle helps hold the clamp locked.

The broach bars (7) straddle the parallel faces of the crank end of the workpiece. Wedges (8) under the broach bars allow their centered 0.679-in. spacing.

In the second station, fixture pads (9) center the workpiece parallel to the faces broached in the first station. Vertical clamping is achieved by the method described above. Broach bars (10) mounted on wedges (11) provide centering and adjustment.

The fixture base is cast iron. Hardened inserts are provided at wear points. Working members are hardened and ground tool steel. Bronze bushings are provided for working shafts.

Piloted Push Broach Layout. A layout for a push broaching with the broach bar guided by a pilot in the fixture is shown in Fig. 9-31.

The workpiece (1) is placed on the bushing (2) which acts as a thrust plate. The pilot (3), an integral part of the broach-bar holder, enters and is centered by a guide bushing (5) before the shell-type broach bar (4) engages the workpiece. A conical surface on the broach bar permits the workpiece to center itself.

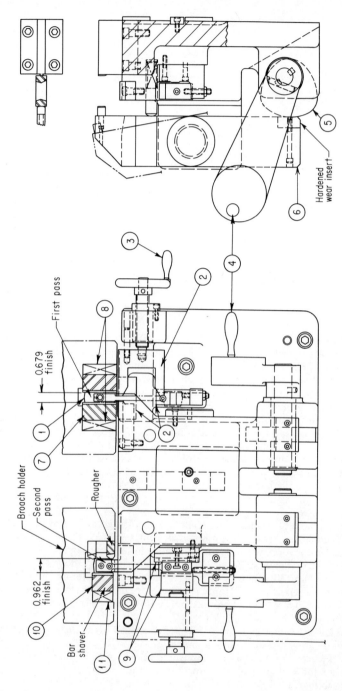

First pass

0.679
finish

Broach holder

Second
pass

Rougher

0.962
finish

Bar
shaver

Hardened
wear insert

Fig. 9-30. Two-station fixture for straddle broaching crank and pin bosses of a connecting rod. (*Detroit Broach and Machine Co.*)

9-34

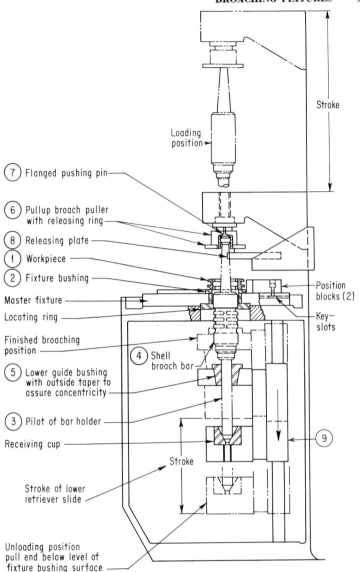

FIG. 9-31. Push broach layout of fixture and pilot-guided broach bar.

At the completion of its stroke, the broach puller (6) with pushing pin (7) strikes the releasing plate (8) and is disengaged from the broach. The lower retriever slide (9) takes the broach below the level of the workpiece which can then be removed.

A layout generally shows the stroke of the ram, the stroke of the retriever slide, and the dimensions of the machine, from which the fixture designer can specify the dimensions of the fixture components and the length and profile of the broach holder and of the broach bar. Broach-holder dimensions must allow the broach holder to clear the workpiece at the upper and lower extremes of the stroke. The broach dimensions must permit the pilot to be centered before cutting starts.

For some applications, the broach is made in one piece instead of two pieces, and it may be piloted by the rough workpiece without a pilot.

Master Push Broaching Fixture. Figure 9-32 illustrates a master fixture which, with interchangeable locating blocks, can position a wide variety of workpieces for push-broaching operations. These locators align the workpiece with the broach center line and allow clearance so that the workpiece is free to center itself on the broach.

The locating blocks (1) are keyed to the fixture base (2) and can be set at various distances from the broach center line to accommodate the OD of various workpieces. The hardened wear plate (3) is subjected to abrasion from the workpiece sliding over it when being loaded and unloaded. Alternate rest bushings (4) accommodate workpieces of different ID.

A locating ring (5) attached to the fixture base mates to and nests in the machine table. A wear bushing (6) between the locating ring and the rest bushing completes the thrust column. The rest bushing is held in place by two standard drill-bushing lock screws (7).

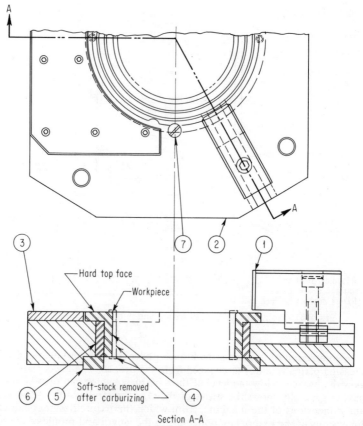

Section A–A

FIG. 9-32. Master push broaching fixture with rest bushing.

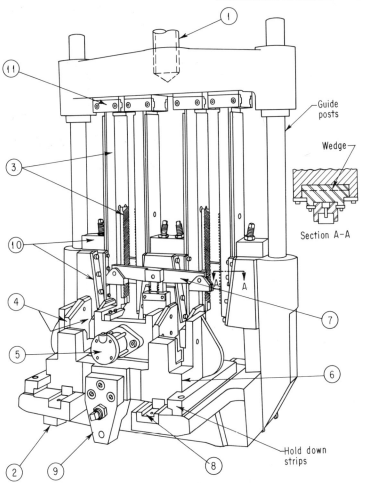

Guide posts

Wedge

Section A–A

Hold down strips

Fig. 9-33. Self-contained broaching fixture. (*Continental Tool Works, Div. of Ex-Cell-O Corp.*)

Self-contained Broaching Unit. Figure 9-33 illustrates a fixture for broaching four surfaces, two per part, of two workpieces. The fixture is a self-contained broaching machine requiring only an external source of reciprocating motion and pressure.

The fixture may be set between the ram and bolster plate of a conventional hydraulic press, with the ram adapter (1) aligned with the press ram. The base of the fixture is then keyed (2) and bolted to the bolster. Ram travel is adjusted so that the broach-bar inserts (3) clear the workpiece at the bottom of the stroke.

Two workpieces are placed between the pair of plates (4). The shuttle cylinder (5) moves the transfer table (6) from the loading position shown to the work position. The clamp bar (7) locks the workpieces in location as the table moves to the work position. The press ram descends, supplying power for the broaching operation, remaining at this lower position while the transfer table retracts to the load position; then the ram returns to its top position. The transfer table travels on hardened ways (8). Travel is limited by an adjustable stop block (9). Each broach holder can be adjusted for position by an individual wedge-and-bar keeper assembly (10) and individual key plates and push blocks (11).

Pull Up Broaching Layout. Figure 9-34 is a layout for pull-up broaching. The broach is shown in the loading position and at the beginning of the cutting stroke. In the loading position, the broach (1) rests in a cup (2) while being held upright and in alignment by a bushing (3) attached to the lower fixture plate (4).

The workpiece (5) is placed on the exposed leading end of the broach. The cycle begins with hydraulic elevation of the broach, cup, fixture plate, and workpiece until the broach engages the puller (6). The workpiece is held up against the thrust plate (7) by the upward motion of the broach. At the end of the stroke, the workpiece drops to the incline (8) and slides off. The broach puller returns the broach

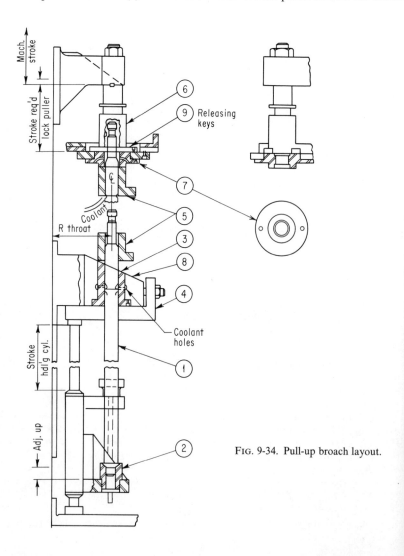

FIG. 9-34. Pull-up broach layout.

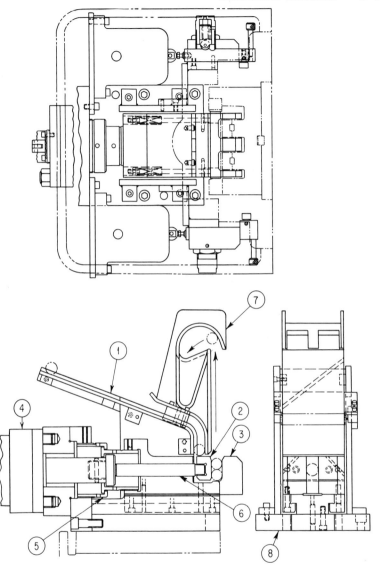

FIG. 9-35. Automatic loading and unloading surface-broaching fixture.

to its original position in the cup and bushing and trips the releasing keys (9). The free broach and lower elements descend to the lower loading position.

The internal surface of the thrust plate (7) and bushing (3) are soft to prevent damage to the broach. Ample clearance is provided between the thrust plate ID and the broach. Adequate coolant should be introduced as close to the point of work as possible, preferably through the thrust plate. Broach length must permit the workpiece to clear the ends of the broach at both upward and lower extremes of its travel.

Fixture for Round Bar Stock. An automatic loading and unloading surface-broaching fixture for round bar stock is illustrated in Fig. 9-35. A gravity loading chute (1) feeds the workpieces into a space between the clamping block (2) and the transfer block (3). The workpiece is moved from the loading position under the chute by the hydraulic cylinder (4) to the broaching position shown. Upon reaching the stop (5), the forward motion of the fixture ceases while continued motion of the cylinder piston clamps the workpiece through the push rod (6).

The descending broaches cut two grooves in the two workpieces and finish them to length. On the upward stroke of the broach holder (Fig. 9-36), two spring-loaded hooks lift the workpieces from the fixture and carry them upward to the unloading hook (7).

Working faces of the hydraulic piston rod, the push rod, and the clamping block are of hardened and ground tool steel. The fixture base (8) and the transfer-block support and retainers are of hot-rolled steel. The loading and unloading chutes are weldments.

The broach holder, Fig. 9-36, has two keyways which position the inserts (1) for cutting the two grooves in the workpieces. Another insert (2) cuts the part to length. Back-up blocks (3) help hold the broach inserts in place. Attached to the

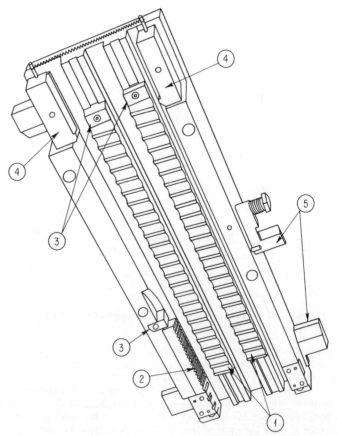

FIG. 9-36. Broach holder for use with fixture of Fig. 9-35.

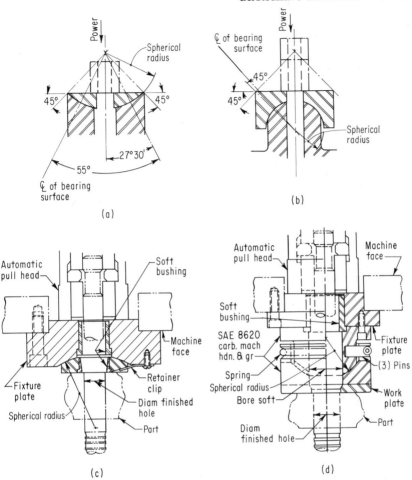

FIG. 9-37. Equalizing fixtures.

side of the holder are cam blocks which actuate the fixture controls. At the top are two unloading hooks (4) for removing the part from the fixture.

Equalizing Fixtures. When it is not possible to properly align a bearing surface for the workpiece, as when broaching a cored hole in a casting or a forging, an equalizing fixture may be employed. Such a fixture usually consists of a hemispherical bushing which rests in a hemispherical cavity. Pressure of the broach against the workpiece is sufficient to move the bushing to the position where the axis of the hole coincides with the axis of the broach.

Shown in Fig. 9-37 are concave and convex hemispherical equalizing fixtures. Figures 9-37a and b suggest the extent and center lines of spherical bearing surfaces. Figures 9-37c and d show representative hemispherical equalizing fixtures. If the broaching operation is in a horizontal or pull-down position, a suitable chip shield should be provided to prevent chips from falling onto the spherical surfaces.

BROACH HOLDERS

A knowledge of broach-holder and broach-insert design and function is invaluable to the fixture designer in coordinating fixture design with these and other machine elements.

It is general practice in surface broaching to design simple broach inserts which are easily produced and easily replaced in case of damage or wear. These inserts are then assembled in broach holders to produce the desired shape in the finished part. Holders are not of universal design but are constructed to suit the particular workpiece and the assembled broach for it.

The broach-holder assembly usually fills the throat of the machine to minimize overhang of the fixture and workpiece.

The holder can be made of ordinary machine steel, high-strength cast iron, or a heat-treatable steel, such as SAE 1045 or SAE 8645 hardened and drawn to Rockwell C 28-36. This hardness permits machining after heat-treating with a minimum of finish grinding. The material selected depends upon the use and amount of handling to which the holder is subjected.

The method of holding the inserts in the holder usually permits their removal, replacement, and adjustment without removing the holder from the machine. However, the assembly may be removed to the toolroom for resharpening of the inserts and resetting to the proper dimensions.

Since the position of the roughing inserts is not critical, they can be brought to the required dimension by using shims between them and the holder. The broach inserts containing the finishing teeth are often set to close tolerances by using an adjusting wedge similar to that shown in Fig. 9-15.

Figures 9-38 and 9-39 show various methods of securing inserts in the holders. The choice of holding method depends upon the accuracy required in the broaching operation, the amount of space and clearance available for the broach-holder assembly, and the frequency with which the inserts must be replaced.

View *a* of Fig. 9-38 shows an insert with a right-angle groove at 30° to the side of the insert. Holes tapped in the holder are spaced at approximately 2½ in. for ¼-

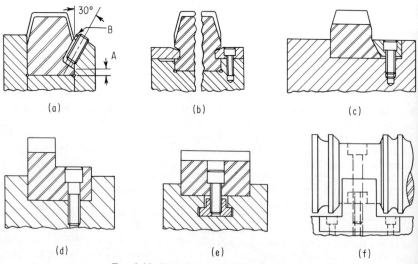

(a)   (b)   (c)

(d)   (e)   (f)

FIG. 9-38. Broach-insert holding methods.

or ⁵⁄₁₆-in.-diam dog-point setscrews. The angle of inclination may be increased to 45° max, thus increasing the stock at B. Dimension A is ⅛ in. min. This method of holding is adaptable to inserts up to 1½ in. wide.

In view b, Fig. 9-38, the insert is held in place by clamping strips along each side. By loosening the strips, the inserts may be removed from the bottom of the holder. This type of holder should be used when the location of the form is not very critical or the surfaces are relatively straight. A more accurate method of retaining the insert is shown in view c. One side of the slot in the holder is accurately machined to position, and the form on the insert is accurately machined. The tapered wedge and insert push the insert to accurate location, as well as clamping it in the holder.

A method of holding an insert for a narrow broached surface is shown in Fig. 9-38d. Holes are drilled and counterbored in the insert and tapped in the holder. Inserts with teeth the full width of the face may also be retained by this method. The use of a T slot is illustrated in view e.

The mounting of a round insert used to surface-broach parts such as bearing caps is shown in Fig. 9-38f. A groove is machined into the holder in which support blocks are mounted. Holes are drilled through the insert and counterbored for socket-head cap screws which attach the insert to the support blocks. When one side is dull, the bar is rotated 180°, and another pass is made with the second side before resharpening. The support-block diameters must be held to $+0.000$ in., -0.0002 in. tolerance, and spaced 3 to 6 in. apart, depending upon the bar-diameter and broaching pressures. The support blocks are separate parts so that the height can be adjusted by grinding or shimming.

Figure 9-39a shows the broach insert mounted on a subholder instead of being mounted directly on the main holder. Each insert has an individual subholder which is slightly shorter than the insert. An advantage of this arrangement is that the machine operator only has to remove the dull insert in its subholder and replace it with a sharp set which has been set to dimensions A and B in the tool-grinding department. Shims are placed between the insert and subholder for proper dimensions. This broach insert has soft-steel inserts which are tapped for the mounting screws.

The wedge and spacers shown in Fig. 9-39b and c provide a means of adjusting broach finishing teeth to the required dimension A. The adjusting wedges usually have a taper of 0.156 in. per ft with a movement of 3½ to 4 in., giving the insert an adjustment of 0.0045 to 0.052 in. The original spacer used with a new insert may be 0.125 in. thick. After the wedge reaches its full adjustment, it is returned to its original position and a thicker spacer replaces the original. Spacers are provided to compensate for the amount ground off the insert during its useful life.

Also illustrated in view b is a tapped plug fitted in a reamed hole to receive the hold-down screw. The positioning rod is removed after the insert hold-down screw has been started.

View c, Fig. 9-39, is section A-A of view b showing the wedge adjusting screw.

An adjustable straddle-broach holder with setting gages is shown in Fig. 9-39d. The inserts (1) are held in a subholder (2) having a close-fitting plug (3) which is tapped for the adjusting screw (4). The end of the plug extends into a T slot to control the movement of the broaches. The adjusting screw has right- and left-hand threads so that each subholder moves the same amount.

Bushings (5) are press-fitted into the holder opposite the first and last teeth of the broach inserts. Using the setting gage (6), the inserts may be easily set to the proper width for the part being broached. With this arrangement one holder and one set of broach inserts can be used for several similar parts requiring only a setting gage for each part.

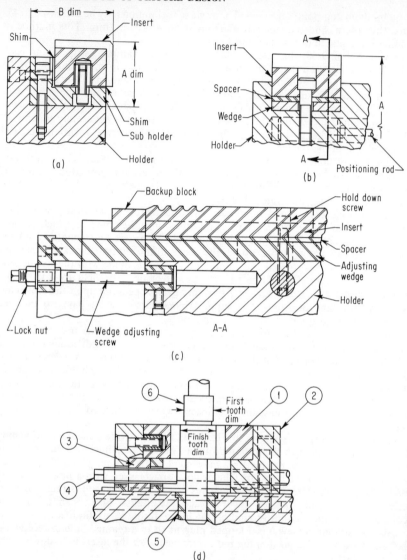

FIG. 9-39. Broach insert holding methods.

CONTINUOUS BROACHING

Fixture for Continuous Broaching. Figure 9-40 illustrates a high-production fixture for a chain-driven broaching machine. The fixture is guided by two channels (1) that move on the slideways of the machine. Drivepins (2) are engaged by a chain to pull the fixture through a fixed broaching station.

The workpiece is placed in a nest (3). Forward travel of the fixture on the slideways actuates cam bars (4, 5). The forward cam bar (4) moves the front slide (6)

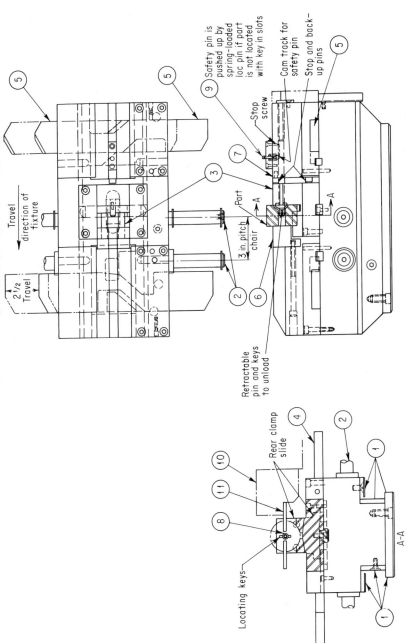

Travel direction of fixture

2½ Travel

⑤

⑤

⑤

③

⑦

②

⑥

⑤

⑨ Safety pin is pushed up by spring-loaded loc pin if part is not located with key in slots

Stop screw

Cam track for safety pin

Stop and back-up pins

Part

A

A

3 in. pitch chair

Retractable pin and keys to unload

⑩

⑪

⑧

④

②

①

①

Rear clamp slide

Locating keys

A-A

Fig. 9-40. Fixture for chain broaching of two slots in a circular workpiece. (*Detroit Broach & Machine Co.*)

against the workpiece. The rear cam bar (5) moves the rear slide (7) forward to engage the vertically positioned workpiece keyway with a locating key (8). The workpiece may be rotated manually to permit engagement of the key. With the key engaged, a safety pin (9) is seated in a cam flat. If, owing to mislocation of the workpiece, the locating key cannot engage the workpiece, the safety pin protrudes to trip a limit switch stopping the machine. The rear slide (7) bears on and supports the nest during broaching.

After the fixtured workpiece is drawn through the fixed broach holders (10) and bars (11), the cam bars are again actuated by being drawn past lugs fixed to the slideways. The forward and rear slides return to their at rest positions, and the finished workpiece falls into an unloading chute.

Continuous Broaching of Connecting Rods. Figure 9-41 illustrates a broaching fixture for a connecting rod. The part is placed against two rough locators (1) with its small end against a work rest (2) and against a back-up block (3) on the bearing end of the part.

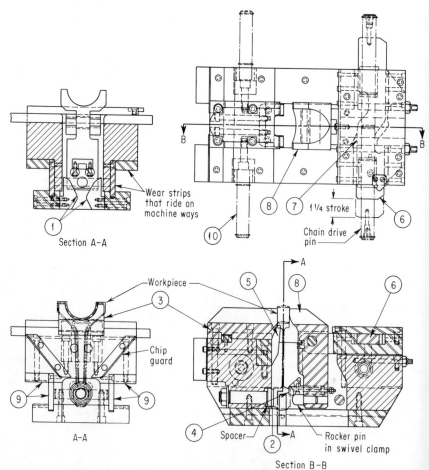

Fig. 9-41. Fixture for continuous broaching of connecting rods. (*The La Pointe Machine Tool Co.*)

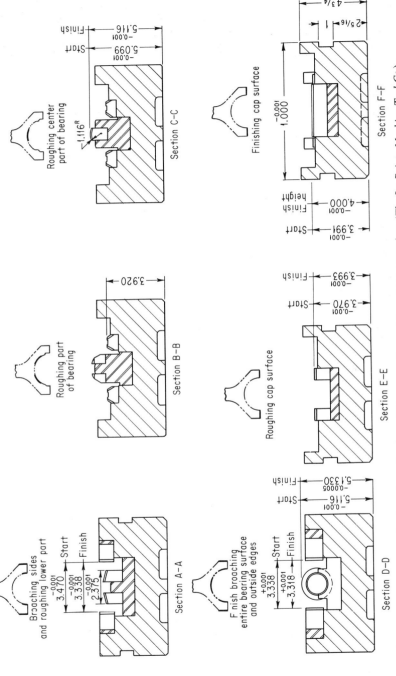

Section C-C

Roughing center part of bearing

1.116^R

5.116 -0.001/+0.000 Finish

5.099 -0.001/+0.000 Start

Section B-B

Roughing part of bearing

3.920

Section A-A

Broaching sides and roughing lower part

Start

Finish

3.470 -0.001/+0.000

3.338 -0.001/+0.000

2.375 -0.001/+0.000

Section F-F

Finishing cap surface

1.000 -0.001/+0.000

4 3/4

2 5/16

1

Finish height 4.000 -0.001/+0.000

Start 3.991 -0.001/+0.000

Section E-E

Roughing cap surface

3.993 -0.001/+0.000 Finish

3.970 -0.001/+0.000 Start

Section D-D

Finish broaching entire bearing surface and outside edges

Start

Finish

3.338 +0.001/+0.000

3.318 +0.001/+0.000

5.1330 -0.0005/+0.0000 Finish

5.116 -0.001/+0.000 Start

Fig. 9-42. Sections through stages of the connecting-rod broaching operation. (*The La Pointe Machine Tool Co.*)

9–47

The small end of the part is held against the work rest by bevel pins (4). The bearing end of the part is supported by a thrust and locating block (5). A cam on the machine drives the cam bar (6) inwardly. A locking angle (7) on the cam bar assists in holding the clamp (8) securely against the part. After the part is broached, a cam on the opposite side of the machine returns the cam bar, loosening the clamp and releasing the part.

Wear strips (9) bear against the ways of the machine. A number of these fixtures are used on a machine and are pulled through and spaced by a motor-driven chain drive. Four chain-drive pins (10) are fastened to each fixture.

The broach holder is in an inverted position in the top of the machine. It roughs and finishes the outside, cap, and bearing surfaces of the connecting rod in one pass. Figure 9-42 illustrates a section through each stage of the broaching operation.

Section 10

PLANING AND SHAPING FIXTURES

By A. G. BAUMGARTNER
Sales Manager, The Cincinnati Shaper Co.

The similarity of many shaping operations to those of planing extends to work-holding methods and devices.

While fixtures are sometimes used for these machining methods, commercially available vises or clamps, stops, angle plates, jacks, toe dogs, hold-downs, alignment strips, and T bolts in various combinations are mounted on the table of the machine by the operator to best suit all conditions of the operation and workpiece.

The shaping or planing of flat surfaces on workpieces held in a vise is common practice, especially if the workpieces are small.

Typical methods of holding work in a vise are shown in Fig. 10-1. Vises are available in a variety of designs from the builders of planers and shapers, as well as from the manufacturers of vises. The double-screw shaper vise (Fig. 10-2) has a tongue that engages one of the grooves in the plate to accommodate work of various sizes. The rear (movable) jaw can be pivoted to hold work with a slight taper. The vise can be rotated and locked down by hold-down bolts in the base at any angle preset on the scale.

Parallels (Figs. 10-1b, c, and 10-3) are supports which are placed underneath the work to raise it for necessary clearances or to simplify the shaping or planing operation. The angular types are for raising or otherwise bolstering or leveling workpieces having nonparallel and/or irregular surfaces, or for presenting a workpiece surface to the tool at an angle other than 90°.

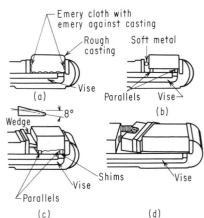

FIG. 10-1. Holding workpieces in vises for shaping and planing (*a*) for machining rough castings; (*b*) for parallel machining; (*c*) for right-angle machining; (*d*) for taper work in a double-screw vise.

10–1

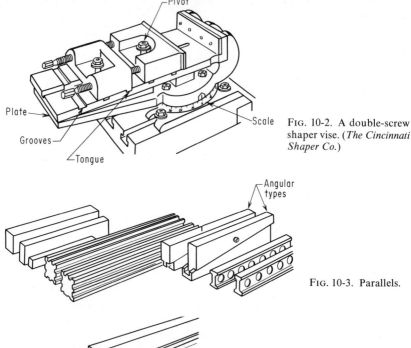

FIG. 10-2. A double-screw shaper vise. (*The Cincinnati Shaper Co.*)

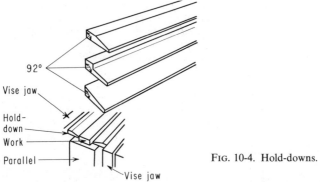

FIG. 10-3. Parallels.

FIG. 10-4. Hold-downs.

Hold-downs, which are thin strips of an approximately triangular cross section, apply a downward force to the work in the vise (Fig. 10-4) in addition to the clamping pressure of the vise jaws.

Workpieces may be clamped directly to the table with T bolts; variations in their designs are shown in Sec. 15.

Workpieces are held by bolts and a wide variety of clamps (see Sec. 15). The plain clamp of Fig. 10-5a may be made adjustable with the addition of a setscrew.

Figure 10-6 shows typical clamping of a workpiece to a shaper table, as well as two end stops for holding the workpiece against the thrust of the tool.

Stop pins and blocks are placed at the ends or sides of the workpiece to prevent its movement on the table. Plain stops (Fig. 10-7a) are round or square pieces of steel to fit T slots or holes in the table; or they are blocks, shown at b, held in slots or held by bolts. The stops illustrated at c, d, and e fit in T slots and incorporate setscrews which can be tightened against the workpiece.

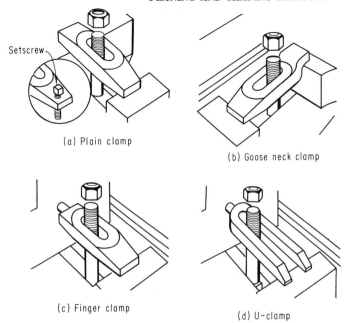

Setscrew

(a) Plain clamp

(b) Goose neck clamp

(c) Finger clamp

(d) U-clamp

FIG. 10-5. Strap clamps.

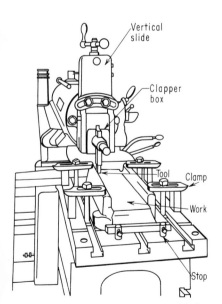

Vertical slide

Clapper box

Tool

Clamp

Work

Stop

FIG. 10-6. Shaper workpiece fastened directly to the table.

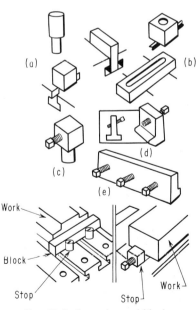

(a)

(b)

(c)

(d)

(e)

Work

Block

Stop

Stop

Work

FIG. 10-7. Stop pins and blocks.

Clamping of a thin, flat workpiece by means of toe dogs is shown in Fig. 10-8. Generally, enough holding pressure will be obtained by setting the toe dogs at an angle of from 8 to 12° from the horizontal.

Aligning strips shown in Fig. 10-9*a, b, c,* and *d* are bolted to the machine table for setting the work on the table, as well as to function as stops. Those shown at *c, d,* and *e* incorporate tongues to fit the table T slots. The angular alignment strip, shown at *e,* can be used in clamping cylindrical workpieces.

Shafting and similar cylindrical workpieces are clamped in V blocks (Fig. 10-10) which are bolted to the machine table.

Workpieces which must be held at a right angle to a finished surface may be secured to an angle plate (Fig. 10-11) with C clamps or other suitable clamps.

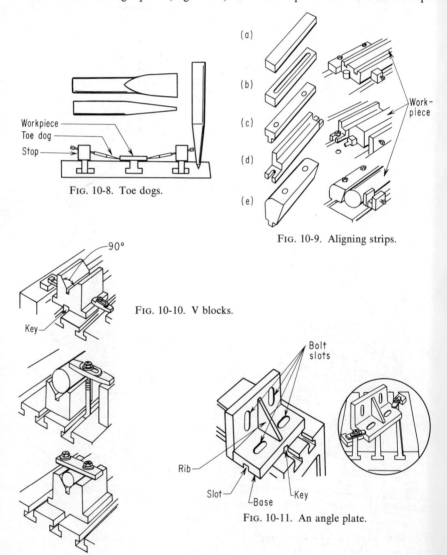

FIG. 10-8. Toe dogs.

FIG. 10-9. Aligning strips.

FIG. 10-10. V blocks.

FIG. 10-11. An angle plate.

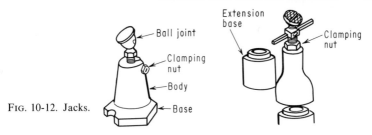

FIG. 10-12. Jacks.

Jacks (Fig. 10-12) are frequently useful in supporting overhanging workpiece sections or in leveling the stock or workpiece. After they are adjusted, jacks should be bolted or clamped to the machine table.

Vises are rarely used with the vertical shaper, but rotary tables are commonly used; various clamps, jacks, etc., are mounted to position on the tables and hold the work.

Flat and tilting as well as supplementary or extension tables are commercially available for the fixturing of workpieces larger than the machine table or for workpieces that are to be set at an angle to it.

Magnetic chucks can be used with suitable stops for holding thin ferrous-metal workpieces.

A first-class planer or shaper hand is generally adept at setting up most work in a vise or directly to the machine table.

References

1. "Shaper Work," New York State Dept. of Education.
2. "Vertical Shaper," The Pratt & Whitney Co.
3. "Shaper Setups," The Cincinnati Shaper Co.

Section 11
GRINDING FIXTURES

By ROBERT W. NEWTON
Associate Engineer, International Business Machines Corp.

The grinding fixtures shown and described in this section are classified according to the grinding process or the type of grinding machine with which they are used, since no standard or quasi-universal classification is presently in use. Although good design practice always applies, these are conditions unique to the grinding process or machine that must be considered in the design of a fixture.

Some of the parts and problems which may affect or be reflected in the design of grinding fixtures are:

1. Coolant nozzles, spray guards, part feeders, and other such devices
2. Coolant escape or control
   a. Coolant delivery through the fixture to the workpiece
   b. Coolant and sludge escape from the fixture
3. Mounting of wheel dressers on or close to the fixture
4. Rotating fixtures and chucks generally require dynamic balancing

FIXTURES FOR CYLINDRICAL GRINDERS

The expansion mandrel of Fig. 11-1a eliminates eccentricity between it and the workpiece. It is run on dead center to grind the small and large ODs of the part concentric with its ID within 0.0003 in. TIR.

The body (1), of hardened, ground, and tempered tool steel, has ground and lapped centers. A setscrew (2), when turned against a rod (3), forces a ball (4) into a tapered hole in the body to expand the Y diameter of the body against the workpiece. The faceplate fixture of Fig. 11-1b has a setscrew (2) which forces wedge rods (1) to expand the arbor.

The mandrel of Fig. 11-2 is used to grind the OD of a part concentric with the tapered bore within 0.00025 in. TIR. The surface Y is previously ground square with the bore and is used in establishing the concentricity specified. Lapped centers in the hardened and ground steel body (1) ensure concentricity. The sleeve (2) pressed on the body has three pins (3), having surfaces Y, which are ground to run true to the centers within 0.0001 in. TIR. A spring-loaded tapered locating pin (4) slides on the body and is retained by a cover (5). A nut (6) spherically seated in a washer (7) clamps the workpiece.

Grinding the OD of a part concentric with its ID within 0.0002 in. is done with the tapered mandrel of Fig. 11-3. The locating diameter of the hardened and ground steel shaft (1), having ground and lapped centers, has a taper equal to the tolerance allowed on the ID of the part.

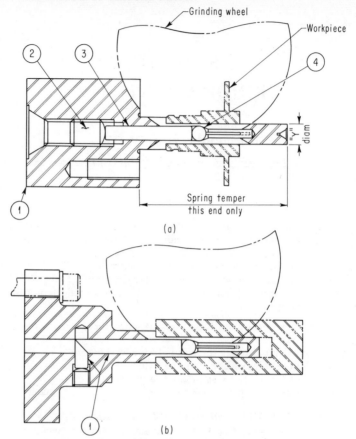

Fig. 11-1. (*a*) Expansion mandrel; (*b*) faceplate expansion fixture.

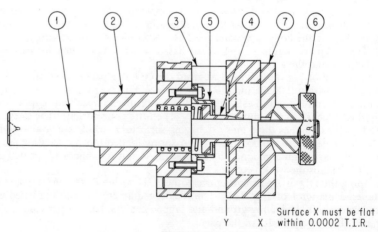

Fig. 11-2. Nut mandrel.

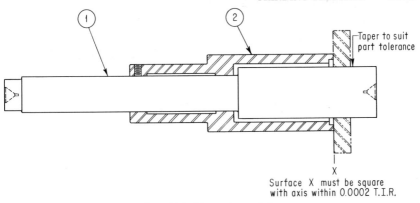

Taper to suit
part tolerance

X
Surface X must be square
with axis within 0.0002 T.I.R.

FIG. 11-3. Tapered mandrel.

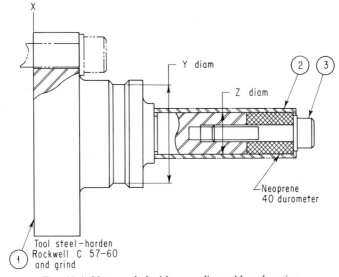

X

Y diam

Z diam

Neoprene
40 durometer

Tool steel—harden
Rockwell C 57—60
and grind

FIG. 11-4. Nut mandrel with expanding rubber clamping.

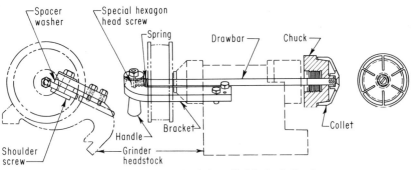

Spacer
washer

Special hexagon
head screw

Spring

Drawbar

Chuck

Handle

Bracket

Collet

Shoulder
screw

Grinder
headstock

FIG. 11-5. Spring chuck for cylindrical grinding.[1]

Surface X of the sleeve (2), which is a tight sliding fit on the shaft, is square with the axis of the arbor within 0.0002 in. TIR.

To prevent distortion of a thin-walled part, it is placed over a closely fitting mandrel (1) (Fig. 11-4) and clamped by expanding the Neoprene bushing (2) with a socket-head cap screw (3).

The fixture of Fig. 11-5, a spring collet, holds the workpiece (Fig. 11-6) during the grinding of its tapered OD. A spring chuck is threaded to fit the headstock of a Norton cylindrical grinder, and its other end is a slip fit in the center hole of the slotted and spring-tempered collet. A drawbar inserted through the grinder headstock and chuck is fastened to the collet with a flat-head cap screw. A compression spring between the headstock and the special hexagon head screw on the drawbar holds the collet in its expanded (work-holding) position. The drawbar is mounted on the grinder headstock. Movement of the draw bar handle releases the workpiece from the collet, which fits the ID on the workpiece.

FIXTURES FOR SURFACE GRINDERS

To position the parts for grinding their angular surfaces, they are held in vise jaws (1, 2) (Fig. 11-7) by blocks (3) against their flat sides. Four self-equalizing plungers (4) located and moving within the stationary jaws (2) compensate for diameter variations in the parts.

The medium for the equalizing system can be oil, clay, or other high viscosity material, but the plungers must be a tight slip fit to prevent leakage of the medium. To prevent cocking of the parts, blocks (5) are machined to closely fit the parts without gripping them.

The cast-iron T-shaped body (1) of the fixture of Fig. 11-8 has three rows of five equally spaced holes in which bolts (2) with eccentric work-holding heads are inserted. A toggle clamp (3) or a clamp similar to the one shown holds the workpiece against the face of the fixture.

The fixture of Fig. 11-9 incorporates a plate (2) which swings on two stripper bolts (3) and a base (1) held on the machine table. The plate is drilled and tapped to receive the bolts of hold-down clamps (not shown) for clamping the work on it. The plate can be fixed at any desired angle by tightening the stripper bolts with a hexagon key.

In the fixture of Fig. 11-10, two flats are ground parallel to each other and to the axis of a hole in a shaft previously ground on centers.

Hardened centers are pressed into angle-iron brackets which are drilled and pinned to the jaws of a grinding vise. The yoke has reamed through holes for the indexing pin. The pin is inserted through the yoke and shaft, and the leg of the yoke is located in an elongated hole in the left-hand bracket. The shaft is placed between

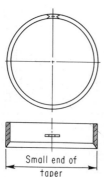

Small end of
taper

FIG. 11-6. Plastic bushing ground in the fixture of FIG. 11-5.

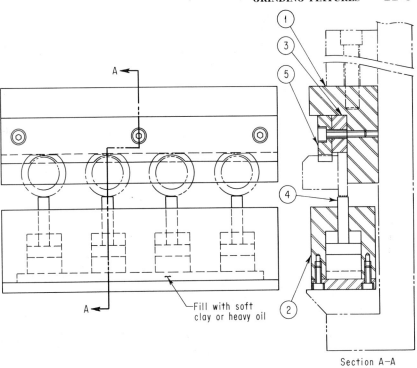

FIG. 11-7. Self-equalizing grinding fixtures for multiple parts.

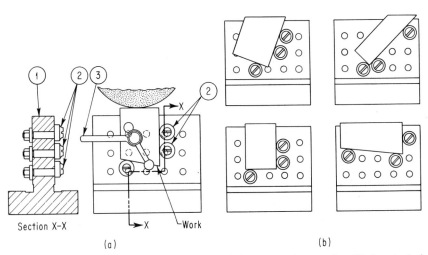

FIG. 11-8. (*a*) Grinding fixture for holding workpieces at various angles; (*b*) four typical setups.[2]

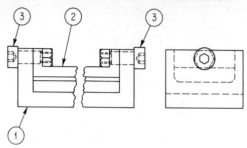

FIG. 11-9. Trunnion-type adjustable grinding fixture.[3]

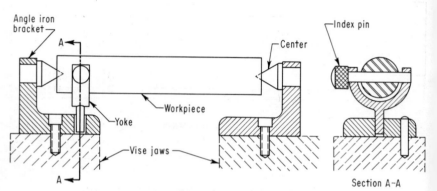

FIG. 11-10. Vise fixture for grinding flats on a shaft.[4]

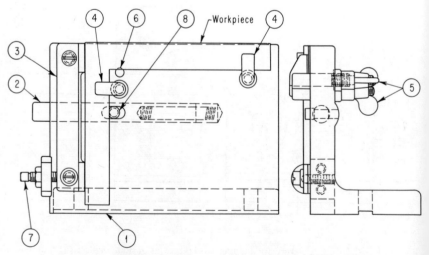

FIG. 11-11. Fixture for grinding a steel try square. (*L. S. Starrett Co.*)

the centers as the vise is tightened. One flat is ground on one side of the shaft; and then the shaft is turned, indexed, and held for grinding the opposite flat.

The cast-iron body (1) of the fixture of Fig. 11-11 can be mounted on any surface grinder for grinding the outer long edge of the workpiece, a steel try square. A pin (8) having a press fit in the spring-loaded plunger (2) holds the edge of the workpiece against the locating block (3) until it is clamped. The part is placed against, and located vertically by, a pin (6) and is held down by hook clamps (4) which are tightened by two wing nuts (5). The locating block is adjusted to a master square with an adjusting screw (7).

The simple angle-plate fixture of Fig. 11-12 was designed for grinding the outside surface of a small stamping (Fig. 11-13) to 0.522 ± 0.001 in. from the center of the 0.156-in.-diam hole and square within 0.003 in. per inch to the inside surface of the part.

The body (1) of the fixture is a cast-iron angle plate to which is fastened a mounting block (7) for the toggle clamp (8). In another block (2) are mounted a locating pin (3), a rest pin (4), a finger jack (5), and its locking thumbscrew (6).

The part is located against the rest pin and on the locating pin engaging the 0.156-in.-diam hole. The finger jack, moved up to support the part, is locked in place by the thumbscrew, which does not change squareness and dimensional relationships of the part. Production is approximately 65 parts per hour.

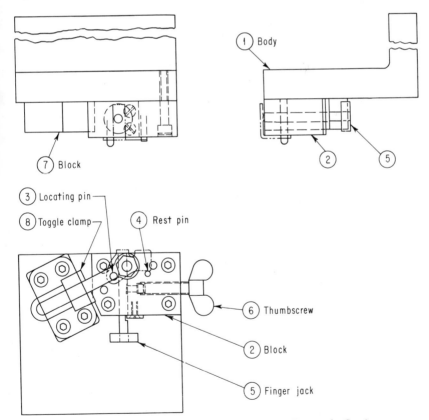

FIG. 11-12. Angle-plate surface-grinding fixture. (*Burroughs Corp.*)

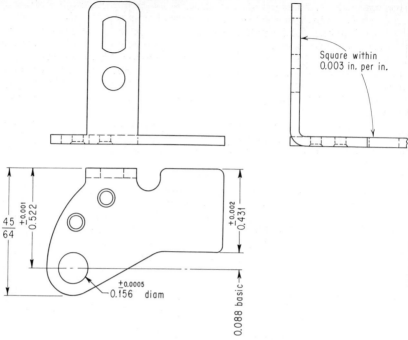

Square within
0.003 in. per in.

$45/64$ $0.522^{+0.001}$

$0.431^{+0.002}$

$0.156^{+0.0005}$ diam

0.088 basic

FIG. 11-13. Workpiece ground in the fixture of Fig. 11-12.

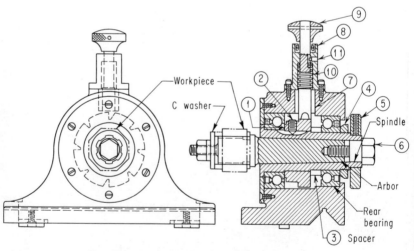

FIG. 11-14. Indexing fixture for an octagonal cam.[5]

All sides of an octagonal cam are ground in the fixture shown in Fig. 11-14. The mandrel has splines that provide a sliding fit in the broached hole in the cam, which is held in place on the mandrel by a C washer and nut. The mandrel is held in the spindle by a drawbolt (6). An index ring (1) is held in contact with the spindle by a setscrew (2). A spacer is fitted between the ring and the rear bearing.

A locknut (4) holds the rear bearing in place. An indexing assembly, consisting of an index plunger (9), a plunger housing (8), a spring (10), and a dog-point setscrew (11) (to prevent plunger rotation), is mounted on the top of the fixture body.

Retraction of the plunger and turning of the handwheel (5) successively bring the notches of the index ring under the plunger. The plunger slides through a bushing (7), engages the notches, and locks the part for grinding each of the eight flat surfaces.

The fixture fits over the V ways of the grinding machine and is held in position by keys and T bolts.

Twenty workpieces (small pump pistons) are vertically placed in the fixture of Fig. 11-15 with their spherical ends on locating pins (1) for grinding the other ends to establish piston lengths of 1.237 to 1.239 in. Rotation of the hand knob (2) clamps all of the pistons between the double V block (4) and two clamping bars (3). Rubber inserts are incorporated in the bars to compensate for variations in diameters of the pistons. Four guide pins (5) set at an angle, as shown, direct a downward component of the clamping force to seat the spherical surfaces of the pistons on the locating pins. A dowel (9) driven through a hole in the head of the clamping stud (6) and into the rear clamping bar prevents the stud from rotating with the hand knob.

After the pistons have been lightly clamped, they are tapped with a rubber mallet to seat them firmly against the locating pins. Further turning of the hand knob sets up full clamping forces.

Each of the six workpieces (Fig. 11-17) held in the fixture of Fig. 11-16 is composed of thin, magnetically soft (Mumetal) laminations which have been stacked to form a small magnetic-core assembly.

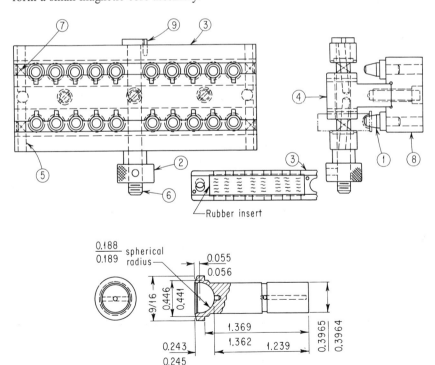

—Rubber insert

Fig. 11-15. Fixture for grinding twenty small pistons.[6]

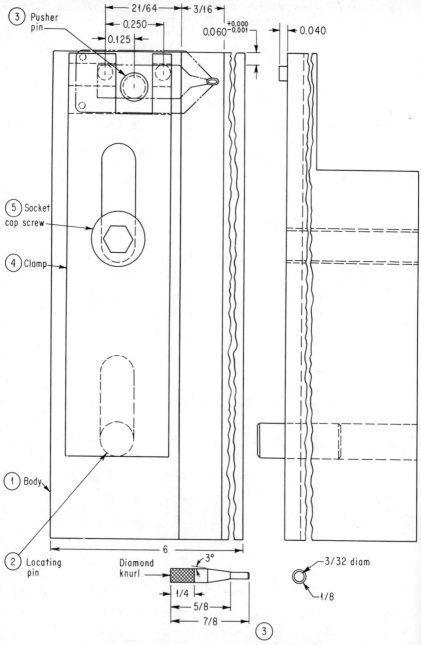

FIG. 11-16. Fixture for grinding six small laminated electromagnet cores. (*International Business Machines Corp.*)

The long inside edge of each stacked core rests against two $\frac{1}{16}$-in.-diam locating pins (2) presenting surface A of the edges of the laminations to the grinding wheel. A knurled, tapered pusher pin (3), which is a slip fit in the fixture body (1), contacts the opposite edge of the core and holds the part snugly against the locating pins. Socket-head cap screws (5) and light steel clamps (4) hold the cores against the vertical surface of the fixture body.

The top surface of the body is ground to establish a distance of 0.060 (+0.000, −0.001) in. between it and the upper edges of the twelve locating pins for setup and for grinding the width of the laminations to 0.061 (+0.001, −0.000) in.

After surface A is ground, each core is removed and reversed in the fixture (with surface B up) for grinding surface B.

Each workpiece of Fig. 11-18, an electrical core assembly, is located by a pin (3) (Fig. 11-19) engaging the 0.022-in.-diam hole. The workpiece is positioned by this pin and a dowel (4) which bears against the outside of the core. A socket-head screw (5) and a small strap clamp (2) hold the assembly against the vertical face of the fixture body (1). Since the fixture holds six workpieces, the distance between the six locating pins and top surface of the body is established at 0.090 (+0.0002, −0.0000) in. by grinding the top of the body and accurately fitting the pins for setup and true location of each workpiece.

A brass insert (6) between the body and the base (1) concentrates magnetic lines of force in the base (which rests upon a magnetic chuck).

The tip of a firing-pin body is ground by a crush-formed grinding wheel in the fixture of Fig. 11-20. The crush-form roll holder is placed in the adapter (1) to crush-form the grinding wheel. The roll holder is removed and replaced by the work-holding assembly. A shoulder on the workpiece is placed against a shoulder on the fixture and held in the groove by a hinged clamp.

The fixture consists of a body (2), a hinged clamp (3), and a clamp bolt (4).

The V grooves in a roll-formed strip (Fig. 11-21) are ground in the fixture of Fig. 11-22 by a four-wheel form grinder.

A filler block, held by T bolts to the base of the grinding machine, supports the fixture and the magnetic chuck and aligns the V's in the sides of the strip with the wheels and crusher rolls.

The magnetic chuck is energized, and four strips are placed in the locating blocks (2) and magnetically held against the vertical faces of the blocks. Their V grooves are located on removable pins (3) and their ends against four stop blocks

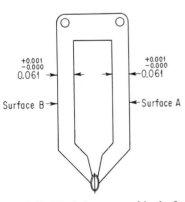

Fig. 11-17. Workpieces ground in the fixture of Fig. 11-16.

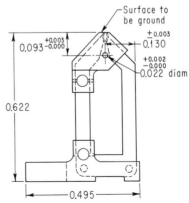

Fig. 11-18. Workpieces ground in the fixture of Fig. 11-19.

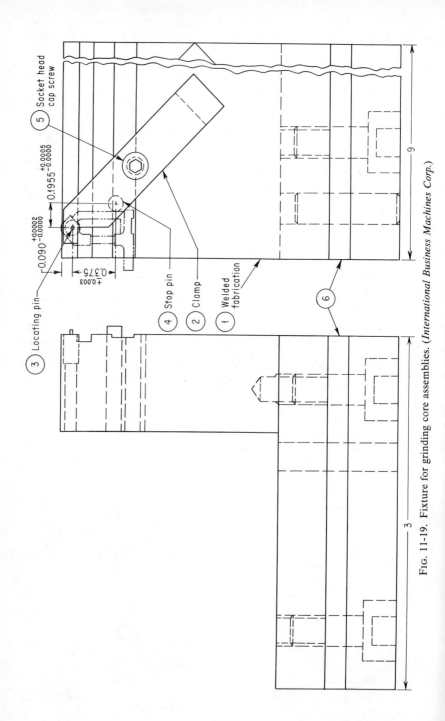

① Welded fabrication
② Clamp
③ Locating pin
④ Stop pin
⑤ Socket head cap screw

0.090 $^{+0.0002}_{-0.0000}$

0.1955 $^{+0.0005}_{-0.0000}$

0.375 $^{+0.0003}_{-}$

Fig. 11-19. Fixture for grinding core assemblies. (*International Business Machines Corp.*)

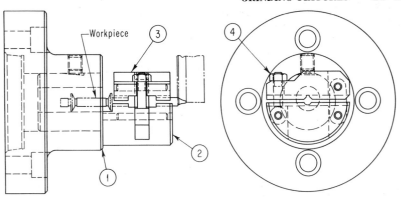

FIG. 11-20. Fixture for crush-form grinding. (*U.S. Naval Ordnance Plant.*)

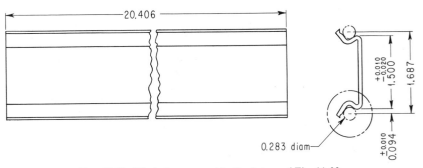

FIG. 11-21. Workpiece ground in the fixture of Fig. 11-22.

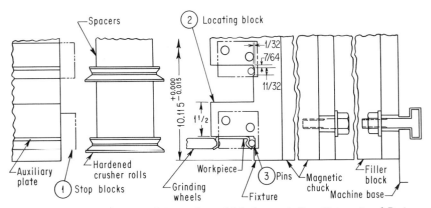

FIG. 11-22. Magnetic chuck and fixture for multiple-form grinding. (*International Business Machines Corp.*)

(1). Four more parts are placed in the locating blocks with their ends butted against the ends of the parts in the fixture. All parts are then rapped with a mallet to force them to be correctly located and seated.

When the V's on one side of the strips are ground, the magnetic-chuck circuit is opened for removal and cleaning of the strips and of the pins. The fixture is cleaned and another set of larger pins, which compensates for stock ground from the V's, is inserted. The strips are reversed in the fixture for grinding the other V's.

The fixture of Fig. 11-23 is a thin metal plate. It can be of cast iron or machine steel with a cutout (1) in which the workpiece is placed. The fixture and workpiece are fed manually or by power between the grinding areas of two double disks for the grinding of two parallel surfaces simultaneously. Other plates, identical except for cutout dimensions, accommodate workpieces of various sizes. Another fixture for double-disk grinders is the rotary carrier, which is a round plate with cutouts around its perimeter. It is mounted on the machine and rotated to successively position each cutout and part between the abrasive disks.

FIXTURES FOR INTERNAL GRINDING

The adapter plate (3) of the fixture of Fig. 11-24 fits the spindle of a Bryant internal grinder for grinding a counterbore in a gear. A hardened and spring-tempered split collet (1) fits on a flanged shaft (2) which is bolted to the adapter plate.

The workpiece, a gear, squares up against the ground face of a stop collar (4) when the gear is clamped. An expansion plug (5) is threaded on a pull bar (6) which exerts a 1,200-lb force on the plug. The expansion plug is adjusted so that it will not interfere with the wheel grinding the counterbore (according to reference dimension, 0.688 to 0.692 in.). A collet OD of 1.251 to 1.250 in., to fit the ID of the gear without distorting it, is also secured by this adjustment.

In the fixture of Fig. 11-25, a chamfer is ground in the hub of a casting. After one chamfer is ground, the part is reversed in the fixture for the grinding of a chamfer in the opposite end of the bore. Locating from the pitch diameter of the splined hub allows the chamfers to be ground concentric with that diameter.

The adapter (5) of the fixture is mounted on a Heald internal grinder and is adjusted by setscrews (6) when the entire fixture is mounted on the grinder.

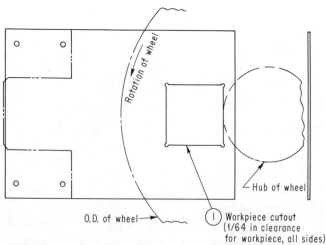

Fig. 11-23. Fixture for a double-disk grinder. (*International Business Machines Corp.*)

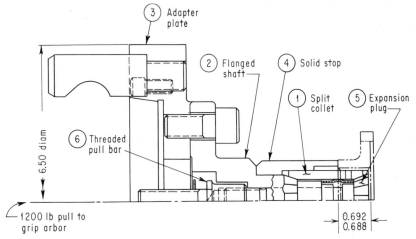

Fɪɢ. 11-24. Split collet to grind a counterbore. (*N. A. Woodworth Co.*)

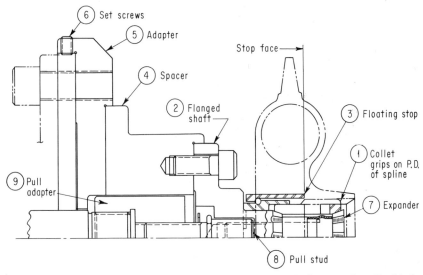

Fɪɢ. 11-25. Collet for grinding chamfers concentric with the pitch diameter of a splined hub. (*N. A. Woodworth Co.*)

A flanged shaft (2) is bolted to a spacer (4) which in turn is mounted on the adapter. A spring-tempered collet (1) fits the internal splines in the hub of the workpiece. The collet and a floating stop (3) are mounted on the shaft.

A collet expander (7) is fastened to a pull stud (8). The stud is connected to the drawbar of the grinder by a pull adapter (9). With the pull stud in the forward position, the expander is adjusted until the OD of the collet is 1.915 in. (for adequate clamping of the part's hub without distorting it).

The cylindrical aluminum part (1) shown in the fixture of Fig. 11-26 is preloaded in a V-bottom carrier against a stop plate (2) for grinding the ID. After the bore on one end of the part is ground, the carrier is unclamped and reversed for grinding the bore on the opposite end. Spare carriers are preloaded for insertion in the fixture to replace carriers with finished parts. The carrier is ground to a close slip fit for the OD of the part, which is held in the carrier by a screw (3).

The carrier is placed in the V ways of a block (4) against a stop pin (5) and is clamped against the V ways with a yoke-clamp assembly (6). The faceplate assembly (7), the block, and a subplate (8) are mounted on a Heald grinder. The entire fixture is adjusted for 0.0000 in. concentricity with the spindle center line by four setscrews (9). Such a fixture should always be balanced with the part in place.

FIXTURES FOR TOOL AND CUTTER GRINDING

The fixture of Fig. 11-27 consists of three cold-rolled-steel plates welded together and then ground to size. The spacing of the tapped holes for the clamp screws permits various sizes of shear blades and similar workpieces to be ground.

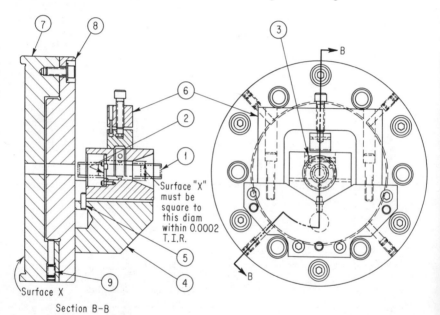

Section B–B

FIG. 11-26. Faceplate fixture for grinding two opposite bores concentrically. (*Thompson Products, Inc.*)

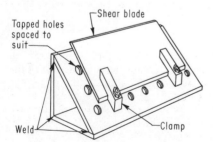

FIG. 11-27. Fixture for grinding shear blade edges. (*The Tool & Manufacturing Engineer.*)

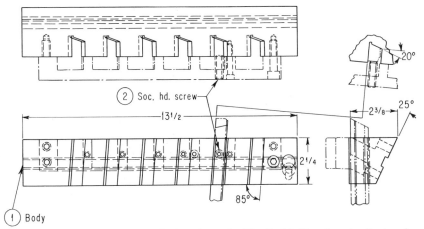

(2) Soc. hd. screw

(1) Body

FIG. 11-28. Fixture for grinding single-point tools. (*The Tool & Manufacturing Engineer.*)

Six single-point tools are clamped in the body (1) of fixture of Fig. 11-28 by socket-head screws (2). A hydraulic surface grinder sharpens the cutting angles on from 28 to 33 tools per hour.

The swinging fixture of Fig. 11-29 consists of two center heads which are adjustable along slots in the base for holding mandrels of different lengths between the centers. A slot across the back of each head at an angle of 45° to the horizontal contains an adjustable slide which is supported by the table center of the grinding machine.

The workpiece (a thin cutter or saw) and a hardened index wheel are clamped on a mandrel which is mounted between the fixture centers.

An adjustable mount holds a two-fingered spring-steel indexing catch which allows the grinding of a cutter having twice as many teeth as the index wheel.

The stop plate can be adjusted to allow the fixture to swing about the table centers and to bring the workpiece only to full cutter depth against the wheel.

The fixture of Fig. 11-30 for grinding lathe and grinder centers has front and rear supports which slide between rails to accommodate tapered centers of different lengths. A hardened and ground tail center supports the small end of the center. Setscrews in a gripping ring attached to a retainer plate securely lock the small end of the workpiece against the tail center.

The large end of a workpiece is adequately supported (for the light grinding pressures involved) by the front edge of the ID of the slip bushing. When changing from one size taper to another, the bushing is interchanged for one of the correct diameter. Rotation of the workpiece is manual.

The fixture may be used on any cutter-grinding machine without the use of a set of accurate tapered adapter sleeves.

The workpiece of Fig. 11-31, a swaging die, is placed on two rest plates and clamped against two relieved locating blocks, which are fastened to a cradle of the fixture.

The turning of the handle positions the cradle, through rotation of the worm gear (2) and wheel (1), to align the outside edge of the conical surface of the die cavity with the direction of grinding-wheel travel.

As the grinding-machine table moves back and forth, a cam-operated air valve, tripped at the end of each stroke, synchronizes the stroke of the air cylinder with the reversal of the table. The cylinder piston, through a ratchet and pawl and

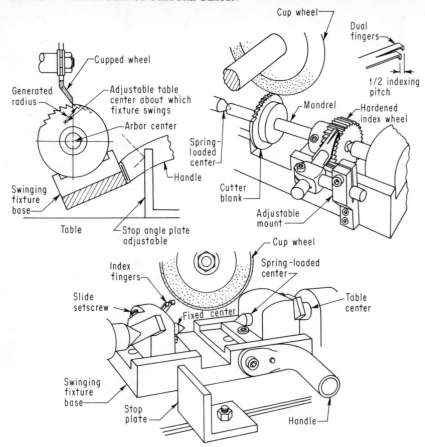

FIG. 11-29. Fixture for grinding cutters and saws.[6]

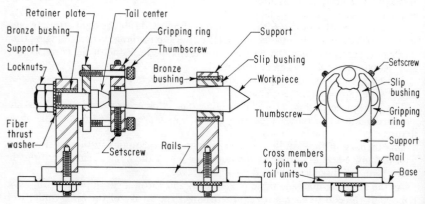

FIG. 11-30. Lathe center grinding fixture.

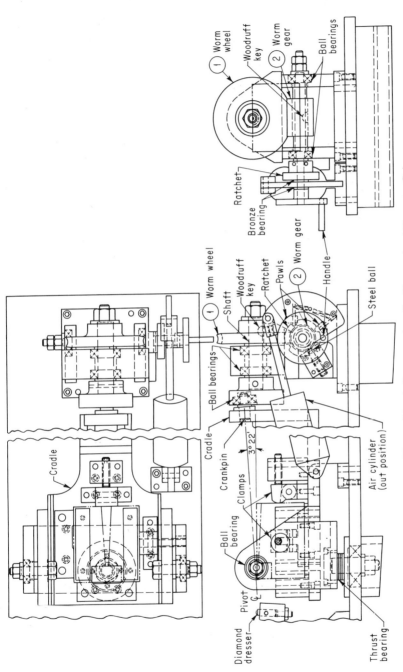

Fig. 11-31. Fixture for grinding a swaging die. (*International Harvester Co.*)

11–19

worm-gear reduction, intermittently revolves the crank pin and the cradle. During each stroke of the machine table, a narrow band along the conical surface of the die cavity is presented to the edge of the wheel.

After each 180° rotation of the crank pin, the pawls are repositioned to produce intermittent rotation in the opposite direction, and the grinding wheel is lowered to remove more die material.

References

1. Newton, R. W.: Spring Chuck and Fixture for Grinding a Molded Plastic Bushing, *Machinery,* December, 1951.
2. Sobkowiak, J.: Grinding Fixture for Holding Work at Any Angle, *Machinery,* March, 1953.
3. Minser, R.: Grinding Fixture Has Adjustable-angle Feature, *Machinery,* October, 1957.
4. Rush, F. L.: Flat-grinding Fixture on Vise, *Am. Machinist,* Dec. 3, 1956.
5. Mawson, R.: Fixture Speeds Critical Grinding, *Iron Age,* February, 1950.
6. Ricker, C. S.: Universal Grinding Fixture Positions Thin Cutters and Saws, *Am. Machinist,* June 25, 1951.

Section 12
ASSEMBLY FIXTURES

Fixtures described in this section, and broadly classified as assembly fixtures, are of two general types:

1. Mechanical assembly fixtures for operations performed at ordinary (room) temperatures with mechanical means
2. Fixtures for hot-joining methods for assembly work using energy in the form of heat as an intrinsic major process factor

MECHANICAL ASSEMBLY FIXTURES

By Committee for Mechanical Assembly Fixtures*

There never has been any standard or unique classification of these types of assembly fixtures. The fixtures in this section have been classified according to the operation or process performed with the fixture. The various categories follow:

1. *Riveting fixtures* hold two or more parts together in predetermined positions while the parts are riveted as specified by the part print.

2. *Drilling and pinning jigs* hold two or more parts to the part-print dimensions while the parts are drilled and pinned to assembly specifications. Drilling is normally done through bushings. This application can also apply to several pinning operations in one jig. Sometimes a means for staking or setting the pin in place is also provided.

3. *Staking fixtures* are designed to hold and position an assembly while a pin or other detail is staked by hand or machine to prevent its loosening during use.

4. *Crimping and swaging fixtures* are used in the assembly of two parts by crimping a portion of one part over another.

5. *Pressing fixtures* are of two types:

a. Holding fixtures hold parts together while an adhesive dries. A means for applying pressure during the drying cycle is provided when necessary. Whenever possible such a fixture holds a multiple quantity of assemblies.

b. Other pressing fixtures hold two parts while one is pressed into another. Usually an arbor press or hydraulic press is used for this purpose. When necessary, various means can be provided in a press-fitting fixture for sizing a part after it is pressed into another. Ball sizing and sizing arbors are most commonly used.

6. *Tab-bending fixtures* are designed for holding parts together, positioning them, and forcing tabs of one part over the other.

* The members of the committee are Robert Carbrey, President, Valley Engineering Co.; Eleonora Freeman, Tool Designer, General Electric Co.; Barry Krumeich, Tool Designer, International Business Machines Corp.; William Mazar, Chief Tool Designer, Link Aviation, Inc.; James Wilson, Chief Tool Designer, Universal Instruments Corp.; Orin Lillie, Tool Engineer, International Business Machines Corp., Assistant Chairman; and Robert W. Newton, Associate Engineer, International Business Machines Corp., Chairman.

7. *Wire-stitching fixtures* hold parts in position for fastening with wire stitches.

8. *Wire-stapling fixtures* hold parts together and position them for fastening with wire staples.

9. *Special holding fixtures* are designed for holding and positioning parts for unique assembly applications, such as assembling a detent ball in a deep hole or locating screws through deep holes.

a. Trunnion holding fixtures hold a part or assembly while other parts not in the same plane are assembled to it.

b. Cradle holding fixtures are for the purpose of holding or nesting a part having an irregular contour in a comfortable working position while other parts are assembled on or in it.

c. Plastic holding fixtures, for assemblies, are usually cradles that fit the irregular contours of a part or assembly and hold or nest them in working position while other parts are assembled on or in it.

d. Support legs are another simple means for holding a part or assembly having an irregular contour in position while other parts are assembled on or in it.

e. Harness boards are heavy boards into which pegs are driven at predetermined locations as an aid in winding and assembling cables and harnesses.

f. Potting or encapsulating holding fixtures hold connectors with cables or harnesses in a cavity while a melted potting compound is poured into the cavity and solidifies.

10. *Masking fixtures* are of several types:

a. Some types are designed for keeping paint or other coatings, such as anodizing compounds, from certain surfaces of the workpiece (see Sec. 14).

b. Other masking fixtures, for the convenience of the assembler, identify different terminal locations on a terminal-board assembly with a template having various color codes around its holes.

Air-clamping Riveting Fixtures. Production from standard riveting machines can be considerably increased for such components as levers with riveted studs by use of the simple holding fixture illustrated in Fig. 12-1.

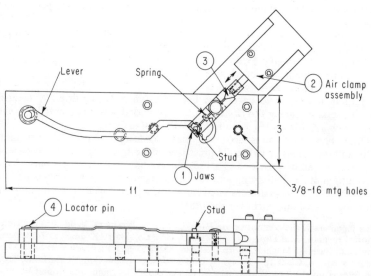

Fig. 12-1. Riveting fixture with air clamping. (*Burroughs Corp.*)

The 0.094-in.-square stud is held securely in the clamp jaws (1) when the air-clamp assembly (2) is actuated, thereby moving a plunger (3) forward. The tapered plunger end causes a scissors action of the jaws which then exert clamping force on the stud. The lever, positioned on the clamped stud and on the pin locator (4), is ready to be riveted by the machine. Retraction of the plunger releases the clamped stud and allows the completed assembly to be removed.

Fixtures for Riveting Both Ends of a Shaft Simultaneously. Upsetting both ends of a shaft simultaneously with a single-head riveting machine can be performed in the fixture depicted in Fig. 12-2.

The parts, two levers and a shaft with flatted ends, are located by pins (1) and blocks (2) on a holder plate (3) which is free to float up and down on an upright (4). A lower anvil (5) (not attached to the machine) is slip-fit in a collar (6) and spring-loaded from the fixture base.

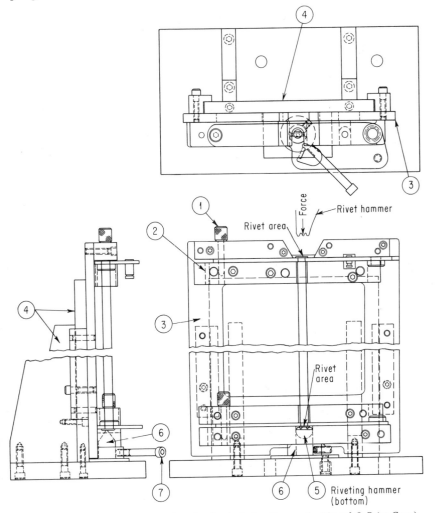

FIG. 12-2. Fixture for riveting both ends of a shaft simultaneously. (*Speed-O-Print Corp.*)

When the rivet hammer engages the top end of the shaft, the resultant pressure forces the floating holder plate down, making the lower end of the shaft contact the lower anvil. The anvil is then rotated by hand with a screw handle (7). Thus the hammer force exerted upon the upper end is used to simultaneously rivet over the opposite shaft end.

A Riveting Fixture with Spring-loaded Adjustable Center Punch. Cold riveting of gold-alloy contacts into electrical-contact assemblies can be performed by an inexpensive riveting fixture which features a standard, purchased, toolmaker's spring-loaded adjustable center punch, illustrated in Fig. 12-3.

Powered by a small air cylinder (1) which compresses the center punch (2), the contact is riveted to the phosphor-bronze spring by a specially ground tip (3). An anvil (4) machined to receive the working end of the contact is interchangeable for

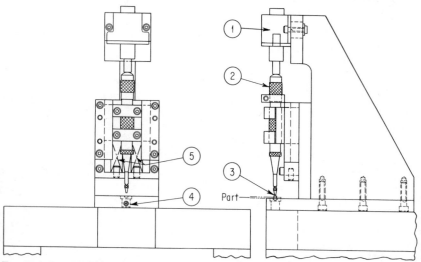

Fig. 12-3. Riveting fixture with a spring-loaded adjustable center punch. (*Link Aviation, Inc.*)

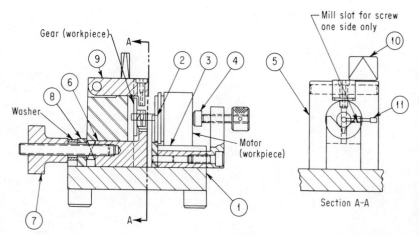

Fig. 12-4. Drill and pin fixture for gear and motor shaft. (*General Electric Co.*)

other contact shapes and sizes. Two springs (5) return the center punch and carrier slide to starting position when the cylinder is released.

A Drill and Pin Fixture for Gear and Motor Shaft. When parts have to be drilled and pinned together at assembly, a fixture such as that shown in Fig. 12-4 can be used. In this application, an aluminum gear is to be pinned to a stainless-steel motor shaft to a predetermined dimension. After the gear and motor are cor-

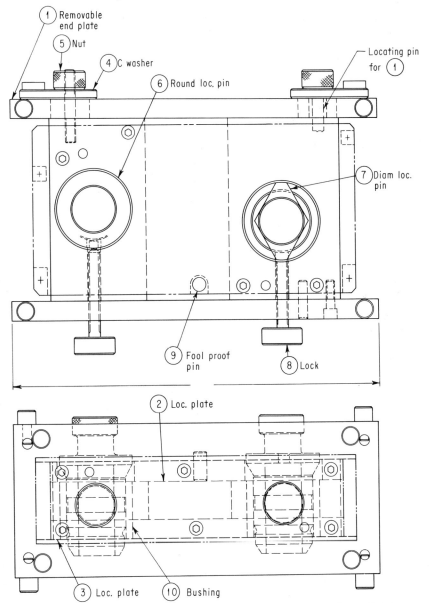

FIG. 12-5. Drill and pin fixture for concentric holes. (*General Electric Co.*)

rectly positioned, they are securely held together by means of a screw through a tapped hole in the gear hub.

The fixture consists of a base (1) on which is mounted a hardened locating plate (2) that is ground to fit the mounting hub of the motor. A soft pad (3) supports the motor, and a thumbscrew (4) with a swivel foot pushes it against the locating plate. A block (5) is also mounted on the base. A locating surface for the gear is ground on the block, and a clearance slot for the motor shaft is also machined in it. The gear is clamped against the locating surface of the block by a sliding V clamp (6) fitted in the block and moved with a stud and hand knob (7) which is threaded through another block (8) mounted on the base. A bushing leaf (9) is also fastened to the block. It is clamped securely with a quarter-turn screw (10). A clearance slot for the motor shaft is also machined in the large block. On one side of the sliding V clamp is a clearance slot for the screw (11) which holds the gear and motor together for drilling through a tapped hole in the gear hub.

To operate, a motor on whose shaft a gear has been loosely assembled is placed on the locating plate while the bushing leaf is open. The motor is then pushed against the locating plate with the thumbscrew. The gear is then pulled against the locating surface by the sliding V clamp. Now the gear can be secured to the motor shaft with the screw (11), and the workpieces are ready for drilling. The bushing leaf is closed and locked by the quarter-turn screw. After the parts are drilled, the bushing leaf is raised and the pin driven in place while the parts are still held securely. Then the clamps are loosened and the assembled workpiece can be removed.

A Drill and Pin Fixture That Controls Concentricity. Specifications for a workpiece, a frame assembly, require holes in the bottom plate and holes in the top plate to be concentric within 0.001 in. TIR so that electrical components can be mounted accurately. The fixture illustrated in Fig. 12-5 positions the workpiece for this purpose and holds it securely for drilling and pinning.

The end plate (1) is removed from the fixture. The frame assembly, which has been loosely assembled with the screws, is slid onto the locating plates (2, 3). An error-proof pin (9) prevents faulty positioning of the workpiece. The end plate is then replaced and secured with a C washer (4) and a knurled nut (5) at each end.

A round locating pin (6) and a diamond locating pin (7) slide into bushings (10) and align the holes in the bottom plate and the holes in the top plate of the workpiece. They are locked in place by means of knurled-head screws (8) to allow

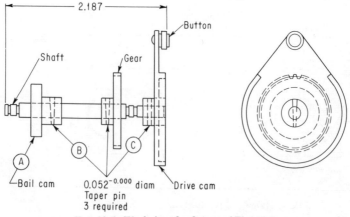

Fig. 12-6. Workpiece for fixture of Fig. 12-7.

tumbling of the fixture, because the frame assembly must be drilled and pinned from both sides.

No drill bushings are required, because the dowel-pin holes are predrilled under-size in the top and bottom plates of the assembly.

After the dowel-pin holes are drilled, the grease-coated dowels are driven in place. Then the end plate is removed and the workpiece taken out of the fixture.

A Drill Fixture to Drill, Ream, and Pin a Geneva Drive Assembly. It is often necessary to assemble parts to predetermined, close-toleranced locations and then pin them together. The Geneva drive assembly, illustrated in Fig. 12-6, requires such a procedure. It consists of a gear, drive cam, and bail cam that are pinned to a shaft.

To drill, ream, and pin this assembly, the two cams and the gear are preassem-bled on the shaft and placed in the fixture, which is illustrated in Fig. 12-7.

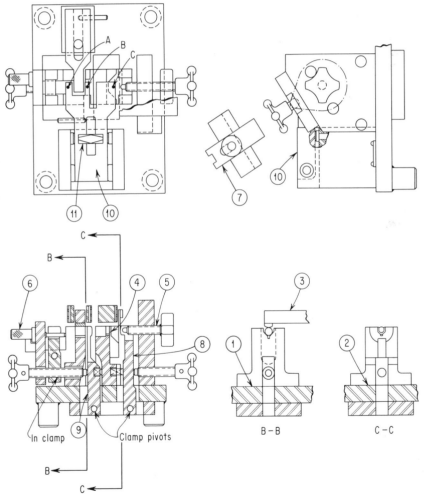

FIG. 12-7. Drill, ream, and pin fixture for Geneva drive assembly. (*International Business Machines Corp.*)

V blocks (1, 2) position the shaft on the center line. It is held in the V blocks with a strap clamp (3). Since all dimensions are taken from the groove in the cam shaft, the surface is positioned in the locator block (4). A spring-loaded pusher (5) ensures that the shaft is held firmly against this locating surface. The angular relationship for the bail and drive cams is set by engaging a locating pin (6) in a hole in the bail cam and by a locator slide (7) on the button of the drive cam. The two cams and the gear are also clamped against their locating surfaces by two clamps (8, 9). A hinged leaf (10) is closed and locked into position with a quarter-turn screw (11). Since limited space prohibits the use of drill bushings, the leaf is hardened and the drill holes (*A, B,* and *C*) in it are ground and lapped. The assembly is now ready for drilling.

After drilling, the bushing leaf is released and swung out of the way. The assembly is now ready for reaming.

While parts are still securely clamped in the fixture, it is advisable to drive and stake the three taper pins to assemble the unit. Then the assembly can be removed from the fixture and stored as one unit.

A Standard Assembly and Staking Fixture for a Hydraulic Press. Figure 12-8 shows a gear that is being pressed onto a shaft and staked prior to copper brazing. The shank of the adapter (1) is made to fit in the ram of a commercial hydraulic press. The punch holder (2) is a slip in fit in the adapter and holds the staking punches (5).

The lower adapter (3) is a slip fit in the base of the press, and the adapter ID is a slip fit for the shaft (workpiece).

When assembling, the shaft is placed in the adapter, and the gear is placed upon the shaft. Spring-tempered fingers (4) are adjusted to hold the gear perpendicular to the shaft. When the press ram is lowered, the staking punches contact the gear and press it onto the shaft until seated against the shoulder. The four staking punches stake the gear to the shaft in four places by the continued pressure of the ram.

Similar gear and shaft assemblies can be staked in this manner by changing the following three items as required: the adapter to hold the shaft, the punch holder (2), and the staking punches (5).

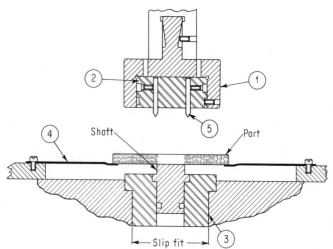

Fig. 12-8. Standard assembly and assembly fixture for a hydraulic press. (*International Business Machines Corp.*)

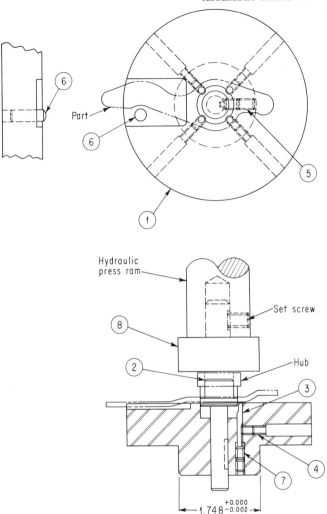

Fɪɢ. 12-9. Assembly and staking fixture. (*International Business Machines Corp.*)

An Assembly and Staking Fixture. In the assembly shown in Fig. 12-9, it is necessary to press a hub into a lever and stake the two parts together before brazing in an atmospheric furnace.

The fixture, also shown in Fig. 12-9, is used in a standard hydraulic press, which has an adapter for a 1.750-in. diam and a pressure pad in the bottom to push a pad (2) upward to eject the completed assembly.

To operate, the lever is placed with its locating diameter on the pad (2) and against a locating pin (6) which prevents the lever from twisting. The hub is then placed with its locating diameter on the pad. By this method the hub is aligned with the hole in the lever.

Pressure is applied to the top of the hub by a flat punch (8) mounted in the press ram. When the ram descends, the hub is pressed through the hole in the lever; the pad is forced down, and the four staking punches (3) stake the lever to the hub in four places. When the press ram is raised, the pad is returned to its normal position by a pressure pad mounted in the press bed, and the completed assembly can be removed.

The staking punches can be adjusted for different staking depths by one setscrew (7) and held in alignment by another setscrew (4).

Movement of the pad is restricted by a dog-point setscrew (5) mounted in a base (1).

A Multiple Staking and Assembly Fixture. Shown in Fig. 12-10 is a standard die set used in a knuckle-action air press. Interchangeable punches and anvils are provided for staking and assembling different parts. To reduce the number of staking punches required, the staking diameter could be standardized with product design.

Two 0.500-in.-diam holes are bored in alignment in the upper and lower shoes of the die set (1). A dowel (9) is press-fitted into the bottom portion with sufficient length left exposed for locating the adapter (3) in alignment with the staking punch (7). The staking punch is a slip fit for the 0.500-in.-diam hole in the upper shoe of the die set. It is clamped by a thumbscrew (8).

The anvil (2) is a slip fit in a hole in the adapter (3). It is clamped by means of the thumbscrew (15). The locating plate (4) is a slip fit over the anvil. It is clamped

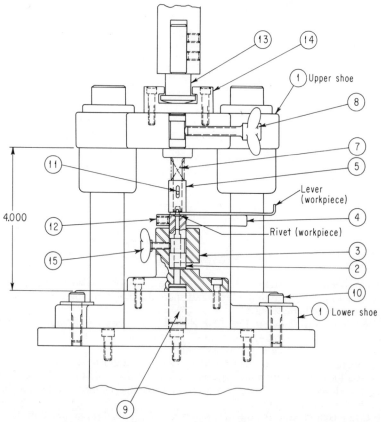

Fig. 12-10. Multiple staking and assembly fixture. (*Argus Cameras, Inc.*)

by a headless setscrew (12). The spring-loaded pressure pad (5) slides on the staking punch (7). Its movement is restricted by the dowel (11), which is press-fit in the staking punch (7) and slides into a slot in the pressure pad.

The lower shoe of the die set is fastened to an adapter plate mounted on the air-press base with fillister head screws (10). The upper shoe of the die set is attached to the press ram with a floating adapter assembly (13, 14).

To operate, the head of a rivet is placed in the recess of the anvil (2), and a lever is placed over the rivet and on the locating plate (4). When the air press is actuated, the ram descends and the pressure pad contacts the lever and holds it firmly against the rivet. Continuation of the press-ram stroke depresses the punch (7) to stake the rivet to the lever, and then the ram returns to the raised or normal position.

Riveting Dies. The riveting of many assemblies can be performed in a punch press with a riveting die similar to that of Fig. 12-11.

The riveting die swages the rivets which secure the upper and lower ball separators, making the ball bearing a completed and permanent assembly. Components for the bearing assembly consist of bearing balls, an inner race, an outer race, an upper ball separator (with rivet holes only), and a lower ball separator (with rivets attached); these are assembled by hand prior to insertion into the die and swaging of the rivet heads.

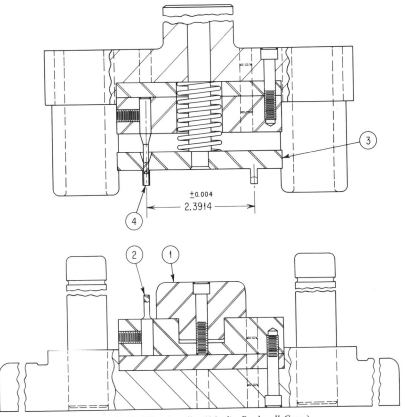

Fig. 12-11. Riveting die. (*Marlin-Rockwell Corp.*)

The die section contains a tapered locator (1) for positioning the inner bearing race. Sixteen punches (2) spaced around the locator support and locate the lower ball separator, which contains the previously staked-in rivets. Swaging is accomplished by the punch section which compresses a spring-loaded pressure pad (3); through the pressure pad sixteen upper punches (4) descend and swage over the protruding rivet ends, joining the separator halves and making the ball bearing a permanent assembly.

A feature of this tool is the consistent pressure which it applies on all rivets in one particular assembly.

A Fixture to Crimp a Latch to a Handle Bracket. The fixture shown in Fig. 12-12 hangs from a retractor so that the parts can be crimped on an assembly line. The workpieces, a latch and handle bracket, are crimped together as shown in the illustration.

The fixture consists of a punch (1) machined to a slip fit for the OD of a shaft (6) and a slip fit in an anvil (3). The shaft and anvil are assembled inside of the punch and held together by a ½-13 thread. A retainer (2) provides guiding surfaces for the punch (1). Plates (4, 5) serve as nests for the workpieces.

To operate, the latch and handle bracket are nested together on the anvil and between the two nest plates. When an air cylinder is actuated, the punch and retainer are forced downward. The anvil, which is fastened to the shaft, remains stationary, thus crimping the latch around the handle-bracket flange. When the air cylinder is reversed, the punch moves up. The assembled workpiece can be removed and another latch and handle bracket positioned for crimping.

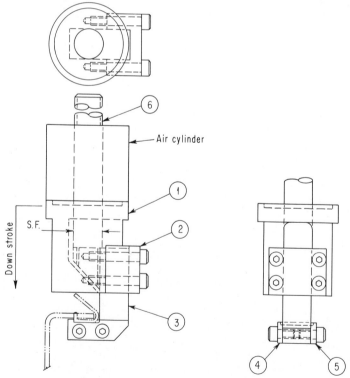

Fig. 12-12. Crimping fixture. (*Lawn-Boy.*)

A Swaging Fixture for Electrical Plug Connectors. Assembling electrical plug connectors to a chassis, previously assembled with other electronic components, requires special treatment such as that performed by a swaging fixture (Fig. 12-13). The chassis has printed circuits, resistors, capacitors, transistors, potentiometers, etc., assembled in a drawn-steel container having a flanged opening for the electrical plug connector (Fig. 12-14). The plastic electrical plug connector is hand-

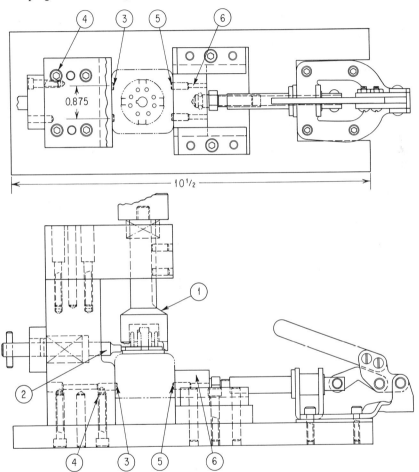

FIG. 12-13. Swaging fixture for electrical connectors. (*Link Aviation, Inc.*)

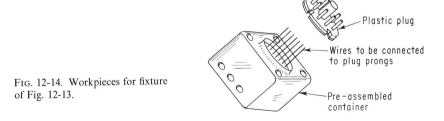

FIG. 12-14. Workpieces for fixture of Fig. 12-13.

placed over the wires protruding from the container and into the flanged hole which receives and seats it. Portions of the hole flange are swaged into the four slots of the plug connector to prevent its removal by a swage punch (1). The swage punch descends and partially lances four segments of the flange and forces them into the slots of the plastic plug. The cutting and swaging angles of the four prongs of the punch must be carefully developed and their surfaces maintained in a sharp condition.

The plastic plug connector is oriented by a retracting locator (2). The assembled chassis is supported by locator pins (3) in a stationary block (4) and locator pins (5) in a movable clamping block (6). Power for operation of the punch can be supplied by any small assembly press, either air, electrical, or hand operated. A stop collar on the upper end of the punch limits travel, preventing damage to chassis components.

A Pressing Fixture for Adhesive Joining. Eight workpieces are clamped during the adhesive-drying cycle in the fixture illustrated in Fig. 12-15. The adhesive is applied to each hub of the gears and to each hole in the clutch plates. The C washer (1) permits fast loading and unloading. Four stop pins (2) together with two locating pins (3) position the upper plate (4) in correct relation to the lower plate (5).

An Assembly Fixture for Cementing and Baking. One way to hold or clamp parts for cementing, baking, or curing is to use weights. Nine workpieces, each consisting of a rectangular plate and a square plate, are held by weights in the fixture shown in Fig. 12-16 while they are cemented and baked.

The fixture consists of a base plate (1) on which are mounted two guide rails (2) for positioning the rectangular workpieces and two guide rails (3, 7) for

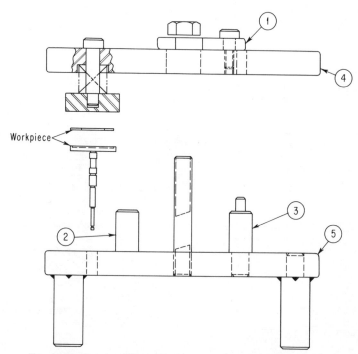

Fɪɢ. 12-15. Pressing fixture. (*International Business Machines Corp.*)

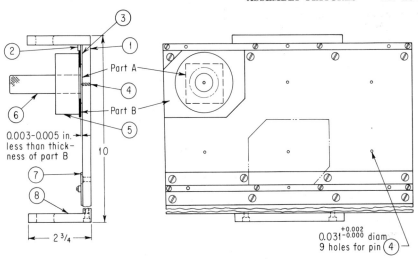

Part A

Part B

0.003-0.005 in.
less than thick-
ness of part B

10

2 ³/₄

$0.031^{+0.002}_{-0.000}$ diam
9 holes for pin ④

FIG. 12-16. Cementing fixture. (*General Electric Co.*)

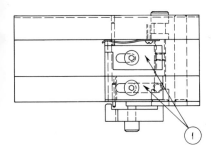

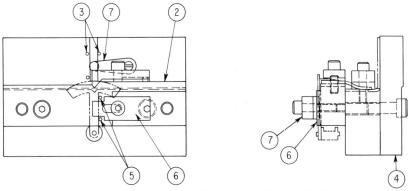

FIG. 12-17. Cementing fixture. (*Link Aviation, Inc.*)

positioning the square workpieces, in which nine 0.031-in. locating holes are drilled. Hubs on the ends of the nine weights (5) are turned to a 1.238-in. diam and to a length of 0.045 in. to fit into the rectangular workpiece. Locating pins (4) pressed into the weights pass through the center holes in the square workpieces and into the locating holes in the fixture base. Knurled handles on the weights and handles on the fixture base are provided for the convenience of the operator.

The number of pieces that can be held in this type of fixture is limited only by part size, loaded-fixture weight, and baking-oven dimensions.

A Cementing Fixture. Figure 12-17 illustrates a fixture designed to hold delicate instrument-pointer components until cured rubber cement has bonded the three components into an integral assembly (Fig. 12-18a).

The tool, which is inexpensively designed for short-run production, uses clamps (1) to secure the V-shaped lever arm which locates in a stepped V groove of the block (2). Pins (3) locate the L-shaped pointer on the base (4) while other pins (5) locate a gear-sector assembly. Another clamp (6) maintains it in the proper position.

The sequence of operations is as follows: cement is applied to the three component parts at the required areas; then the pointer is placed into position between pins (3) and held by a spring (7). Next, the lever arm is placed in the V groove and secured by the clamps. Then the gear-sector assembly is positioned by the pins and secured by a top clamp. Parts make contact with each other at the cemented areas. The fixture is then placed in an oven at 280°F for 2½ hr to cure the cement. The fixture parts and body are fabricated from CRS.

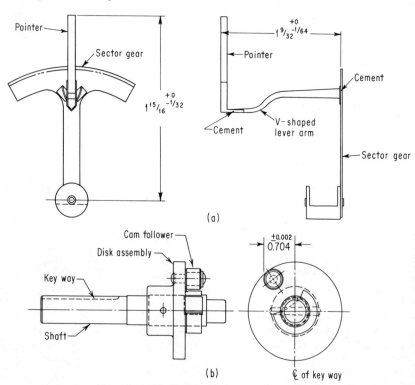

FIG. 12-18. Workpieces for fixture of Fig. 12-17.

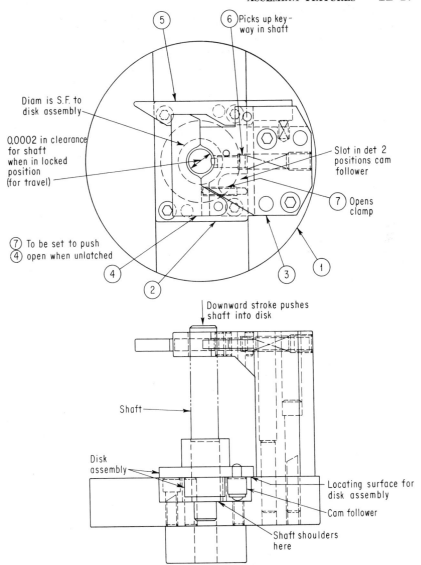

FIG. 12-19. Hydropress fixture. (*International Business Machines Corp.*)

A Fixture to Assemble and Align a Drive Pulley Shaft in a Disk Assembly. In Fig. 12-18*b* is shown a disk and pulley-shaft assembly. The cam follower has been riveted to the disk in a previous operation. As shown, the keyway in the drive pulley shaft has a linear relationship to the cam follower of the disk assembly. The hydropress fixture shown in Fig. 12-19 maintains this relationship during the assembly of the two workpieces.

The fixture consists of a base (1) on which is turned a hub that fits a center hole in the ram of a hydraulic press. A locating block (2) to position the disk and cam-follower assembly is mounted on the base. Also mounted on the base is a block

(3). A locating hole in this block and one in the clamp (4) are ground to allow 0.0002 in. clearance for the shaft when they are clamped and locked by a latch (5). A spring-loaded pin (6), also contained in the block, positions the keyway in the correct relationship with the cam follower of the disk assembly.

To operate, a disk assembly is placed on the locating block with the cam follower in the slot provided. While the clamp is open, a drive pulley shaft is placed in the locating hole with the locating pin in the keyway. Then the clamp is closed and locked by the latch. When the press is actuated, the downward stroke of the ram presses the shaft into the disk until its shoulder rests on the bottom of the step in the base. The length of the locating block controls the relationship of the shaft and the disk assembly. When the latch is opened, a spring plunger (7) forces the clamp open, which facilitates the removal of the completed assembly.

Air-operated Fixtures for Assembly Operations. Air-operated fixtures sometimes improve assembly operations by applying a desired amount of pressure at a predetermined rate with a simple and inexpensive fixture. Air-operated fixtures can also reduce a tedious, time-consuming assembly operation to an easy part-loading task.

The assembly fixture illustrated in Fig. 12-20 is used to insert bearing sleeves into each end of the workpieces shown and to burnish the bearing holes to the finished dimension after assembly.[1]* The workpiece is located on two V blocks

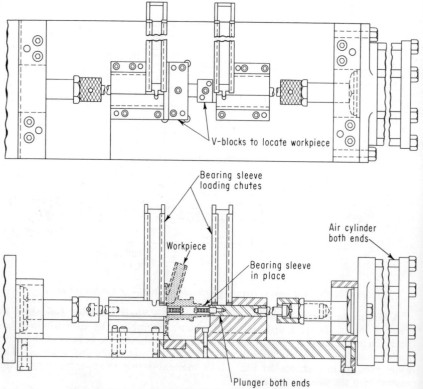

FIG. 12-20. Air-operated fixture for bearing sleeve insertion.[1]

* Superior numbers indicate references listed at the end of this section.

which hold it in alignment with two square plungers. The plungers slide in guide blocks and are moved by actuating double-acting cylinders on both ends of the fixture. The piston travel and pressure applied by the air cylinders can be preset or adjusted to prevent damage to the workpiece.

A burnishing tool is mounted on the end of each plunger. It serves as a pilot for the bearing sleeve during insertion into the workpiece and finishes the bore in the sleeve during the completion of the air-cylinder piston's forward stroke.

The bearing sleeves are fed through two chutes, each of which drops a bearing into position in front of the plunger when it is retracted.

To operate, the two chutes are loaded with bearing sleeves. A workpiece is positioned on the two V blocks. Two bearing sleeves are now in position in the path of the plungers. The burnishing tools on the ends of plungers pick up the bearings and insert them into the workpiece simultaneously from both ends when the air cylinders are actuated. As the plungers continue moving through the full stroke of the air cylinder, the burnishing ends are forced into the bearings which finish the bores to the proper size and alignment. When the plunger retracts completely, two more bearing sleeves drop into position. The workpiece can then be removed and another positioned on the V blocks for another assembly cycle.

An Air-operated Jewel-setting Press. "Miniaturization," the design and manufacture of extremely small parts, is fast gaining widespread use outside of the watchmaking industry. Aircraft, missile, and space-vehicle weight and space limitations require the packaging of smaller and smaller electronic units for bombing and navigational instrument controls.

The jewel-setting press illustrated in Fig. 12-21 is an example of assembly tooling for miniature work. Five jewel bearings are pressed into a watch-pillar plate to exact depths at one and the same operation. The jewels must not be canted in the holes. Although they can be set individually by hand, it would be impossible to achieve the required depth precision by doing so.

The lower part of the press has a workpiece plate (1) with locating pins (2) to ensure radial orientation of the pillar. Five feeding tubes (3) are vertically arranged in the base to coincide with the holes in the pillar. Inside each tube is a push rod (4) located below the end of the tube to form a pocket or nest into which a cylindrical jewel is manually inserted.

The depth to which the jewels are lowered is controlled by the position of the push rod. Each of the five push rods is individually adjusted for height by an adjustment screw (6) and a jam-lock mechanism (7). Any play or flexing of the pillar at the instant of jewel insertion would result in loss of control of seating depth. To prevent this, the upper die element mates perfectly to the pillar and has five support rods (8) which press on the pillar at the jewel-setting points. The support rods are also individually adjusted by cam rods (9) for control of penetration.

In operation, five jewels are placed in the feeding tubes, the pillar is carefully positioned, and a spring-loaded hand cam (10) is moved to close the die and lock all components in place. An air cylinder (11) in the base of the press bears against and raises a plate (12) to which the lower ends of the five push rods are fastened. The upward motion of the plate and push rods simultaneously seats the five jewels in the pillar.

A cam-type ejector (13) is provided to free the workpiece after the operation. Turning the handle forces the cam plate (14) to raise three ejector rods (15) which push the workpiece out of the nest.

An Arbor Press Fixture. A bushing is to be press-fitted into a casting at a location shown in Fig. 12-22. The fixture consists of a sizing plug (1) which is mounted in the ram of an arbor press (not shown). Two strippers (5) are mounted to a plate (2) which is fastened to the base (7) by studs (8). A block (6) is pressed into this base on the center line of the ram and plug. The top of this block is a positive stop for the bushing when it is pressed into the casting. The casting is positioned on the base by a round pin (3) and a diamond pin (4) for peripheral location.

The sizing plug has two functional diameters and a quill end used for mounting it in the arbor press. Diameter A is ground to a slip fit for the bushing and chamfered on the end for easy loading of the workpiece. Diameter B is ground

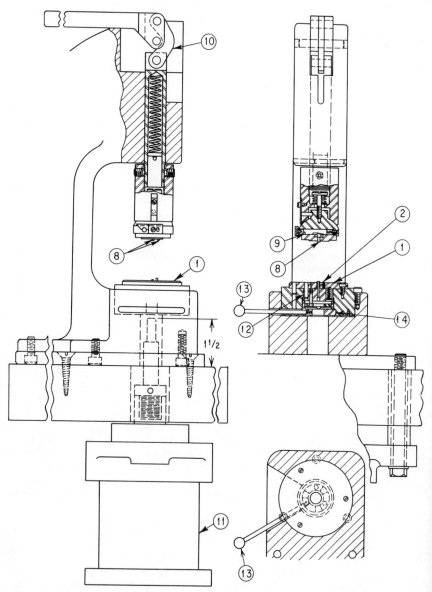

FIG. 12-21. Jewel-setting press. (*Hamilton Watch Co.*) (U.S. Patent No. 2,602,986.)

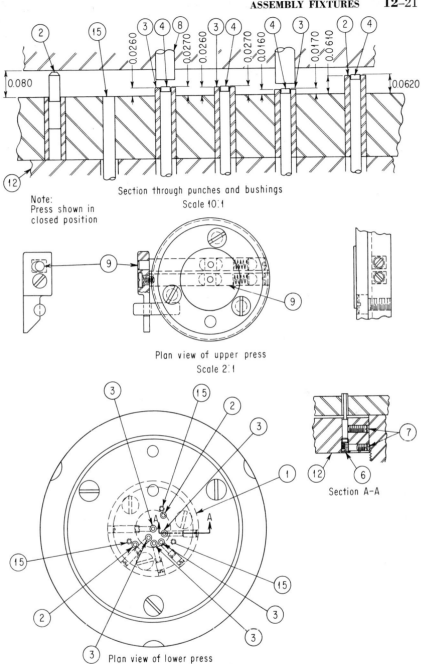

Section through punches and bushings
Scale 10:1

Note:
Press shown in
closed position

Plan view of upper press
Scale 2:1

Section A-A

Plan view of lower press
Scale 2:1

FIG. 12-21 (*continued*)

to the ID of the bushing. When the bushing is seated on top of the block, it will be sized as diameter B is forced through it by the downward stroke of the press.

To operate, a casting is positioned on the base. A bushing is also loaded on the sizing plug with its lower end above the stripper plate while the press is at top of its stroke. During the downward stroke of the press, the bushing is seated on top of the block and sized by diameter B of the plug. On the return stroke of the press, the completed workpiece is lifted from the locating pins and stripped from the plug by the stripper block.

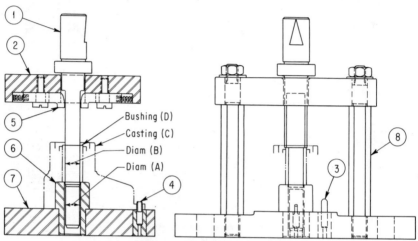

Bushing (D)
Casting (C)
Diam (B)
Diam (A)

FIG. 12-22. Pressing fixture. (*Millers Falls Co.*)

A Fixture to Crimp Four Tabs on a Resistor Assembly. After internal components are assembled inside a sheet-metal can (Fig. 12-23), four tabs on its end must be crimped to retain them. With the simple fixture illustrated in Fig. 12-24, the assembly can be held and the tabs crimped.

It consists of a base (5) on which is mounted a block (1). A bushing (2) is a sliding fit in the loading hole in the block and serves as a stop for the workpiece. A clearance hole is provided in the bushing for wires that protrude from the assembly. By means of four levers (3) and an anvil assembly (6), the workpiece is crimped. A lever mechanism (4) provided in the base raises the bushing to eject the part.

To operate, the four levers must be in the horizontal or loading position. The can assembly is loaded into the hole in the block until it rests on the top of the bushing. When the levers are raised to the vertical or crimping position, the angular faces of the anvils bend and crimp the tabs on the workpiece to approximately a 90° setting. The operation of each lever crimps one tab.

The completed assembly is easily removed from the fixture when the handle of the ejector assembly is depressed. This forces the bushing and the workpiece to rise so that the end of the workpiece is above the top of the block.

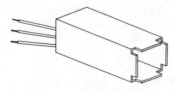

FIG. 12-23. Workpiece for fixture of Fig. 12-24.

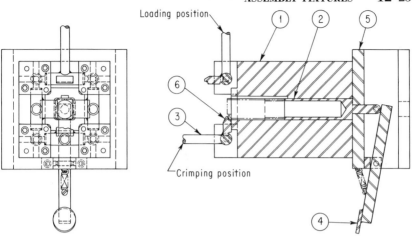

FIG. 12-24. Tab-crimping fixture. (*International Business Machines Corp.*)

An Indexing Fixture for Stitching. The indexing fixture for stitching shown in Fig. 12-25 presses ten wire terminals through both sides of a terminal strip and bends them to form the terminal shown in Fig. 12-26. This fixture is used on a double-headed stitcher.

It consists of a plate (29) upon which are mounted two holder plates (1, 2) for the flat terminal strip. A clamp plate (1) pivots on a pin (27) and is held open for loading by a spring plunger (28). A plate (2) slides between guide blocks (21, 22) and is connected to the indexing mechanism by a bracket (20). The workpiece is centered against an adjustable stop (3). A handle (4) containing a starting switch (7) pivots on a pin (5) to clamp the workpiece between the plates. The handle is held in the clamping position by a spring (6). The indexing mechanism consists of a rack (14) and two pawls (12, 13) which are moved by two solenoids (10, 11) through a toggle pivot (15). A double-acting air cylinder (8) powers the indexing mechanism through connecting linkage (9). An upper limit switch (17) tripped by an adjustable setscrew (16), which is attached to the rack (14), starts the forward cycle of the operation. A lower limit switch (19) opened by an adjustable setscrew (18), also attached to the rack, stops its movement and ends the cycle. The fixture can be aligned with adjusting and locking screws (23, 24). It is clamped to the stitching machine by a block (26) and an arm (25). The two open areas in the fixture plate, *A* and *B* (29), provide clearances for the movement of the stitching anvils when the terminal wires are being assembled.

To operate, a flat terminal strip (workpiece) is inserted between the two holder plates (1, 2). The clamp plate (1) is held open for loading by raising the handle (4). After the workpiece is centered against the adjustable stop, it is clamped by releasing the handle and allowing pressure to be exerted against it by the spring. When the starting-switch button is pressed, the air cylinder which exerts continuous pressure during the forward cycle retracts the plate (2) to the starting position. As soon as the setscrew (16) on the indexing rack (14) contacts the upper limit switch, the forward cycle begins. Two pawls (12, 13), alternately moved by the two solenoids, engage the first notch, second notch, etc., in the indexing rack. At the completion of the cycle, a setscrew (18), also on the indexing rack, contacts the lower limit switch and shuts off the machine's motor. Then the handle is raised and the terminal assembly removed.

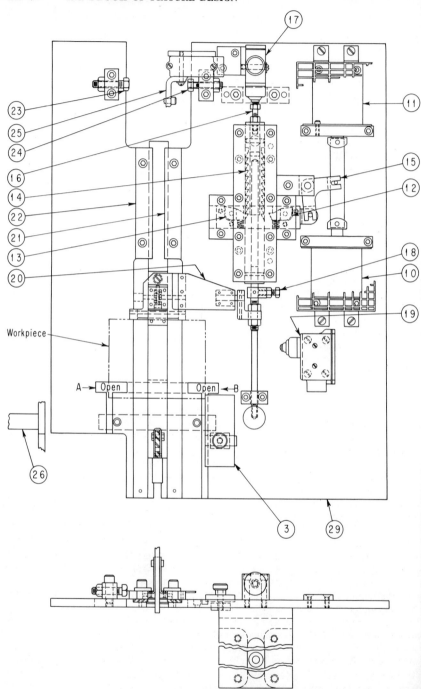

Fig. 12-25a. Indexing stitching fixture. (*Western Electric Co., Inc.*)

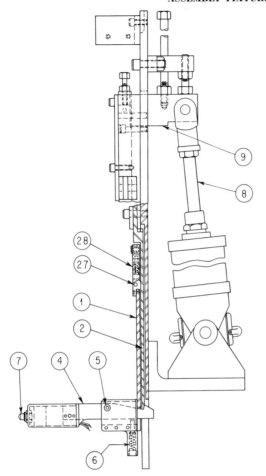

FIG. 12-25*b*. Indexing stitching fixture. (*Western Electric Co., Inc.*)

Wire-stapling Fixtures. A plastic cover is to be assembled on a switch and held in place by a formed wire staple (Fig. 12-27). The staple is fitted in grooves over the cover and through holes in the switch body; finally it is crimped under the body.

The staple is formed into a U shape by the stapling machine before it is inserted in the parts.

The fixture illustrated in Fig. 12-28 has a work-holding anvil (1) which locates workpieces. This anvil has two crimping grooves (2) which crimp the staple under the switch body. The anvil is mounted on a slide (3) which rides in a track (4). Two spring-loaded plungers (5) are located on the anvil assembly on the center line of the crimping grooves. These plungers guide the formed staple into the parts. Two cam plates (6) are mounted on either side of the track and, when the slide is pushed in, engage the plungers and push them toward the center of the anvil. A socket-head cap screw (8) and check nut, mounted on the back of the track, are adjusted to stop the slide when it is under the head of the stapling machine. The

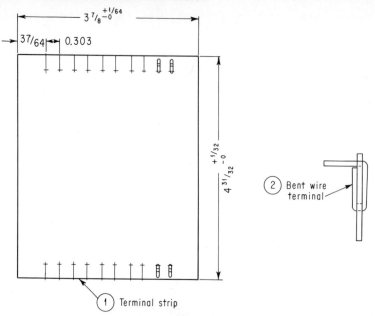

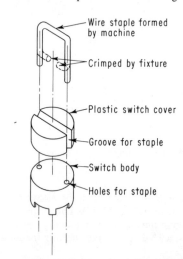

FIG. 12-26. Workpiece for fixture of Fig. 12-25.

FIG. 12-27. Workpieces for fixture of Fig. 12-28.

fixture is mounted on the table of the stapling machine by the mounting block (7).

To operate, the plastic cover is prepositioned on the switch body. This preassembly is then positioned on the anvil with the slide pulled out toward the operator in the loading position. When the slide is pushed in, the plungers engage the cam plates which force them in toward the anvil. When the slide contacts a stop screw (8), a limit switch (not shown) in the stapling-machine circuit is closed and the stapling head with the formed staple descends. The staple fits between the grooves in the cover and the guides on the plungers and through the holes in the switch body; it is crimped by the crimping grooves on the anvil. When the stapling head retracts, the slide can be pulled back for convenient unloading of the completed assembly and the loading of another cover and switch body.

The fixture illustrated in Fig. 12-29 holds a fiber terminal strip (Fig. 12-26) in a coiled position so that a steel end cap may be inserted into each end and then wire-stapled in three positions (120° apart), thus securing the caps and maintaining a cylindrical part.

The assembly illustrated in Fig. 12-30 is a case for loading coils for telephone circuits. The body of the stapling fixture holds the eyelet, end cap, and coiled terminal strip under pressure exerted by a toggle clamp (1). The opposite and unclamped end of this assembly has an end cap inserted by hand which is then presented to the wire-stitching machine for stapling in three places. Orientation of the staple positions is facilitated by two keys (2) attached to the body of the fixture, which are presented to the machine with a handle (3).

After stapling one end, the assembly is released, and the stapled end is inserted into the fixture and clamped. The required coils and insulators are inserted into the tubelike case; then the end cap is inserted and similarly stapled in three places.

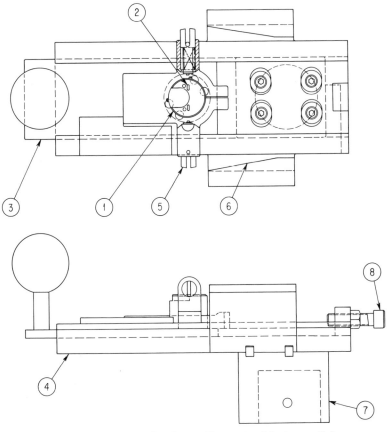

FIG. 12-28. Wire-stapling fixture. (*International Resistance Co.*)

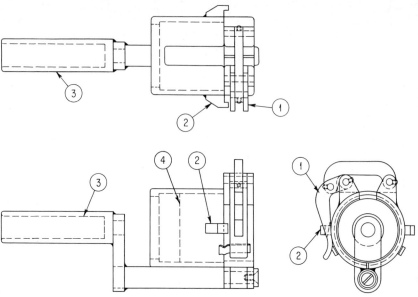

Fɪɢ. 12-29. Wire stapling fixture. (*Western Electric Co., Inc.*)

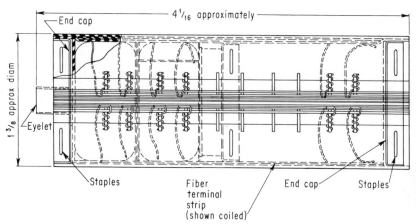

Fɪɢ. 12-30. Workpiece for fixture of Fig. 12-29.

Spacers (4) placed in the body of the fixture permit locational adjustment for different length eyelets. End caps can also be stapled and positioned at any point within the case.

Assembly Fixtures Using Ball-and-Socket Arms. Figures 12-31 through 12-33 show holding fixtures for various parts during assembly. These fixtures securely hold a main component of an assembly at a convenient angle in order that other parts can be assembled to it. With the main component held securely, the assembly operator has the use of both hands in performing the assembly operations. An adjustable arm or work positioner, commercially available, is used with all three of these fixtures. The arm has a simple ball-and-socket joint which is clamped by friction locking force. When the locking pressure is released, the ball can move freely in three planes and can be locked at any desired angle and position. These arms can be obtained in different sizes that will hold up to 1,000 lb.

The fixture shown in Fig. 12-31 is adjustable for different sizes of assemblies, since the arms (1, 2) can be adjusted to different widths on the slide bar (3). The arms are then clamped in place with screws (4). Hooks (5) can be moved in and out in the slots of the arms for parts of different lengths. The slide bar is attached to the positioner (6). It can be raised or lowered to different heights on a post (7) and clamped with a handwheel (8). The post is assembled to a suitable base.

The holding fixture shown in Fig. 12-32, in addition to the movements provided by the positioner, permits 360° rotation of the workpiece about a vertical axis.

The workpiece is located on locating pins (1, 2) and then secured with clamps (3). The rotary-table base (4) can turn 360° through a post (5) and a bushing (6). The base is then clamped in the desired position by a clamp arm (7).

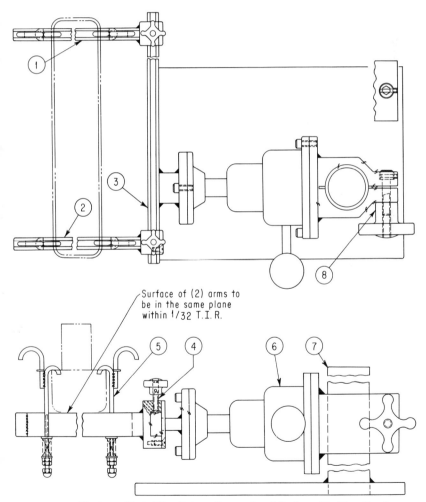

Surface of (2) arms to be in the same plane within 1/32 T.I.R.

FIG. 12-31. Assembly-holding fixture. (*International Business Machines Corp.*)

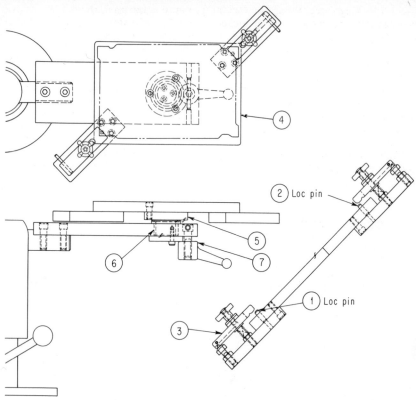

FIG. 12-32. Assembly-holding fixture. (*International Business Machines Corp.*)

The fixture shown in Fig. 12-33 holds a connector and electronic assembly while wires are being soldered into the connector. The connector is inserted into the holder (1), and the electronic assembly is held above the connector by pins (2, 3). These pins go through the mounting holes, raising the assembly above the normal mounting height from the connector. This provides clearance to solder the wires into the connector pins.

A (Ball Detent) Assembly Fixture. When a ball detent is to be assembled in a blind hole between an inner housing and an outer housing, the ball is spring-loaded from the outer housing to a spherical seat in the inner housing.

The inserting tool shown in Fig. 12-34 is an arbor (3) whose pilot diameter *B* is a slip fit for the bore of the outer housing. The diameter *A* is a slip fit for the smaller bore of the inner housing. A slot in the arbor holds a pivoted lever (2). A magnet (1) is press-fit into a hole in this lever.

To operate, the steel ball is placed on the cupped end of the magnet in the lever. The outer housing is slipped on the arbor, locating on the *B* diameter, and stopped against the shoulder *F*. The ball is now correctly positioned from the end of the outer housing. The lever is pressed, and the housing is rotated until the ball contacts the blind hole. Pressing on the lever holds the ball in the hole against the spring tension. The inner housing is next guided into the outer housing by the *A* diameter of the arbor. After the inner housing contacts the surface *C*, it is pushed from the opposite end of the outer housing. The ball is held in the blind

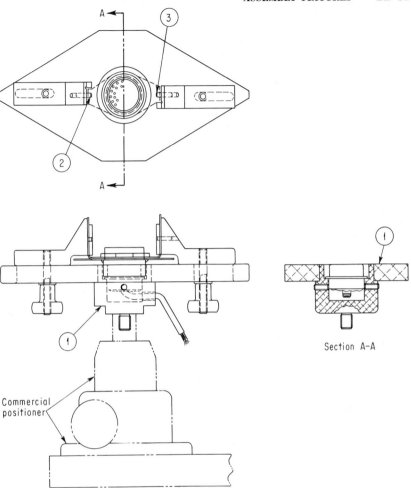

FIG. 12-33. Assembly-holding fixture. (*International Business Machines Corp.*)

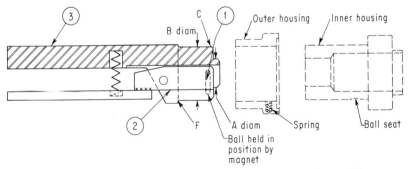

FIG. 12-34. Ball-detent assembly fixture. (*ASTME Denver Chapter 77.*)

hole by the OD of the inner housing. When the inner housing is seated in the counterbore of the outer housing, it is rotated until the ball rests in the spherical seat. The assembly is now complete.

An Internal Retaining-ring Assembly fixture. A snap ring is compressed, inserted into a length of tubing, and seated in a groove inside the tube with the fixture illustrated in Fig. 12-35. It consists of two spring-loaded slides (1) which have a circular groove for the snap ring (workpiece). The outer edges of the slides are tapered.

The base (2) of the fixture, which is mounted on a small arbor press, locates the tubing under the ram inserting tool (3).

The inserting tool, which is mounted in the arbor press, mates with the outer edges of the slides and has a pilot that is a slip fit in the ID of the tubing.

The tubing is placed down into the base and against the locating surfaces (5, 4). The snap ring is then positioned by hand between the slides and located in the circular groove. When the ram is brought down, the inserting tool engages the slides, forcing them in and squeezing the snap ring into a diameter small enough to fit inside the tubing. As the inserting tool continues down, it pushes the snap ring out of the slides and down into the tubing until it snaps into place in the groove inside the tubing.

The tool is then retracted and the slides move out to loading position for insertion of another snap ring. The assembled tube and ring can then be removed from the base of the fixture.

A Setscrew-loading Fixture. A socket setscrew (1), illustrated in Fig. 12-36, is to be inserted and partially threaded into the recessed hub of a workpiece. The tapped hole in the hub is too deep in the recess for convenient loading of the setscrew by hand.

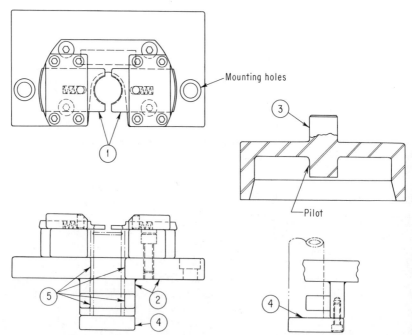

Fig. 12-35. Retaining-ring assembly fixture. (*ASTME Denver Chapter 77.*)

The fixture consists of a drum (2) fastened to a right-angle plate which can be secured to a stand or bench. The OD of the drum is a slip fit for the inside of the workpiece. A spring-loaded plunger (3) is mounted in a hole in the drum that is a slip fit for the hub (4) on the workpiece. The plunger is retained with a pinned collar (5). Also in the drum are a hole for loading the setscrew and a slot by means of which the workpiece, with its setscrew protruding from the hub, can be removed from the fixture.

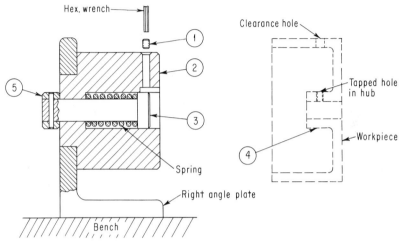

FIG. 12-36. Setscrew-loading fixture. (*Torrington Co.*)

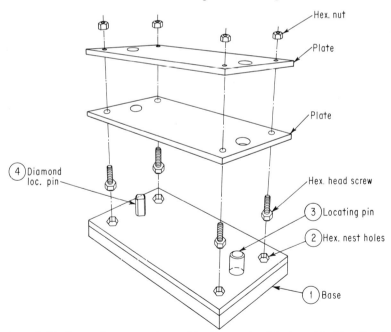

FIG. 12-37. Fixture for a screwed assembly. (*International Business Machines Corp.*)

To operate, a setscrew is dropped into the hole in the drum. The spring plunger, in released position, covers this hole and prevents the screw from falling through. Then the workpiece is loaded onto the drum. When the workpiece is seated against the end of the drum, the hub retains the setscrew. It may be necessary to rotate the part until the setscrew drops into the tapped hole. A hex wrench can then be inserted through a clearance hole in the part and through the loading hole in the drum to turn the setscrew. When the screw is partially set, the part can be removed. The slot in the drum allows the setscrew to pass without being turned all the way into the part.

Assembly Fixtures for Screw Fastening. The simple design of the fixture of Fig. 12-37 can be adapted for the assembly of various types of parts held together by screws or bolts. The bench assembly of parts by unskilled labor using air-operated or manual nut spinners or screwdrivers can be easily and speedily accomplished with modifications of this fixture design. The base incorporates nests for hexagon head screws and locators for the two plates that correctly align the plates while the nuts are tightened. The completed assembly is lifted off the locators, and the fixture is again loaded with screws and plates.

The fixture shown in Fig. 12-38 is used when two or more parts are to be fastened together with standard head screws. The parts must also be held in correct relation to each other. Parts *A, B,* and *C* are to be fastened together in this manner.

The fixture consists of a base (1) machined to nest parts *A* and *B.* Three holes are located in the base for loading screws. Two locating pins (3) are positioned on the base to locate part *C.* An error-proof block (4) correctly orients part *B.* A hinged leaf (2) has three holes for loading screws and is machined to hold the three parts together. The leaf also serves as a rest surface when screws are being loaded through the base.

To operate, the jig is set on the base with the leaf open. The parts are positioned, and the leaf is closed. The leaf now holds the parts together. Three screws are dropped into the holes in the leaf and driven with a power screwdriver. The jig is turned over, and three screws are driven through the base in the same manner. The leaf is opened, and the assembly is removed.

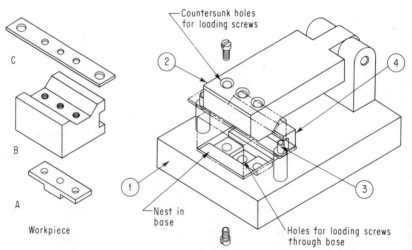

FIG. 12-38. Fixture for screwed assembly. (*South Bend Controller Co.*)

A Deep-hole Multiple O Ring Inserter. The problem of inserting O rings into internal grooves in internal bores increases as the depth of the bore increases in proportion to the ID.

An assembly calling for six O rings to be more or less equally spaced along the inside of a ⅞-in. bore that is over 7 in. in length is shown in Fig. 12-39. As this is part of a production-valve assembly, a fast means of inserting the O rings was devised to assure complete seating of all six O rings.

A mandrel (1) is made up of nylon sections equally spaced and eccentrically located along the length of a steel rod and attached by setscrews. For ease of handling, the mandrel has a knurled head. The length of the nylon sections corresponds to the O-ring seat spacing in the valve body (workpiece), and the OD of the nylon sections is slightly less than the ID of the O rings. The OD of the thin-walled steel tube (2) is made a sliding fit for the valve-body bore, and the ID is made a sliding fit over the nylon sections of the mandrel.

To operate, six lubricated O rings are loaded onto the mandrel, each hanging loosely in its slot. The steel tube is then started over the end of the mandrel. As shown in section X-X, each O ring is doubled back into its slot and trapped as the tube slides over it until the tube stops against the mandrel knob.

The assembled mandrel and tube are then inserted into the bore of the valve body (workpiece) until the knurled head of the mandrel is against the end of the workpiece. The tube is then pulled out of the far end of the bore. The released O

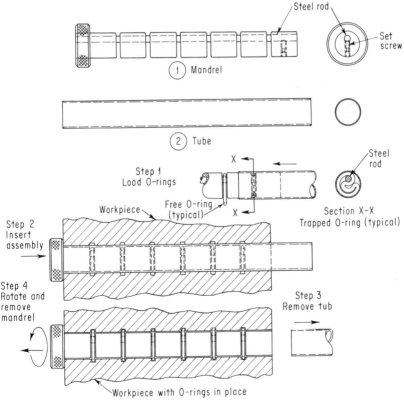

FIG. 12-39.   O ring insertion fixture. (*Sundstrand, Denver.*)

rings pop into their respective grooves. The mandrel is then removed, and the assembly is complete.

Should any of the O rings not be fully seated, the mandrel cannot be removed. Rotation of the mandrel by its knurled knob will force the off-center steel rod to remove any kinks in the O rings, allowing the mandrel to be easily removed and indicating 100 per cent seating of the O rings.

A Plastic Holding Fixture. Figure 12-40 shows a holding fixture made from layers of plastic casting resins and glass cloth. It nests a casting having irregular contours in a comfortable working position while another part is assembled to it. The molding of plastic fixtures around a part is often inexpensive compared with the required machining of fixtures to hold some irregular contours. The best sequence to follow when making plastic tooling is to build the tool and then draw the design according to the existing tool.

A form or mold is made from cardboard to the outside contour of the fixture (1). The mold and the part (2) are coated with wax. After the casting resin is mixed according to the manufacturer's directions, it is poured into the bottom of the mold, together with three or four alternate layers of glass cloth, to the required depth. The parting line of the part should be approximately ½₂ in. above the top of the fixture. Then a part is pressed into the plastic and glass-cloth mixture and leveled. The plastic is allowed to cure. After curing is completed, the plastic fixture is removed from the mold. The base of the fixture is machined parallel with the top of the part. A pick-out slot is also machined in the fixture, which completes its fabrication.

Support Legs. When components must be assembled to both sides of a panel, three sets of simple leg assemblies, such as those shown in Fig. 12-41, can hold the

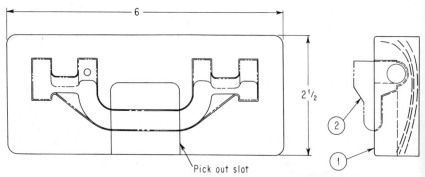

FIG. 12-40. Plastic holding fixture. (*International Business Machines Corp.*)

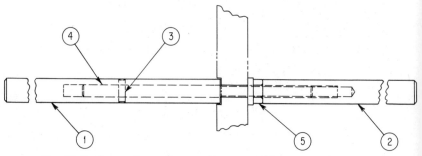

FIG. 12-41. Support legs as fixtures. (*International Business Machines Corp.*)

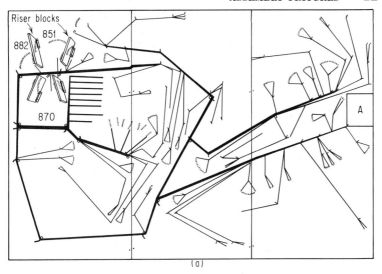

(a)

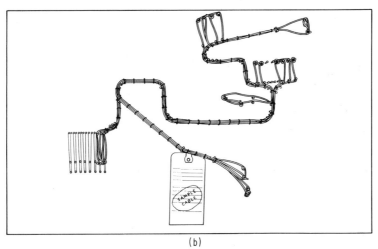

(b)

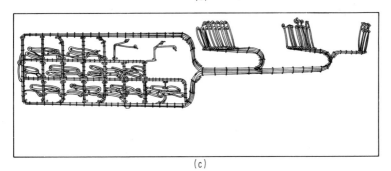

(c)

FIG. 12-42. Wire harness boards. (*Link Aviation, Inc.*)

assembly securely. The assembly can then be turned over easily for working from the opposite side. These legs can be left on until this subassembly is assembled into the final unit, as it provides a way for the assembly to be stored on a shelf without damage.

Top and bottom legs (1, 2) are made from aluminum bars. A stud (4) is a slip fit in each leg and pinned in place by a pin (3), or it may be brazed in place. The extended portion of each stud is threaded into each top leg. A flanged nut (5) secures each leg to the assembly (workpiece).

Wire Harness Boards. The assembly of single wires into a completed harness or cable is facilitated by a wire harness board. Figure 12-42a illustrates such a tool, which is composed of three sheets of ¾-in.-thick plywood, each 4 by 8 ft. Nails or special pins with grooves are driven into the board at terminal and bend positions. The paths of the wires are painted on the boards.

Riser blocks with pins at areas 851, 870, and 882 provide for special terminal and contouring considerations in another plane. Wire code number applied to the layout and a wiring list at A complete the tool. The assembled wires are laced and taped before removal from the tool.

Smaller harness layouts, Fig. 12-42b and c, on smaller plywood boards are made with an actual-size print of the part drawing glued to the base. Varnish or shellac is applied to the surface to reduce wear. Nails or special pins are driven into the base at the terminal and bend positions through the attached part print.

Harness areas or terminal sections in which variations are required from one part to another can be facilitated by modules. These are removable and replaceable board sections which can be accurately relocated to provide the harness with such variations as a terminal fan of 6, 12, or 20 wires.

Potting or Encapsulating Fixtures. In the electronics industry, many types of electrical connectors are potted. Potting is the process of enclosing soldered connections, as in a connector, with a protective material, such as plastic, rubber, or similar material.

The potting fixture shown in Fig. 12-43 is actually a holding fixture for a cable with six connectors on it (one of which is shown).

The connectors are placed in the holes in the holding block and retained by the thumbscrews along the sides. The potting compound can then be poured into the connectors while they are held rigidly in place. The holes in this type of fixture can be varied to suit any combination or position of connectors on a cable.

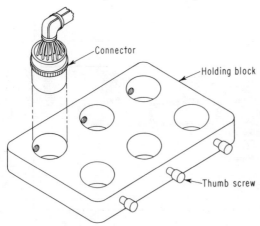

Fig. 12-43. Potting fixture. (*International Business Machines Corp.*)

A Lens and Holder Assembly Fixture. The fixture of Fig. 12-45 is used with an operation to twist and crimp four ears to hold a lens on a holder plate, as shown in Fig. 12-44.

A loose lens is positioned on a spring-loaded plunger (1). A mounting plate with four vertical tabs is inverted and nested between three pins (2) and a pusher spring (3). The four tabs to be twisted and crimped are in line with slots in four anvils (4). Each anvil serves as a shaft within a spur gear (5) which is meshed with a ring gear (6).

After a platen (7) is brought down lightly by a foot-treadle assembly, an air cylinder (8) is actuated and an end pad (9) contacts an arm (10). This motion rotates the ring gear, forcing the anvils to revolve. Thus, the tabs are twisted to a preset position which can be varied by the adjustable stops (11).

After the tabs are twisted, platen pressure can give additional crimping action if required.

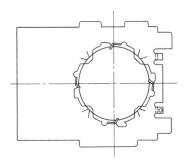

Twisted tab   Lens   Holder

FIG. 12-44. Workpieces for fixture of Fig. 12-45.

Trunnion Holding Fixture for Rotating a Large Assembly. A trunnion holding fixture, such as the one illustrated in Fig. 12-46, is designed to hold a large part or assembly in several different planes while other parts are assembled to it.

The fixture shown consists of a body or framework (1) which is made from square tubing of welded construction.

On one end of the fixture, a mounting plate (4) is fastened to a shaft (5) that is rotated by a worm gear (2) and a worm pinion (3). With a worm-gear drive, an assembly can be rotated 360° without operator fatigue. Heavy unbalanced parts or assemblies can be easily turned and will not slip past a stop. A handle (6) may be placed on either end of the worm for right- or left-hand operation of the fixture.

The workpiece is positioned and clamped to the mounting plate with two screws (7) which are threaded into tapped holes in the mounting plate through two locating holes in the workpiece.

The support block (8), mounted on the opposite end of the fixture, is machined to fit a hub on the end of the workpiece. A very long or extra-heavy part or assembly needs support at both ends. The block may be replaced with a free-turning mounting-plate assembly to be clamped to a workpiece.

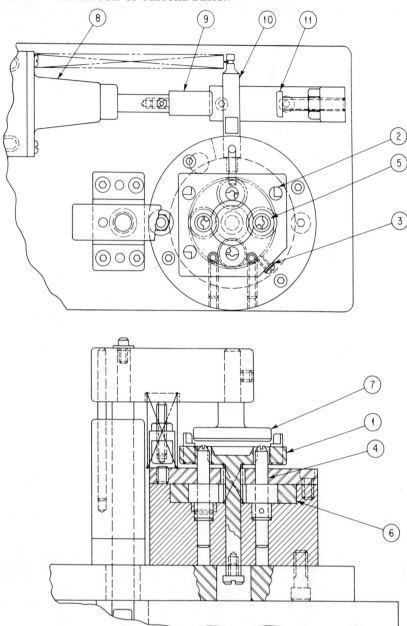

FIG. 12-45. Lens and holder assembly fixture. (*Argus Cameras, Inc.*)

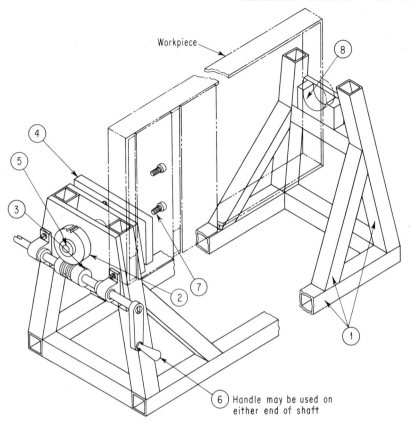

Workpiece

Handle may be used on
either end of shaft

FIG. 12-46. Trunnion fixture.

FIXTURES FOR HOT-JOINING METHODS

*By Committee for Fixtures for Hot Joining**

Fixtures described here are those for the assembly or union of two or more metallic workpieces with heat energy directed to or induced in the areas of the workpieces to be joined.

Fixture designs include only those used with various conventional welding, brazing, and soldering methods but not those for joining without heat by applied pressures or vibratory forces.

The primary function of fixtures for these assembly methods is that of holding and orienting workpieces for their correct joining.

* The members of the committee are Frederick N. Abel, Tool Designer, Universal Engineering Co.; John G. Anderson, Square D Electric Co.; James F. Goodall, Industrial Engineer, Collins Radio Co.; Kenneth W. Hamlin, Mechanical Engineering Dept., State University of Iowa; Norman E. Hinkel, Tool Designer, Square D Electric Co.; Steve Konz, Industrial Engineer, Collins Radio Co.; R. A. Lubbock, Tool Engineer, Universal Engineering Co.; I. L. Rabourn, Tool Engineer, Square D Electric Co.; and Allan I. Young, Industrial Engineer, Collins Radio Co., Chairman.

Except for electrode pressures, fixtures need not be designed to withstand the torque and other forces of cutters, drills, and other tools.

Stresses resulting from thermal expansion of workpieces and/or fixtures must be considered in the design of clamps and locators and in the proper positioning of the workpieces before and during assembly, depending upon the necessary distribution of heat to the work and fixture. Fixtures for some operations must absorb considerable heat and provide clamping pressure to prevent excessive thermal expansion of the work and of fixture elements.

The thermal conductivity and coefficient of expansion of some metals will result in cracking adjacent to the weld when tightly clamped. This difficulty may be overcome with a fixture for tack welding or through final welding performed without a fixture. Under the same condition, the distortion of other metals may be difficult or impossible to control and must be corrected by a subsequent operation to produce uniform workpieces.

Welding Jigs and Fixtures

In general, welding fixtures and jigs are grouped in three classifications: tacking jigs, welding fixtures, and holding fixtures.

Tacking Jigs. A tacking jig locates the components of a weldment in their correct relationship with proper fit-up, while a tack welder tacks them together prior to their final welding. The workpiece is usually then removed from the tacking jig and transferred to a separate fixture for completion of the welding. A tacking jig need not be exceptionally strong or of heavy construction, since heat of the few short tacking welds induces only slight thermal stresses in it.

Welding Fixtures. A welding fixture properly locates and holds workpieces for a complete welding operation. It simplifies and/or eliminates handling and moving of the workpieces and of associated tooling, but it necessitates construction to withstand thermal pressures and stresses within the weldment. It is often impracti-

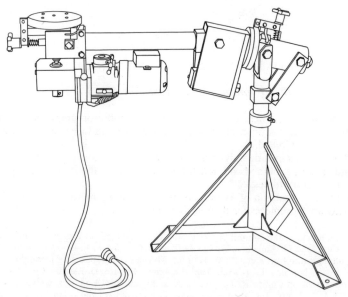

FIG. 12-47. Welding positioner. (*Aronson Machine Co.*)

cal or even impossible to design satisfactory welding fixtures for intricate, complex assemblies and heavy, bulky weldments; hence in general practice, the parts are initially tacked together in a tacking jig and then the workpiece is transferred to a holding fixture, usually used in conjunction with a welding positioner, for completion of the work.

Holding Fixtures. A holding fixture is a device specifically designed to hold previously tacked assemblies in place on a positioner. The fixture itself can often be adapted for positioning by the addition of an economical trunnion stand with index plate and plunger of suitable design. Counterweights may be used to make positioning easy, and if necessary, dolly mounting will make the entire unit more readily portable. Like the welding jig, the holding fixture must be strongly and rigidly constructed to withstand the cumulative stresses generated within the workpiece in the process of welding.

A simple, economical positioning device, such as that shown in Fig. 12-47, incorporates a circular plate to which a workpiece or a fixture can be attached. The table can be rotated in three planes and locked in any position by hand screws.

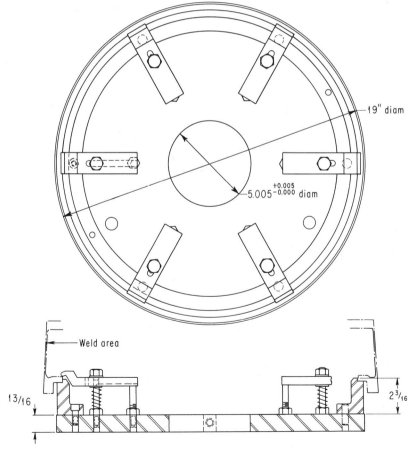

FIG. 12-48. Fusion-welding fixture for tack-welded workpieces. (*Pratt & Whitney Aircraft.*)

umentate, and
General Design Considerations

Jigs and fixtures for welding may incorporate standard clamps, locating buttons, pins, and blocks employed in machining and assembly fixtures. Clamping and locating devices should be basically simple and strong. Simple, nonbinding locators are essential.

Figure 12-48 illustrates standard strap clamps for clamping tack-welded workpieces in a holding fixture. The holding fixture can be mounted on a standard revolving positioner.

Interference Considerations. Clamps and locators required to position and secure components must be carefully placed to preclude interference with the welding tool. Provision must be made to prevent its fusion to the fixture or burnthrough by including slots, relief areas, or back-up bars. Burn- and fusion-resistant materials may be used.

Unloading Workpieces. Unlike machining fixtures, where the size and shape of the workpiece remain essentially the same at loading and unloading, workpieces for welding fixtures generally are separately loaded, individually located, welded together, and finally removed as a single and often an unwieldy, unyielding unit. Unless the locators have been properly placed for easy removal of the finished workpiece, it can be difficult, or even impossible, to remove the weldment from the fixture.

Workpiece Expansion. Expansion, contraction, and distortion from welding may further complicate workpiece removal by tightly forcing the workpiece against locating devices, or the fixture frame, and thereby binding the finished weldment. Fixed locators may locate on one and the same side of all components in the weldment, and removable or retractable locators and clamps may locate on the other sides whenever it is expedient or necessary to locate a workpiece from several sides to maintain accuracy and critical dimensions. The threaded shoulder pin, of suitable length and design, is a simple and economical retractable locator, readily adaptable, and often utilized for such applications; but it must be designed and positioned to adequately protect its threaded portions during tacking and welding operations against damage from weld spatter. Distortion and expansion from welding that can force the workpiece against such threaded locators or pins, or other removable and retractable locators, thereby making their removal difficult, must be anticipated.

Figure 12-49 illustrates a fixture to maintain critical internal dimensions and parallel relationship of the sides of a box type of machine-base weldment. The fixture can quickly be disassembled for easy removal from the welded structure. The threaded members are at a distance adequate to prevent damage from weld spatter. The fixture design affords rigidity and strength to withstand the strains generated in the welding.

Cylindrical Workpieces. Expanding or collapsible mandrels may be adaptable for weldments incorporating cylindrical and tubular sections of relatively small diameter. Trunnion devices are readily adaptable to locating and easily revolving and positioning large, unwieldy cylinders.

Figure 12-50 shows a simple air-operated expanding fixture which incorporates a bicycle tube as an economical and trouble-free expanding member.

Figure 12-51 shows a positioner for large cylindrical workpieces.

Clamping Considerations. Quick-acting and cam-actuated clamps offer secure and positive initial pressure, rapid release, adequate clearance, and low susceptibility to damage from weld spatter. A wide variety of mechanical clamping devices are advantageously adapted to welding fixtures, including screw, strap, cam, toggle, hydraulic, air, and many other clamps, the choice depending upon application, pressure requirements, etc. Screw clamps, which are relatively simple, can exert great

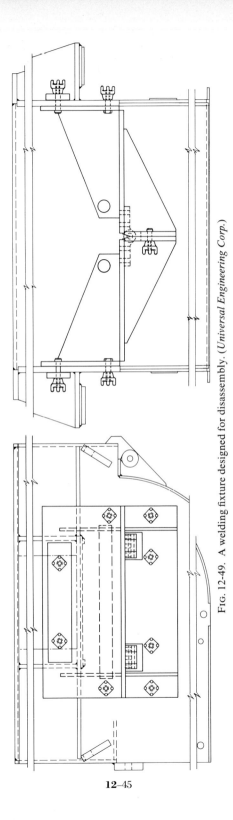

Fig. 12-49. A welding fixture designed for disassembly. (*Universal Engineering Corp.*)

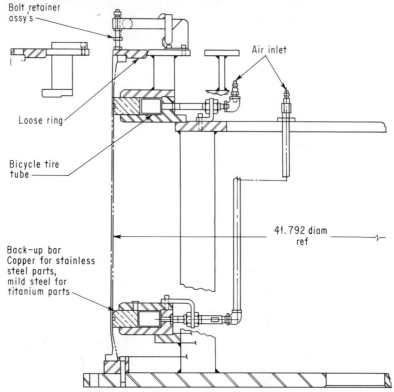

Bolt retainer
assy's

Air inlet

Loose ring

Bicycle tire
tube

41.792 diam
ref

Back-up bar
Copper for stainless
steel parts,
mild steel for
titanium parts

FIG. 12-50. Air-operated expansion-type welding fixture. (*Pratt & Whitney Aircraft.*)

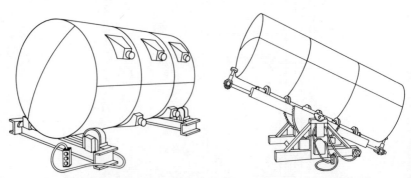

FIG. 12-51. Positioner for welding large workpieces. (*Aronson Machine Co.*)

pressure but should be avoided unless the threads can be adequately protected from weld spatter. Heavy toggle clamps are well suited to welding fixtures. Air and hydraulic clamps are fast-acting, positive, and readily obtainable in pressure ratings to suit most requirements. Clamp handles and knobs should be large enough and long enough to allow easy manipulation by the welder's gloved hands.

Figure 12-52 shows a simple clamping and locating wedge which can be instantly closed or opened by a hammer blow.

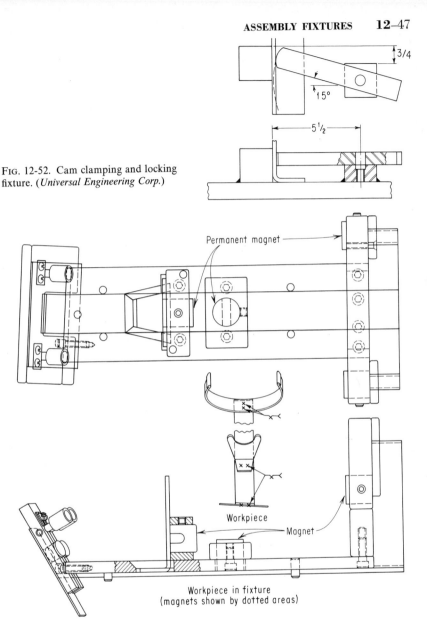

FIG. 12-52. Cam clamping and locking fixture. (*Universal Engineering Corp.*)

FIG. 12-53. Magnetic welding fixture. (*The Tool Engineer.*)

Magnetic Retention. Magnetic holding devices, both electromagnets and permanent magnets, are adaptable, economical, and timesaving. Fixtures incorporating magnets and fabricated from nonferrous metals or plastics permit the magnetic holding forces to be directed to ferrous-metal workpieces.

Figure 12-53 shows a magnetic welding fixture in which aluminum is used wherever possible, since the magnets should not be in contact with other ferrous metals than the workpiece. If it is impractical to construct the entire fixture of aluminum, the magnets may be inserted in aluminum blocks or bushings attached to the fixture. Magnets may be retained in the aluminum blocks by setscrews or cap screws.

Plastic Fixtures. Welding fixtures made of cast epoxy or phenolic tooling resins may also be used with conventional locating and clamping devices, but the inherent close nesting of the workpiece often makes other locating and clamping means unnecessary. Plastic welding fixtures can also afford a substantial cost advantage over metal fixtures. Design time and problems are minimized; fabrication time is substantially reduced; and positive nesting of the assembly in the cast fixture ensures dimensional accuracy sometimes not obtained in fabricated metal construction and even permits use of the fixture as an initial inspection device. Epoxy and phenolic resins retain dimensional stability, have minimum deterioration, will not support combustion, and will shatter rather than permit distortion in the workpiece.

Flexibility. If feasible, all locating devices should permit some adjustment for changing locating dimensions necessitated by design changes and engineering revisions or to compensate for expected weld distortion. Locating areas should be carefully correlated with any subsequent machine operations, since welding and machining must often index and originate from the same locating points.

Utility. All jigs and fixtures must be strong enough to withstand the abuses of loading and unloading and the built-up stresses from welding within the workpiece. They should be simply designed to permit easy accessibility for part positioning and permit the welder to work from the most advantageous angle, generally downhand, with no part of the fixture located to interfere with the electrode or torch.

Jigs and fixtures should be readily operated by welders of varying skill and should incorporate error-proof pins or elements to prevent inverted or reversed loading of workpieces or other welders' errors.

Large fixtures may be made in sections for ease of handling and construction, for replacement of worn sections, for change of sections to accommodate product revision, or for the interchange of sections with several weldments of similar basic design.

Duplicate Fixtures. Duplicate jigs and fixtures are often economically justified, since they can substantially increase the output of a work station by allowing a helper to fit up the next assembly and load and unload it in one fixture, while the welder devotes a major portion of his productive time and ability to actually welding the assembly in the other fixture.

Basic Design

Some design principles listed by the Canadian Welding Bureau are:

1. Whenever possible, a fixture should be a positioner; that is, a fixture should enable all welds to be brought to a convenient welding position. Indexing positioners are accurate and convenient for the welder.

2. A fixture should be easily and quickly positioned (by one hand if possible); balancing may be necessary to enable this to be done. The use of light alloys will reduce the weight of moving parts. Air motors or electric motors can be used for revolving heavy, cumbersome fixtures, and air or hydraulic rams or racks can be used for tilting them.

3. Design must be simple and inexpensive; accuracy and elaboration must be no greater than required. Welded construction is best; toolroom work should be avoided, and machining should be kept to a minimum.

4. A fixture should be built around the workpiece and should locate and clamp it in position for assembly, tacking, and welding.

5. The tool designer should attempt to control only essential workpiece dimensions in a fixture.

6. A fixture should permit freedom of workpiece movement in one direction to avoid locked-in stresses. A floating anchorage is recommended.

7. Joints must be readily accessible for welding. Slots, cutouts, or openings in the fixture should readily present to the welding tool any seams, spots, etc., located on the reverse side of the workpiece.

8. To compensate for thermal distortion, the parts may be bent in the welding fixture before welding, or they may be bent or sprung in a separate fixture.

9. Heat distortion should release rather than bind the workpiece in the fixture. Rams or bumpers may assist in unloading parts that are heat-bound in the fixture.

10. For safe handling, fixtures should be kept cool with air, water, fins, or insulated handles.

11. Convenient positioning of the operator with ladders, trestles, cradles, or trolleys is sometimes advisable for efficient operation.

12. If necessary, the fixture may be mounted on a separate positioner, form, or cradle.

13. To facilitate the flow of weldments, fixtures or positioners may be mounted on wheels or used with floor-mounted or overhead conveyors.

14. Use either integral or separate copper backing bars for poor-fitting or light-plate workpieces to prevent blowout of molten filler metal and ensure proper fusion.

15. Revolving the fixture is preferable to removing and turning the workpiece.

16. Vertical or overhead welding should be avoided.

Economics can be effected by designing the fixture to accommodate several identical small weldments, permitting the welder to progressively weld them with a single loading and unloading sequence. This practice becomes even more productive when duplicate fixtures are utilized.

There is no universal jig entirely satisfactory for the welding of a number of diverse parts. Each workpiece requires and merits individual consideration and presents unique problems.

RESISTANCE WELDING

Resistance welding includes spot, seam, projection, and flash welding. A resistance welder is a combined electrical and mechanical machine tool having electric power to heat the work at the weld location and mechanical power to press or forge the heated materials together.

During the resistance-welding process, an electric current flows through the parts to be welded and meets resistance which heats and softens the parts. Then the mechanical power presses the soft parts together to make the weld. The current that melts the parts should not melt the jig. The jig can be prevented from melting in four basic ways:

1. By ensuring that current-carrying parts of the jig are of low electrical resistance

Copper is the most-used metal. Rolled copper (which will carry 1,800 amp per sq in.) in flats, rounds, and copper tubing is almost indispensable. Also, based on a 50 per cent duty cycle, cast copper will carry 1,500 amp per sq in. Water cooling will approximately double allowable current flow. Tubing is especially valuable, since it can be connected to the welder's water supply and the generated heat removed by the water.

Aluminum bronze and similar copper-base alloys can be used when higher strength is desired for bases, arms, clamping devices, and stops. They should not be annealed during fabrication of the fixture and thus lose their higher strengths.

Aluminum and its alloys can be used to conserve weight but not for actual current-carrying parts, because oxidation will develop at the joints or clamps.

Nonmagnetic cast iron (nickel iron) is sometimes used as a cheap, strong material for a portion of the jig that is in or around the magnetic field of the machine. Magnetic materials cut down the flow of current, reduce machine efficiency, and become hot owing to induced currents.

The resistance of some metals can be reduced by silver-plating them. This is especially helpful at joints.

2. By water-cooling the jig

Water flowing through copper tubing is an excellent coolant. A system in which water floods into a drain pan is very efficient, particularly for seam welding.

3. By keeping materials out of the throat area of the machine

The magnetic field of the machine will heat any metal in this area, but metals of high electrical conductivity will not become as hot as magnetic materials.

4. By keeping the number of joints to a minimum

When connections have to be made, their clamped surfaces must be at least twice the area of the cross section carrying the current. It is a good practice to bridge the connections with flexible members, such as braided copper wire.

Projection-welding Fixtures

Essentially, a projection-welding fixture is that part of the die exclusive of the electrodes. For all practical purposes, the die and fixture may be considered to be the same. A die is a device, usually shaped to the work contour, which clamps the parts being welded and conducts the welding current from the machine platens to the workpiece. The lower die consists of the necessary work-locating and clamping devices and will either contain or comprise the lower electrode, depending upon the nature of the parts being welded.

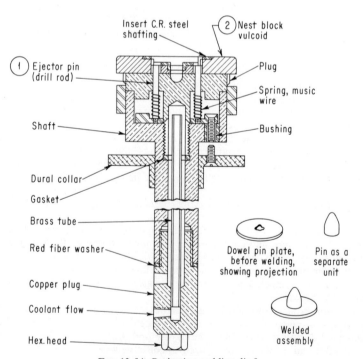

FIG. 12-54. Projection-welding die.[2]

Assembly fixtures and electrodes for projection welding differ in several respects from those designed for conventional spot welding. For projection welding, the fixtures usually become a part of the welding dies, which are mounted on the machine platens; for spot welding, it is necessary to move the fixture and work when more than one weld must be made. Projection-welding dies are designed to allow multiple welds to be made in one cycle of the machine. The stationary fixture locates and holds the work during the welding cycle, after which the completed work is removed. Since a portion of the projection-welding fixture forms part of the secondary-current path during the welding cycle, its current-carrying components must be insulated from the rest of the die. Figure 12-54 shows a projection-welding die for welding a dowel-pin assembly. The die was designed for mounting into the horns of a combination press-type welding machine, rather than directly to the machine platens.

It is necessary to use a welding machine with as small a throat as possible, as well as to keep the height of the fixture to a minimum, for maximum welder efficiency resulting from the minimum of metal mass in the magnetic field of the throat.

All gage pins, clamps, locators, index pins, etc., should be insulated from current-carrying components. Figure 12-55 shows a locating pin pressed into an insulating sleeve, which in turn is pressed into the lower die. Fabricating these parts out of insulating materials, such as fiber, micarta, vulcoid, Bakelite, etc., will eliminate the insulating of metal-fixture parts. If abrasion resistance is important or if long production runs are encountered, an insulated metal part may be required. If a locating pin contacts both workpieces, as shown in Fig. 12-55, current shunted across the pin will pit and burn it; therefore, it should be easily replaceable. Pin life can be prolonged in such cases by chromium-plating the pins.

Electrode contact faces are subject to considerable wear, and when worn, they will fail to maintain a constant pressure contact with the work. It then becomes necessary to adjust them by raising the lower arm or fixture or to replace them with refaced or new electrodes. Figure 12-56 shows the component (1) of Fig. 12-54 and illustrates a recessed electrode for refacing when worn. The plug allows $\frac{1}{16}$-in. wear and can be refaced four times before complete replacement is necessary. The die shown in Fig. 12-55 has a knockout hole to drive out the worn electrode.

In addition to electrode or die wear, consideration must be given to stops, gage points, and pins to assure their proper functioning at both new and worn electrode heights.

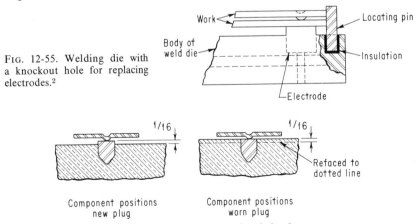

Fig. 12-55. Welding die with a knockout hole for replacing electrodes.[2]

Work — Locating pin
Body of weld die — Insulation
Electrode

1/16   1/16
Refaced to dotted line

Component positions new plug

Component positions worn plug

Fig. 12-56. Refaceable-plug design.[2]

Internal cooling of the electrodes is necessary to avoid overheating and wear during the welding cycle. Water at 70° F, introduced at a rate of 1 to 5 gal per min, will provide proper cooling. Figure 12-54 illustrates a method to cool projection-welding dies in which water is fed through a tube to the electrode faces. When coolant must pass through a cast copper die or electrode, cast copper tubing or stainless-steel or seamless-steel high-strength annealed tubing cast in the die or electrode is preferred to drilling holes in the cast metal, because holes drilled in cast copper may permit difficult-to-stop water leakage. Electrode design should be kept as simple as possible, since the more complicated electrodes usually require more intricate water-cooling passages. On high-production jobs involving high-duty cycles (speed of operation of the welding machine), separate cooling lines should be run to upper and lower electrodes. When dial feeds are used, welding under water with a suitable container built onto the table has been used to simplify the water-line circuits.

Current-carrying fixture components should be as close to the electrodes as possible.

The high-amperage low-voltage welding currents in projection welding necessitate sizes of current-carrying fixture components having electrical properties conforming to the welding current required. When sizing such conductors, whether they be one of the copper-base alloys or other nonferrous materials, the current-carrying capacity of the metal is available from electrode manufacturers. The electrode contact on parts welded should extend a minimum of five times the diameter of the projection in all directions from the weld to assure uniform heat distribution.

There should be no alternative path for the welding current. Non-current-carrying fixture components must be insulated from those carrying current to ensure that all of the current goes through the welds. The die of Fig. 12-54 utilizes an insulating nest block (2) so that the current follows a path from the dowel-pin plate directly through the projection into the dowel pin. All die components are insulated from the current-carrying copper alloy.

All moving slides, bearings, index pins, adjusting screws, and any accurate locating devices should be protected against flash. Some flashing is inevitable and the current can arc across insulated pins, creating a short circuit.

The fixture components must accurately locate the parts to be welded, since the simultaneous formation of multiple welds requires that all projections be in uniform contact with the mating material. The upper and lower dies must be parallel and must register accurately in a manner similar to punch-press dies. Proper registration prevents slippage and ensures good electrical contact and is one of the reasons that press-type machines are used for multiple-projection welding.

The effect of welding pressure on the machine, the part, and the fixture components and their resistance to deflection are fixture-design considerations. One part can be accurately positioned to another by punching holes in one part and matching them to semipunchings in the other, thus avoiding the necessity of having the fixture control the location of both parts.

Ease of loading and unloading the fixtures and the safety of the operator are particularly important with hand-loaded dies to protect the operator's hands. Air jets or ejector pins, operated through a lever coupled with air knockouts or mechanical strippers, lower unloading time and contribute to operator safety, especially when the work tends to stick to the electrode faces. The upper electrode may be designed to pick up the part from the lower die. In the die of Fig. 12-54, rapid unloading of the welded assembly is accomplished by means of the spring-loaded ejector pins (1).

Electrical shock is a remote hazard to the operator during loading and unloading of the fixture. To protect the operator, the machine base should be insulated from the secondary circuit on one side only, at either the upper electrode or the fixture base. Additional protection can be provided by guards for hand-loaded dies and by dual push buttons requiring both hands to control the machine.

Workpiece Considerations for Fixture Design

Some parts to be welded may be nested in a recessed electrode without auxiliary clamping, over a pilot pin pressed into the electrode, or into an insulating sleeve mounted on the electrode. Parts produced on screw machines, having the projection formed as a radiused projection, an annular ring, or a beveled, annular edge, are frequently fused to a flat sheet or stamping. Specialized parts of fasteners are in the form of weld bolts, weld nuts and pads, weld pins, and weld brackets and are normally commercially available forged products designed to be components of a welded fastener assembly.

A smaller fastener part can be held in a recessed lower electrode with the larger part on top. To locate the smaller part on top, additional holding devices may be required. For example, parts may be nested into the upper electrode and held by spring clips assembled on either the inside or outside of the electrode. A spring-loaded ball or plunger bearing on the part through a hole drilled in the electrode may hold small parts. Vacuum may also be used to hold small parts in the upper electrode. Examples of electrode design for welding this type of part are shown in Fig. 12-57. Such parts are readily adaptable to hopper or magazine feeds which feed the parts automatically into the upper or lower electrode; the mating part is manually added.

Figure 12-58 shows a fixture for welding two stamped sheet-metal parts. The channel-shaped workpiece is placed on the lower platen in a nest formed by a plate (1), the locating dowels (2), and the lower electrodes (3). The rectangular work-

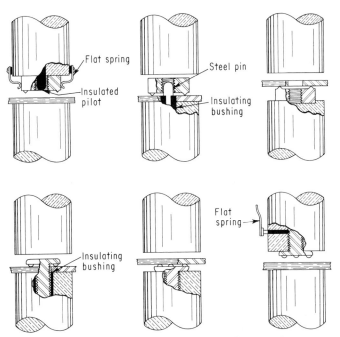

Fᴵɢ. 12-57. Electrode designs. (*The Tool Engineer.*)

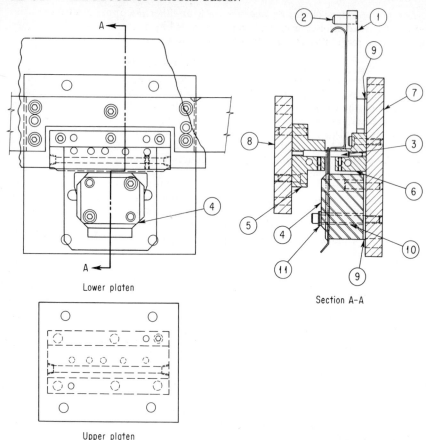

Lower platen

Section A–A

Upper platen

FIG. 12-58. Welding two stampings. (*American Metal Products Co.*)

piece, having projections at the weld areas, is positioned by a locating block (4) ensuring contact of the projections with the other workpiece. Upper and lower electrodes are pressed into machined copper bars (5, 6) which are cross-drilled for water circulation. The bars are mounted directly to copper base plates (7, 8) which are fastened to the machine table and ram.

A steel plate (1) and locating block (4) are insulated from contact with the copper base (7) by micarta inserts (9). Attaching bolts are insulated by micarta sleeves (10) and washers (11). The outboard fixture elements for location of the channel-shaped workpiece are not shown.

Spot-welding Fixtures

Some workpieces can be spot-welded without fixtures. They can be manually oriented and placed between the machine electrodes. When the two assembled workpieces have a common straight edge, a block may be mounted adjacent to the electrodes against which the workpieces can be held during joining.

Spot-welding Fixtures. Figure 12-59*a* shows a mainspring-and-brace assembly for a watch. The two workpieces are held in alignment while being joined by a single spot weld. Figure 12-59*b* shows the fixture in which the two workpieces are placed in a common nest.

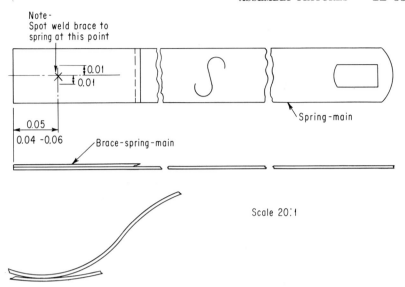

Note-
Spot weld brace to
spring at this point

0.05

0.04 -0.06   Brace-spring-main

Spring-main

Scale 20:1

FIG. 12-59a. Workpieces for the fixture of Fig. 12-59b.

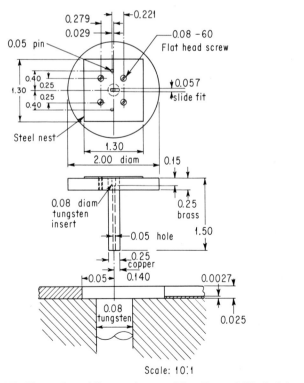

0.279   0.221
0.029

0.05 pin

0.08 -60
Flat head screw

0.40
0.25
1.30
0.25
0.40

0.057
slide fit

Steel nest

1.30
2.00 diam   0.15

0.08 diam
tungsten
insert

0.25
brass

0.05 hole   1.50

0.25
copper

0.05   0.140   0.0027

0.08
tungsten   0.025

Scale: 10:1

FIG. 12-59b. Fixture for welding watch parts. (*Elgin National Watch Co.*)

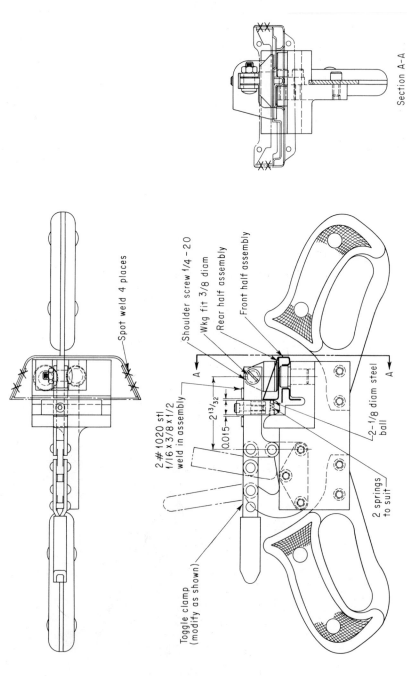

Section A-A

Spot weld 4 places

Shoulder screw 1/4 – 20

Wkg fit 3/8 diam

Rear half assembly

Front half assembly

2 # 1020 stl
1/16 x 3/8 x 1/2
weld in assembly

2 13/32

0.015

2-1/8 diam steel
ball

2 springs
to suit

Toggle clamp
(modify as shown)

FIG. 12-60. A manual spot-welding fixture. (*Western Electric Co., Inc.*)

12–56

Figure 12-60 shows a small portable fixture for spot-welding two small stampings. This simple fixture incorporates two handles removed from purchased hacksaws and a proprietary toggle clamp. The stampings are designed and formed to nest within each other. They are positioned and clamped in the fixture, which is placed between the electrodes.

Figure 12-61 illustrates a fixture for holding a circular, dome-shaped workpiece while brackets are welded to its outer perimeter at four places. The fixture has an aluminum base plate (1) with two locating dowels (2) which radially locate the workpiece (3). At three points on the base-plate circumference, screw clamps (4) hold the workpiece. Attached to the base plate is an aluminum locating ring (5) which locates in the ID of the workpiece. A micarta guide (6) has eight cutouts which are in turn placed against the lower electrode for location during welding. The fixture is placed over the horn of the spot welder with the micarta cutout against the lower electrode. The bracket is located, and the two workpieces are spot-welded. The sequence is repeated for two spots in each of four brackets.

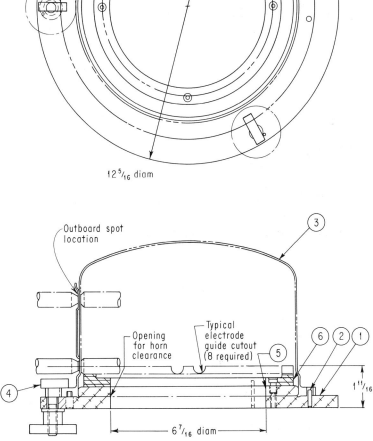

Fig. 12-61. Fixture for spot-welding circular workpieces. (*Pratt & Whitney Aircraft.*)

Figure 12-62 shows a sizing and spot-welding fixture for a receptacle-cover assembly. The four stampings are placed in the fixture, and four cam clamps (1) press against them to bring the assembly to its required size and alignment. The fixture (2) is removed from its base (3) and is manually positioned to accomplish the welding. The fixture is replaced on its base, the clamps are released, and the fixture is pressed down on its spring-loaded mounting against ejector pins (4) which push the finished workpiece out of the fixture.

Figure 12-63 shows a spot-welding jig consisting of a slotted plate with two locating pins. Symmetrical right- and left-hand parts are placed on the pins as

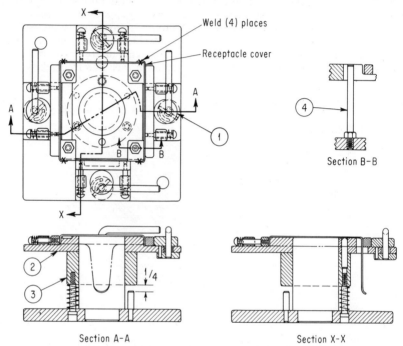

FIG. 12-62. Sizing and spot-welding fixture. (*Western Electric Co., Inc.*)

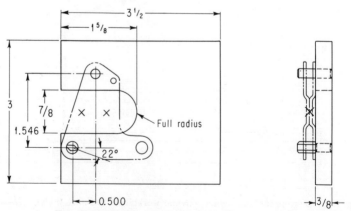

FIG. 12-63. Simple spot-welding jig. (*The Vendo Co.*)

shown, and the jig is placed between the electrodes for spot welding. The slot in the plate permits the lower electrode to contact the workpiece.

Figure 12-64 illustrates a special electrode which fits a small space between two toroidal workpieces. A solenoid-actuated clamp (1) holds a small workpiece (2) in position against the lower-electrode button (3). The larger workpiece (4) is placed over the lower electrode, and the machine is cycled to spot-weld the two workpieces. The magnetic clamp is attached to, but insulated from, the lower electrode.

Figure 12-65 illustrates a method of equalizing the pressure of several spot-welding tips simultaneously pressing on workpieces of varying thickness.

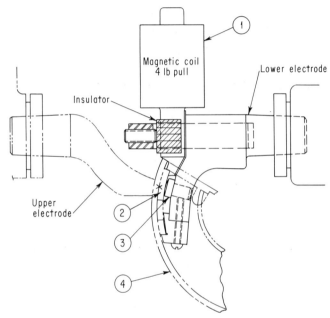

FIG. 12-64. Special spot-welding electrode assembly. (*Detroit Transmission Div., General Motors Corp.*)

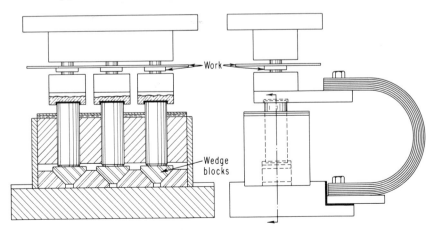

FIG. 12-65. Welding fixture with equalized electrode pressures.

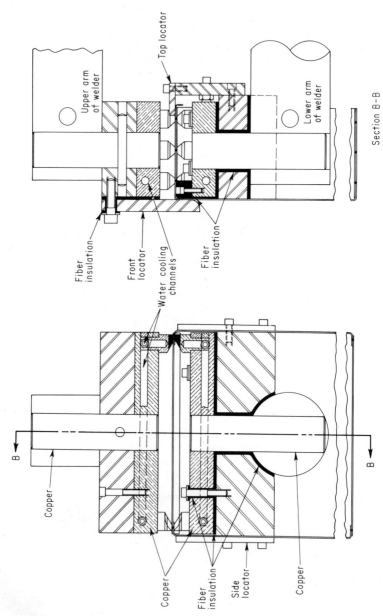

Upper arm of welder

Top locator

Lower arm of welder

Section B-B

Fiber insulation

Front locator

Water cooling channels

Fiber insulation

Copper

B

B

Copper

Fiber insulation

Side locator

Copper

FIG. 12-66. Fixture for spot-welding a rectangular box. (*Craft Mfg. Co.*)

If a workpiece heavier than the rest is inserted, it will force the electrode and its wedge block down, displacing the other wedges until the pressure at all electrodes is equal.

The fixture of Fig. 12-66 holds an open box for spot-welding it to a top plate in six places. Top, front, and side locators align the box and top plate and, with the box inverted, align it with the bottom plate for again spot-welding it in six places. Water-cooling passages are machined in the heavy current-carrying members of the fixture, which are insulated from the other metallic parts with heat-resistant vulcanized fiber.

Brazing and Soldering Fixtures

Fixtures for furnace brazing and torch soldering may be of cast heat-resisting alloy supports, of graphite blocks, or of heat-resisting alloy wire to hold the components together.

Tungsten disks to be copper-brazed to steel shanks are placed in the holes in the graphite base of the fixture of Fig. 12-67a. A slight clearance between the holes and the shanks allows gravity, as the copper shims melt, to move them downward against the tungsten disks. Thin sheets of asbestos paper between steel parts and graphite fixture blocks generally prevent carbon diffusion into the parts and their possible melting.

Figure 12-67b shows steel and tungsten carbide components held by clamps made of heat-resisting alloy bolts and bar stock. The mica insert prevents the tungsten carbide component from being brazed to the alloy bar.

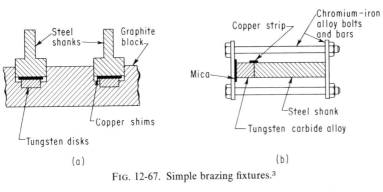

FIG. 12-67. Simple brazing fixtures.[3]

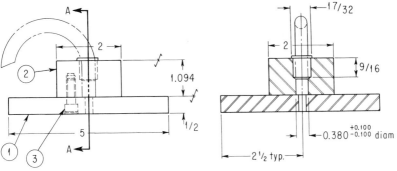

FIG. 12-68. Fixture for acetylene-torch brazing. (*The Vendo Co.*)

Figure 12-68 shows a fixture for the acetylene-torch brazing of a siphon-tube and washer assembly. This simple fixture consists of a base (1), a block (2), and two screws (3). The fixture holds the tube and washer in the position required for the operation.

References

1. Lessman, G. W.: Air Power Saves Assembly Time, *Am. Machinist,* p. 89, Aug. 7, 1950.
2. Ochieano, M. L.: Design of Fixtures for Projection Welding, *Iron Age,* p. 55, May 2, 1946.
3. Webber, H. M.: Holding and Supporting Assemblies in Electric Furnace Brazing, *Iron Age,* Sept. 15, 22, 1938.

Section 13

INSPECTION FIXTURES

By ASTME BOOKS STAFF

An inspection (qualifying, gaging) operation is any examination of a workpiece that determines whether or not it meets standards of quality.

Standards of quality considered in this section are all permissible linear and angular dimensions and relations, including specified tolerances, as defined or implied by the engineering or manufacturing drawings and specifications. Other standards of quality such as surface finish, hardness, etc., are not considered.

An inspection fixture generally holds or nests a workpiece but may be placed on or clamped to it. A fixture facilitates the manipulation and observation of a gaging device separate from or incorporated in the fixture.

Inspection fixtures need not be designed to withstand forces, such as shock and vibration, associated with machining or with some other fabricating and assembly processes, such as riveting, staking, and stitching. Inspection fixtures are not required to resist temperatures present in welding, brazing, soldering, and heat-treating. Clamping forces in an inspection fixture are generally too small to affect its design, but they should not distort the workpiece.

The accuracy of the construction of an inspection fixture and the design of gaging devices and any linkage associated with them are dependent upon the standards of quality specified for the workpiece.

Problems coupled with chips and coolants, with hazards of cutting tools, hot electrodes, and electric currents, or with rapid fixture loading need not be considered in the design of inspection fixtures.

GAGING DEVICES

Gaging is the process of investigating and determining whether or not a workpiece conforms to dimensional quality standards specified.

A *limit gage* only determines whether or not a dimension of a workpiece is within its prescribed dimensional limits.

A *flush-pin gage* is a limit gage which checks a distance between surfaces and/or points on a workpiece for deviations from that distance that are within the limits specified. It is made with a step on one end (the indicator or exposed end) of the pin equal in depth to the tolerance on a part's dimension (Fig. 13-1). The opposite or contact end of the pin bears against a gaging point or surface of the workpiece. A workpiece is within tolerance if the surface of (1) the end of the pin, (2) the step, or (3) any portion of the pin between its step and indicator end is in the same plane as the gaging surface of the fixture. For all other positions of the pin, a workpiece is out of tolerance. The operator, either visually or by touch, judges coincidence of these surfaces. Flush-pin gaging is not generally used for checking total tolerances under 0.010 in.

An *indicator gage* measures and shows on a suitable scale the extent of the deviation in a workpiece dimension.

An indicating gage of the mechanical type, commonly called a dial indicator, is a device that detects, amplifies, and presents visually on a scale any change in the position of its probe. The travel of the probe is generally amplified mechanically and is seen on a circular scale calibrated in angular increments corresponding to the linear motion of the probe. The accuracy of a dial indicator is limited by the tolerances of its components as well as by any lost motion, such as backlash in a gear and rack. This type of gage is not generally used for measuring total tolerances of less than 0.0015 in.

Dial indicators are available with balanced and with continuous dials, with or without revolution counters. If the tolerances are bilateral, such as ±0.002 in., the balanced dial indicator is preferable. If they are unilateral, such as −0.000 in., +0.001 in., either type is convenient. The continuous type of dial is particularly useful for measurements which rotate the indicator hand more than a half turn. When several complete turns are involved, the revolution counter indicates to the user the number of revolutions made by the large hand.

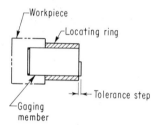

Fig. 13-1. Flush-pin gage.

Standard dial indicators come in four sizes ranging from 1⅜ to 3¾ in. diam. The size selected usually depends upon the application and the distance the indicator must be from the eye. Even though the larger-diameter indicators may seem to be easier to read, it has been found that more accurate readings are obtained (less mistakes are made) when a smaller-size indicator is chosen (a 2½-in. dial is best for all-round use). The smaller-size indicator requires the user to concentrate more on reading, thus producing a more reliable result.

The choice of graduations is next in the selection of dial indicators. It is best not to require the operator to estimate a reading closer than half the distance between dial divisions. If an indicator with 0.001-in. divisions requires the user to estimate the reading closer than 0.005-in., a dial with 0.0005-in., 0.0001-in., or 0.00005-in. graduations should be ordered. When working tolerances in ten-thousandths of an inch must be checked, the 0.0001- or the 0.00005-in. indicator is used.

Most dial indicators have a range equal to 2½ times the number of divisions on the dial. One of the desirable features of the dial indicator is the addition of minimum-maximum limit hands.

Inspection fixtures themselves, and particularly their gaging devices, require inspection and recalibration schedules to maintain accurate inspection of parts.

Hole Relation Checking Fixtures. This type of fixture is an important tool used in the production of interchangeable parts and assemblies to check the location of bored, drilled, reamed, or tapped holes.

When the part is placed in position on the fixture, the pins that do not enter the hole give an indication of which holes are out of location, and the part is rejected.

In designing this type of fixture, the mean dimension of the workpiece is used for the fixture dimension with 10 per cent of the workpiece tolerance as the fixture-dimension tolerance. The pin diameters may depend directly on the minimum hole size and hole spacing.

Figure 13-2 shows a simple workpiece and its hole-location fixture. If the workpiece has four holes within the diameter tolerance, this fixture will indicate their location in relation to the center hole and to each other within +0.001 in. The fixture cannot differentiate between oversize, undersize, tapered, or elongated holes.

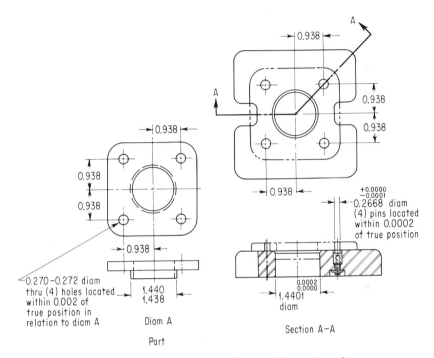

FIG. 13-2. Hole-location fixture. (*Pratt & Whitney Aircraft.*)

The fixture of Fig. 13-3 checks the size of the flange and hole locations on an automobile parking lamp casting.

A die casting having an oversize flange will not fit between the six locating blocks (1, 2, 3, 4) of the fixture. Two pins (5) inserted through headless bushings (6) and into the three tapped holes of the casting inspect their locations with respect to each other and to the flange.

The distances from six mounting holes to the outside flange surfaces of a sheet-aluminum chassis, as well as interhole distances, are checked in the fixture of Fig. 13-4. The chassis is loaded with the edges down between seven gage blocks (1), and hole location is checked by six pins (2). An oversize chassis will not fit between the gage blocks, while an undersize chassis permits the insertion of a 0.030-in. feeler gage between the blocks and the flange surfaces.

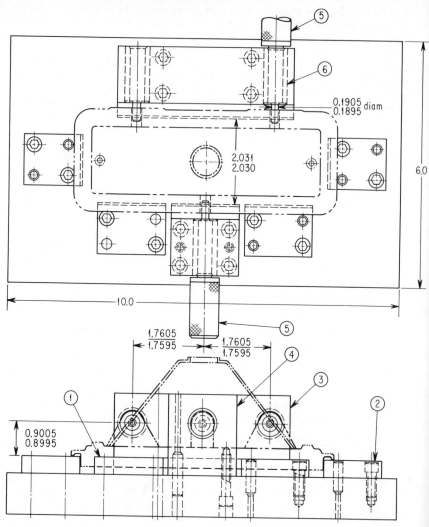

FIG. 13-3. Fixture for checking flange dimensions and hole location. (*Ford Motor Co.*)

Dimensions of a stamped part (Fig. 13-5) are inspected in the fixture shown in Fig. 13-6 together with a conventional dial indicator and stand. Base *A* of the fixture is placed on a surface plate and all go pins are retracted. The sliding gage (1) is opened by pushing on the fixture surface marked "push here to load and unload." The part is placed on pin locators (2) with part surface *V* parallel to the fixture base *A*. The inspection procedure consists of the following major steps:

1. The sliding gage (1) is released, and the entry of the pin (3) into the 0.134-in. notch is checked.

2. With the gage (1) on part surface *W*, the insertion of the go pins (4) checks the 0.166-in. dimension.

3. With the go pins (4) inserted, the flush-gage surfaces check the 1.103-in. dimension between the locating holes and holes in which pins (4) are inserted.

4. The insertion of go pins (5) checks the 1.187- and 0.593-in. dimensions for the two holes in the tabs opposite the locating holes.

5. The 0.265-in. notch width is checked by the insertion of the sliding gage (6).

6. The insertion of the four go pins (7) checks the location of the four No. 6-32 tapped holes.

7. The tip of a dial indicator is passed over the part surface X to check its flatness.

8. The insertion of another go pin (8) checks the 0.468-in. dimension locating the 0.190-in.-diam hole in the end of the stamping.

9. The fixture is turned to rest on its base B. The dial indicator is set to zero with its probe on top of the indicating pins (9); then the indicator probe is passed over the part surface Y to check the 1.192-in. dimension.

10. The fixture is turned to rest on its base C. The indicator is set to zero with its probe on the indicating surface (10) of the fixture. The part surface V is held against the fixture while the part width, 0.937 in., is checked.

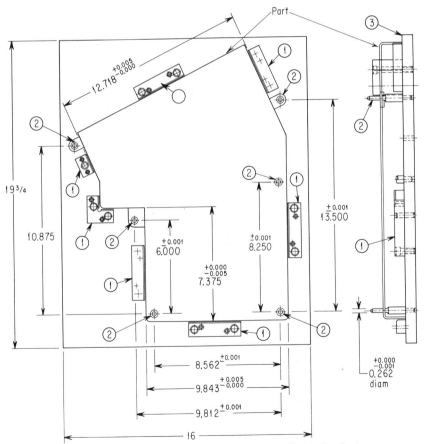

FIG. 13-4. Chassis-inspection fixture. (*Western Electric Co., Inc.*)

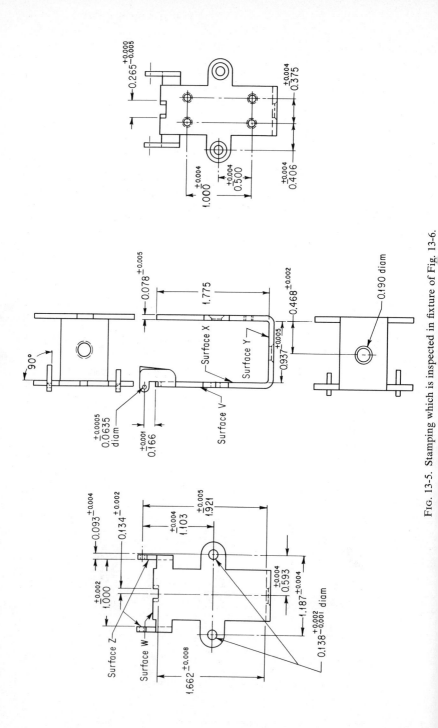

FIG. 13-5. Stamping which is inspected in fixture of Fig. 13-6.

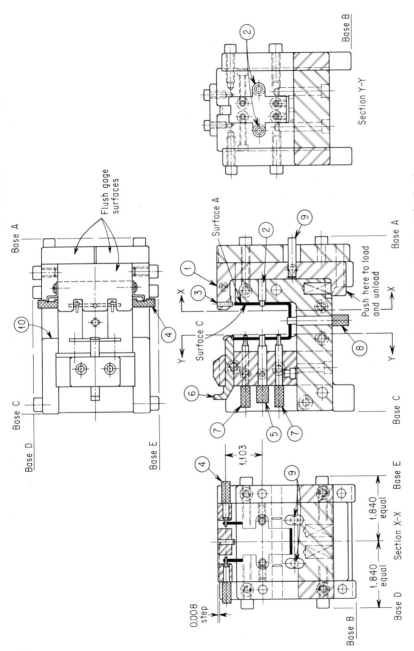

FIG. 13-6. Fixture for inspecting a stamped part. (*Harig Mfg. Corp.*)

11. With the fixture resting on its base *D*, the indicator is brought to zero with its probe on top of the lower indicating pin (9). Surface *Z* of the bent tabs is indicated to check the 1.000-in. spacing dimension. This procedure is repeated with the fixture resting on base *E*.

During the inspection procedure, the checking pins are held in place by spring detents or screws bearing on flatted surfaces of the pins. Each base has hardened and ground rest buttons to support the fixture.

The hole-relation gage of Fig. 13-7 is used to check the distance from the center line of the two large holes to the shoulder of the inside bore in the neck. Also, it is used to check the distance from the outside face of the larger hole (left hand) to the center line of the bores in the neck.

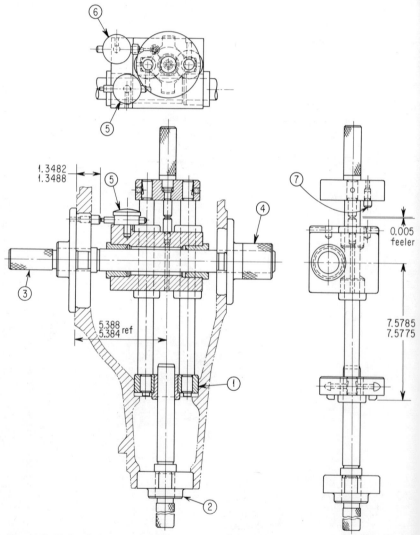

FIG. 13-7. Hole-relation gage for gearbox. (*New Holland Machine Div., Sperry Rand Corp.*)

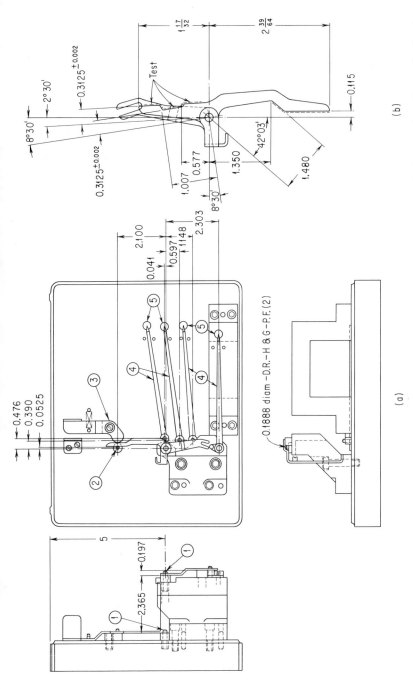

(b)

(a)

Fig. 13-8. (a) Fixture for checking dimensional tolerances and relations of four surfaces of a stamping; (b) the stamping. (*Burroughs Corp.*)

The central portion of the gage is inserted into the workpiece with the plug (1) in the bore of the neck bearing on the shoulder. The pin assembly (2) is inserted in the outer bore of the neck and through the plug (1). A second pin assembly (3) is placed in the cross bore through the bushings in the central portion of the gage. A locator plug (4) supports the end of the pin.

The indicator gage (5) is used to determine the distance from the center line of the neck bores to the outside face of the large bore. A second dial indicator (6), acting through linkage bearing on a pin (7), checks the distance from the center line of the two large bores to the shoulder of the inside bore in the neck.

All the locating plugs are relieved to have a four-point bearing on their locating surfaces.

Surface Relationship Fixture. The inspection fixture of Fig. 13-8a establishes dimensional tolerances and relations of four surfaces of a stamping (Fig. 13-8b).

The stamping is located on pins (1) which are 0.0002 in. under the low limit of the 0.1895-in. holes. The 0.115-in. dimension is maintained by a spring-loaded clamp (3) which holds the stamping against a pin (2).

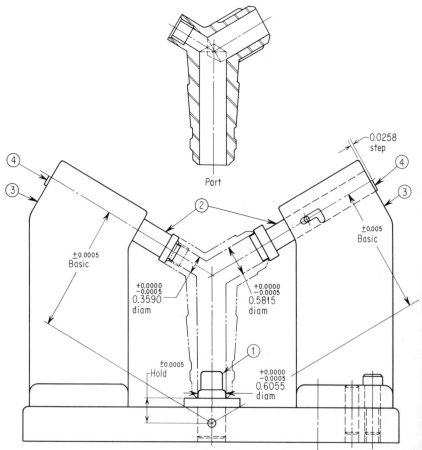

Fig. 13-9. Flush-pin fixture for inspecting elbows and T-shaped workpieces. (*Pratt & Whitney Aircraft.*)

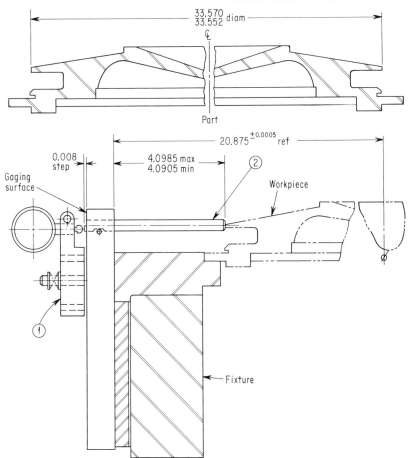

Fig. 13-10. Fixture for inspecting diameters. (*Pratt & Whitney Aircraft.*)

Variations in the surfaces to be inspected are reflected in the movement of the pointer-type indicators (4). These indicators are levers with ratios of 15 to 1.

The fixture is calibrated with a master part, and the tolerances for production parts are scribed in white plastic inserts (5) located under the indicator points.

Flush-pin Fixtures. This type of fixture checks workpiece surface relations.

Figure 13-9 shows a typical fixture to check hole and face location on elbow and T-shaped workpieces. The workpiece is placed on the base locator (1); then two movable locators (flush-pin gages) (2) are pushed into the workpiece. When they are fully inserted, the ground faces of the mounting blocks (3) must be coincident with or between the steps ground on the locators (4), or the workpiece is rejected.

Figure 13-10 shows a flush-pin fixture in which a workpiece diameter is checked by inspection of the radius. The acceptable diameter range is 33.552 to 33.570 in., or a total tolerance of 0.018 in. The radius range must then be 16.776 to 16.785 in., or a total tolerance of 0.009 in. The fixture-construction tolerance of 0.0005 in. results in a net acceptable tolerance of 0.0085 in. The 0.008-in. step of the gage pin (2) establishes workpiece acceptability if either step of the gage pin or any part of it between the steps is aligned with the outer ground face of the gaging surface. As tolerances decrease, the flush-pin method must be changed to one of amplification. A typical dial-indicator assembly (1) is mounted to the fixture. Using either a master part or a precise linear measurement, the indicator is brought to zero at the mean radius. Workpiece acceptability is then determined by indicator deviation from the mean in accordance with design tolerance.

The fixture shown in Fig. 13-11 incorporates a dial indicator (1) which slides in a slot (2) in the base to gage various shoulder lengths. Separate adapters and masters are provided for different workpieces. The master is inserted into the adapter, and the indicator reading is noted. Production workpieces then inserted must duplicate the indicator reading within the prescribed tolerance. A tapped hole in the adapter provides storage for the master.

The inspection fixture of Fig. 13-12 incorporates a flush pin (3) to check the contour of a parabolic (dish) shaped radar reflector which is mounted on a swinging arm (1).

The parabolic surface of the workpiece is checked by placing the stepped flush pin in a hole in each step of the gaging member (2). The part is rotated, and the relation of the step in the pin to the gaging surface is noted.

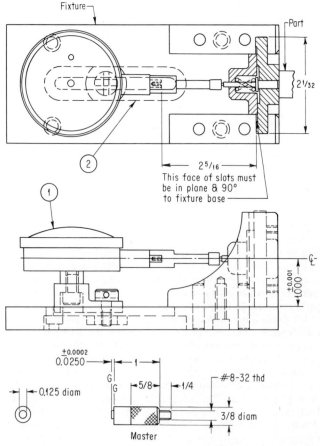

FIG. 13-11. Flush-pin fixture for inspection of shoulder lengths. (*Argus Cameras, Inc.*)

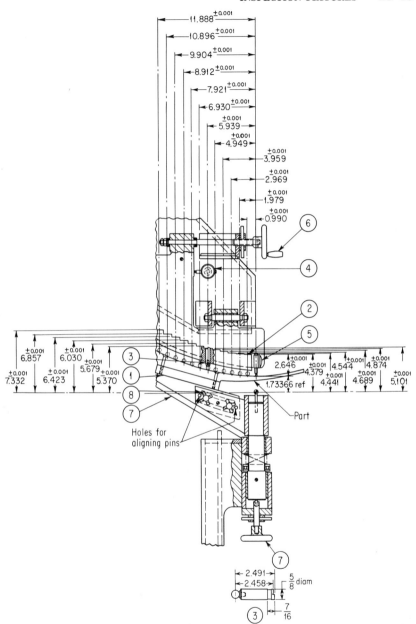

Fɪɢ. 13-12. View of operating mechanism for inspection fixture of Fig. 13-13. (*The Emerson Electric Mfg. Co.*)

The dial indicator (5) is placed on the dead center of the workpiece by rotating the handwheel (6) which controls lateral movement of the gaging member. The dial indicator is set to zero by turning a lower handwheel (7) which controls vertical movement of the workpiece. The dial indicator (4) checks the position of the mounting screws in relation to the part center.

Figure 13-13 illustrates the entire fixture.

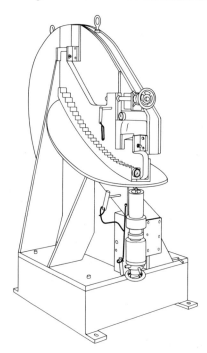

FIG. 13-13. Fixture for checking contour of a parabolic-shaped workpiece. (*The Emerson Electric Mfg. Co.*)

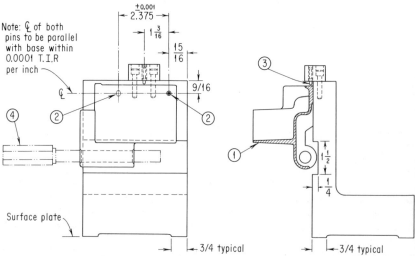

FIG. 13-14. Inspection for parallelism of holes in an aluminum casting. (*Universal Winding Co.*)

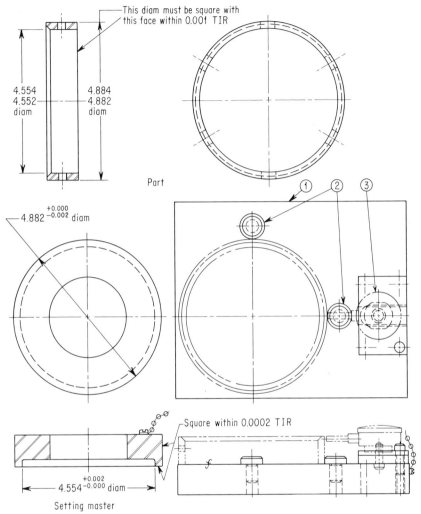

This diam must be square with
this face within 0.001 TIR

4.554
4.552
diam

4.884
4.882
diam

Part

4.882 $^{+0.000}_{-0.002}$ diam

Square within 0.0002 TIR

4.554 $^{+0.002}_{-0.000}$ diam

Setting master

FIG. 13-15. Fixture for inspecting squareness. (*Pratt & Whitney Aircraft.*)

Squareness Checking Fixtures. Workpieces are often placed in fixtures to check the squareness of surfaces or parallelism of holes to surfaces.

The fixture shown in Fig. 13-14 is placed on a surface plate together with a dial indicator and its stand. The workpiece (1), an aluminum die casting, is placed on two pin locators (2) and held in position by a spring plunger (3). A ground plug (4) is inserted in the casting to project the center line of the bored hole.

An indicator reading shows whether or not the plug center line is parallel to the base and consequently to the locator center lines and the two holes in the workpiece within the required tolerance of 0.0005 in. per inch.

Figure 13-15 shows a fixture to check the squareness of an OD with the face of the workpiece. The fixture consists of a ground plate (1), two locators (2), and a dial indicator (3). A setting master is provided to zero the indicator. The workpiece is placed face down on the plate against the two locators and manually rotated. Indicator deflection must not exceed 0.001 in. TIR.

The workpiece of Fig. 13-16 is a rectangular pipe formed in a U shape. Its flanges are parallel but have an axial twist of 90°.

The fixture for this workpiece (Fig. 13-17) has a fixed rectangular locator (1) that fits in one flange while the other flange determines the position of the other rotatable locator assembly (2). The fixture base has ground side rails (3) and a movable indicator assembly (4). A dowel pin (5), serving as an indicator setting gage, permits the operator to zero the indicator by passing it between the rail and the dowel. Measuring the distance from the rear locator assembly to the two side rails checks the 3.624 ± 0.015 and 2.450 ± 0.015 part dimensions. The axis of a pin (6) is coincident with the center line of the rear locator.

Measuring the distance between the pin and a fixed bar locator (7) checks the 90° angle between the rectangular openings of the workpiece.

The bases of the rectangular locators are parallel but differ in elevation by 0.285 in. A workpiece with flanges closer together than that distance cannot be clamped in position. If a positioned workpiece has its flanges more than 0.291 in. apart, a 0.007-in. feeler gage can be inserted between the flange and the locator base.

To assure the tight fitting of the locators in the flanges, the locators are tapered and spring-loaded along the long side. For endwise location, screw-actuated pins are provided.

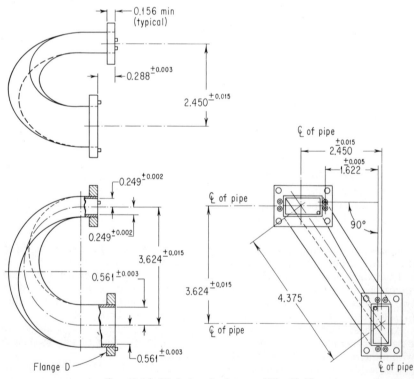

FIG. 13-16. Workpiece for fixture of Fig. 13-17.

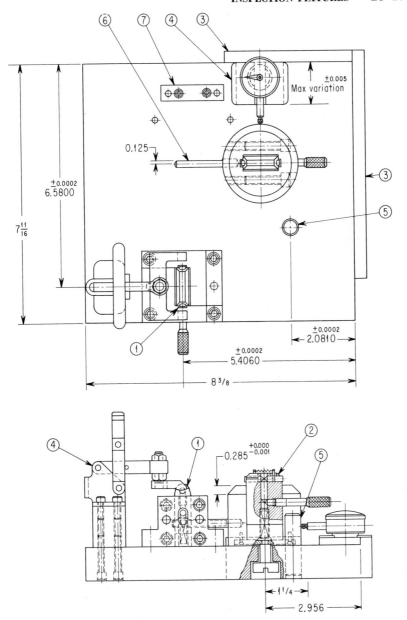

F<small>IG.</small> 13-17. Inspection fixture for a rectangular pipe. (*Western Electric Co., Inc.*)

Concentricity and Squareness Checking Fixtures. The extent of the concentricity of bores, bearing surfaces, etc., and the squareness of these surfaces to shoulders or mounting surfaces are quite commonly specified. The checking of these characteristics can be done with a dial indicator and a means of holding or rotating the workpiece.

The fixture shown in Fig. 13-18 incorporates a ground V locator in which the workpiece is placed and manually rotated. A dial indicator (1) with its probe bearing on an ID checks concentricity between the ID and the OD of the workpiece. A second dial indicator (2), mounted on a slide, allows its probe to contact the internal face which shows squareness of the face. Concentricity of the ID is checked by placing the probe on the surface to be checked and rotating the workpiece.

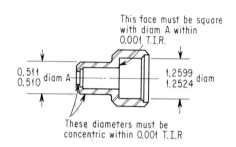

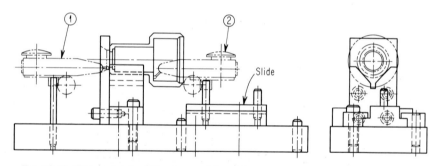

FIG. 13-18. Fixture for checking concentricity and squareness. (*Pratt & Whitney Aircraft.*)

Figure 13-19 shows a typical bushing having an ID and an OD which must be concentric within 0.001 in. Both diameters have a tolerance of 0.0005 in., and both bushing faces must be square to the center line of the bushing within 0.0005 in. TIR. Any two points on either face can each vary up to 0.0005 in. in squareness with a total indicator reading of no more than 0.001 in.

The fixture consists of a relieved mandrel (1) on which the workpiece is manually rotated while seated against a second locator (2) which bears on the face being inspected. A dial-indicator probe (3) contacting the OD of the rotating part allows any difference in wall thickness to be registered directly on it. The probe (4) of a second indicator bears on the workpiece face to detect lack of squareness during rotation.

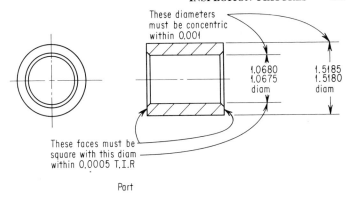

These diameters
must be concentric
within 0.001

1.0680
1.0675
diam

1.5185
1.5180
diam

These faces must be
square with this diam
within 0.0005 T.I.R

Part

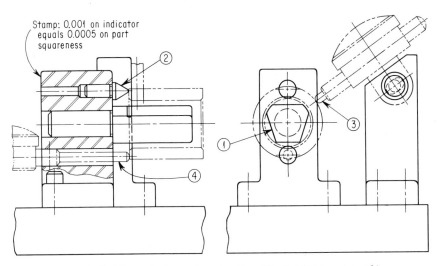

Stamp: 0.001 on indicator
equals 0.0005 on part
squareness

FIG. 13-19. Fixture for inspecting a bushing. (*Pratt & Whitney Aircraft.*)

The workpiece of Fig. 13-20 is a hollow cylinder. The fixture here utilizes an expanding and centering mandrel (1) with its allowable runout held within 0.001 in. TIR. The workpiece is mounted on the mandrel and manually rotated while a dial-indicator probe (2) bearing on the OD detects concentricity variation. A second dial-indicator probe, bearing on the face of the workpiece through a linkage (3), checks its squareness.

The centering mandrel is a standard proprietary item designed to allow rotation of the workpiece about the best average bore center line. If the bore of a workpiece is slightly out of round, this type of mandrel will allow correct gaging, while a solid type will not.

Two internal diameters, Y and Z, of an aluminum casting (Fig. 13-21) must be concentric within 0.002 in. TIR and must be square with the X surfaces within 0.002 in. TIR.

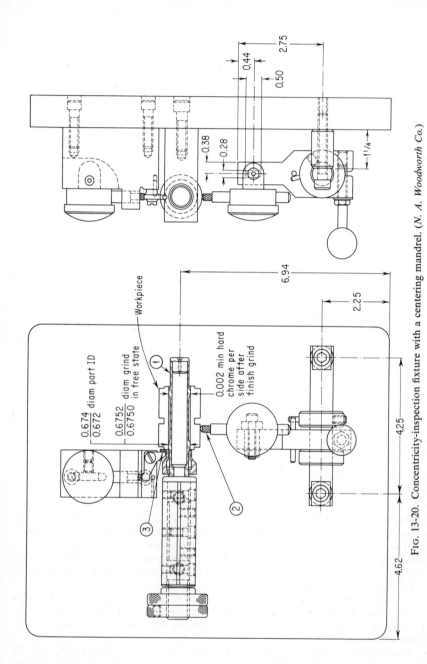

FIG. 13-20. Concentricity-inspection fixture with a centering mandrel. (*N. A. Woodworth Co.*)

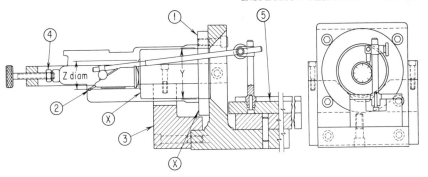

Fig. 13-21. Squareness- and concentricity-checking fixture. (*Thompson Products, Inc.*)

The inspection fixture (Fig. 13-21) for the casting has a ground plate (1) against which the workpiece base is held by a clamp (4). A dial-indicator probe (2) is moved against each ID. Revolving the workpiece in the V locator (3) permits checking the concentricity of the two diameters and their squareness to the X surfaces by moving the indicator mounted on a slide (5).

An aluminum casting is checked for the proper relationship between its bore and its outside surface contacted by the indicator probe. The part is placed on the tapered spring-loaded locator (1) and clamped against a fixed locator (2) with the strap clamp (3). A jig leaf (4) carrying a dial indicator (5) is closed and locked with a quarter-turn screw. The indicator assembly is rotated in its bushing (6) which revolves the indicator probe around the external surface of the part, thereby measuring any runout. A construction hole in the base is used by the tool inspector to check the position of the locator and indicator assembly. (See Fig. 13-22.)

A part consisting of a curved aluminum cylinder, a flared sleeve with a counterbalance, and a thick ring is inspected in the fixture of Fig. 13-23. After assembly, the OD of the ring should not run out more than 0.010 in. in relation to the center line of the sleeve. The distance from the base of the sleeve to the outer edge of the ring must be 7.282 ± 0.005 in.

The inspection fixture includes a hollow mandrel (1) in which the assembly is mounted. The mandrel is rotated in a V locator (2), and runout of the ring is shown by the indicator (4). The distance between one end of the cylinder and the inner surface of the sleeve's flange is checked with a flush pin (3).

The workpiece inspected in the fixture of Fig. 13-24 is a ball-bearing assembly which is checked for width of inner race, runout, and position of grooves in outer race. Five dial indicators are used to check the part dimensions.

A master setup ring is placed on the spring-loaded locating mandrel (1), and the indicators are set to zero. An air cylinder supplies clamping pressure to the bearing's inner race equal to its average-application preload rating of 6.5 to 7.5 lb.

After the bearing has been placed on the mandrel and the clamping pressure applied, the variation in the width of the inner race is measured by the indicator (2) as it bears against the indicator arm. The inspector rotates the outer bearing race manually and checks the concentricity of the bore of the bearing within 0.0015 in. TIR by watching indicators (3, 4). As the workpiece is rotated, any variation in the location of the grooves moves the checking rolls (7) longitudinally. This movement is registered on two dial indicators (5, 6).

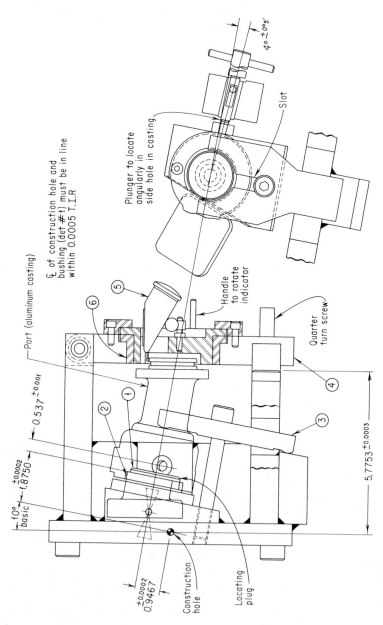

Part (aluminum casting)

₵ of construction hole and
bushing (det #1) must be in line
within 0.0005 T.I.R

Plunger to locate
angularly in
side hole in casting

Slot

$4° \pm 0°5'$

Handle
to rotate
indicator

Quarter
turn screw

$0.537 {}^{+0.001}$

$1.8750 {}^{+0.0002}$

10°
basic

$0.9467 {}^{+0.0002}$

Construction
hole

Locating
plug

$5.7753 {}^{+0.0003}$

Fig. 13-22. Runout-inspection fixture. (*Thompson Products, Inc.*)

13–22

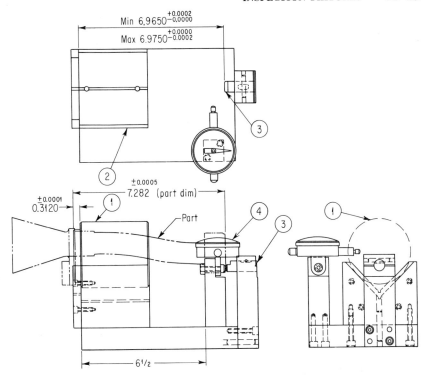

Fig. 13-23. Inspection fixture for a flared pipe. (*Western Electric Co., Inc.*)

The spindles of the checking rolls are mounted on miniature ball bearings (8) in a spring-loaded sleeve (11) which permits axial (longitudinal) movement. The checking-roll units are mounted on ball slides (9) permitting lateral movement. Cone-point setscrews (10) are used to adjust and align the ball slides.

Pressure Testing Fixtures. When a workpiece is primarily a container or conveyor of a liquid or gas, a pressure test may be necessary. The test may consist of only filling it with a liquid and noting any leakage after application of gas or fluid pressure. When filling a workpiece with a liquid for pressure testing, it is necessary that an air vent be provided at the extreme top point so no air can be trapped in the workpiece. The air vent is closed while the hydrostatic pressure is applied.

All pressure tests must be carefully controlled and performed under company, local, or state safety regulations.

Openings in the workpiece may be sealed against leakage by using a synthetic-rubber O ring as a gasket or as a packing. O-ring gaskets have been used for pressures up to 15,000 psi, but O-ring packings are recommended for pressures up to and including 1,500 psi. At pressures from 1,500 to 3,000 psi, the O-ring packing should be supplemented by a leather or special plastic back-up washer, commonly known as a nonextrusion ring. The sizes of grooves for the O rings are listed in manufacturer's catalogues; the manufacturer's recommendations should be followed for successful operation.

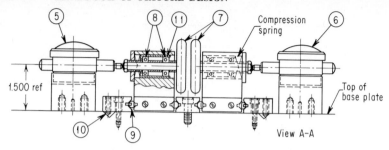

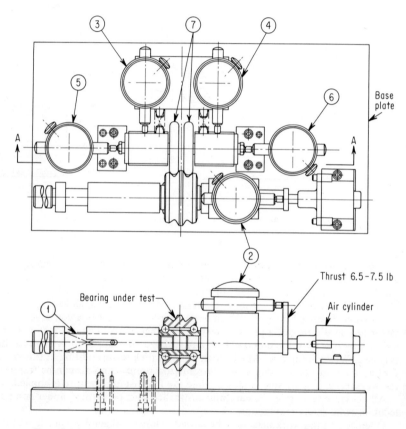

FIG. 13-24. Fixture for inspecting ball bearings. (*Marlin-Rockwell Corp.*)

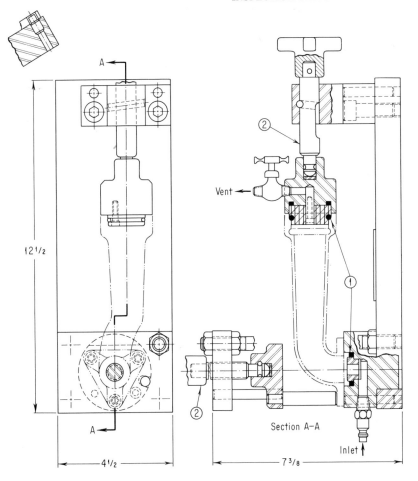

FIG. 13-25. Pressure-test fixture for a small casting. (*Pratt & Whitney Aircraft.*)

The pressure-test fixture shown in Fig. 13-25 holds a machined elbow with all its openings sealed with O rings (1). Two commercial-fixture jacks (2) hold the workpiece. The fluid enters this workpiece from the bottom while the air is expelled at the top through a valve which is closed during the pressure test.

Figure 13-26 shows a pressure-test fixture in which four surfaces of the workpiece must be sealed.

The outer ring of the part rests on a ring (1) which is part of the fixture base, and the outer ring is sealed by an O-ring gasket. The inner ring of the part is sealed by O-ring gaskets in the floating ring (2) and a removable ring (3). Strap clamps (4) hold the workpiece securely between the two rings (2, 3). The cover (5) is placed around the removable ring and is held against the top surface of the part by a drawbolt (6).

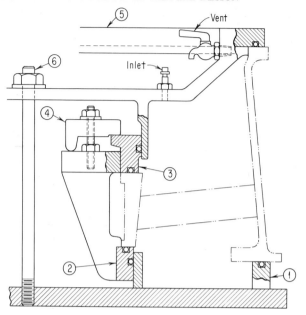

Fig. 13-26. Pressure-test fixture. (*Pratt & Whitney Aircraft.*)

An inlet for the testing fluid and a vent for the trapped air are located in the cover. Four O-ring gaskets and two O-ring packings are used as seals in this fixture.

Contour Checking Fixture. The fixture of Fig. 13-27 has a master cam for checking the contour of a workpiece which is located directly above the master cam.

A dial indicator (1), a master-cam tracer (2), and a workpiece tracer (3) are mounted on a guidepost (4). The workpiece is held in the fixture by a strap clamp (5) and a swiveling two-point contact clamp (6). Two dog-point setscrews (7) serve as part locators.

Manual rotation of the guidepost simultaneously causes the master-cam tracer to follow the surface of the master cam (8) and the workpiece tracer to follow the corresponding surface on the workpiece. The workpiece tracer is spring-loaded and bears against the contact tip of the dial indicator; therefore any deviations between the master- and workpiece-cam contours are shown on the indicator dial.

During loading and unloading of the workpiece, the guidepost is raised and turned to the left, allowing the lower tracer arm to rest on the support (9). During storage the tracer arm is held by a safety clamp (10).

The tracers incorporate ½-in.-diam fixture-construction balls. The master cam is made of tool steel, hardened and ground.

Staging Fixtures. When using optical instruments for inspecting workpieces, the surfaces to be checked are positioned in the light beam with work holders known as staging fixtures. Fixtures having centers hold shafts and other cylindrical parts containing machined centers.

Most fixtures designed specially for holding individual parts can be classified as single-position, step-shift, multiple-position, interposer, and tracer fixtures.

The single-position fixture is loaded to present a workpiece to a light beam for the inspection of certain outlines with only one positioning.

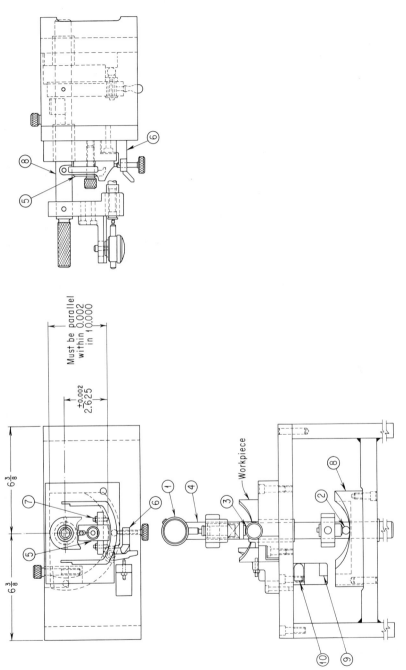

FIG. 13-27. Cam-inspection fixture. (*The Emerson Electric Mfg. Co.*)

13–27

A step-shift fixture is advantageous when it is desirable to see all dimensioned outlines of a workpiece, although the workpiece may be larger than the lens field area can cover.

The work-holding components of the multiple-position fixture are mounted on a sliding base. Controlled movement is obtained against end stops if two positions are needed or against various indexing stops if three or more positions are needed.

When views of a part from more than one direction are needed, workpiece loading blocks can be designed to present various faces of the work effectively to the light beam.

Auxiliary interposers may be used to inspect indirectly the position of a remote surface. For example, a pin of known length may be placed in a hole with the end of the pin extending into the light beam. Thus the distance the pin extends above the surface around the hole, or any other reference surface, may be used to inspect the hole depth.

Large or hidden contours may be inspected by means of a tracer fixture. By using accurate floating heads capable of coordinate movements in two perpendicular directions, a contour staged at some distance from the projector light beam can be reproduced on the screen for study of its magnified movement and shape.

The fixture of Fig. 13-28 is held on an optical comparator table by a clamping screw (1) and its hand knob (2). A chuck (3) holding a small part is rotated to project the form of the workpiece on the screen of the comparator. Rapid and accurate inspection of small, complex parts is practical with similar staging fixtures mounted on a comparator table.

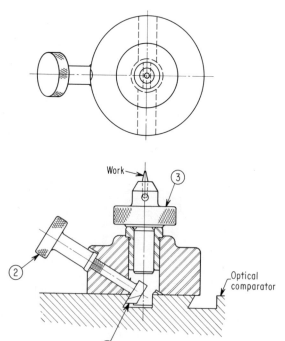

Fig. 13-28. Staging fixture for optical inspection of a small part. (*ASTME Northern Massachusetts Chapter 100.*)

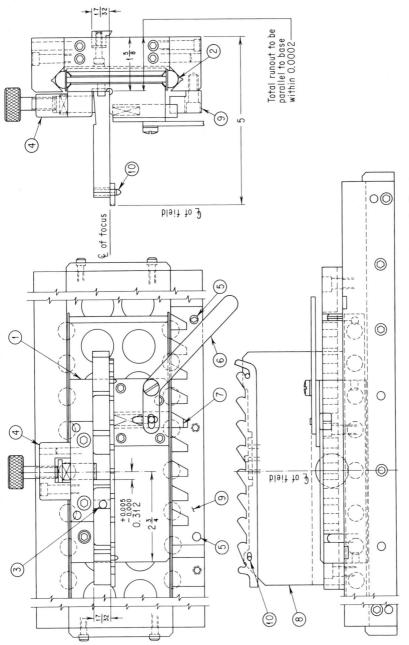

Total runout to be parallel to base within 0.0002

Fig. 13-29. Multiple-position staging fixture. (*Burroughs Corp.*)

The inspection fixture of Fig. 13-29 comprises a carriage (1) which moves on bearing balls (2) in V-shaped ways that are parallel to the base within 0.0002 in. The fixture is mounted on a comparator.

Two locating pins (10) incorporated in a mounting plate (8) engage two 0.159-in. slots in the workpiece (Fig. 13-30). The mounting plate is positioned with its %₂-in. slot over a locating dowel (3) in the carriage. The lower edge of the mounting plate is held in the carriage by a clamp assembly (4).

A notched spacing bar (9) is located on the carriage by two locating pins (5). Positioning of the bar and carriage is controlled by an indexing detent (7) which engages notches in the bar corresponding to the inspection positions for each of the workpiece teeth. Detent contact with and retraction from the notches is manually controlled by a lever (6).

The detent, the spacing bar, and the mounting plate can be modified to accommodate racks and similar workpieces having teeth or other contours along their edges.

A workpiece may have dimensional or other tolerances so small that magnification is required for inspection. The location of the features to be inspected may not permit projection of their shadows with an optical comparator, but a shop microscope can be used.

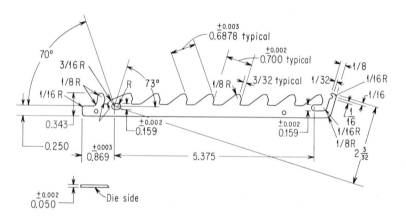

FIG. 13-30. Part for inspection in fixture of Fig. 13-29.

The fixture shown in Fig. 13-31 features a microscope (1) mounted on a carriage (2). A dial indicator with a wheel-type probe (3) is mounted on the carriage with its probe bearing on the ground edge of a worktable (4). As the carriage is moved along the table, the indicator shows the position of the microscope with reference to the table edge. The workpiece, a printed-circuit board, is clamped down in position against a locating block (5). The entire workpiece edge is visually inspected through the microscope eyepiece (6).

The fixture of Fig. 13-32a has a binocular microscope incorporating reticles with engraved lines (Fig. 13-32b) that agree with the specified skew angles (3½° and 7°) for the slots of small armatures (in this case, 0.760 in. diam) under inspection. Other lines on the reticle are spaced at distances equal to commutator widths.

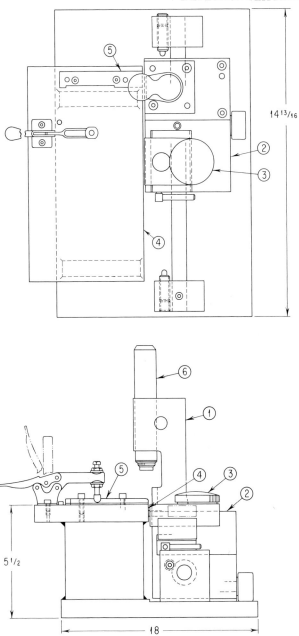

Fɪɢ. 13-31. Fixture for inspection of printed-circuit boards. (*The Emerson Electric Mfg. Co.*)

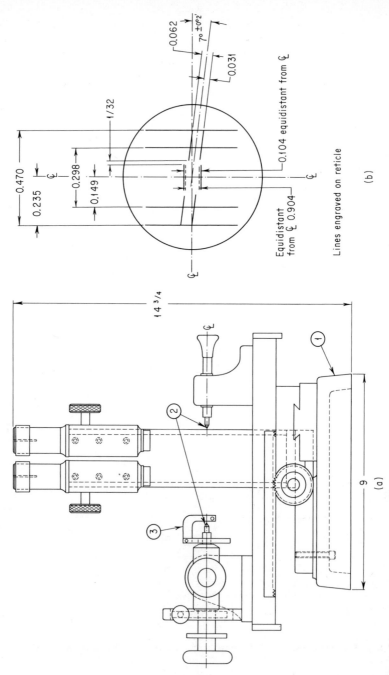

0.062
7° ±0°2'
0.031

1/32

0.470

0.235

0.298

0.149

0.104 equidistant from ℄

Equidistant from ℄ 0.904

Lines engraved on reticle

(b)

14 3/4

1
2
3

9

(a)

Fig. 13-32. (a) Fixture for armature inspection; (b) engraving on reticle. (*Western Electric Co., Inc.*)

A commercial table (1), with suitable slides and an indexing plate, provides movement of the centers (2) which engage the shaft ends of the armature. A bracket (3) has a chrome-plated hole (0.204 + 0.001, − 0.000 in. diam) in which a shaft diameter (0.2030 in.) is held.

Plastic Contour Checking Fixtures. Compared with all-metal fixtures, plastic types are light and therefore easier to handle and transport. Construction costs are generally lower, and plastic compounds may cost less than some metals. Although many plastics are wear-resistant, metal wear plates and bushings can be cast in or attached to a plastic fixture. Elements of a fixture which must duplicate a surface of a workpiece can be cast against or built up to such a surface.

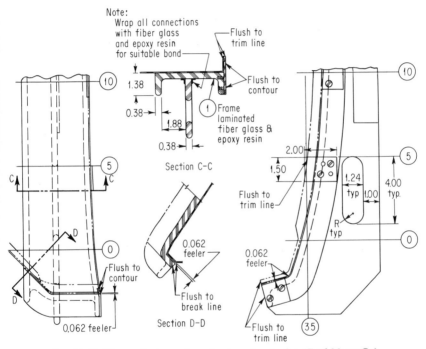

FIG. 13-33. Fixture for inspection of automotive fender. (*Ford Motor Co.*)

Shown in Fig. 13-33 is part of a fixture for checking the door-line contour of an automotive fender. This fixture, approximately 34 in. long and weighing less than 12 lb, can easily be moved into checking position. Allowable deviations are checked by inserting feeler gages at the points shown.

Figure 13-34 shows a large checking fixture of epoxy resin and fiberglass for checking the contour of a stamping and also the size and location of cutouts in it. The bed and frame members are of 2-in.-OD thin (⅛ in.) wall tubing. The fixture provides a locator (2) for the workpiece and provides a contour bar (1) located alongside the positioned workpiece. A 0.120-in. feeler is used to check required clearance between the contour bar and the workpiece.

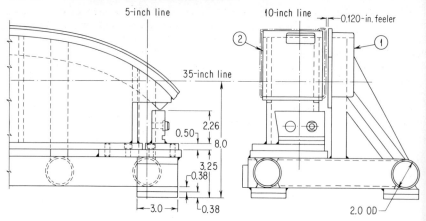

FIG. 13-34. Plastic inspection fixture for an automotive stamping. (*Cadillac Motor Car Div., General Motors Corp.*)

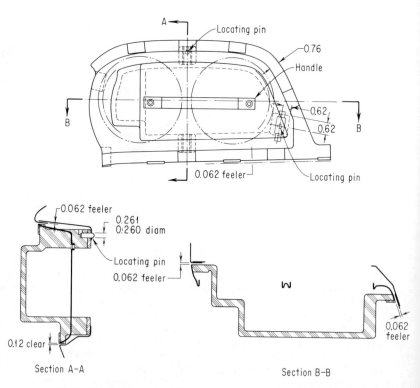

FIG. 13-35. Plastic fixture for inspection of head-lamp area. (*Ford Motor Co.*)

Figure 13-35 shows a portion of a fixture of laminated fiberglass and epoxy resin by which the contour of a head-lamp area of an automotive front fender is checked. The fixture is made in both the right-hand version (shown) and one of the opposite hand. Bullet-nose metal locating pins and metal pads are incorporated at wear points. When the fixture is placed in its gaging position, its edges coincide with the contour of the workpiece. Clearance between the workpiece and fixture at locations shown is checked by a 0.062-in. feeler gage.

Figure 13-36 shows a portion of a large contour- and hole-location-checking fixture of epoxy resin and fiberglass construction. It is approximately 40 in. long, 13 in. wide, and 10 in. high but weighs only 26 lb.

The bed and frame members are lengths of fiberglass tubing. Metal hardware is added at contact surfaces and hole locations. Contours are checked by inserting feeler gages between the workpiece and fixture. Hole locations are checked by their alignment with bushing-guided metal plug gages.

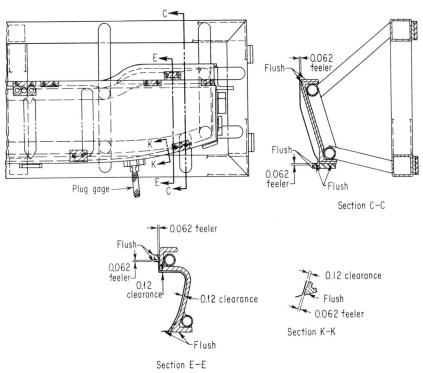

FIG. 13-36. Contour- and hole-location fixture. (*Ford Motor Co.*)

Checking Rotors and Impellers. The fixture of Fig. 13-37 incorporates a flat circular-index plate (3) that carries four rest buttons (2) upon which the workpiece is clamped. The central hole of the workpiece (a 22-blade forged-aluminum impeller) is placed on a locating plug (4) in the center of the fixture. The outer edge of the reference blade of the impeller is located by a sliding V locator (5).

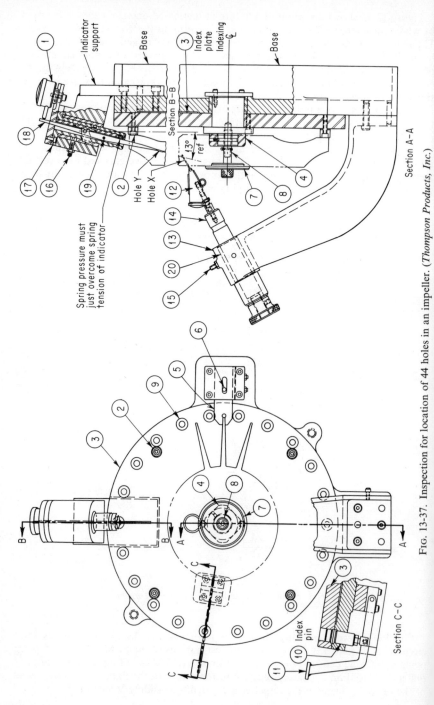

Fig. 13-37. Inspection for location of 44 holes in an impeller. (*Thompson Products, Inc.*)

13–36

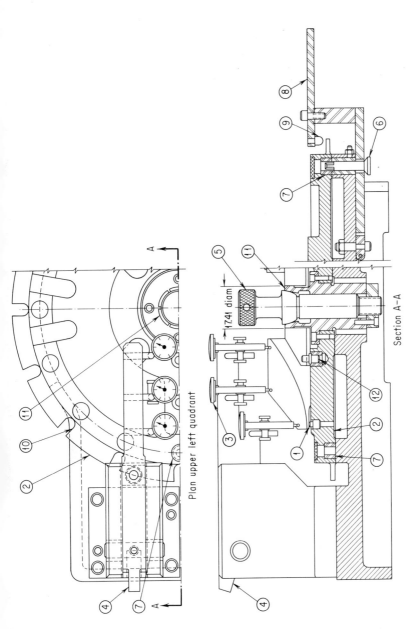

Plan upper left quadrant

Section A–A

Fig. 13-38. Inspection fixture for rotor-blade spacing and thickness. (*Thompson Products, Inc.*)

1.741 diam

The impeller is held down on the rest buttons by a clamp plate (7) and a knurled socket-head cap screw (8). Twenty-two bushings (9) equally spaced around the circular-index plate, an indexing pin (10), and a handle (11) comprise the indexing mechanism (see section C-C).

Each of the 22 X holes between blades is successively checked within 0.005 in. of its specified position by an indicator (12) (see section A-A). An indicator arm (13) mounted to the cast fixture base holds an indicator mounting slide (14) which can be retracted and revolved in a slide bushing (20).

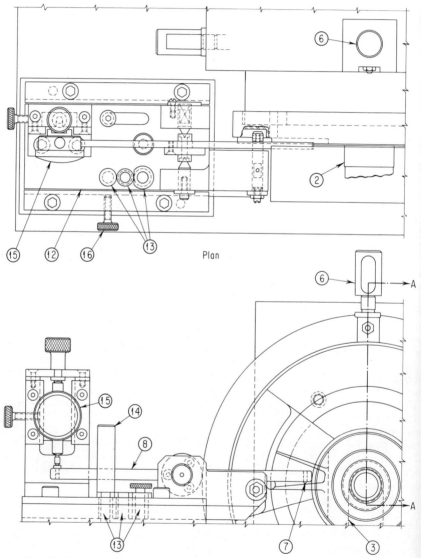

Fig. 13-39. Contour-inspection fixture for rotor blades. (*Thompson Products, Inc.*)

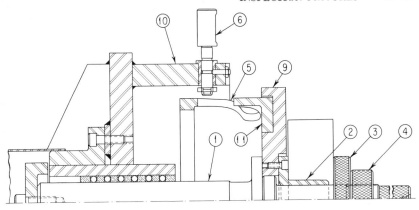

Section A-A

FIG. 13-39 (*continued*)

A spring plunger (15) engages a groove in the indicator slide to hold it up during rotation of the index plate and during loading and unloading of the fixture.

Shown in section *B-B* is another spring plunger (16) which similarly holds a second slide (17) that carries a dial indicator (1).

Each of the 22 *Y* holes adjacent to an *X* hole is checked by this indicator as the index plate is rotated to an index station for each pair of holes.

The indicator assembly has an indicator lever (18) which pivots around a dowel (19). The two indicator assemblies are mounted 180° apart on the circular base of the fixture. The indexing assembly and the sliding V locator are also mounted on the circular base 180° apart but exactly between the indicator assemblies.

The design of this fixture can be modified to check the location of holes (or teeth, bosses, etc.) circularly spaced at various radial distances from a central point on workpieces which are not necessarily of circular outline.

In the fixture of Fig. 13-38, each of the 16 blades or vanes of a forged-aluminum rotor is checked for correct spacing and thickness. A setting master is used to set the indicator dials to zero. The rotor is placed on an expanding slotted collet (11) and is located by a pin (12). Outward clamping pressure on the center hole of the workpiece is provided by rotation of the knurled end of an expander (5).

When the lever handle (8) is depressed, it pulls an index pin (6) out of one of 16 index bushings (7) circularly spaced around an index plate (2) and pushes a bullet-nosed pin (9) into an indexing notch (10).

The handle is swung to bring the notch in alignment with the next index station. Release of the lever allows the index pin to be pushed upward by a flat spring (not shown) and into the index bushing, which locates the plate and workpiece vane in the inspection position below six dial indicators (3). At the inspection position, each of the 16 blades is checked for correct spacing and thickness.

Two indicator latches, or mounting arms (4), each carrying three dial indicators, are swung upward to allow rotation of the index plate and to allow for loading and unloading of the workpiece.

The workpiece (Fig. 13-40) to be inspected in the fixture of Fig. 13-39 is a 16-bladed aluminum rotor. It is clamped on a locator (2) and against a ring (9) by a C clamp (3) and a knurled nut (4). A roller follower assembly (6) is lowered into a spiral-cam track (5). The follower is held by an arm (10) welded to the fixture base (not shown).

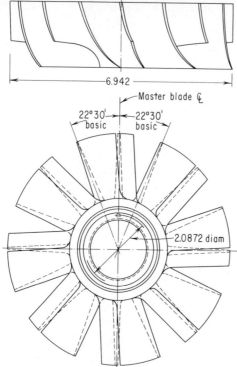

FIG. 13-40. Rotor for inspection in fixture of Fig. 13-39.

The diamond point of the locating stylus (7) mounted on one end of the indicator arm (8) rests on the first of three inspection points on the surface of a rotor blade.

As the operator turns the knurled end of the shaft (1), the shaft and the workpiece move in a spiral path about the shaft center line. Rotation of the shaft also guides the stylus along the initial inspection surface of the rotor blade.

Deviations from the specified contour of the blade result in vertical movements of the indicator arm which actuate a dial indicator (15). If the blade contour is within the specifications there will be little or no movement of the stylus point, since its travel is synchronized with that of the roller cam follower in the spiral-cam track.

For inspection of two other blade surfaces, two other separate spiral-cam tracks are ground in the cam ring (11). The slide (12) on which the indicator assembly is mounted is shifted to any one of the corresponding inspection positions. The slide is located by a plug (14) which is pushed into the correct locating bushing (13) and clamped in that position by the knurled screw (16).

Gear Checking Fixtures. Permissible tolerances for gear blanks, particularly on surfaces used for locating in the gear-cutting machine, are determined by the accuracy requirements for finished gears.

Gear blanks of small and medium size are frequently inspected by using fixtures similar to that shown in Fig. 13-41. The gear blank is placed over a locator (1) and rests on a spacing collar (2); these are mounted on a sliding block (3). The fixture base (4) has a T slot to guide and retain the sliding block. The stop (5) positions the gear blank in proper relation to the dial gages (6). Any deviation in the work-

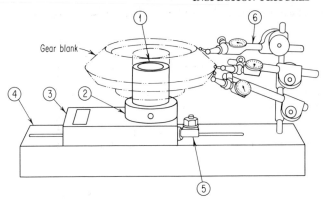

Gear blank

Fig. 13-41. Fixture for inspecting bevel-gear blanks.

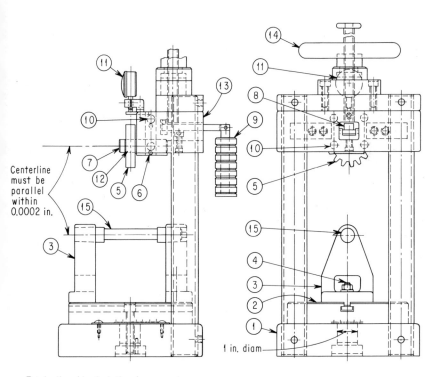

Centerline
must be
parallel
within
0.0002 in.

1 in. diam

Total allowable deviation from exact
℄ of 1.000 diam hole in detail 1
and of detail 12 in 3 in.
movement of detail 13
is 0.0005 in.

Fig. 13-42. Gear-inspection fixture. (*Western Electric Co., Inc.*)

piece surfaces can be read on the indicator dials. A master gear blank is used to set the indicators to zero.

Finished gears may be checked on commercial gear-checking machines; however, special fixtures are sometimes required.

The fixture of Fig. 13-42 checks spur, helical, and worm gears for size, tooth characteristics, and eccentricity.

A master of the gear to be checked is slipped on a mandrel (15) held between two sliding headstocks (3), each of which is clamped to the fixture table (2) by a T bolt (4).

A second master (5) is held on a master shaft (12) by a knurled nut (7) and meshed with the first master. Rotation of a handwheel (14) vertically positions an

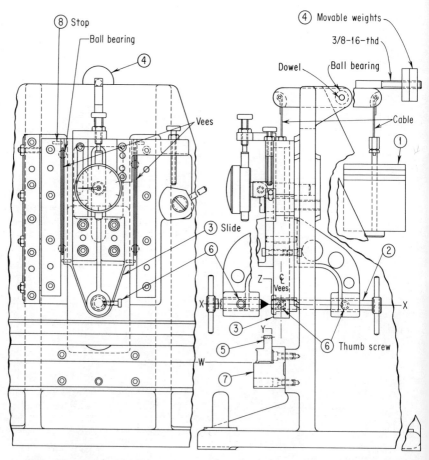

The weight of all details on one end of the cable to be balanced by weight of all other details on other end of assembly

Note: center line X-X to be parallel & square with surfaces W,Y,& Z within 0.00005 maximum for entire length

FIG. 13-43. Gear-checking fixture using a rack as a master gear. (*International Business Machines Corp.*)

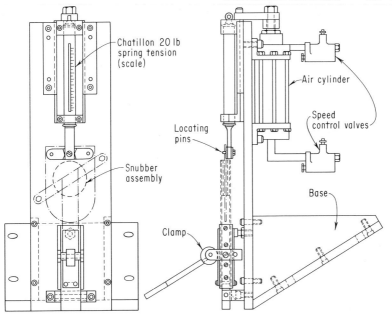

FIG. 13-44. Fixture for checking snubber tension.[1]

adjustment block (13) and sets an indicator (11) to zero when the required counter-balance weight (9) is placed on a weight rod (14) suspended from a balance bar (8). Counterbalances permit only specified pressures on the mating gears as they are revolved.

The master gear on the mandrel is then replaced by the gear to be inspected. Size, smoothness, and irregularities of a gear are transmitted by a follower block (6) and are measured by the dial indicator (11). The V ways of the follower block, incorporating bearing balls (10), permit small variations in gears under test to be shown on the indicator.

The base (2), having a vernier scale, may be swiveled for checking mating gears having nonparallel axes of revolution.

Gears having a tolerance of 0.0002 to 0.0003 in. are checked on the fixture of Fig. 13-43. A gear rack, having a tooth-to-tooth tolerance of 0.0005 in. with a maximum accumulated tolerance of 0.0002 in., is used as the checking gear.

The gear to be checked is placed between the carbide-tipped centers (2) and locked in place with the thumbscrew (6). The master gear rack (5) is held by the supporting bar (7). The slide (3) is counterbalanced by weights (1, 4).

Sliding the movable master gear rack horizontally checks the angularity of a gear by the movement of the indicator, which is indirectly in contact with the work-piece. If the indicator reading is minus, the gear teeth have been cut at an angle; if the indicator reading is plus, the gear teeth are straight.

Tension Checking Fixture. Fixture 13-44 illustrates a fixture for checking the spring tension of snubber pads against a steel plate. This is accomplished by apply-ing a predetermined pressure to the snubber assembly. It would be very tiring for an operator to apply this pressure by hand.

The fixture consists of a double-acting air cylinder connected by an arm to the spring scale. Speed-control valves at each end of the air cylinder are connected to single, foot-operated control valves which move the gage slide up and down. The plunger of the scale is equipped with a crossbar on which are mounted two pins for locating and holding a steel plate. Directly under the spring scale is a quick-acting cam-clamp assembly for holding the snubber. The fixture is mounted on a tilted faceplate for the convenience of the operator.

The steel plate is positioned on two locating pins, and the snubber assembly is clamped to the base. When the foot-operated control valve is pressed, the air cylinder pulls the spring scale up to the specified pressure, regulated by the speed-control valves at each end of the double-acting air cylinder. The operator then determines whether the assembly will pass the inspection by checking the tension gage. Close-limit adjustment of a snubber assembly can be made while it is in the fixture.

Reference

1. Lessman, G. W.: Air Power Saves Assembly Time, *Am. Machinist,* Aug. 7, 1950.

Section 14

MISCELLANEOUS FIXTURES

By ASTME BOOKS STAFF

A Multipurpose Fixture. Accurate but inexpensive tooling is needed for low production. In this type of work, economies can be effected by designing one tool or fixture to do the work of several.

The stainless-steel part shown in Fig. 14-1 must have both faces ground perpendicular to the bore. There are three milled slots in the periphery of the workpiece, one of which must be ground to close tolerances; there is also a milled slot in one of the faces. There are five drilled holes, two of which are counterbored, and four end-milled slots.

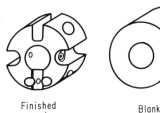

FIG. 14-1. Stainless-steel part machined in fixture of Fig. 14-2.

Finished part

Blank

As shown in the exploded view of Fig. 14-2, the fixture consists of a steel body with several accessories. Squareness of the body facilitates location for all operations. For most operations, the part is held on the locating post by a clamping screw and washer. Since the locating post is equidistant from all sides of the body, the body can be turned over for different operations without affecting machine settings or stops.

Drill bushings are held in removable blocks ground to fit accurately located slots in the tool body. A tongue on the end of one of the drill-bushing blocks orients the part for many of the operations. An indexing pin orients the part for drilling holes in the periphery at an angle of 45° to the slots. The bushing blocks clamp the part for grinding two faces and milling a slot when it cannot be held by the clamping screw and washer. A third bushing block for locating three holes in the face of the part is inverted for drilling one of these holes, since the holes are too closely spaced for inserting bushings of adequate wall thickness.

A Hand Milling Template. The fixture illustrated in Fig. 14-3a was made for milling the edge of an irregularly shaped opening in a small casting in a hand milling machine. Components of the fixture are a base plate with the necessary clamps

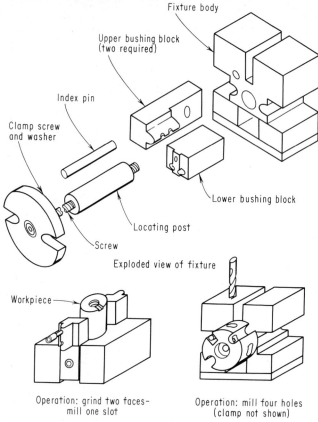

FIG. 14-2. Multipurpose fixture for machining stainless-steel part. (*The Tool Engineer.*)

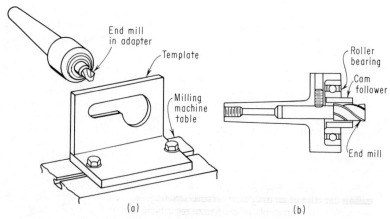

FIG. 14-3. Profile-milling template and follower. (*The Tool Engineer.*)

to hold the workpiece and an upright plate having a cutout the same shape as the opening in the workpiece.

Cutting is done with an end mill mounted in a special adapter shown in Fig. 14-3*b*. The cutter is locked in place so it will rotate with the adapter. A ball bearing, pressed into the adapter, carries a hardened cam-follower roller. This roller does not touch the cutter.

The cutout area in the template is made larger than the desired opening by the difference between the radius of the cutter and the radius of the roller. In use, the roller runs along the edge of the template opening.

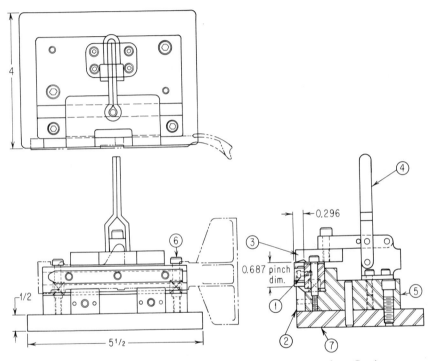

Fig. 14-4. Sanding fixture for magnesium die casting. (*Dictaphone Corp.*)

A Sanding Fixture. The fixture of Fig. 14-4 is used to machine the underside of a magnesium die casting to the dimension of 0.296 in. This surface will be used as a locating surface for subsequent operations.

A slot in the part is placed over the spring-loaded locator (1) and forced down to the stationary clamping surfaces (2) by the block (3) attached to the toggle clamp (4). The angles ground on the clamping blocks contact the workpiece outside the parting line and force it against the spring-loaded locator. The locator block is backed up by a filler block (5) and guided by two stripper bolts (6). The base plate (7) is large enough to permit clamping to the sanding-machine table with strap clamps.

A Rope-cutoff Fixture. The fixture of Fig. 14-5 is used to sear and cut off 16 nylon lawn-mower-engine starter ropes in one setup. A gas flame is used to heat the nylon fibers so that they can be cut with a sharp knife.

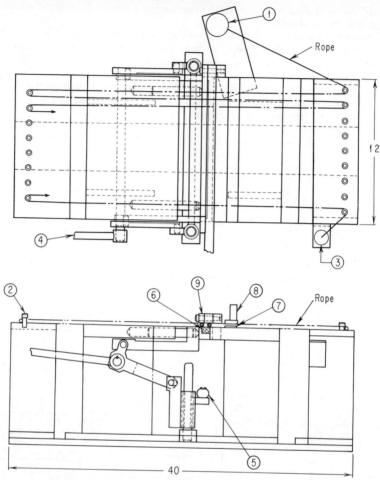

FIG. 14-5. Fixture to sear and cut off nylon rope. (*Lawn Boy.*)

One end of the rope is held in the clamp (1), laced around the studs (2), then clamped in a second clamp (3). The handle (4) is depressed, raising the gas burner (5). The cutter block (6) is also retracted, permitting the flame to sear the nylon fibers. Two coarse files are used as rope rollers to rotate the ropes for even heating. One file (7) is bolted to the frame of the fixture, and a second file (8), a loose piece, is reciprocated across the ropes by hand. When the rope is seared, the flame is lowered and a combination hold-down bar and knife guide (9) is swung into place; this puts pressure on the rope while a sharp knife is drawn through the slot to cut the ropes.

A Plastic-tube-cutoff Fixture. Plastic tubing of various diameters and lengths is cut off in the fixture shown in Fig. 14-6. The tubing is inserted into one of the ten bushings in the bushing carrier and index head (1) and is cut with a cut-off blade (2). An air-actuated drill-press feed mechanism (3) moves the cutoff-blade carrier assembly (4), which is guided by two rods (5), into the tubing.

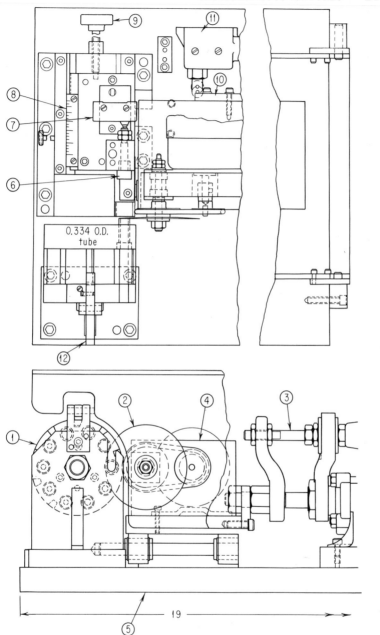

FIG. 14-6. Cutoff fixture for plastic rod and tubing. (*International Business Machines Corp.*)

The fixture is actuated by pushing the tubing through the bushing and against the plunger (6) which contacts a limit switch (7). The length of the tubing is indicated by the scale (8). The plunger, limit switch, and scale are mounted on a slide whose travel is controlled by the screw (9).

The return motion of the cutoff blade is controlled by an adjustable cam (10) and limit switch (11).

The position of the bushings is controlled by an index lever (12) which engages notches in the index head. For the operators' convenience, the bushing size is marked on the bushing carrier 90° counterclockwise from the bushing location.

A hinged plastic hood covers the entire fixture to protect the operator from the cutoff blade and flying chips.

A Wire Brushing Fixture. Adoption of the fixture shown in Fig. 14-7 eliminated a considerable safety hazard caused by the old method of wire-brushing small parts. The old method required that the operator hold the parts to be brushed in contact with a rotating wire brush. This frequently caused the parts to be thrown from the operator's hands, and it also required the operator's hands to be close to the brush.

This fixture is mounted in such a way that the high-speed wire brush contacts the parts at the opening in the fixture tube. The tube is mounted at a slight angle from the horizontal. Cylindrical parts are inserted in the higher end of the tube; as the parts pass through the tube and past the opening, they are cleaned and buffed without danger to the operator.

The size of tubes used in this fixture may be changed to accommodate various-sized parts, but the tubes must be from $\frac{1}{32}$ to $\frac{1}{16}$ in. larger than the OD of the parts. The speed at which parts progress through the tube is controlled by its inclination. Too great a pitch will result in parts leaving the tube at excessive speed. The amount of tilt also determines the length of time the workpiece is presented to the wire brush or buffing wheel and is consequently a means of controlling the degree of finish produced.

Heat-treating Fixtures. The heat-treating of large numbers of parts in a single cycle may be accomplished with the fixture shown in Fig. 14-8. This fixture was designed to repeatedly resist long exposure to high temperatures and the thermal shock of quenching, in addition to providing a solid support for a heavy load.

Type HT cast alloy (35 per cent Ni, 15 per cent Cr, 0.50 per cent C, balance Fe and small amounts of Si and Mn) was used in fabricating the fixture.

The fixture was designed as a group of individual leaves, forming a flexible grid that is loosely pinned together through box members.

The fixture shown in Fig. 14-9 is designed to hold gear plates and similar flat parts during heat-treating. This fixture was made of type 302 stainless steel. The parts are clamped between the base (1) and a top plate (2) by a swinging strap clamp (3). The workpieces are centered in the fixture by two movable studs (4).

Induction hardening of one end of a stud is accomplished with the fixture of Fig. 14-10. The holder illustrated is mounted directly above the heating coil, and a quenching tank is located directly below the coil.

Workpieces (studs) are fed into the holder through a guide spring. An adjustable stop is set so that when a stud is loaded, the bottom stud in the holder is correctly positioned in the coil. The operator then takes his finger off the guide spring and inserts a new stud in position for loading. When the stud in the coil has reached the correct temperature, the operator pushes the new stud into the holder, ejecting the heated stud which falls into the quenching tank.

At the end of each run, untreated studs remaining in the holder can be cycled through by loading a number of previously heat-treated parts into the holder. These studs can be released by lifting the holding spring.

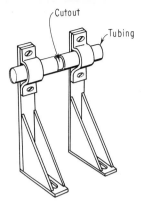

FIG. 14-7. Fixture for wire-brushing cylindrical parts. (*The Tool and Manufacturing Engineer.*)

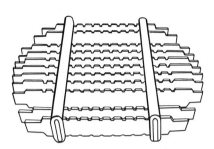

FIG. 14-8. Grid type of heat-treating fixture.[1]*

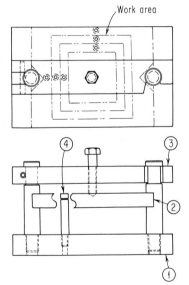

FIG. 14-9. Heat-treating fixture for gear plates and similar flat parts. (*Eclipse-Pioneer Div., Bendix Corp.*)

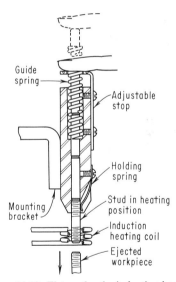

FIG. 14-10. Fixture for the induction heating of studs. (*The Tool Engineer.*)

A Masking Template for Part Placement. The fixture illustrated in Fig. 14-11 is simply a mask or template that is placed over a terminal board. Pins line up with the workpiece (1). Terminals (electrical) are inserted by hand in the metal terminal board through holes in the template. A spot-faced area around each hole in the template is painted an identifying color (2) to ensure correct positioning of each

* Superior numbers refer to specific references at the end of this section.

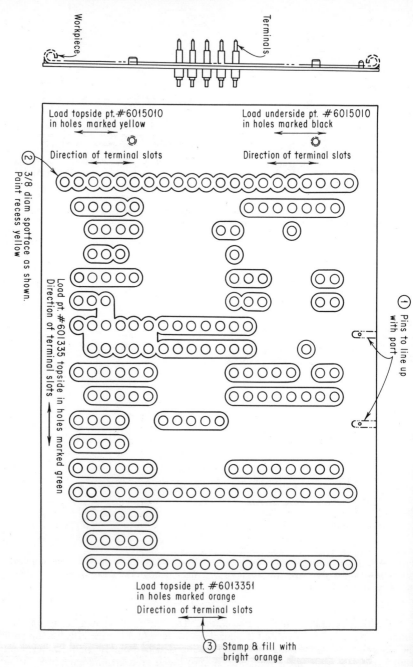

FIG. 14-11. Masking template for part placement. (*International Business Machines Corp.*)

terminal. Directional arrows (3) for alignment of the terminals are also painted the same identifying color.

A Masking-and-Holding Fixture for Painting. The fixture shown in Fig. 14-12 combines the features of hanging an electronic sealed-can assembly for spray painting with masking two surfaces to keep them free of paint.

On each side, a Dzus fastener strip (5) is fastened to a block (6) with socket-head cap screws (3). A chain (4) looped through a hanging ring (1) is fastened to each end of the block with socket-head cap screws and washers (2). The washers, cap screws, and chain ends are soft-soldered to a block.

Each Dzus fastener strip is inserted under the rim of the can (workpiece), and four Dzus fasteners are quarter-turned to their locked position. The can is now masked and ready to hang in a spray booth for painting.

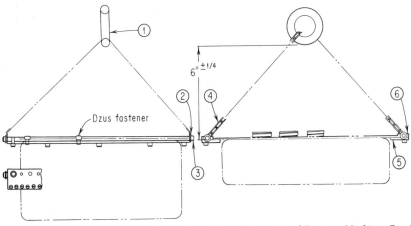

FIG. 14-12. Masking-and-holding fixture for painting. (*International Business Machines Corp.*)

A Contact-adjusting Fixture. Accurate contact pressures and maximum phasing adjustment of an electrical-contact assembly for a variable wire-wound potentiometer are facilitated by means of the fixture illustrated in Fig. 14-13. The requirements of the electrical assembly include an accurate spring-contact force or pressure of 20 grams to a tolerance of plus or minus 3 grams at a radius of 1.400 in. The required angular spacing between the contacts is $90°$.

The fixture consists of a shaft (1) upon which the electrical-contact assembly is mounted. It is rotatable to bring the contact brushes of the workpiece in line with the engraved marks *B* or the gram-gage finger (4). When the part is positioned, the shaft can be locked by a screw (2) to prevent any further movement of the workpiece.

Fine bending adjustment of the brush holders is made by moving a slide block (3). The shaft is rotated, and the brush holders on the electrical-contact assembly are adjusted until the contact pressure indicated on the gram gage is within the specified limits.

A Marking Device for Tubing. The device shown in Fig. 14-14 was used in a foot-operated press to stamp identification numbers on a piece of thin-walled brass tubing. The working parts consist of a roller (1) which acts as a mandrel to hold the parts and a marking roller (2) having the same OD as the workpiece. A gear

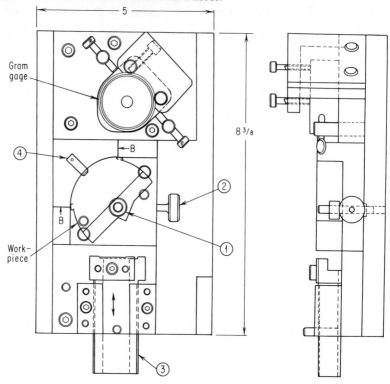

FIG. 14-13. Electrical-contact-assembly adjusting fixture. (*Link Aviation Inc.*)

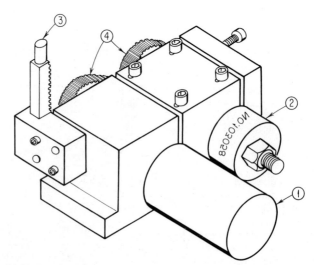

FIG. 14-14. Marking device for tubing. (*The Tool and Manufacturing Engineer.*)

rack (3) connected to the ram of the press actuates the two rollers through mating gears (4). The mounting block for the marking roller is adjustable to control the depth of the impression. Use of coarse pitch gears permits the spacing of the rollers to be adjusted a small amount.

Tube-bending Fixtures. If a suitable standard bending machine is not available, a simple fixture for each size and shape of tubing can be made. Each fixture has a base plate that can be clamped to a bench, and each base plate has blocks or pins about which tubes can be bent. Hand bending tools form the tubing about the blocks or pins.

Figure 14-15 illustrates a fixture for making one bend in a tube. A clamp holds the tube while it is being bent. A pencil mark is aligned with a scribed line on the base plate to locate the bend. The bending tool has a hole in the end to fit over the

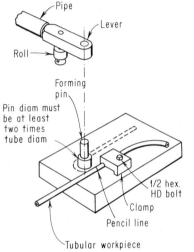

FIG. 14-15. Fixture for bending tubing 180°.[2]

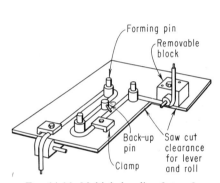

FIG. 14-16. Multiple-bending fixture.[2]

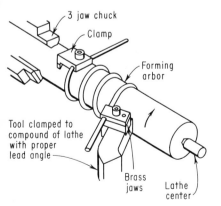

FIG. 14-17. Forming tubing into a spiral on a lathe.[2]

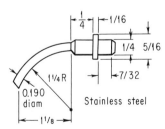

FIG. 14-18. Stainless-steel part formed in fixture of Fig. 14-19.

forming pin. The roller is grooved to hold the tube against the base plate. The space between the roller and tubing should be from ⅛ to ¼ in. The minimum radius of bend is equal to the tubing diameter.

A fixture for making multiple bends is shown in Fig. 14-16. When making several bends, it is best to start forming near the center of the part and form progressively out to the ends. All pins and blocks must be removable so that they will not interfere with the making of other bends. A clamp is needed only at the first bend to keep the tubing from slipping while being bent. Subsequent bends may need a back-up pin to keep the tube from bowing while it is being formed around the pin.

A helix or spiral may be formed about a pin with the hand bending tool; however, the tubing may be more satisfactorily formed on a lathe. A piece of CRS may be used as a forming arbor, as shown in Fig. 14-17. Usually the arbor must be smaller than the ID of the coil because of the springback in the tubing.

The 1¼-in. radius on the part shown in Fig. 14-18 is formed on the fixture of Fig. 14-19. The part is held on the bending roll (1) with the U-shaped clamp (2). The knurled pin (3) holds the clamp to the bending roll. The pressure block (4) forms the part around the roll as it rotates. The bending roll, clamp, and pressure block are of tool steel, hardened and ground.

Sheet-metal-forming Fixtures. Customary methods for bending limited numbers of small metal stampings involve the use of press brakes with universal-type tooling or bending dies mounted in mechanical presses. Bending fixtures can also be used for such operations and have many advantages, particularly when workpieces are too small for handling in a press brake or mechanical press, when stamping shapes are irregular, or when compound forming shapes are required. In addition, bending fixtures are portable and eliminate the need for die setting; their production rate equals or sometimes exceeds that obtained from conventional forming dies.

The simplest type of bending fixture is shown in Fig. 14-20a. It is used for square bending of a workpiece with legs of unequal length. An alternate design for making the same bend is shown in Fig. 14-20b; the workpiece is bent directly by means

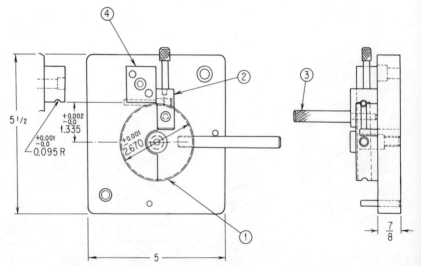

Fig. 14-19. Forming fixture for stainless-steel part. (*Koehler Aircraft Co.*)

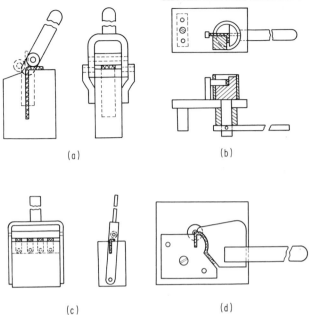

(a)

(b)

(c)

(d)

FIG. 14-20. Sheet-metal forming fixtures. (*The Tool Engineer.*)

of a slot in the bending spindle. Both designs are satisfactory because the moving component's center of rotation coincides with the bend in the workpiece, and there is no appreciable relative movement or friction between the workpiece and fixture components.

If such an arrangement is not possible, the arc of the moving component should be made to coincide as much as possible with the corresponding chord. This is illustrated by the multiple-bending fixture shown in Fig. 14-20c.

The ease of forming compound bends, which are difficult or impossible to form with one press stroke on standard bending dies, is illustrated by the fixture shown in Fig. 14-20d. With one movement of the handle, three successive bends are effected in the workpiece: a bend with an angle smaller than 90°, a curve, and a second bend with an obtuse angle.

References

1. Alloy Extends Fixture Life, *Steel,* July 7, 1958.
2. Burton, Dudley K., and Charles W. Wertz: 4 Rules for Forming Your Own Tubular Heaters, *Am. Machinist,* Dec. 15, 1958.

Section 15

COMMERCIAL FIXTURES AND ELEMENTS

By ASTME BOOKS STAFF

Commercially available fixtures, components, and hardware can reduce jig and fixture design time and cost. Many fixturing problems can be solved with vendor components and services. Constant research and development resulting in new offerings makes it impractical to provide a complete index of available vendor items.

Costs will be increased if every fixture component is designed and fully detailed. Standard items seldom need to be drawn other than in outline form on assembly drawings. Many vendors furnish templates for their products to allow outlines and other dimensional data to be easily and quickly traced onto an engineering drawing.

A standard component will generally be of certified quality and structural adequacy, while original component design may include some analysis of probable load, which may result in overdesign to compensate for variables in workmanship and materials.

The purchase price of a mass-produced component is usually considerably less than the cost of its fabrication in the plant. Purchased components also reduce assembly labor costs because they are designed for ease of assembly. Fixture maintenance costs are reduced by standardization and off-the-shelf availability of components.

The designer often assumes responsibility for the decision to make or buy a fixture. He can survey the complete range of fixtures that are commercially available and consider the advantages of standardization, cost, and off-the-shelf availability, with or without minor in-plant rework. If a complete unit is unavailable, it may be fabricated of purchased major components. Even in the case of a complex fixture, standard hardware, such as bushings, clamps, buttons, straps, etc., should be considered.

The make-or-buy decision will be further influenced by the availability of skilled manpower and facilities and by consideration of the probable work load at the proposed fabrication time. In the toolroom, the heavy work load accompanying product change will usually preclude doing major fixture work. At other times, fixture work might be a profitable way to use required stand-by technicians.

Complete Proprietary Fixtures. The fixtures shown in Figs. 15-1 and 15-2, with the addition of interchangeable jaws, locators, bushings, etc., are suitable for high-production drilling, tapping, threading, and milling operations on small parts.

The hand-operated vise fixture (Fig. 15-1a) incorporates self-centering horizontal master jaws that are held open by a spring and closed by turning the clamping screw. Interchangeable jaws hold small round parts ($\frac{3}{16}$ to 1 in. diam) for vertical drilling or tapping. A support arm for drill bushings may be mounted to the top plate, and special jaws may be made to fit contoured parts.

15-1

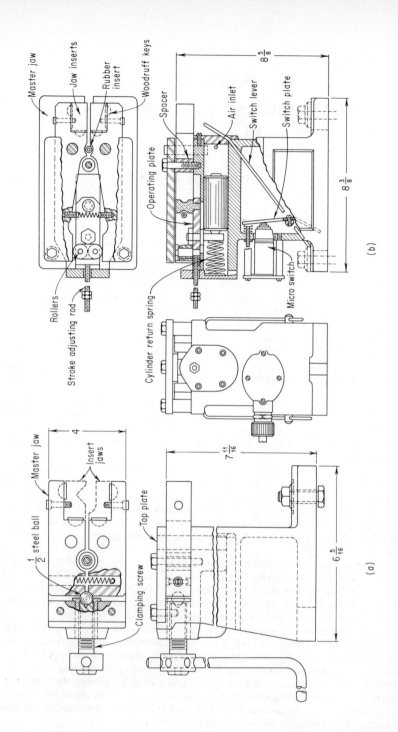

Master jaw

Jaw inserts

Rubber insert

Woodruff keys

Spacer

Air inlet

Switch lever

Switch plate

$8\frac{5}{8}$

$8\frac{3}{8}$

Operating plate

Micro switch

Rollers

Stroke adjusting rod

Cylinder return spring

(b)

Master jaw

Insert jaws

$\frac{1}{2}$ steel ball

Top plate

4

$7\frac{11}{16}$

$6\frac{5}{16}$

Clamping screw

(a)

15–2

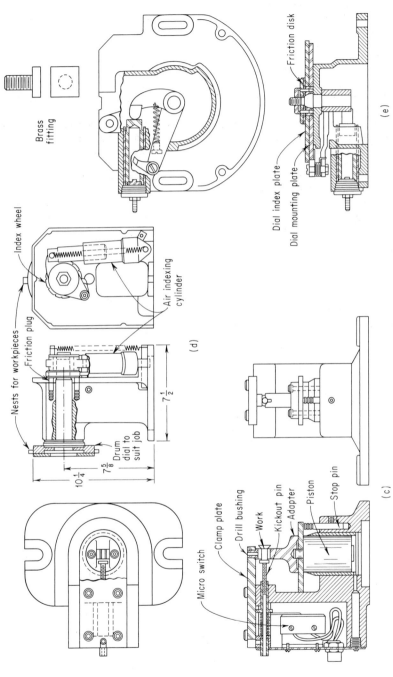

Fig. 15-1. Master fixture bases: (*a*) hand-operated vise fixture; (*b*) pneumatic vise fixture; (*c*) lift-clamping fixture; (*d*) drum-type horizontal indexing fixture; (*e*) dial-type indexing fixture. (*Snow Manufacturing Co.*)

The air-operated vise fixture (Fig. 15-1b) is suitable for drilling and tapping small parts (up to 1⅛ in. diam). An air cylinder closes the jaws by moving a roller between them. The limit-switch lever, contacted by the workpiece or tripped by the operator, releases air pressure through a solenoid valve.

Another fixture operated by air pressure (Fig. 15-1c) vertically clamps the workpiece and incorporates an automatic spring-loaded kick-out pin for part ejection. The clamp plate and work adapter can be modified, and the bushings are interchangeable for different workpieces and hole sizes. Insertion of the workpiece trips the limit switch which controls travel of the lift-clamping piston.

An air-operated horizontal-indexing fixture (Fig. 15-1d) is particularly suited for die-head threading, drilling, or tapping. Brass fittings are threaded (⅛ in. NPT) at a net production rate of 2,800 pieces per hour with the die head operating at 1,250 rpm. The drum dial is automatically indexed by an air cylinder and valve interlocked with the machine cycle. Nests, located away from the rotating tool, are close to the operator for manual loading.

The dial type of air-operated fixture in Fig. 15-1e has a 7½-in. dial plate, which may have from 10 to 36 stations for drilling and allied operations on small parts.

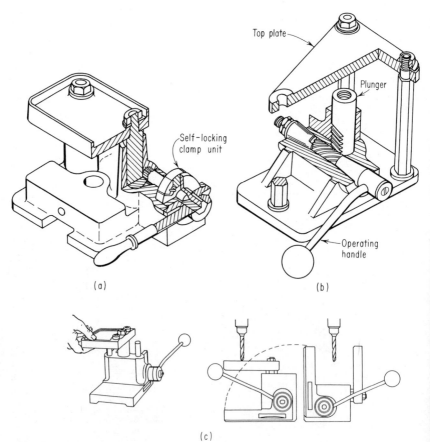

(a)   (b)

(c)

FIG. 15-2. Pump jigs: (a) typical rack-and-pinion type; (b) plunger-operated post type; (c) swiveling type. (*Accurate Bushing Co.*)

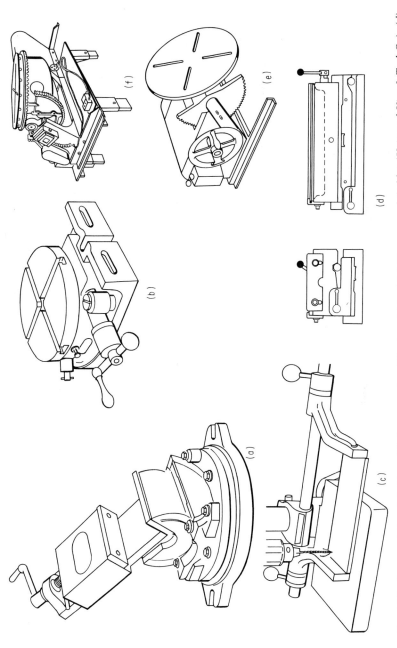

FIG. 15-3. Commercial work holders: (a) three-way vise; (b) rotary table; (c) drill-press work holder (*Universal Vise & Tool Co.*); (d) magnetic sine plate (*Omer E. Robbins Co.*); (e) bench-type positioner; (f) trunnion-type rotary table.

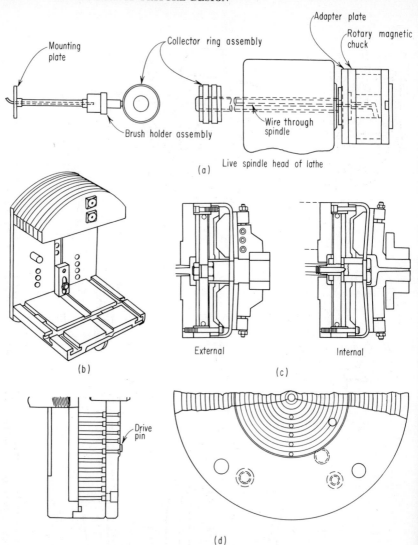

Fig. 15-4. Commercial chucks: (*a*) rotary magnetic chuck (*Magna-Lock Corp.*); (*b*) adjustable lathe fixture (*Universal Vise & Tool Co.*); (*c*) diaphragm chuck (*N. A. Woodworth Co.*); (*d*) vacuum chuck (*Cushman Chuck Co.*).

The air cylinder may be interlocked with the machine circuit for timing automatic indexing with the spindle cycle.

A pump jig (Fig. 15-2) is essentially a quick-acting vise. It incorporates hand-lever actuation of either a rack and pinion or a cam mechanism to vertically move a top plate or a plunger. Lever movement clamps the workpiece between tooling attached to the plate and the moving member. Locking devices, built into the jig, control clamping pressure. Pump jigs may be used for different parts and drill sizes by interchanging locators, plates, drill bushings, etc.

One type of fixture (Fig. 15-2c) incorporates a swiveling top plate which facilitates loading and unloading. When equipped with a double-end top plate, multiple operations such as drilling and reaming are facilitated in a small area at the same location. This type of jig has two finished faces perpendicular to each other, permitting operations at right angles to the initial operation. Pump jigs are available in a variety of styles, sizes, and types.

Major Commercial Components. The cost of a single-purpose compound-angle fixture precisely made in the toolroom might well exceed that of its commercial equivalent shown in Fig. 15-3a. Low-production quantity or frequent workpiece design changes often justify the use of and prove the versatility of standard components.

The vise shown in Fig. 15-3a can be obtained in different sizes. The locking means can be the conventional method shown, a quick-lock mechanical system, or a high-production pneumatic device. Blank metallic or nonmetallic jaws can be profiled to the workpiece contour.

The rotary table shown in Fig. 15-3b is revolved horizontally; it can be end-mounted to permit operations in a vertical plane.

The drill-press work holder shown in Fig. 15-3c is another of the many fixturing aids found in current catalogues. A sine plate (Fig. 15-3d) is available in different sizes with either a permanent magnet or an electromagnet. Figures 15-3e and f show typical positioning devices.

The equipment shown in Fig. 15-4 is for turning and related processes. Holding equipment for turning operations includes magnetic, conventional three- and four-jaw mechanical chucks, and collet devices. The same devices with minor variations are available for fixtures which may be designed for indexing.

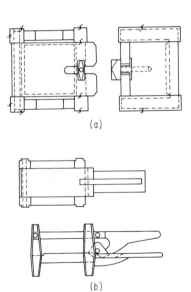

Fɪɢ. 15-5. Commercial jigs: (a) box jig; (b) leaf jig. (*West Point Mfg. Co.*)

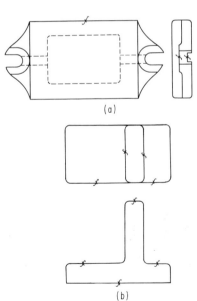

Fɪɢ. 15-6. Fixture bases: (a) mill-fixture base; (b) T-angle plate (*Standard Parts Co.*).

Stop elements

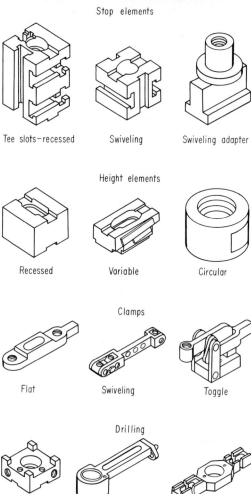

Tee slots-recessed   Swiveling   Swiveling adapter

Height elements

Recessed   Variable   Circular

Clamps

Flat   Swiveling   Toggle

Drilling

Sliding base   Bush holder   Bush holder

Base plates

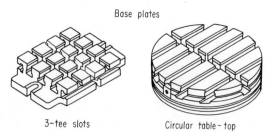

3-tee slots   Circular table-top

FIG. 15-7. Universal jig and fixture system. (*Wharton & Olding, Ltd.*)

It is sometimes advantageous to enclose the workpiece, thereby retaining the desired relationship between operations performed in any of the surrounding planes. Shown in Fig. 15-5 are square and rectangular box jigs and tumble jigs of cast aluminum and cast iron. The jigs are available in lengths up to 8 in. and in widths up to 4 in., as well as in leaf jigs up to 2 × 6 × 6 in. A single box or tumble jig can be designed to hold the workpiece during a series of operations, thereby eliminating individual fixtures for each operation.

Mill-fixture bases (Fig. 15-6a) are available in lengths of 9 to 15 in., while T-angle plates (Fig. 15-6b) can be purchased in lengths, widths, and heights of 2 to 15 in. Both bases and plates are normalized precision-ground castings; the former are supplied with standard keyways or jig-bored holes. The addition of clamps, locators, etc., to a base or plate makes a complete fixture at low cost.

One currently available base features pneumatic support of the upper plate during its movement or rotation. By introducing air pressure, the base and plate are separated a few thousandths of an inch, the plate being supported by the column of air. In this position, the heaviest load can be repositioned by hand. With release of the air pressure, the plate seats on the base for subsequent machining operations. Pneumatic-type fixture plates are available in many sizes, including some plates that are capable of supporting over 28,000 lb.

One proprietary system utilizes approximately 450 elements or blocks of varying function, enabling a toolmaker to construct a jig or fixture much on the building-block principle. The blocks are held to a tolerance of 0.0003 in., have case-hardened wear surfaces, and have T slots for positive location. Illustrated in Fig. 15-7 are base, height, stop, clamp, and location elements. A fixture can be assembled, used, photographed for reference or later reconstruction, and then returned to stock in its elemental form.

A solution to the problems of clamping relatively large workpieces for machining operations is found in the clamp-and-jack system (Fig. 15-8). The kit includes

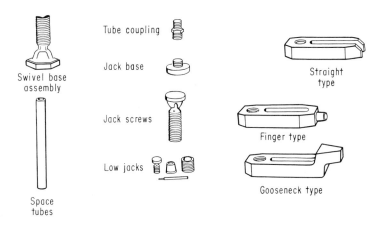

FIG. 15-8. Universal clamp and jack system. (*Universal Vise & Tool Co.*)

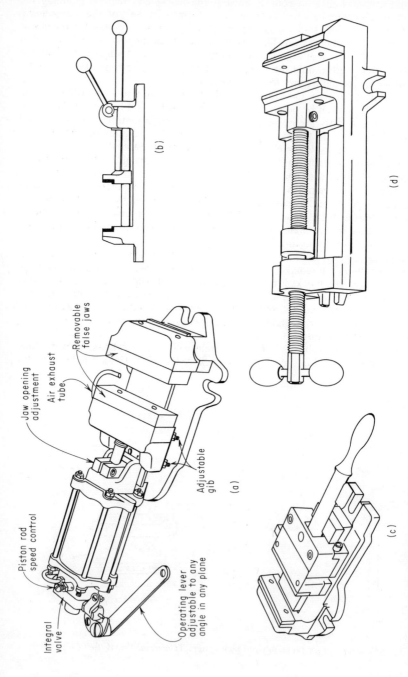

Jaw opening
adjustment

Air exhaust
tube

Removable
false jaws

Piston rod
speed control

Adjustable
gib

Integral
valve

Operating lever
adjustable to any
angle in any plane

(a)

(b)

(c)

(d)

Fig. 15-9. Commercial vises: (a) automatic air vise (Bellows Co.); (b) screwless vise (National Machine Tool Co.); (c) wedge-lock vise (Universal Vise & Tool Co.); (d) interrupted screw-type vise (Universal Vise & Tool Co.).

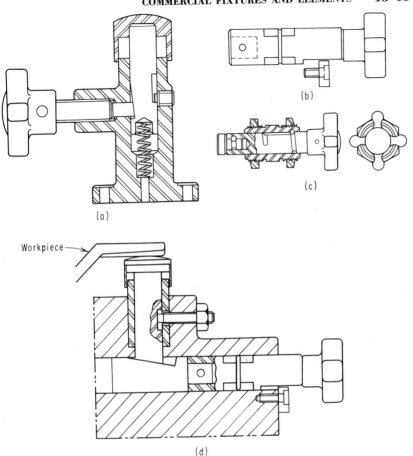

FIG. 15-10. Jacks: (*a*) fixture jack; (*b*) jack lock; (*c*) cam lock jack; (*d*) typical jack-lock application.

clamp elements, jack elements, spacer tubes, straps, etc., and greatly simplifies machine setup.

When process considerations and/or workpiece characteristics suggest the holding of a workpiece rather than its nesting, a vise can be incorporated as a major component. If positioning in all planes (Fig. 15-3*a*) is not a required or desirable feature, a simple vise (Fig. 15-9) can be utilized. A number of pneumatic or hand-actuated types are available in many sizes.

Some workpieces, such as castings, vary dimensionally. Retention and support of such workpieces in a fixture can require adjustable locating pads. A standard-fixture jack in either unit or component form (Fig. 15-10) can be incorporated to compensate for workpiece size difference.

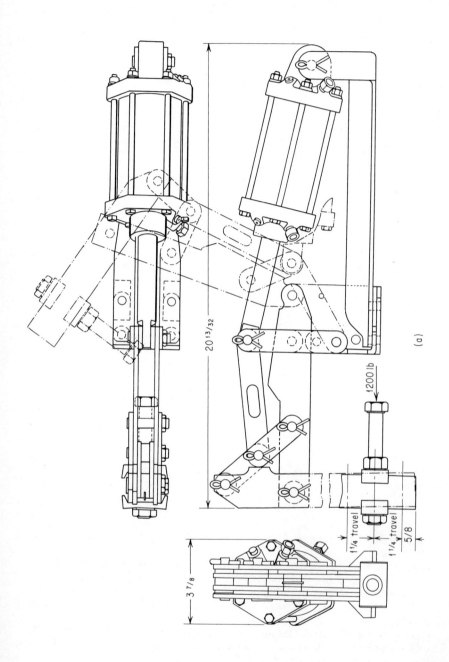

(a)

20 13/32

1200 lb

1 1/4 travel

1 1/4 travel

5/8

3 7/8

15-12

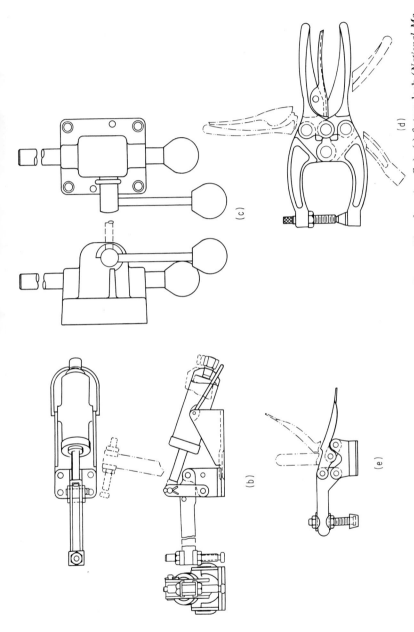

Fig. 15-11. Clamps: (a, b) pneumatic single- and double-action clamps (*Lapeer Manufacturing Co.*); (c) fixture lock (*National Machine Tool Co.*); (d) plier-type toggle clamp (*Detroit Stamping Co.*); (e) conventional toggle clamp (*West Point Mfg. Co.*).

15–13

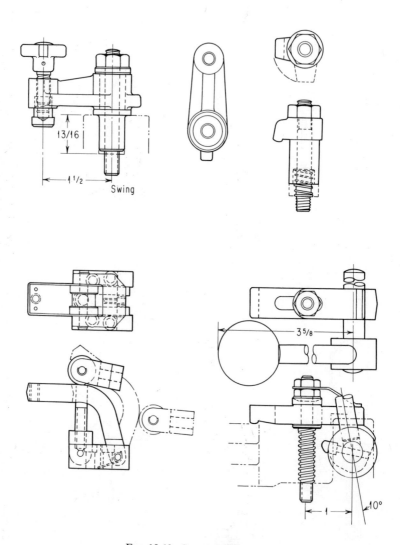

13/16

1 1/2

Swing

3 5/8

1

10°

Fig. 15-12. Commercial clamps.

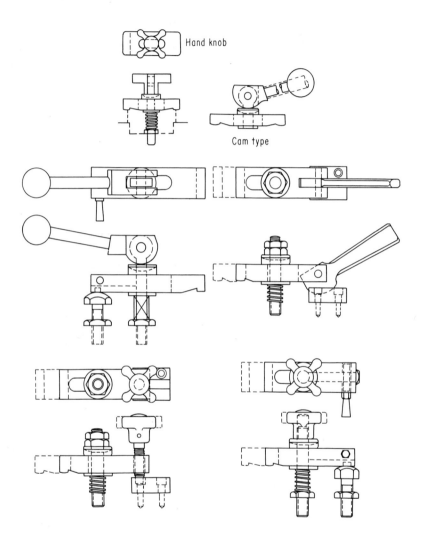

Hand knob

Cam type

FIG. 15-13. Commercial clamps.

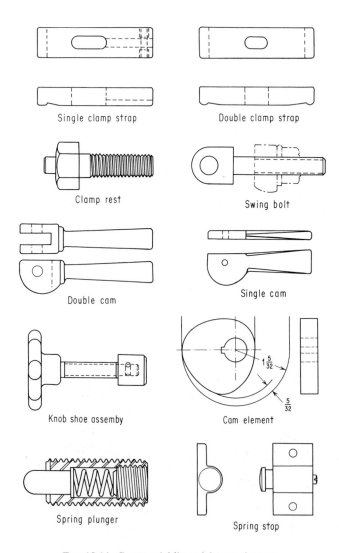

Single clamp strap

Double clamp strap

Clamp rest

Swing bolt

Double cam

Single cam

Knob shoe assemby

Cam element

Spring plunger

Spring stop

Fig. 15-14. Commercial jig and fixture elements.

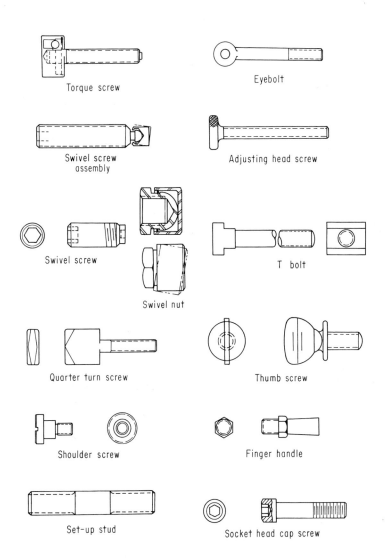

Torque screw

Eyebolt

Swivel screw assembly

Adjusting head screw

Swivel screw

Swivel nut

T bolt

Quarter turn screw

Thumb screw

Shoulder screw

Finger handle

Set-up stud

Socket head cap screw

FIG. 15-15. Commercial jig and fixture elements.

FIG. 15-16. Commercial jig and fixture elements.

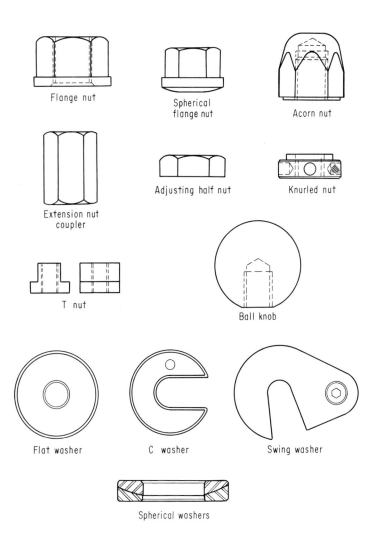

FIG. 15-17. Commercial jig and fixture elements.

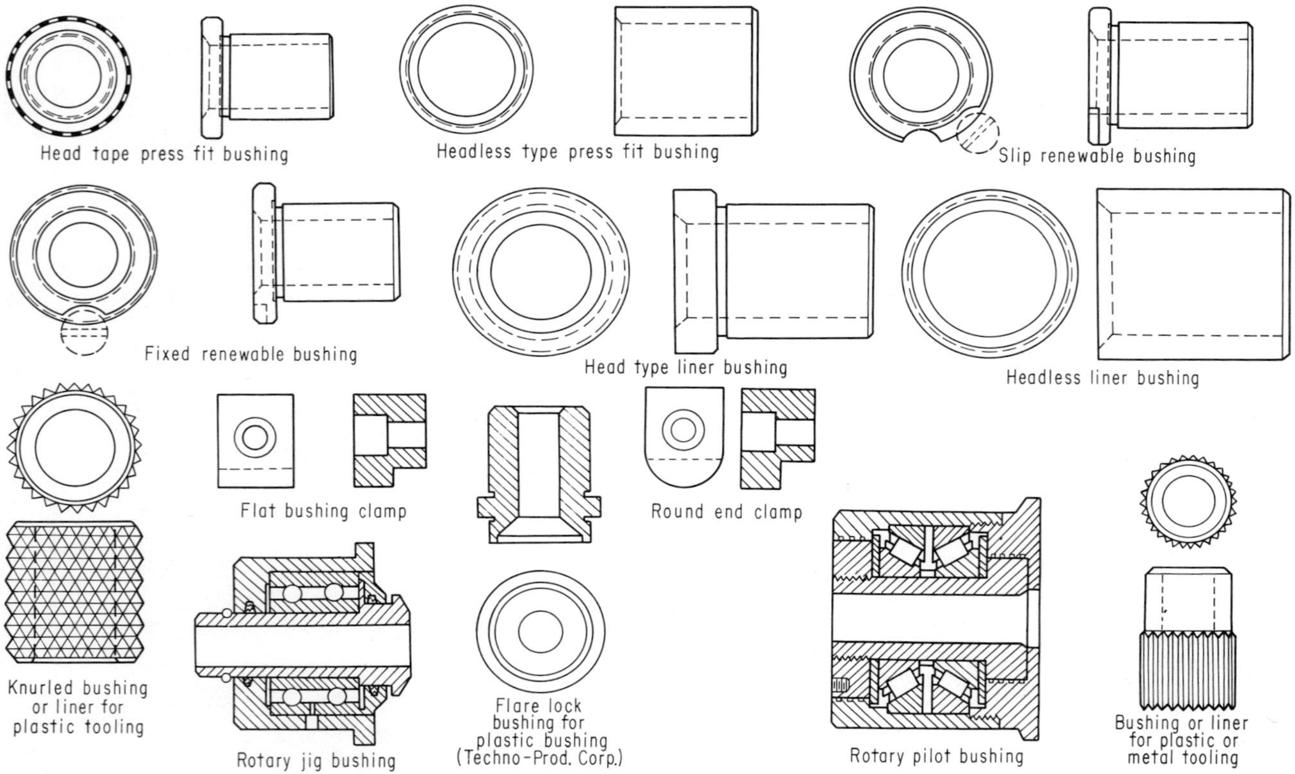

Slip renewable bushing

Headless liner bushing

Bushing or liner for plastic or metal tooling

Rotary pilot bushing

Headless type press fit bushing

Head type liner bushing

Round end clamp

Flare lock bushing for plastic bushing (Techno–Prod. Corp.)

Head tape press fit bushing

Fixed renewable bushing

Flat bushing clamp

Rotary jig bushing

Knurled bushing or liner for plastic tooling

Fig. 15-18. Commercial jig and fixture elements.

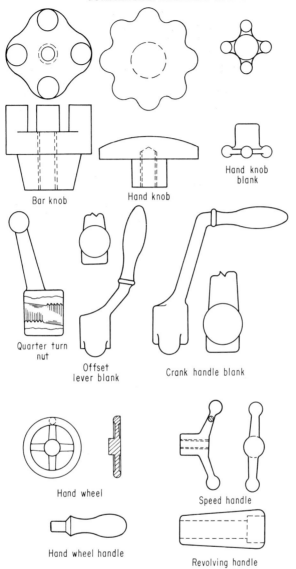

Bar knob

Hand knob

Hand knob blank

Quarter turn nut

Offset lever blank

Crank handle blank

Hand wheel

Speed handle

Hand wheel handle

Revolving handle

FIG. 15-19. Commercial jig and fixture elements.

Miscellaneous Jig and Fixture Components. A workpiece having a specified reference point or plane, such as a locating pad or tooling hole, may require the application of adequate clamping pressure directed toward that point or plane. Forces induced by an operation may necessitate positive retention of the workpiece in the fixture, but space limitations may not permit inclusion of the many available clamping devices. Some of the compact designs of Figs. 15-11, 15-12, and 15-13, with many variations commercially available, may be suitable. Not only are the units available, but all components are also offered (Fig. 15-14).

Typical male-thread hardware is shown in Fig. 15-15. Figures 15-16 and 15-17 show minor hardware. Figure 15-18 shows types of bushings, etc. Figure 15-19 shows types of handles, wheels, and cranks. The sizes of these items are found in current catalogues.

Inspection Fixture Components. Many of the components and devices described for production fixtures can be used or modified for inspection operations.

Examples of flush-pin gages are shown in Sec. 13. Gaging elements consisting of pins and bushings are commercially available in a wide range of sizes.

Many inspection fixtures incorporate dial indicators as combined probe and measuring tools. They are available from many sources in a wide range of sizes.

INDEX

1